DATE DUE

Since 1990, at least sixty-seven former heads of state or government have been prosecuted for serious human rights or financial crimes. The majority of these leaders were brought to trial in free and fair judicial processes, and some served time in prison as a result. This book explores the reasons for the meteoric rise in trials of senior leaders and the motivations, public dramas, and intrigues that accompanied efforts to bring them to justice. Drawing on an analysis of the sixty-seven cases, the book examines the emergence of regional trends in Europe and Latin America and contains eight case studies of high-profile trials of former government leaders – Augusto Pinochet (Chile), Alberto Fujimori (Peru), Joseph "Erap" Ejercito Estrada (the Philippines), Frederick Chiluba (Zambia), Pasteur Bizimungu (Rwanda), Slobodan Milošević (former Yugoslavia), Charles Taylor (Liberia and Sierra Leone), and Saddam Hussein (Iraq) – studies written by experts who closely followed the trials and their societal impacts. This is the first published book to examine the global rise in the number of domestic and international trials, telling the tales in readable prose and with fascinating details.

Ellen L. Lutz is the executive director of Cultural Survival, an international human rights organization that works on behalf of indigenous peoples. She previously directed the Center for Human Rights and Conflict Resolution and taught international human rights law, international criminal law, and other international law subjects at Tufts University's Fletcher School. From 1989 to 1994, she served as the California director for Human Rights Watch and as that organization's principal researcher on Mexico. She has written widely on human rights and conflict resolution, international and transnational accountability for human rights violations, indigenous rights, and human rights in Latin America. Lutz received her J.D. from the University of California, Berkeley (1985), and her M.A. in anthropology from Bryn Mawr College (1978).

Caitlin Reiger, a recognized expert on international prosecutions, is deputy director of the Prosecutions Program at the International Center for Transitional Justice (ICTJ). From 2003 to 2005, she was the chambers senior legal advisor to the judges of the Special Court for Sierra Leone. In 2001, she cofounded and served as legal research coordinator of the Judicial System Monitoring Program in East Timor and later appeared as defense counsel before East Timor's Special Panels for Serious Crimes. Reiger has provided extensive policy advice and comparative research on national-international tribunals for serious human rights violations. Reiger manages the ICTJ's Cambodia program and managed the ICTJ's former Yugoslavia program. She received a B.A. in history and an LL.B. from the University of Melbourne (1996) and an LL.M. (in international law/human rights) from the London School of Economics (2003).

Prosecuting Heads of State

Edited by

ELLEN L. LUTZ

CAITLIN REIGER

CAMBRIDGE UNIVERSITY PRESS
Cambridge, New York, Melbourne, Madrid, Cape Town, Singapore,
São Paulo, Delhi, Dubai, Tokyo

Cambridge University Press
32 Avenue of the Americas, New York, NY 10013-2473, USA

www.cambridge.org
Information on this title: www.cambridge.org/9780521756709

First published 2009
Reprinted 2009

Printed in the United States of America

A catalog record for this publication is available from the British Library.

Library of Congress Cataloging in Publication Data
Prosecuting heads of state / edited by Ellen L. Lutz, Caitlin Reiger.
    p. cm.
Includes bibliographical references and index.
ISBN 978-0-521-49109-9 (hardback)
1. Trials (Political crimes and offenses).   2. Heads of state – Legal status, laws, etc.
I. Lutz, Ellen L. 1955–   II. Reiger, Caitlin, 1970–
K543.P6P76   2009
345'.0231 – dc22   2008038066

ISBN 978-0-521-49109-9 Hardback
ISBN 978-0-521-75670-9 Paperback

Just as we have depended on each other and our colleagues for inspiration and analytic rigor, we have also depended on the support of our families who encouraged us and filled in for us so that this book could come to fruition. Caitlin particularly extends her thanks to Adrian Morrice for his ongoing support and for reminding her why she does this. She dedicates this book to her daughters Havana and Lia, whose lives to date have accompanied the entire process. Ellen's gratitude similarly goes to Theodore Macdonald, Jr. She dedicates this work to Martina Couto and to David and Julia Randall, who, for her, are the reason for everything.

Contents

List of Contributors

EDITORS

Ellen L. Lutz is the executive director of Cultural Survival, an international human rights organization that works on behalf of indigenous peoples. She previously directed the Center for Human Rights and Conflict Resolution and taught international human rights law, international criminal law, and other international law subjects at Tufts University's Fletcher School. From 1989 to 1994, she served as the California director for Human Rights Watch and as that organization's principal researcher on Mexico. She has written widely on human rights and conflict resolution, international and transnational accountability for human rights violations, indigenous rights, and human rights in Latin America. Lutz received her J.D. from the University of California, Berkeley (1985), and her M.A. in Anthropology from Bryn Mawr College (1978).

Caitlin Reiger, a recognized expert on international prosecutions, is deputy director of the Prosecutions Program at the International Center for Transitional Justice (ICTJ). From 2003 to 2005, she was the chambers senior legal advisor to the judges of the Special Court for Sierra Leone. In 2001, she cofounded and served as legal research coordinator of the Judicial System Monitoring Program in East Timor and later appeared as defense counsel before East Timor's Special Panels for Serious Crimes. Reiger has provided extensive policy advice and comparative research on national-international tribunals for serious human rights violations. Reiger manages the ICTJ's Cambodia program and managed the ICTJ's former Yugoslavia program. She received a B.A. in history and an LL.B. from the University of Melbourne (1996) and an LL.M. (in international law/human rights) from the London School of Economics (2003).

CONTRIBUTORS

Ronald Gamarra is a Peruvian lawyer who specializes in legal defense of victims of human rights violations. Currently he serves as the executive secretary of the Peruvian National Human Rights NGO Coordination Body and is one of the legal representatives of the victims in the trial against ex-President Alberto Fujimori for crimes against humanity. He was a member, and later director, of the Legal Section at the Institute for Legal Defense (1988–2000). He served as special ad hoc solicitor for cases of corruption and human rights violations committed by former President Alberto Fujimori, presidential advisor Vladimiro Montesinos, and individuals belonging to Fujimori's criminal organization (February 2001–December 2004). From 2005 to 2007, he returned to work at the Institute for Legal Defense. He is the author of various articles and books in his field and has a master's degree in criminal law.

Paul Lewis is a journalist for the *Guardian* newspaper. His work includes investigations on homegrown terrorism, human trafficking, and immigration. He was the Stern Fellow at the *Washington Post* in 2007, the Henry Fellow at Harvard University in 2004, and president of Cambridge University Students' Union in 2002. He has a First Class B.A. degree in Social and Political Science.

Naomi Roht-Arriaza is a professor of law at the University of California Hastings College of Law. She is the author of *The Pinochet Effect: Transitional Justice in the Age of Human Rights* (2005) and *Impunity and Human Rights Violations in International Law and Practice* (1995); is coeditor of *Transnational Justice in the Twenty-First Century: Beyond Truth versus Justice* (with Javier Mariezcurrena) (2006); and has written numerous articles and book chapters on justice and accountability. She has lived and worked extensively in Latin America and is a member of the Legal Advisory Council of the Center for Justice and Accountability.

Miranda Sissons is the deputy director for Middle East Programs at the International Center for Transitional Justice (ICTJ). An Australian, she is a specialist in human rights and international humanitarian law (IHL) in the Middle East. Before joining the ICTJ, Sissons worked as a researcher and consultant at Human Rights Watch, helped develop Arab civil society networks on the International Criminal Court, and served in the Australian diplomatic service. She has authored numerous publications on human rights and IHL issues in the Middle East and elsewhere. Sissons holds a B.A. from Melbourne University and an M.A. in international relations from Yale University, where she was a Fulbright Scholar.

Emir Suljagić is a Srebrenica survivor, journalist, and author born in 1975 in Ljubovija, Serbia. In 1995, the lives of nearly every man he had ever known – and those of many women too – were wiped out in the Srebrenica genocide. He published a book about the experience called *Postcards from the Grave*. After the war, he went to the University of Sarajevo to read political science. From September 1996 through January 2006, he worked as a reporter and staff writer at the Sarajevo-based weekly magazine *Dani*. Between 2002 and 2004, he worked in the Hague as a correspondent from the International Criminal Tribunal for the former Yugoslavia for *Dani*, and for the London-based Institute for War and Peace Reporting. He is currently a doctoral candidate at University of Hamburg.

Abdul Tejan-Cole is the chairman of the Anti-Corruption Commission of Sierra Leone. He has an LL.B. (Hons) degree from Fourah Bay College, University of Sierra Leone, and an LL.M. from University College London. He was a human rights teaching Fellow at Columbia University in New York and a Yale World Fellow. He worked as a trial attorney and appellate counsel in the Special Court for Sierra Leone and taught law at the University of Sierra Leone. Tejan-Cole also headed the Cape Town office of the International Center for Transitional Justice in 2006–2007. He has written extensively on human rights and transitional justice issues.

Lars Waldorf is the director of and a lecturer at the Centre for International Human Rights, Institute of Commonwealth Studies, University of London. He ran Human Rights Watch's field office in Rwanda from 2002–2004 and covered genocide trials at the United Nations International Criminal Tribunal for Rwanda in 2001. He currently is writing a book on *gacaca*, Rwanda's traditional, community-based approach to resolving disputes and allowing reconcilliatory justice, with generous support from the United States Institute of Peace. He received a B.A. (1985) from Harvard College and a J.D. (1989) from Harvard Law School. After clerking for the New Jersey Supreme Court (1991–1992), he worked at Bet Tzedek Legal Services in Los Angeles and the Washington Lawyers' Committee for Civil Rights as a Skadden Fellow (1992–1994). He was a senior trial attorney at the Civil Rights Division of the United States Department of Justice in Washington, D.C. (1994–1999). He has also taught at The New School and Harvard College.

Marieke Wierda is a Dutch citizen born and raised in the Republic of Yemen. She studied law at Edinburgh (LL.B.) and New York University (LL.M.) and is a member of the New York Bar. Wierda joined the International Criminal Tribunal for the former Yugoslavia in its early years (1997–2000) and worked with the judges in chambers. Subsequently she joined the International Center for Transitional Justice (2001–present), where she is Director of Prosecutions. She has worked on prosecutions-related issues in a wide variety of contexts, including Sierra Leone, Uganda, Afghanistan, Iraq, and Lebanon. She has numerous publications including, with Richard May, a book titled *International Criminal Evidence* (2002).

Abby Wood is a graduate of Harvard Law School and The Fletcher School for Law and Diplomacy at Tufts University. She is currently a doctoral student at the Travers Department of Political Science, University of California at Berkeley. Her research interests include comparative politics, institutional design, and democratic theory.

About the International Center for Transitional Justice

The International Center for Transitional Justice (ICTJ) assists countries pursuing accountability for past mass atrocity or human rights abuse. The center works in societies emerging from repressive rule or armed conflict, as well as in established democracies where historical injustices or systemic abuse remain unresolved.

To promote justice, peace, and reconciliation, government officials and nongovernmental advocates are likely to consider a variety of transitional justice approaches including both judicial and nonjudicial responses to human rights crimes. The ICTJ assists in the development of integrated, comprehensive, and localized approaches to transitional justice comprising five key elements: prosecuting perpetrators, documenting and acknowledging violations through nonjudicial means such as truth commissions, reforming abusive institutions, providing reparations to victims, and facilitating reconciliation processes.

The center is committed to building local capacity and generally strengthening the emerging field of transitional justice, and it works closely with organizations and experts around the world to do so. By working in the field through local languages, the ICTJ provides comparative information, legal and policy analysis, documentation, and strategic research to justice and truth-seeking institutions, nongovernmental organizations, governments, and others.

The ICTJ Prosecutions Program has worked for several years with domestic and international justice initiatives, drawing on staff with experience in such tribunals. It maintains as its goals the promotion and strengthening of domestic and international(ized) criminal prosecutions for systemic crimes, seeking to define further the concept of a "fair trial," and influencing policy makers by producing high-quality analysis of key developments in the field, including monitoring of significant trials such as those of Alberto Fujimori, Charles Taylor, and Hissène Habré. The program is also dedicated to analysis and advice on the impact of the International Criminal Court on the countries and regions where it is active and the strengthening of the capacity of local actors to engage in informed decision making on prosecution options and strategies.

Foreword

by Mary Robinson

One of the most important developments in the slow but determined journey of the international community toward a system of justice and accountability is the increasing acceptance of the duty to prosecute those responsible for mass human rights violations, regardless of rank or position. The historical unspoken presumption that heads of state may act with impunity has finally begun to crumble, but progress continues to be extremely difficult, unsteady, and hard fought.

The strong and conflicting reactions in Sudan and elsewhere to the request by the prosecutor of the International Criminal Court for the arrest of President Omar Hassan Ahmad al-Bashir of Sudan, and the response in Bosnia and Herzegovina to the arrest of Radovan Karadžić, show the political sensitivities that can become significant bumps in the road.

It is important that the lessons learned on this difficult journey are available to us all. However, until now there has been no detailed review of major attempts at bringing national leaders to justice.

Prosecuting Heads of State fills this void and is a fascinating and readable account of efforts to bring senior political leaders to justice for human rights and financial crimes. It considers the background and political circumstances that have enabled these cases to proceed and the effect they have had on transitions to peace and democracy in the countries concerned. The book analyzes the broader impact of these prosecutions within the affected communities in terms of satisfying victims' demands for justice, establishing an historical record of the crimes, and reestablishing a normative framework of respect for human rights and trust in state institutions. *Prosecuting Heads of State* illustrates the increasing institutionalization and respect for the rule of law throughout the world.

While serving as president of Ireland, I traveled to Rwanda soon after the genocide of 1994 in the hope of bringing attention to the tragedy that occurred there and focusing on the collective responsibility of those who caused such appalling brutality. My concern for putting an end to impunity in the case of gross violations of human rights continued when I had the honor to serve as United Nations High Commissioner for Human Rights. With my colleagues, our work included striving to achieve accountability and assistance to victims of numerous atrocities throughout the world, and we often felt frustrated.

Visiting East Timor in late 1999, I heard firsthand accounts from victims of their suffering at the hands of the Indonesian military and militias and urged the Indonesian government to help bring senior leaders to account for the systematic violence they inflicted during this period. Other situations of mass human rights violations during my tenure included Chechnya, the Great Lakes region of Africa, Sierra Leone, the Balkans, and the Middle East. In each situation of conflict, the tragic reality is that those who are least powerful – very often women and children – routinely become innocent victims of those who abuse the power with which they have been entrusted.

The growing international consensus toward prosecuting heads of state that is evidenced by the creation of the UN-backed and hybrid tribunals, as well as indictments from regional and domestic courts, is encouraging. Before 1990, only a handful of ex-leaders throughout history had been prosecuted, and most of them in "political trials" without the benefit of due process or an independent judiciary. Since 1990, more than sixty former heads of state have been indicted in various jurisdictions. Most were accused of egregious human rights or financial crimes for which there was legitimate evidence and were tried in free and fair judicial processes. Many have served time in prison. Side by side with this transformation has been increasing state willingness to overturn or find loopholes in past amnesties, to waive official immunities, and to remove other impediments to trial.

All individuals, regardless of official rank or capacity, are legally bound to refrain from committing such horrific crimes as genocide, war crimes, and crimes against humanity. This principle is rooted in the ancient laws and customs of almost all cultures and throughout history. A strong global response announces to all those in positions of power and leadership that they can no longer use terror tactics, systematic rape, ethnic cleansing, mutilation, and indiscriminate killing of noncombatants as weapons of war or for any other purpose. The deterrent effect of prosecuting those in power cannot be underestimated. The marked increase of indictments since the fall of the Berlin Wall should send a strong message to those in power to conduct themselves within the framework of the norms of international law. Impunity for committing crimes while in office is no longer guaranteed, and the contemporary movement toward prosecuting heads of state indicates that no one is above the law.

The cases described in this volume show that we still have some way to go, yet as a former head of state, I can attest to the fact that, symbolically at least, the successful examples detailed herein send a very powerful message indeed.

Preface

This book owes its origins to Ferdinand Marcos, former dictator of the Philippines and a tyrant who died with the blood of some ten thousand victims of torture, disappearance, and extrajudicial execution on his hands. In early 1986, just a few months after an Argentine court found five of that country's nine former dictators guilty of torture, disappearance, and extrajudicial execution, Marcos was deposed by a populist uprising and fled to Honolulu. Then an idealistic new lawyer with some human rights experience, I was determined that he would pay for his crimes, if not in the Philippines then in the United States. In law school, I had studied the landmark *Filártiga v. Peña-Irala* decision, in which a U.S. appellate court ruled that an alien can be sued for human rights abuses that violate "the law of nations" even if those acts took place in another country. If Marcos could not be criminally charged in the United States, his victims could at least enjoy a measure of justice by suing him here for damages.

One of America's great human rights lawyers, Paul Hoffman, a colleague who then was the legal director at the American Civil Liberties Union of Southern California, offered to lead the litigation team and our twelve-year battle against Marcos in U.S. federal courts began. Our odyssey was so fraught with legal challenges that a good professor could base an entire year of law school instruction on that case alone. It was the political challenges that arose during the Honolulu-based trial that were most perturbing, however.

Although the creation of an international tribunal was unimaginable when we first filed our lawsuit, by the time the litigation wound down (technically it still hasn't ended; even though a jury awarded Marcos' victims a $1.2 billion judgment, his assets have yet to be recovered), the international community was in active negotiations to establish an International Criminal Court (ICC) with jurisdiction to try future leaders who behaved as Marcos had done. As an observer at the 1998 Rome conference that established the ICC, I couldn't help pondering that the planned new court was bound to face the same problems we had faced in the Marcos case. What was most amiss with that litigation was its location, far away from where the crimes had occurred or where the victims still lived. In contrast to the junta trial in Buenos Aires, where the counsel and judges were Argentine, the media had a stake in closely monitoring the proceedings, and the survivors and the loved ones of those who died could testify or be present in the courtroom, only a handful of the Marcos regime's ten thousand victims had any connection with the proceedings, and the media barely noticed the trial was taking place.

For me the most important lessons learned from the Marcos lawsuit were that whenever possible, justice for human rights crimes must be as accessible as possible to those who suffered most and that the best kind of justice leads to national acknowledgment of the wrongs that occurred and societal involvement in righting them. Those lessons prompted me to begin asking some of the questions that this book addresses: To what extent were sovereign states trying leaders who had committed serious human rights or other crimes while in power? What were their motivations? What were the outcomes of such cases? What was the impact on society of doing so or not doing so?

Queries of this magnitude cannot be fully explored in isolation, and I was fortunate to have many friends and colleagues who were wrestling with related questions and were eager to confer or collaborate. My deepest gratitude goes to Naomi Roht-Arriaza and Kathryn Sikkink, both dear friends and sometimes coauthors, who were as captivated by these issues as I was and always eager to reexamine them from a fresh perspective.

Despite several years of preliminary exploration, this book did not begin to take shape until 2004 when the U.S. Institute of Peace (USIP) awarded me a grant to write it. Then, just as the work was getting off the ground, the circumstances of my life changed, forcing me to face the fact that it would be impossible for me to write the book I had originally proposed. Fortunately, I also realized that there was a much better book to be written by collaborating with the International Center for Transitional Justice (ICTJ), and particularly the deputy director of the ICTJ's Prosecutions Program, Caitlin Reiger. To my eternal gratitude, USIP grant officer Taylor Seybolt, a champion throughout, agreed to the revised project plan, and the present volume was born.

Since evolving into a joint project, the collaboration between us – and the ICTJ as a whole – has been a joy. Marieke Wierda, Pablo de Greiff, and Graeme Simpson deserve particular thanks for encouraging Caitlin to take on the project. In October 2006, drawing on the ICTJ network of prosecution experts working on mass crimes, Caitlin and I cohosted a conference to enable the chapter authors to discuss their cases with one another and benefit from the insights and feedback of practitioners, many of whom had been involved in litigation against heads of state as prosecutors, activists, monitors, or victims' representatives. For their firsthand insights and reflections, we both thank Geoffrey Nice, Stuart Alford, Reed Brody, Nehal Bhuta, as well as ICTJ colleagues Ruben Carranza, Eduardo Gonzalez, Vasuki Nesiah, and Marieke Wierda. Tiasha Palikovic undertook the painstaking task of recording the conference proceedings, and the ICTJ's Richard Bailey and Laila Pedro pitched in during the conference and well beyond in ways too numerous to count, as did Nisma Zaman. Caitlin and I are deeply grateful for the help they provided.

The project also benefited enormously from the research assistance of Cambridge, Massachusetts–based research assistants Adam Day, Laura Roht-Arriaza, William Brennan Thomas, Abby Wood, and Paul Lewis, who researched the sixty-seven cases, and, in the case of Abby and Paul, contributed chapters to the volume. ICTJ interns Niki Ganz Moss and Eric Vang provided extraordinary service in the final days of the project, checking references and filling in missing citations, and Geoff Dancy assisted with the preparation of the charts and provided a fresh perspective on making sense of the numbers. Extra special thanks are due to our editor, Mark Cherrington, who is a grand master at saying things as simply as they can be said, and no simpler.

Thanks also are due to my former colleagues at Tufts University's Fletcher School, particularly Peter Uvin, director of the Institute for Humanitarian Studies, which sponsored the USIP grant and identified many of the outstanding interns who worked on the project; the many Fletcher students who assisted with the pre-grant research; Wendy Lekan and Fran Parisi who helped prepare the grant proposal and manage the grant; and Eileen Babbitt for her support throughout.

At the ICTJ, we had the benefit of many colleagues' enormously rich range of expertise and knowledge of the country situations considered in the book, which added to the depth of perspective that the authors' own firsthand experiences brought to the recounting of the case studies. For their generous responses to urgent queries and comments on drafts, Caitlin's and my heartfelt thanks go to Paul James Allen, Patrick Burgess, Javier Ciurlizza, Cristian Correa, Thierry Cruvellier, Leonardo Filippini, Eduardo Gonzalez, Priscilla Hayner, Bogdan Ivanišević, Juan Méndez, and Michael Reed.

Finally, the authors deeply appreciate the assistance of John Berger, our editor, and Paul Smolenski at Cambridge University Press, and of Mary Paden, Elizabeth Budd, James Diggins, and Diane Scent for their invaluable help in readying the manuscript for publication.

Ellen L. Lutz

1

Introduction

Ellen L. Lutz and Caitlin Reiger

In September 1985, nine members of Argentina's military junta, whose successive regimes covered the period in Argentine history known as the "dirty war," walked into a courtroom in downtown Buenos Aires. Until that day, they had absented themselves from their trial, which had already gone on for months and during which hundreds of witnesses testified about their torture, the disappearance of loved ones, arbitrary arrest, cruel detention, and even crueler methods of extrajudicial execution. The city was mesmerized by the trial. Long lines for seats in the observation gallery formed days in advance of each court session. By eight in the morning, all the copies of *El Diario del Juicio*, the unofficial newspaper report of the testimony of the previous day, were sold out.

Entering the courtroom, some of the generals and admirals were stone-faced. Others whispered among themselves. None displayed any signs of remorse, and only one, Lieutenant General Lami Dozo (who later was acquitted), appeared agitated. The two most notorious of the accused made the greatest impression on the gallery. Admiral Emilio Eduardo Massera, an imposing figure who had been head of the navy – which ran the Navy Mechanics School where some five thousand disappeared persons were held between 1976 and 1979 – appeared in court in full navy dress regalia. By contrast, his army co-junta member, General Jorge Videla, appeared in court in civilian clothes and refused to appoint counsel for his defense (a court-appointed defender represented him). He buried his nose in a book while the prosecutor read out the indictment and described the evidence against him. Some thought it was a Bible; others suggested it was a mystery novel. Whichever it was, Videla made clear his contempt for the proceedings that ultimately condemned him and became the springboard for the global transitional justice movement.

Fast forward to October 2006: Saddam Hussein, whose reign of terror spanned nearly a quarter century, shuffled into a Bagdad courtroom to learn his fate. Although he might have been put on trial for waging aggressive wars against Iran and Kuwait, for using chemical weapons against both Iranians and tens of thousands of Iraqi Kurds, or for murdering countless Iraqi Shiites, this trial focused on a single set allegations relating to the attacks against 148 Shiite men and boys from the town of Dujail in the 1980s in retaliation for an alleged assassination attempt on his life. A five-judge Iraqi judicial panel of a tribunal that was funded and heavily influenced by the United States had found Hussein and his codefendants responsible for crimes against humanity for the attack on the Dujail villagers.

As Hussein sank into his seat, presiding judge Ra'uf Rashid Abd al-Rahman commanded, "Make him stand up!" Six guards hustled the ex-dictator to his feet and held his arms behind him while the judge read out his sentence of death. Hussein shouted defiance in reply: "Go to hell! You and the court! You don't decide anything, you are servants of occupiers and lackeys!" The judge shouted back, "Take him out!" As he was led away, Hussein bellowed, "Long live the Kurds! Long live the Arabs!"[1]

Before 1990, only a handful of former or current heads of state or government had ever been indicted for serious human rights violations or other abuses of authority while in power. As a rule, former chief executives who had committed crimes, like those who had fallen from political favor, went into exile or in some cases were summarily executed. Since then, no fewer than sixty-seven heads of state or government from around the globe have been, at a minimum, criminally charged for their misconduct while in office.

This book is an effort to understand what changed, and why. Has humanity indeed entered an era in which heads of state and other senior government officials are as vulnerable as common criminals to arrest, trial, and punishment for their crimes? Is this a global phenomenon, or one of selective application? If the latter, which leaders are "at risk" and which are likely to escape with impunity?

The book builds on the body of work that examines criminal trials as a means of achieving accountability for serious violations of international human rights or humanitarian law. It also builds on work that explores the creation and development of the various international criminal tribunals over the past decade, as well as the contemporary willingness of some states to exercise "universal jurisdiction" for the most heinous of such crimes. It considers the interface between domestic decision making regarding criminal prosecutions and international interest in trying government leaders, including the establishment of international tribunals with jurisdiction to do so. In addition, it examines the international movement against political corruption that began to gain traction during the same time period. It explores the extent to which these trends have influenced sovereign states to create the political space for independent domestic courts to try senior officials for human rights and economic crimes. Ultimately, this book considers the significance of pursuing these leaders for their victims and for the societies they once ruled.

Hundreds of government and military officials around the globe have now been indicted for the kinds of crimes covered in this book. We limited our study to heads of state or government so that we could examine a complete data set without the need for statistical sampling. Although indictments and trials of heads of state or government are inevitably more politicized than those of their underlings, there is no other global subset of perpetrators who are similarly situated that we could have selected.

In addition to the cases we examine here, there have been many more in which a former head of state or government has been the subject of some sort of criminal investigation. For example, after Belgium enacted its universal jurisdiction law in 1993, victim complaints flooded in against former dictators and even sitting heads of state, including Mauritanian president Maaouya Ould Sid'Ahmed Taya, Iraqi president Saddam Hussein, Israeli prime minister Ariel Sharon, Ivory Coast president Laurent Gbagbo, Rwandan president Paul Kagame, Cuban president Fidel Castro, Central African Republic president Ange-Felix Patassé, Republic of Congo president Denis Sassou Nguesso, Palestinian Authority president Yasir Arafat, former Chadian president Hissène Habré, former Chilean president General Augusto Pinochet, and former Iranian president Ali Akbar Hashemi-Rafsanjani.[2] Official investigations into these cases were opened, but most never progressed beyond this exploratory phase. We limited our analysis to those instances in which a leader was the subject of some level of formal charges or was indicted, depending on the requirements of the particular legal system, to ensure that we were addressing only those cases for which there was official intent to prosecute the accused.

Because of the high publicity value of prosecutions of top political figures, the news media carries more information about criminal prosecutions of heads of state or government than it does for prosecutions of lower-ranking officials. In terms of responsibility, heads of state or government are at the top of the chain of command. In cases of corruption crimes, which are usually committed for personal gain, these leaders most likely were directly involved in the criminal acts. In cases of human rights crimes, even if they did not directly order them or carry them out, they often were in positions to know what was going on, even if they deliberately insulated themselves from knowledge of the facts. Finally, at a symbolic level, these cases often represent far more than the individuals on trial. Especially in situations in which the prosecutions have followed a political transition or the end of a regime, pursuing the highest individual in the hierarchy is also about marking a break with the past and sometimes condemning an entire system that facilitated the commission of serious crimes in the name of the state.

FROM AMNESTIES TO ADJUDICATION: NATIONAL RESPONSES TO HUMAN RIGHTS CRIMES

Since the trial of the nine junta members in Argentina during the 1980s, the subject of trying senior governmental officials for serious violations of human rights has riveted the attention of the international human rights movement. Before then, aside from hesitant efforts in Western Europe to punish those responsible for atrocities committed during World War II and Greece's trial of the leaders of its authoritarian regime, which fell in 1974, the world gave little thought to what consequences should be brought to bear against dictators and others who were responsible for egregious wrongs. The transitions from dictatorship to democracy that took place in Latin America throughout the 1980s, and particularly Argentina's conviction and sentencing of five of the former junta members to lengthy prison terms, changed that. Overnight, the human rights movement embraced the aim of ensuring that leaders who perpetrated human rights abuses faced justice. The issue was no longer whether there should be accountability, but how much and what kind of accountability, as well as what compromises were acceptable to keep the peace or prevent a return to authoritarian rule.

In 1988, the Aspen Institute's Justice and Society Program hosted a ground-breaking conference to explore the dimensions of meaningful accountability for gross violations of human rights. The participants, mostly scholars and human rights advocates, agreed that accountability minimally requires a successor government to investigate and establish the facts so that the truth is known and acknowledged as a part of the nation's history. Although there was disagreement about acceptable trade-offs, there was consensus that meaningful accountability requires individuals who perpetrated the abuses to be held responsible. The participants also recognized that accountability, by itself, is neither sufficient nor possible absent other functioning democratic institutions, including an independent judiciary, the removal of impediments to a flourishing civil society, and a commitment to the rule of law.[3]

Over the next few years, the subject of accountability continued to gain traction. With the end of the Cold War, many Eastern European countries were compelled to confront what to do about those who had committed human rights abuses during decades of Communist rule. Their responses varied widely. Some states opted for nonjudicial accountability solutions such as "lustration," or banishment from political life. Romania summarily executed its former dictator Nicolae Ceausescu and his wife Elena, although the generals who had taken charge of the country claimed that they had first convicted them in a military trial. Others filed charges against ex-leaders – some for financial and others for human rights crimes. A fuller analysis of the newly democratic governments' responses to Cold War–era crimes can be found in Chapter 2.

In South Africa, the negotiated end of apartheid created a similar quandary. In coming to terms with the necessity of compromising to achieve peace, both the ruling National Party and the African National Congress (ANC) embraced international human rights discourse and norms as the best means to achieve common ground, write a constitution, and craft a power-sharing agreement.[4] Yet as is so often the case in negotiated ends to long-standing conflicts,[5] throughout the process the topic of how to deal with criminal violations of human rights during the apartheid era was shelved until all other contentious issues were resolved and the parties had agreed on a draft constitution text. Only then did National Party and ANC negotiators, in a secret process, craft the language of "National Unity and Reconciliation" that laid the groundwork for South Africa's 1994 interim constitution and the subsequent enactment of legislation that mandated the establishment of the Truth and Reconciliation Commission (TRC).[6] An integral part of the agreement was the provision of a conditional amnesty that enabled perpetrators of past violations to apply to swap criminal and civil liability for testimony before the TRC's Amnesty Committee. Amnesty would only be granted upon satisfaction of various conditions, including disclosure of all known aspects of their crimes that were related to "a political objective," including the names of those higher up in the chain of command. Somewhat counterintuitively, remorse was not among the determinative criteria for amnesty.[7] Despite the fact that the "amnesty for truth" deal was predicated on the basis that prosecutions would follow for those who did not submit to the process or were refused amnesty, with the exception of the 1996 conviction of former Vlakplaas commander Eugene de Kock, South Africa's apartheid-era leaders all managed to escape indictment.[8] While the South African TRC amnesty arrangements were much lauded at the time, the question of prosecution for those who escaped the process continues to be a live one, and it is questionable whether such a compromise would be acceptable under international law today.[9]

In Latin America, sensing the turning tide toward greater accountability, authoritarian leaders of countries transitioning to democracy went to great lengths to issue decrees, pass laws, and even hold national referenda to immunize themselves from prosecution. These "self-amnesties" became topics of interest for the Organization of American States' (OAS) human rights machinery.[10] Indeed, the rulings of the Inter-American Commission and Court both reflected and helped to stimulate the global attitude shift toward greater accountability. Thus, in its 1985–86 Annual Report, the Inter-American Commission on Human Rights adopted the measured view that it was up to the appropriate democratic institutions of the state concerned to determine whether and to what extent amnesty was to be granted.[11] Yet even then the commission took the view that amnesties should not be used as a shield to prevent victims from obtaining information about human rights abuses.

As more and more American states passed amnesty laws in the late 1980s, the commission found itself inundated with petitions from human rights victims alleging that amnesty laws violated their right to judicial protection. In its 1992 Annual Report regarding a massacre by security forces of seventy-four people in El Salvador, the commission concluded that the Salvadoran government had a duty to investigate and punish the perpetrators, notwithstanding an El Salvadoran Supreme Court ruling that those who carried out the massacre were protected from prosecution by that country's amnesty laws.[12] In the same report, in recommendations concerning amnesty laws in two other countries – Uruguay and Argentina, the commission reemphasized that regardless of whether amnesty laws had been adopted, states had a duty under the American Convention on Human Rights to clarify the facts and identify those responsible for human rights abuses.[13] In September 2006, in a case involving Chile, the Inter-American Court of Human Rights ended this legal ambiguity by holding that amnesties for those responsible for crimes against humanity violated the American Convention on Human Rights.[14]

As these national developments were slowly taking form in Latin America, there was a parallel development in national courts in Europe that helped continue the momentum for change during the late 1990s. Victims, human rights advocates, and investigating magistrates creatively used universal jurisdiction laws that were on the books in Spain, Belgium, and other European countries. These are discussed further in Chapter 2 of this volume.

THE RAPID EVOLUTION OF INTERNATIONAL CRIMINAL TRIBUNALS

By 1993, just five years after the Aspen Institute conference, accountability became the subject of debate at the pinnacle of global political power. The international community was under pressure to forge an effective response to what was becoming a bloody and intractable conflict in the former Yugoslavia, yet it was reluctant to send in troops. In July 1992, Human Rights Watch had issued a report concluding that the war was an international armed conflict to which the Geneva Conventions applied – including the requirement that war criminals be tried.[15] Around the same time, journalist Roy Gutman published an article in *Newsday* exposing, for the first time, the Bosnian Serb death camps.[16] In response, the Security Council commissioned a panel of experts to investigate, and two major human rights funders – the Soros Foundation and the MacArthur Foundation – ensured that the commission was adequately funded.[17] Meanwhile, the administration of U.S. President George H. W. Bush, having lost a tough election battle, began to worry about its legacy if it did not take positive action to stop the violence that was tearing Bosnia apart. At a December 1992 conference in London, U.S. acting Secretary of State Lawrence Eagleburger called for a war crimes tribunal for the former Yugoslavia. The incoming Clinton administration endorsed Eagleburger's proposal.[18]

In the spring of 1993, the United Nations Security Council established the Ad Hoc Tribunal for the Prosecution of Persons Responsible for Serious Violations of International Humanitarian Law Committed in the Territory of the Former Yugoslavia since 1991 (ICTY) in response to the continuing widespread and systematic murder, rape, and ethnic cleansing of civilians in Bosnia.[19] In doing so, the Security Council asserted that massive human rights abuses were a threat to international peace and security and judicial accountability for perpetrators was a prerequisite for ensuring that peace and the protection of human rights are guaranteed in the future.[20] Although the establishment of the ICTY did not bring about peace in the region, its existence did alter the playing field.

In 1999, at the height of the war in Kosovo, that tribunal became the first international court to announce that it had indicted a sitting head of state – Slobodan Milošević – for war crimes and crimes against humanity in connection with the deportation and murder of Kosovo Albanians. These charges were later expanded to include genocide and crimes against humanity and to cover the earlier conflicts in Bosnia and Croatia. Even though Milošević was ousted from power six months later, Serbia took almost two years before it turned him over to the ICTY for trial. A detailed analysis of the Milošević trial before the ICTY and its implications for the former Yugoslavia and international justice can be found in Chapter 9.

Eighteen months after the establishment of the ICTY, the Security Council, again pressed to respond to an international crisis to which it was reluctant to send troops, established a similar court to prosecute genocide and other systematic, widespread violations of international humanitarian law in Rwanda.[21]

The Rwanda Tribunal faced the challenge of coordinating its efforts with those of domestic courts in Rwanda that also had jurisdiction and a powerful interest in trying those responsible for the genocide. Tensions arose between the two systems over resources, jurisdiction, and punishment, and for a while the tribunal was plagued with scandal and inefficiency. However, the tribunal also issued the first-ever decision that a former head of government was guilty of genocide. On May 1, 1998, at his initial appearance before the ICTR, Jean Kambanda, who was prime minister of Rwanda from April 8 to July 17, 1994, pleaded guilty to charges of genocide, crimes against humanity, and related crimes.[22] He was sentenced to life imprisonment.

In subsequent years the international community has established an assortment of other ad hoc judicial processes, including hybrid domestic-international courts like the Special Panels for Serious Crimes in East Timor, the Special Court for Sierra Leone, a specialized war crimes chamber in Bosnia, the Extraordinary Chambers in the Courts of Cambodia, and the Special Tribunal for Lebanon.[23] These courts either have already faced or will face similar challenges in tackling high-level leaders, as shown by the current proceedings against Liberia's Charles Taylor and Cambodia's Khieu Samphan.

The creation of the Yugoslav and Rwandan tribunals in the mid-1990s also stimulated international efforts to establish a permanent international criminal court. The United Nations sponsored an international diplomatic conference in Rome in 1998 where the statute of the International Criminal Court (ICC) was adopted. Today the ICC is a fully functioning court. Judges and prosecutors have been selected, and, notwithstanding U.S. government efforts to undermine it, 106 states have committed themselves, and their financial wherewithal, to making the ICC a meaningful institution. The new court has the benefit of the jurisprudence and the experience of the ad hoc tribunals for the former Yugoslavia and Rwanda, as well as the hybrid tribunals. At this writing, three cases are under investigation: Uganda and the Democratic Republic of the Congo (DRC), which were referred by those states parties, and the Darfur region of Sudan, which was referred by the UN Security Council. Three defendants from the DRC and Jean-Pierre Bemba Gombo from the Central African Republic, Thomas Lubanga Dyilo, Germain Katanga, and Mathieu Ngudjolo Chuiof, have been arrested and surrendered to the court in the Hague.

DOMESTIC CORRUPTION PROSECUTIONS

The institutionalization of international criminal judicial processes coincided with a less-heralded phenomenon in national courts: the rise in indictments, prosecutions, and convictions of often high-level public officials for corruption crimes including bribery, extortion, misappropriation of public or private funds, and other acts that involved using public power for private gain. Corruption is as old as war, and in many cases nearly as devastating. The World Bank estimated that in 2006 the global cost of corruption reached $1 trillion. Yet until the end of the Cold War, prosecution of top public officials for corruption was no more common than their prosecution for human rights or humanitarian law violations.

The shift owes its origin, in part, to the Watergate scandal at the end of the Vietnam War. In its aftermath, the U.S. Congress uncovered slush funds used by U.S. multinational corporations to finance U.S. elections, as well as to bribe foreign government officials. In the same reform-driven mind-set that led to the first federal laws governing U.S. foreign policy with respect to countries engaged in violations of human rights, the Congress unanimously passed the Foreign Corrupt Practices Act (FCPA) in 1977, which was aimed at curbing corrupt business practices by U.S. corporations overseas.[24]

However, it quickly became apparent that the United States' good intentions were undermining the competitive position of U.S. businesses in the international marketplace. In 1988, the Congress amended the FCPA. Proclaiming the need for a global response to foreign bribery, the Congress called on the president to pursue the negotiation of an international agreement, "among the largest possible number of countries," to govern acts now prohibited under FCPA.[25]

Meanwhile, in Europe during the 1990s, a string of corruption scandals touching senior officials, including heads of state and government, was creating embarrassment. Allegations of corruption cost some leaders their public offices, including President Felipe González of Spain and Helmut Kohl of Germany, both of whom were voted out of office in the wake of corruption scandals.[26] In Italy, long a haven for official corruption, a group of Milanese prosecutors and magistrates initiated a campaign in 1992, called Mani Pulite (Clean Hands), to undercut institutionalized corruption that transcended political parties and allegedly was linked to the Mafia. Several prime ministers, including Silvio Berlusconi, found themselves in the dock for corruption, as is detailed in Chapter 2.

By the turn of the millennium, what began as an American housecleaning exercise had become a global movement. First the Americas (1996), then Europe (1999) adopted treaties criminalizing corruption.[27] The 1997 treaty of the intergovernmental Organization for Economic Cooperation and Development (OECD), the thirty member countries of which are home to the majority of the world's multinational corporations, requires members to enact laws prohibiting corporate bribery and extortion. It entered into force in 1999.[28] Africa followed in 2003, and in the interim, Asia, the Pacific Island states, and the Middle East declared interest in creating regional instruments or structures to impede corruption. Meanwhile, the United Nations promulgated the UN Convention against Corruption (UNCAC), which entered into force on December 14, 2005.[29] As of February 4, 2008, 107 countries had ratified it, and 140 had signed it.

Although UNCAC does not define "corruption," it does require, among other means to curb corruption, states to criminalize intentional bribery of national or foreign public officials, and intentional embezzlement, misappropriation, or other diversion for private gain by a public official of any property, funds, or anything else entrusted to the official by virtue of his or her position. It also requires states to criminalize influence trading and calls on them to "consider adopting legislation" to criminalize other official abuse of functions and illicit enrichment. Responding to a spate of cases in which public officials used legal maneuvers to evade the administration of justice, UNCAC calls on states to establish long statutes of limitations for corruption or adequate suspensions of existing statutes, to ensure that those accused of corruption cannot outrun the clock.

Corruption is a complex issue. It necessarily involves multiple actors and can take place on many levels. Official corruption is often seen as a victimless crime, because it usually is hard to measure the costs to individual members of the public. Depending on the corrupt activity, the cost to the public at large can range from modest to monumental, but is often outweighed by the expense of investigating it, particularly when the parties control all the relevant evidence and have no incentive to cooperate with investigators.

Although the coincidence of the trends to prosecute perpetrators of human rights abuses and government officials who engage in corruption has been largely unremarked by the international justice movement, its significance is worth exploring, particularly on account of the avenue that corruption cases have opened for holding heads of state or government accountable for at least some of the excesses of their regimes, as several of the cases in this volume demonstrate.

A NEW KIND OF POLITICAL TRIAL

Those in possession of power have long used courts to humiliate or distract their political opponents. In 1964, Judith N. Shklar defined a political trial as "a trial in which the prosecuting party, usually the regime in power aided by a cooperative judiciary, tries to eliminate its political enemies. It pursues a very specific policy: the destruction, or at least the disgrace or disrepute, of a political opponent."[30] These types of cases remain a feature of political life around the globe but increasingly are becoming a small minority of the overall number of judicial processes against heads of state or government.

Although still highly politicized, the kinds of trials that have been occurring since the fall of the Berlin Wall are less often vehicles for grabbing or retaining power, or for bullying opponents. Instead, they appear to be responses to public pressure for accountability for official misconduct while in office. More and more, prosecutions are occurring before randomly chosen judges serving in judiciaries that are relatively independent of the politicians or political forces holding power. Some of these recent indictments of heads of state are for serious human rights violations.[31] Others involve corruption charges. Sometimes corruption charges are brought as surrogates for rights-violation charges that are too politically sensitive to prosecute. In other circumstances, misappropriation of state funds is itself the rationale for the indictment. In many of these cases, graft may have facilitated the abuse of human rights, in that it impeded the country from meeting the immediate economic, social, and cultural rights needs of its population, or had longer-term consequences, such as increasing the country's debt burden or ability to attract new development aid, or causing social unrest or political instability. In other cases, corruption may have been one of the key means leaders used to finance the mechanisms through which human rights crimes occurred, such as the procurement of weapons or the funding of death squads or militias.

Indictments and trials are occurring notwithstanding the existence of the same complex countervailing pressures that were often used as a justification against pursuing accountability in the past. This is particularly true for countries transitioning to democracy after an extended period of violent conflict, or authoritarian or totalitarian rule. Perpetrators may have been active participants in settlement negotiations or are participating now in democratically elected governments. Trying perpetrators may have to compete with other democratic transition priorities such as maintaining order, placating a restive military or other armed fighters (especially those loyal to a potential defendant), demobilizing and reintegrating ex-combatants, or staving off economic collapse. Sometimes the infrastructure and capacity to stage complex, high-profile trials is lacking. This can also affect decisions on when, where, or how to proceed. Even under the worst circumstances, however, lip service is usually paid to the importance of trying those leaders most responsible for serious human rights and financial crimes.

Other challenges, such as legal or procedural immunities, statutes of limitations, or the principle against retroactive application of the law, have interfered with trials or have restricted the scope of prosecution to a handful of narrowly defined or time-limited charges. In many countries, the public seems to have a high tolerance for what it perceives as the eccentricities of the legal process, provided that ex-leaders who are popularly accused of crimes face judgment for at least some their misdeeds. At times, the perception of progress may not translate into concrete results. Recognizing that justice must at least be seen to be done, many governments have investigated or indicted former heads of state for crimes committed while in office, only to allow the process to bog down, sometimes for years, in the courts. Others have seen judicial processes through to conclusion but have quietly arranged for ex-leaders to serve their sentences under comfortable house arrest or while retaining other publicly provided benefits. In cases in which ex-leaders have gone into exile, some governments have made a big show of seeking their extradition, without following through on the legal or political steps necessary to obtain the return of the accused. Nonetheless, momentum to try former leaders for their human rights or corruption crimes is spreading around the globe.

SIXTY-SEVEN CASES

Between January 1990 and May 2008, sixty-seven heads of state or government from forty-three countries around the globe had been formally charged or indicted with serious criminal offenses: there have been thirty-two defendants from Latin America, sixteen from Africa, ten from Europe, seven from Asia, and two from the Middle East. Additionally, Figure 1.1 shows the percentage of defendants from each of the world's five regions. Some faced a single charge or set of charges, whereas others were indicted multiple times over a period of years. The cases are about evenly divided between human rights and corruption crimes, although in Asia only two countries, South Korea and Cambodia, have indicted their former leaders for human rights crimes. Some leaders faced both human rights and corruption crimes. Only a handful of cases, ranging from sodomy to treason, were not related to human rights or economic crimes. The breakdown of the types of charges is contained in Figure 1.2. A full list of all of these cases is contained in the Appendix at the end of this book. As noted earlier, although there may have been other types of proceedings against heads of state or government during this time, such as constitutional challenges or impeachment efforts, these have not been included for the purposes of this study, nor have those criminal complaints that may have been filed but that were never formally pursued.

Although our purpose is not to attempt a detailed statistical analysis, some observations are worth noting. Of the sixty-seven heads of state or government

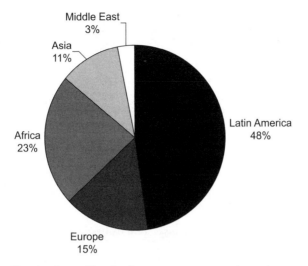

FIGURE 1.1. Prosecutions of heads of state or government by region.

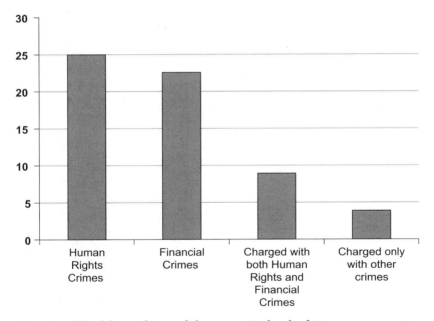

FIGURE 1.2. Breakdown of types of charges against heads of state or government.

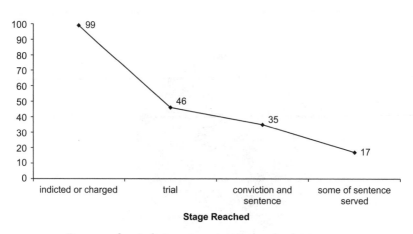

FIGURE 1.3. Progress of 99 indictments against 67 heads of state or government as of July 2008.

charged in criminal cases since 1990, most indictments and trials were concentrated in the period between 1995 and 2002, after which the number of new cases in most parts of the world decreased. The period between 1995 and 2002 coincides with the headiest days of international justice institution building, with the United Kingdom's arrest and extradition proceedings of Augusto Pinochet and the Belgian and Spanish universal jurisdiction laws.[32] The reduction in new cases coincides with the international "war on terror," which has arguably heightened popular acceptance of strong leaders and strong-armed tactics to maintain security. It is worth noting that in Latin America, the one region that (aside from Colombia) has been relatively free of terrorist activity in the past decade, the number of new indictments of heads of state did not lessen after 2002.[33]

The percentage of those sixty-seven individuals who were formally charged who subsequently were tried, convicted, and served some form of sentence, as illustrated by Figure 1.3, highlights the ambiguous nature of the trend. Roughly half of the 99 separate criminal proceedings examined proceeded to trial. Almost half of all heads of state or government whose trials have been completed were convicted, but only half of these served some form of sentence. Only one, Saddam Hussein, was executed. The rest were sentenced to either fines or house arrest, the terms of which varied widely. Many benefited from policies prevalent in Latin America and Europe allowing anyone over the age of seventy who is convicted of a crime to serve his or her sentence at home. One former head of state, Nicaragua's Arnoldo Alemán, who was convicted of embezzling and laundering $100 million from the public coffers of his deeply impoverished country, had his twenty-year sentence reduced to five years of "Nicaraguan arrest," meaning that he was not allowed to leave the country. Alemán was permitted to campaign for his party in the spring 2007 elections.[34] Although there may be increasing resolve to commence prosecutions against former leaders, this resolve still seems to wane as the process progresses.

CASE STUDIES OF PROSECUTIONS OF HEADS OF STATE

We begin this book by surveying the historical rise of judicial accountability for heads of state and government for human rights and corruption crimes in the two regions where accountability has been most salient: Europe and Latin America. In Europe, the trend toward holding heads of state responsible for their actions coincided with post–World War II political transformations that led the region to embrace democracy and restructure itself as a federated union of states. In Western Europe, most countries have not had to deal with rights-violating regimes (at least not domestically) since World War II, although in recent years the region has confronted the challenge of what to do about the surviving Nazi war criminals before they, or their direct victims, pass away. For countries that were governed by dictatorial regimes, the record is mixed: in 1974, Greece chose to try the colonels who carried out a military coup and used torture as a tactic of social control; Spain, in contrast, chose to sweep crimes committed by Franco's regime under the rug after his death in 1975.

Since the end of the Cold War, the former Soviet bloc European states have similarly had a mixed record with respect to the legacy of human rights violations during the Soviet era. In some cases this involved political sanctions, but in others, particularly the former East Germany, it involved criminal trials for past rights abuses. With the exception of the countries that were part of the former Yugoslavia, most governments' desire to be accepted as part of the European Community has outweighed any contemporary repressive inclinations.

Nevertheless, many European countries are still struggling with accountability for financial or ethical crimes that embroil political leaders, although the countries of the region have enthusiastically embraced international and regional anticorruption treaties. On a regional basis, Europe is also the world leader in ratifying international human rights and humanitarian law treaties and in embracing international judicial processes for persons accused of the most egregious human rights and humanitarian law crimes. In addition, Europe is leading the world in its willingness to extend the jurisdiction of domestic courts to try criminals whose human rights crimes happened elsewhere in the world.

Like Europe, Latin America's interest in accountability for heads of state predates the end of the Cold War. Both Europe and Latin America established extensive human rights machinery at the regional level to address violations of regionally accepted human rights norms. Although the European system advanced and became institutionalized more rapidly, the cases brought before it tended to be less egregious than those that the Inter-American human rights system faced. Thus, many international juridical pronouncements relating to accountability were first articulated by the Inter-American Commission on Human Rights or the Inter-American Court of Human Rights. However, national systems of justice also were confronted with what to do about criminal leaders and occasionally explored trials as a solution. For example, in 1963, Venezuela persuaded the United States to extradite former president Marcos Pérez Jiménez to stand trial for financial crimes committed while he was in office, including "peculation, malversation, and related felonies."[35] Five years later, a closely divided Venezuelan Supreme Court convicted him of the minor crime of continuous profit from public office (*lucro de funcionarios*) and sentenced him to four years, one month, and fifteen days in prison. Because he had already served that amount of time, he went directly from his sentencing hearing to exile in Spain.[36]

In the intervening years, most countries in Latin America had military dictatorships that were engaging in human rights and corruption crimes. In that era, it was dangerous to talk about the return to democracy, let alone trials. The Argentine junta trials changed all that, raising hopes among human rights and pro-democracy advocates that justice might indeed become an international value. Within a couple of years, however, Argentina backtracked by blocking further prosecutions of perpetrators of "dirty war" crimes, and in 1990, president Carlos Menem pardoned the junta members who had been convicted.

Trials of political leaders further suffered a black eye when the United States captured Manuel Noriega, military dictator of Panama, after it invaded that country in 1989. Although he was technically a prisoner of war, the United States carted him to Miami to stand trial for drug trafficking, racketeering, and money laundering in a U.S. federal court. Noriega was sentenced under U.S. federal law to forty (later reduced to thirty) years in prison; the U.S. invasion, which cost the lives of at least two hundred Panamanians and twenty-three U.S. troops, was globally condemned. The Organization of American States passed a resolution deploring the invasion and calling for the withdrawal of U.S. troops. A similar measure in the UN Security Council died only after it was vetoed by the United States, France, and the United Kingdom.[37]

For a time, many assumed the accountability movement had hit a brick wall. However, as Roht-Arriaza describes in Chapters 3 and 4 and in her book

The Pinochet Effect,[38] the untiring efforts of human rights activists who were determined to see justice done turned the tide. In the past decade, criminal investigations or judicial proceedings against former senior officials have occurred in Argentina, Brazil, Chile, Colombia, Ecuador, Guatemala, Mexico, Paraguay, Peru, Uruguay, and Venezuela. In Argentina, President Néstor Kirchner dissolved the amnesty laws. New cases, as well as revised cases against those previously given amnesty, are progressing through the courts. Roht-Arriaza cautions in her chapters, however, that legal and political obstacles to trials are strewn across the Latin American landscape, and the two often are so interlaced that it is difficult to determine in which domain they lie. This is the circumstance of former Peruvian president Alberto Fujimori, whose case Ronald Gamarra describes in Chapter 5. In 2005, the sixty-nine-year-old former president attempted to make a victorious return to Peru to run again for the presidency. Instead he found himself in custody in Chile, from where he was later extradited to Peru to stand trial for human rights, financial, and abuse of authority crimes. On December 11, 2007, the Supreme Court of Peru sentenced him to six years in prison for ordering an illegal search. A separate trial on charges of ordering two infamous massacres as well as the torture and unlawful detention of a journalist could each result in additional sentences of fifteen or more years.

In Asia, it is increasingly commonplace for states to try senior officials for corruption and other financial crimes that occurred during their incumbency. South Korea, India, Pakistan, Nepal, the Philippines, and Indonesia have done so. However, there is little demonstrated political interest in trying senior officials for human rights crimes. For example, the Indonesian government indicted former president Suharto for embezzling $570 million from several charities that had been under his charge but not for the massive human rights abuses that occurred during his thirty-year reign. That indictment was quashed by the courts. In Cambodia, Khmer Rouge former head of state Khieu Samphan is now in pretrial detention, but it has taken almost thirty years and an internationally assisted court to bring him there.

As Abby Wood discusses in Chapter 6, after President Ferdinand Marcos's 1986 ouster and exile to Hawaii, no criminal indictment against him was issued on the technical grounds that while he was not on Philippine soil, he was beyond the reach of the law. The government of Corazon Aquino, however, refused to permit Marcos to return to the Philippines, even after he expressed willingness to face a Philippine jury. The closest Marcos came to prosecution was a civil suit filed against him in the United States for torture, disappearance, and extrajudicial execution during his dictatorship. Although the victims eventually won a $1.2 billion judgment, Marcos died long before the lawsuit was tried. Since that time, the international climate has changed, trials of former heads of state have occurred in neighboring countries, other senior political officials have been indicted and tried in the Philippines, and the Philippines has ratified the ICC Statute. But no senior official from Marcos's administration or any subsequent one has faced criminal charges for human rights violations. Former president Joseph Estrada was convicted on corruption charges in 2007 and then pardoned by President Gloria Macapagal Arroyo. He never faced charges for human rights crimes, even though his adminis-tration engaged in a military campaign against Muslim separatists that led to the internal displacement of some 400,000 civilians and reports of human rights violations including extrajudicial executions, disappearances, and torture.[39]

Given the extent of atrocities that have occurred in Rwanda, Liberia, Sierra Leone, Sudan, the Democratic Republic of the Congo, and many other African countries, and the international judicial response to each of these crises, one might expect to see evidence of a "justice cascade" in Africa. In fact, the opposite is true. Certainly there have been bona fide trials, such as the trial of former Zambian president Frederick Chiluba, who was arrested and charged with corruption and theft of $40 million while in office. As Paul Lewis demonstrates in Chapter 7, Chiluba's prosecution was a home-grown anomaly in a region where most countries have shunned legitimate trials for senior officials unless pushed into them by powerful international actors.

There have also been political show trials aimed at eliminating threats to the political power of those holding office. Lars Waldorf illustrates this in Chapter 8 with a case study on the Pasteur Bizimungu prosecution in Rwanda. For nearly a decade, international attention focused on justice in Rwanda, including an international criminal tribunal, massive international assistance to revitalize the country's judicial system, and an alternative justice mechanism called *gacaca* that was based on traditional dispute resolution mechanisms and constructed to deal with all but the most responsible participants in Rwanda's genocide. Despite that attention, Bizimungu's trial was Rwandan president Paul Kagame's way of demonstrating that political dissent would not be tolerated, ethnic discourse would be criminalized, and the international community would not, and could not, protect political dissidents and human rights defenders.

Three of the heads of state or government whose indictments took place since the end of the Cold War – Jean Kambanda (Rwanda), Slobodan Milošević (the former Yugoslavia), and Charles Taylor (Liberia) – were brought before international or special hybrid national-international tribunals. In all three cases, the United Nations Security Council took the view that the worst of the crimes committed during these conflicts could not or should not be tried by domestic courts. In each case, the international community had committed international troops to quell conflicts, crimes against humanity, and alleged genocide and therefore had its own vested interest in seeing justice done. Although domestic and international human rights advocates had called for prosecution of all three of these defendants as well as the establishment of the institutions that facilitated their prosecution, ultimately it was the creation of impartial, professional tribunals and the appointment of independent prosecutors and judges who were free from domestic political concerns that ensured these former leaders faced justice.

As Miranda Sissons and Marieke Wierda show in Chapter 11, a similar scenario occurred with respect to the trial of Saddam Hussein in Iraq, although there the relationship was one between the occupying power and the postoccupation Iraqi leadership notwithstanding the fact that international human rights groups had been campaigning for justice for the victims of the Ba'athist regime for many years. After the U.S. invasion of Iraq, human rights advocates also called for an international or hybrid court. This was rejected by the Bush administration which, despite the political chaos and lack of experienced judicial personnel, wanted an Iraqi-led special court over which it would have substantial influence.

These cases illustrate the complex web of geopolitics within countries, regions, and farther afield that involved the waxing and waning of international support for leaders who finally were held accountable for their crimes. Other politicians whose cases are surveyed in this book also faced international political ups and downs, but what distinguished Slobodan Milošević, Charles Taylor, and Saddam Hussein was their willingness to wage war on their own people and their neighbors, and the cruelty and corruption associated with their doing so. When international politics turned against them, the response was the same as it was in Nuremberg.

Yet in all three cases, politics continued to overshadow the judicial proceedings to varying degrees. As Abdul Tejan-Cole highlights in Chapter 10, the same states that promised Charles Taylor safe exile in Nigeria for relinquishing power in Liberia later pressured Nigeria to turn him over to the Special Court for Sierra Leone. Once he got there, those states further exerted pressure to remove his trial from the region, citing fears of regional instability that could result from holding the trial so close to his continued support base in Liberia. Furthermore, the accusations he faces before the court relate to the impact of his activities on the conflict in Sierra Leone, not to crimes he committed in Liberia.

In Chapter 9, Emir Suljagić highlights a similar scenario that played itself out in the former Yugoslavia. In 1995, Milošević was hailed by the West as a peacemaker for bringing about and participating in the Dayton Peace Accords that brought about an end to the war in Bosnia. It was only after he turned his nationalist fervor against ethnic Albanians in Kosovo that the international community showed any appetite for his arrest. Even after power transferred to a new president, Vojislav Koštunica, Serbia continued to protect Milošević from trial by the ICTY. At a point when international pressure was mounting, Koštunica and Milošević cut a deal allowing for his arrest and domestic trial on corruption charges in Serbia in exchange for Koštunica's promise never to send him to the ICTY. Again, however, international pressure intervened, and this promise was broken.

Taylor, Milošević, and Hussein were all charismatic leaders who continued fighting long after the international community assumed that facing justice would render them submissive. All three did their best to use their trials (or in Taylor's case, the proceedings leading up to trial) to their political advantage. To a degree, they succeeded. Milošević, acting as his own attorney, used his trial in the Hague as a political platform for an audience back home while dragging out the proceedings so long that they concluded with his death rather than a verdict. Hussein tried the same tactic but was thwarted by a judicial process that was fundamentally compromised by extensive political interference. His trial focused on only a limited example of the many crimes of which he was accused, and to outsiders unused to the brevity of Iraqi trials, it appeared to have been ramrodded through. The political authorities ensured that the process was brought to an end with Hussein's hasty execution, presumably to prevent him from doing further political damage from the dock. The mockery he faced at his execution further diminished the legitimacy of the judicial proceedings against him.

FINAL QUESTIONS

Although this book focuses on contemporary efforts to prosecute heads of state, it also is an inquiry into the broader impact of justice. The authors of the case studies explore whether trials of heads of state relieve victim or societal suffering and anger produced when officials violate human rights or raid the state treasury. They also examine the impact of restraints on achieving justice imposed by legal or procedural rules. For example, can justice be realized if the accused is tried only for a limited number of crimes that occurred after a certain date, when more serious crimes are proscribed on account of amnesties or statutes of limitations? Can justice be achieved if the accused is charged only with financial crimes when he is also responsible for massive human rights crimes? Do procedural protections for the accused undermine the public's need for truth or victims' needs to have their day in court and a judgment at the end? What is the impact on victims and the public when indicted or convicted heads of state enjoy disproportionately favorable conditions of confinement (e.g., house arrest or luxurious detention on military bases) or when a state is unable to recover the assets they stole or wasted?

The chapters in this book also explore the ways in which states juggle competing interests when crimes are committed by powerful politicians in a highly charged political environment. Is there a significant difference in the way states make decisions about whether to indict heads of state for corruption or other financial crimes, and the way they make decisions about whether to prosecute heads of state for human rights crimes? When there is an overlap between financial and human rights crimes, what makes some crimes more palatable to try than others? When there is an extended series of crimes, what makes certain crimes indictable and others off-limits? Under what circumstances are trials intended as serious efforts to achieve retribution, deterrence, reparation, or some other legitimate justice goal? Alternatively, under what circumstances are they "political trials," as defined by Shklar?

The chapters in this book also explore the interrelationship between international pressures and domestic interests when it comes to criminal trials of former heads of state. The intensity of international involvement in trials varies widely. In some cases, like those of Estrada and Chiluba, international influences were minimal. In others, including Pinochet, Fujimori, Bizimungu, and Hussein, transnational or international pressures strongly influenced the milieu in which the decision to try a former leader was made. In still others, such as Taylor and Milošević, the international community created the judicial tribunal and then pressured the states harboring the defendants to turn them over for trial. In Rwanda, international interests relating to trials competed directly with domestic interests. Elsewhere, such as in the nations of the former Yugoslavia, they compromised justice by limiting the range of options or meddling in domestic processes. However, international interests have also contributed to strengthening domestic judicial processes. For example, the ICC's requirement that states adapt their domestic law to conform to their obligations under the ICC Statute forced many states to improve the domestic legal laws and procedures for trying human rights crimes.

Finally, the chapters in this book explore the relationship between criminal accountability and future human rights protection. There is no perfect correlation between trials and justice. If anything, the connection between trials and the prevention of violence or rights abuses is even less certain, and certainly less well understood. Nevertheless, in countries that conducted relatively just trials of heads of state for human rights violations or corruption, only one – Iraq, where the trial of Saddam Hussein was among the least just of all of the trials examined in these pages – experienced subsequent diminutions in human rights protections or destabilizing political violence. The correlation, however, cannot be ascertained because the causes of the escalating violence in Iraq may have been similar to the causes that provoked the political interference in Hussein's trial, rather than one influencing the other. History will tell whether just trials – or the political will to pursue accountability – are indicators for democratic consolidation, solidification of the rule of law, or the independence of the judiciary, or whether it is these factors that make just trials possible. It is our hope that this book will significantly advance the inquiry.

NOTES

1. Ellen Knickmeyer, "Hussein Sentenced to Death by Hanging," *Washington Post*, November 6, 2006 , p. 1.
2. See, for example, "Belgium: Questions and Answers on the 'Anti-Atrocity' Law," Human Rights Watch, Revised, June 2003. http://www.hrw.org/campaigns/icc/belgium-qna.pdf.
3. The Justice and Society Program of the Aspen Institute, "State Crimes: Punishment or Pardon," papers and report of the conference, November 4–6, Wye, MD: The Aspen Institute (1989).
4. Richard A. Wilson, *The Politics of Truth and Reconciliation in South Africa: Legitimizing the Post-Apartheid State*, Cambridge: Cambridge University Press, 2001, 8–9.
5. See Christine Bell, *Peace Agreements and Human Rights*, Oxford: Oxford University Press, 2000.
6. *The Promotion of National Unity and Reconciliation Act*, no. 34 of 1995.
7. Wilson, *Politics of Truth and Reconciliation*, 23.
8. One of the witnesses the TRC did try to depose was former South African president P. W. Botha. After he ignored three subpoenas and publicly called the TRC a "circus," the TRC referred the matter to a South African court. Although Botha was found guilty, the judge cited the ex-strongman's ill health at age eighty-two as the reason for imposing only a 10,000 rand (about $1,600) fine and a suspended twelve-month prison sentence. That sentence was later overturned on appeal on the technical grounds that TRC's mandate had expired when the subpoena was issued. Wilson, *Politics of Truth and Reconciliation*, 72.
9. For a comprehensive evaluation of the failure of post-TRC prosecutions in South Africa, see Harvard Law School International Human Rights Clinic and Institute for Justice and Reconciliation, *Prosecuting Apartheid-Era Crimes? A South African Dialogue on Justice* (2008).
10. This machinery derives from the *American Convention on Human Rights* (1978) O.A.S. Treaty Series No. 36, 1144 U.N.T.S. 123.
11. Robert K. Goldman, "Amnesty Laws, International Law and the American Convention on Human Rights," *The Law Group Docket* 6, no. 1 (1989).
12. *Massacre Las Hojas v. El Salvador*, Case 10.287, Report No. 26/92 (24 Sept. 1992), IACHR Annual Report 1992–1993, 83.

13. IACHR Annual Report 1992–1993, 41 Report No. 28/02 (Argentina); and 154 Report No. 29/92, (Uruguay).
14. *Almonacid Arellano et al. vs. Chile*, Judgment of November 26, 2006, Inter-Am Ct. H.R. Ser. C No. 154 (2006).
15. Human Rights Watch, *War Crimes in Bosnia-Hercegovina* (Volume I), August 1, 1992.
16. Roy Gutman, "Tales of Hunger, Torture at Camp in Northern Bosnia," *Newsday*, July 19, 1992, p. 7.
17. S.C. Res. 780, October 6, 1992, U.N. Doc. S/RES/780 (1992).
18. Interview with Aryeh Neier, President, Open Society Institute, January 4, 2008; see also, Samantha Power, *"A Problem from Hell": America and the Age of Genocide*, New York: Basic Books, 2003, 290–296, 481–485.
19. S.C. Res. 827, May 29, 1993, U.N. Doc. S/RES/827 (1993).
20. Report of the Secretary-General pursuant to Paragraph 2 of Security Council Resolution 808 (1993), U.N. Doc. S/25704, May 3, 1993.
21. S.C. Res. 955, November 8, 1994, U.N. Doc. S/RES/955 (1994).
22. *The Prosecutor v. Jean Kambanda*, ICTR 97-23-S, Judgment and Sentence, September 4, 1998.
23. (Cambodia) Agreement between the United Nations and the Royal Government of Cambodia Concerning the Prosecution under Cambodian Law of Crimes Committed during the Period of Democratic Kampuchea, June 6, 2003; (Sierra Leone) Agreement between the United Nations and the Government of Sierra Leone on the Establishment of a Special Court for Sierra Leone, January 16, 2002; (East Timor) Regulation on the Establishment of Panels with Exclusive Jurisdiction over Serious Criminal Offences, June 6, 2000, UNTAET/REG/2000/15; (Lebanon) S.C. Res. 1757, May 30, 2007, U.N. Doc. S/RES/1757(2007); (Bosnia) Law on the Court of Bosnia and Herzegovina, *Sluzbeni glasnik Bosne I Hercegovine* No. 29/00, 15/02,16/02, 24/02, 3/03, 37/03, 61/04. For a close look at the East Timor Serious Crimes Unit, see Caitlin Reiger and Marieke Wierda, *The Serious Crimes Process in Timor-Leste: In Retrospect*, International Center for Transitional Justice, March 2006; for a close look at the Bosnian War Crimes Chamber, see Human Rights Watch, *Narrowing the Impunity Gap: Trials before Bosnia's War Crimes Chamber*, February 2007.
24. *Foreign Corrupt Practices Act*, U.S. Code, Title 15, Chapter 2B, sec. 78dd-1-3 (1977).
25. *Omnibus Trade and Competitiveness Act of 1988*, U.S. Code, Title 19, Chapter 17, sec. 2901.
26. Arnauld Miguet, "Political Corruption and Party Funding in Western Europe," April 2004, prepared following the Transparency International Western Europe group meeting, Athens, Greece, September 13–15, 2002.
27. Inter-American Convention against Corruption, OAS (1996), signed March 29, 1996, entered into force March 6, 1997; Criminal Law Convention on Corruption, CETS no. 173 (1999), signed January 27, 1999, entered into force July 1, 2002.
28. OECD Convention on Combating Bribery of Foreign Public Officials in International Business Transactions, 37 ILM 1 (1988), signed 17 December 1997, entered into force February 15, 1999. See generally, Ethan S. Burger and Mary S. Holland, "Why the Private Sector Is Likely to Lead the Next Stage in the

Global Fight against Corruption," *Fordham International Law Journal* 30, no. 45 (December 2006).

29. United Nations Convention against Corruption, signed October 31, 2003, entered into force December 14, 2005.

30. Judith N. Shklar, *Legalism: Law, Morals and Political Trials*, Cambridge: Harvard University Press, 1964, 1986.

31. For the purposes of this study "serious human rights violations" includes acts that would be crimes under the Rome Statute of the International Criminal Court, as well as other serious violations of rights protected by the International Covenant on Civil and Political Rights and related international human rights treaties that attract criminal liability under domestic or international law.

32. See generally Naomi Roht-Arriaza, *The Pinochet Effect: Transitional Justice in the Age of Human Rights*, Philadelphia: University of Pennsylvania Press, 2005.

33. In an article surveying all human rights trials in all countries of the world since 1979, Kathryn Sikkink and Carrie Booth Walling similarly find a decrease in the number of trials after 2002. "Errors about Trials: The Emergence and Impact of the Justice Cascade," presented at the Princeton International Relations Faculty Colloquium, February 13, 2006 (on file with authors).

34. Tim Rogers, "Why Nicaragua's Caged Bird Sings," *Time* in partnership with CNN, May 2, 2007, www.time.com/time/world/article/0,8599,1616952,00.html.

35. Judith Ewell, *The Indictment of a Dictator: The Extradition and Trial of Marcos Pérez Jiménez*, College Station: Texas A&M University Press, 1981, 123. *Black's Law Dictionary* gives the following definitions for these crimes: Peculation – "embezzlement, especially by a public official." *Blacks Law Dictionary*, Abridged 7th ed., s.v. "peculation"; Malversation – "[French "ill-behavior"] Official corruption . . . especially by someone exercising an office." *Blacks Law Dictionary*, Abridged 7th ed., s.v. "malversation."

36. Ewell, *Indictment*, 141.

37. Paul Lewis, "Fighting in Panama: United Nations; Security Council Condemnation of Invasion Vetoed," *New York Times*, December 24, 1989.

38. Roht-Arriaza, *The Pinochet Effect*.

39. Amnesty International, *Philippines: Torture Persists: Appearance and Reality within the Criminal Justice System*, ASA 35/001/2003, January 24, 2003.

2

Prosecutions of Heads of State in Europe

Ellen L. Lutz

Europe has had a long tradition of calling for criminal prosecutions of senior officials for grave crimes committed while in office. Since the end of the Cold War, the "justice norm" has become further embedded. Europeans' willingness to try their own leaders is illustrated in several lines of cases: (1) the prosecutions of aging former Nazi officials for crimes they committed during World War II; (2) the prosecutions of former Eastern European leaders for Cold War–era crimes; (3) the Slobodan Milošević trial (and related trials) in the International Criminal Tribunal for the former Yugoslavia and subsequent domestic and international trials of perpetrators involved in war crimes and crimes against humanity in the former Yugoslav countries; and (4) the prosecutions of heads of state and other top government officials on corruption charges. In addition, Western European countries have opened their courts to trials of perpetrators of genocide, crimes against humanity, and other serious human rights violations from Argentina, Chile, the former Yugoslavia, Rwanda, and numerous other countries. Almost all of the countries of Eastern and Western Europe are members of the International Criminal Court (ICC) and to regional and international human rights and anticorruption treaties; in addition, most have conformed their domestic legislation to the ICC statute's provisions.

EUROPEAN ANTECEDENTS TO CONTEMPORARY TRIALS OF POLITICAL LEADERS

Even before the end of World War I, there was intense Allied interest in trying German leaders responsible for war crimes. The Versailles Treaty of 1919 called for the trial of German emperor William II by an international tribunal for "a supreme offense against international morality and the sanctity of treaties" (especially the violation of the German-guaranteed neutrality of

Belgium and Luxembourg). The treaty called for the kaiser to be tried before a special tribunal of five judges from the United States, Great Britain, France, Italy, and Japan. However, the Netherlands, where the kaiser had fled, refused to extradite him on the grounds that the offense charged was unknown in Dutch law. The trial never took place.

In the early 1920s, the Europe-dominated League of Nations took up the question of creating a permanent international criminal court. Its Advisory Committee of Jurists submitted a resolution calling for the establishment of a High Court of Justice that would, upon referral by the League of Nations, be "competent to try crimes constituting a breach of international public order or against the universal law of nations."[1] The resolution was ignored. The matter was revived after the assassination of King Alexander of Yugoslavia in 1934, and in 1937 a treaty was drafted to create an international criminal court that would try persons accused of offenses established in the Convention for the Prevention and Punishment of Terrorism. World War II intervened, however, and it never entered into force.[2]

Trying World War II–era Nazi war criminals was first discussed in the early years of the war. Initially, the Allied leaders were not in agreement about what to do with Hitler and his most senior henchmen. Winston Churchill took the view that their "guilt was so black," it was "beyond the scope of any judicial process"[3] and argued for summary execution of the Nazi leaders once their identities were confirmed. By the end of war, however, he was persuaded by the Americans, with whom Stalin was in accord, to participate in formal trials.

Final agreement on the Charter of the International Military Tribunal did not come until August 8, 1945, after the war in Europe had ended. The tribunal's statute had just thirty succinct articles, which set forth the structure and powers of the court and defined the crimes over which it had jurisdiction: crimes against peace, war crimes, and crimes against humanity. The statute also provided guarantees of a fair trial for the defendants and established the scope of punishment for those found guilty. The defendants were to be tried by the International Military Tribunal, composed of prosecutors and judges from the four Allied powers.

The indictment issued on August 24, 1945, named twenty-four defendants. The list did not include the three most senior Nazi leaders, Adolf Hitler, Joseph Goebbels, or Heinrich Himmler, all of whom had committed suicide. The most senior defendant was Hermann Goering, whom Hitler had designated to be his successor. At the conclusion of the trial, twenty-two defendants remained.[4] Of these, three were found innocent. Twelve were sentenced to death by hanging – an issue in itself, not because any of the four Allied powers opposed the death penalty, but because, at that time, European military officers considered it dishonorable for military officers to be executed by any means other than firing squad. On October 16, 1946, ten of the twelve were hanged. Goering committed suicide the evening before his scheduled execution. Another defendant, Martin Bormann, who was tried in absentia, was never found. Of the remaining defendants, three received life terms, the rest terms ranging from ten to twenty years. At the insistence of the USSR, all served their sentences in full.

DOMESTIC TRIALS FOR WORLD WAR II CRIMES

Following the International Military Tribunal trial at Nuremberg, additional trials of high-ranking Nazis and others implicated in Third Reich crimes were carried out by the victorious powers in their respective occupied zones. These included specialized trials targeting judges, doctors, and industrialists, as well as trials that addressed specific population targets, methods of murder, or specific concentration camps.

Less well known are the trials that Germany and formerly occupied countries conducted themselves. In the Enabling Treaty of March 30, 1955, the Allies gave Germany full jurisdictional power to try German war criminals. Trials proceeded for more than two decades. As one German legal scholar wrote in 1976, more than 50,000 Nazi criminal cases have been prosecuted, in many instances successfully: "Very few of the Nazis in responsible places have . . . escaped adjudication in one form or another."[5] Nevertheless, because of a lack of political enthusiasm, a judiciary tainted by its own involvement in the Nazi regime, laws that favored findings of lesser levels of culpability, dispersed control over individual trials, and disparities in the availability of evidence, most Nazi criminals who were actually found guilty received sentences that made "a mockery of the victims' suffering."[6]

France, Italy, Belgium, and other European countries also tried collaborators. In France trials initially were a sidebar to purges by former Resistance activists to root out collaborators and ensure that they paid for their crimes. Tens of thousands were summarily executed. More than one hundred thousand were jailed. Women accused of having had sexual relations with German soldiers had their heads shaved. Yet as the initial zeal for retribution faded and order was reestablished, liberation courts were set up to try Vichy officials and collaborators. These courts were less than impartial because justices and jurors were drawn from Resistance groups. They were less than efficient because of the enormous volume of cases, the inexperience of the jurists, and the complex procedural rules they were required to follow. Nonetheless, by 1951, 124,751 cases had been tried. Of these, 2,853 of the accused were sentenced to death (767 were executed), 38,266 received prison sentences, and 46,145 were found guilty of *indignité national* and punished with loss of political or economic rights.[7]

Among those tried was Field Marshall Philippe Petain, a World War I hero who was enlisted at age eighty-three to lead the Vichy government and granted extraordinary powers after the Germans invaded France in the spring of 1940. After the war, Petain insisted on returning to France from Switzerland, where the Germans had unceremoniously deposited him in the waning hours of the war. As his biographer described it, "The main burden of complaint, and the one on which de Gaulle laid particular emphasis, was not what had happened at Vichy but that Petain in person was responsible for the ignominious 'capitulation' of 1940 – in other words, responsible for France's shame."[8] He was tried for treason, but not for the worst crimes of the Vichy regime, including the deportation of French Jews, the forced labor of French citizens sent to German concentration camps, or the "anti-terror" campaign of the Milice, or French Gestapo.[9] Although sentenced to death, Charles de Gaulle commuted his sentence to life imprisonment on account of his advanced age. He died in prison in 1951.

POST–WORLD WAR II EUROPEAN TRIALS OF SENIOR POLITICAL FIGURES

Calls for trials of senior political leaders who commit crimes while in power have since been heard frequently in Europe. Popular demand for trials has often forced the hands of political leaders who owed favors to rights-violating or corrupt predecessors or who, for other reasons, considered filing indictments against political leaders to be too sensitive politically. This, in part, results from the tradition in many civil law jurisdictions of empowering individuals who have been the victims of crimes to initiate private prosecutions against alleged perpetrators. Although the details of this system vary from country to country, in essence, when individuals file credible criminal cases, state prosecutors or investigating magistrates must investigate them as if they had been brought by a state prosecutor.

In Greece, in the wake of the collapse of the authoritarian regime of the colonels on July 23, 1974, Constantine Karamanlis's transitional government immediately faced the problem of what to do about the crimes committed by its military predecessors. The colonels believed that they had fire-walled themselves from prosecution with an amnesty decree they had negotiated with conservative and centrist political parties before leaving office. Karamanlis, whose main interest during his initial months in office was to hold elections to consolidate democracy and his own legitimacy as head of state, was hesitant to take on the military by filing charges against its leaders. His hand was forced by an Athens attorney, Alexandros Lykourezos, who initiated a private prosecution.

As two Greek scholars have noted, Lykourezos's action "allowed the government to have its cake and eat it too" by relieving it of the political costs of both inaction and initiating proceedings.[10] Indeed, the case provided Karamanlis with the opportunity to showcase democracy at work and opened the door for other private citizens to file cases. Four major criminal cases were tried in Greece the following year: twenty leaders of the 1967 military coup were charged with high treason for their illegal seizure of power;[11] thirty-two individuals, including junta leader George Papadopoulos and his successor Dimitrios Ioannides, were charged with the bloody suppression of the student uprising at the National Technical University of Greece on November 17, 1973; and fifty-five active and retired military officers and conscripts were tried in two trials for torture by the military police. The three most culpable coup leaders were sentenced to death, fifteen others received lengthy prison terms, and two were acquitted. Significant prison terms were also meted out to those convicted in the other two cases. Karamanlis commuted the three death sentences to life imprisonment. Papadopoulos died in prison in 1999; as of January 2008, Ioannides was still serving time.

The fall of the Berlin Wall provided a fresh opportunity to try former leaders for human rights and other crimes committed while in office. The response of post-Communist states varied widely. Some states, such as Czechoslovakia, Hungary, and Poland, initially opted for nonjudicial accountability solutions such as "lustration," or banishment from political life. Romania summarily executed its former dictator Nicolae Ceausescu and his wife Elena, although it publicly declared that they had been convicted and sentenced to death by an extraordinary military court for grave crimes against Romania, including "genocide, subversion of the state, theft of public assets, destruction of the national economy, and an attempt to escape."[12]

In Bulgaria, public clamor led to Todor Hristov Zhivkov becoming the first former Communist leader in Eastern Europe to be tried, convicted, and punished. Yet instead of facing charges for a five-year forced-assimilation campaign against ethnic Turks in Bulgaria that led to the mass exodus of some 310,000 people, Zhivkov was charged with embezzlement and corruption. According to Helsinki Watch, the prosecutor general's office probably chose to focus on economic crimes because of Bulgaria's political climate in the early 1990s, which included widespread popular support for Zhivkov's anti-Turkish policies.[13] He was convicted of corruption for rewarding cronies with cars and apartments. Charges of embezzling millions of dollars and transferring them to personal Swiss bank accounts were not proved. Because of his frail health, he was permitted to serve his seven-year sentence under house arrest. Zhivkov was acquitted of the charges by the Bulgarian Supreme Court in 1996 and died two years later.

In Albania, Ramiz Alia, who became his country's head of state in 1985 and led the reclusive hard-line Communist state until March 1992, when the Democratic Party won in a national election, was charged, after he left office, with misappropriating government property and funds, misusing power, and abusing the rights of citizens. Although credited with bringing democracy to Albania, Alia had become unpopular by the time he lost power in September 1992. He was found guilty two years later and sentenced to nine years in prison. Although his sentence subsequently was reduced to five years, he served only one, because the Court of Appeals ruled that the Albanian Criminal Code exempted him from serving his term. In March 1996, Alia was charged with crimes against humanity and again imprisoned. A year later, in the midst of his trial, a riot broke out. Prison guards deserted the prison where Alia was being held, and he escaped. His whereabouts are still unknown.

In 1997, the Czech Republic indicted Jozef Lenárt, prime minister of Czechoslovakia from 1963 to 1968, for his role in suppressing the Prague Spring uprising. He was accused of summoning Soviet forces in 1968 to crush the uprising. Seventy-two people died as a result. Although the court rejected Lenárt's claim of head-of-state immunity, he was acquitted in 2002 for lack of evidence. His acquittal was upheld on appeal, but not in popular public opinion. President Vaclav Havel publicly expressed disappointment at the acquittal, and Lenárt's death in 2004 was barely covered in the Czech press.

Public clamor to try former German Democratic Republic leaders came from both sides of the Berlin Wall rubble. East German former dissidents called on Bonn to prove its commitment to their revolution by aggressively pursuing justice, even if doing so meant relaxing the rigid procedural and due-process rules of the German legal system. A backlash occurred, however, when the united German government moved ahead with indictments of four border guards for shooting East Germans who were trying to escape to the West. Critics complained that in its eagerness to try somebody, the government was engaging in the same sort of "victor's justice" that the Allies imposed on Germany at Nuremberg. The judicial spotlight turned to the top-level decision makers who were responsible for making the laws or giving the orders under which the border guards acted. In May 1992, four senior officials, including Erich Honecker, the former state council and Socialist Unity Party chairman, were charged in an 800-page indictment with collective manslaughter.

Trying Honecker was a delicate matter for Germany's political elite because, in the final years of the Cold War, he had been on cordial terms with and welcomed during an official state visit by Chancellor Helmut Kohl. Yet the bigger problem was what to do about the defendant's deteriorating health as a result of aggressive liver cancer. In January 1993, the German constitutional appeals court dismissed the charges against Honecker for health reasons, and he flew to Chile, where he died the following year. In May 1993, his codefendants were found guilty as accessories to the crimes committed by the border guards, who already had been found guilty of being the direct perpetrators. Honecker's codefendants received prison terms of four-and-a-half to seven-and-a-half years.

The matter did not end there. In 1995, Egon Krenz, East Germany's last president, who served for only six weeks in 1989, was indicted along with two former government colleagues on similar charges. Krenz played no part in any of the border-patrol shootings, nor was he involved in drafting the law that authorized their doing so. Critics contended that he was selected for prosecution because, unlike most East German leaders, he was still relatively young and healthy. Nonetheless, Krenz was convicted and sentenced to six-and-a-half years in prison. He appealed for years but gave himself up in 2000 after the European Court of Human Rights and Germany's highest court turned down his appeals; he served four years before his sentence was commuted.[14]

The latest Communist-era indictment involves Poland's Cold War–era strongman, General Wojciech Jaruzelski. On April 17, 2007, Jaruzelski, now eighty-three and repentant, was charged with committing a "communist crime" by declaring martial law in 1981 to curb the rise of the Solidarity movement, the Soviet bloc's first free trade union that directly challenged the Communist order. Poland's parliament cleared him in 1996 of all constitutional responsibility for imposing martial law, but the new charges focus on his creation of a criminal military organization with the aim of conducting crimes. If he is found guilty, Jaruzelski could be sentenced to ten years in prison, although on May 8, 2008, a Polish regional court called on prosecutors to revise their indictment against him, further delaying the elderly ex-leader's trial.[15]

CASES AGAINST AGING NAZIS

In the waning years of the twentieth century, Europe confronted the prospect of a generation of Nazi atrocity victims who were dying without the satisfaction of knowing that their persecutors had faced justice, and of Nazi war criminals who were escaping justice through their own deaths. Beginning in the 1980s, European prosecutors expanded their efforts to extradite and try those Nazi perpetrators who were still alive.

Because by then the most senior Nazis had been tried or were dead, these trials focused on those at the intermediate levels of the chain of command who were believed responsible for specific horrific acts, deportations, or massacres. Although trials took place, the passage of time played havoc with the interests of justice. Elderly witnesses desperate to see justice done, supported by sympathetic and zealous prosecutors, introduced evidence that fading memories and physical aging rendered practically worthless.[16] In some cases, the alleged perpetrator was so old or infirm that a court found it would be inhumane to put him on trial.[17] France is the one country where national courts have conducted high-profile trials of ex-Nazis, the third of which had tentacles that reached into the highest ranks of contemporary French politics.

In 1984, France put Klaus Barbie on trial. Barbie, a German who was the head of the Gestapo in Lyon, was accused of torturing prisoners and ordering the deportation of thousands of Jews, including a group of forty-four Jewish children from an orphanage. Within France, his best-known crime was the torture and murder of Jean Moulin, a leader of the French Resistance movement. After the war, Barbie worked for U.S. counterintelligence forces. The Americans helped him relocate to Bolivia, where he lived under the pseudonym of Klaus Altmann and had close ties to brutal Bolivian dictator and cocaine trafficker Luís García Meza Tejada. After García Meza was stripped of power, Bolivia turned Barbie over to the French to stand trial. Barbie's trial was infamous for his defense strategy, which included both Nazi apologists and defense lawyer Jacques Verges's attempt to put France on trial for war crimes it had committed in Algeria and other French colonies after World War II. Barbie was found guilty and sentenced to life imprisonment. He died in prison four years later at age seventy-seven.[18]

The first contemporary trial of a Frenchman implicated in Nazi-era crimes involved the head of intelligence in the Milice, Paul Touvier, who served under Barbie. In 1946, Touvier was tried in absentia and sentenced to death by a French court for treason and collusion with the enemy. By remaining in hiding, he managed to outwait the twenty-year statute of limitations on French sentences. A 1971 decision by President Georges Pompidou to pardon him inflamed public opinion, and two years later new charges of crimes against humanity for the assassination of seven Jews were filed against Touvier. In 1989, he was finally caught hiding in a monastery in Nice. He was arrested, and additional charges for other wartime-era crimes were filed against him. He was convicted in 1994 at age eighty-one and sentenced to life imprisonment; his conviction was upheld on appeal the following year. Touvier died in 1996.[19]

The final case in this trilogy involved Maurice Papon, a civil servant in the Vichy government who provided the French Resistance with important intelligence. In 1998, at age eighty-seven and after the longest trial in French history, he was found guilty of "complicity in crimes against humanity" for participating in the arrest and deportation of 1,560 Jews to Germany. He was sentenced to ten years' imprisonment. As one reporter described it, "The Papon trial called an individual collaborator to account, but he stood in the dock as a representative of thousands of other French people faced with similar dilemmas in the Vichy period."[20]

Unlike Touvier, who spent most of his life fleeing from French justice, Papon held a post near the pinnacle of the French political system. He was chief of the Paris police during the 1960s, had the French Legion of Honor bestowed upon him by President Charles de Gaulle, and later served as budget minister under Prime Minister Raymond Barre and President Valéry Giscard d'Estaing from 1978 to 1981. Papon's disgrace, against which he doggedly fought, came with the changing of the contemporary political guard. After fourteen years of legal wrangling, he was finally convicted in 1998.[21] Still fighting, he fled to Switzerland while his conviction was appealed but was returned by the Swiss authorities. The penalty for his flight was summary dismissal of his appeal.[22] Initial appeals for clemency to French president Jacques Chirac were denied, and Papon served three years in prison. However, in 2002, invoking a French law that provided for the early release of aged prisoners to receive medical care, Papon prevailed upon a French court to free him. He died in February 2007.

In 1986, Austria, long notorious in the region for not investigating or prosecuting its Nazi war criminals, elected former United Nations (UN) Secretary General Kurt Waldheim president. Shortly thereafter, Waldheim's past as a Wehrmacht officer in Yugoslavia and Greece came to light. An international commission of historians asserted in a 1988 report that Waldheim had been "in close proximity" to some Nazi atrocities and knew that they were going on. Further, it said he deceived the international community about his service and tried to make it seem harmless.[23] Although he refused to step down as president and Austria made no attempt to prosecute him, the court of international public opinion did so. Foreign leaders shunned the country to avoid meeting him, and the United States placed him on the "watch list" of persons banned from entering the country.

THE INTERNATIONAL CRIMINAL TRIBUNAL
FOR THE FORMER YUGOSLAVIA

In 1993, in response to widespread and systematic murder, rape, and "ethnic cleansing" of civilians in Bosnia, the UN Security Council, acting under the peace enforcement provisions of the UN Charter (Chapter VII), established the Ad Hoc Tribunal for the Prosecution of Persons Responsible for Serious Violations of International Humanitarian Law Committed in the Territory of the former Yugoslavia since 1991 (ICTY). As such, all member states are required to cooperate with it pursuant to their obligations as members of the United Nations. The tribunal has jurisdiction over four crimes: grave breaches of the Geneva Conventions, violations of the laws or customs of war, crimes against humanity, and genocide committed in the territory of the former Yugoslavia from the start of the war in 1991 until "a date to be determined by the Security Council upon the restoration of peace."[24]

On May 27, 1999, the ICTY became the first international court to indict a sitting head of state for war crimes and crimes against humanity.[25] Slobodan Milošević was indicted by the tribunal at the height of the war in Kosovo for the deportation and murder of Kosovo Albanians. These charges were subsequently expanded to include genocide, crimes against humanity, grave breaches of the Geneva Conventions, and violations of the laws or customs of war in Bosnia and Croatia as well as Kosovo. The saga of Milošević's arrest, trial, and untimely death, along with the impact of those events on justice in Serbia, Bosnia, and other affected countries, is dealt with in Emir Suljagić's chapter in this volume.

In 2005, the ICTY also indicted Kosovo's former prime minister, Ramush Haradinaj, a former commander in the Kosovo Liberation Army, for his alleged role in systematically murdering and ethnically cleansing Serb civilians during the war in Kosovo.[26] All of the charges – and indeed Haradinaj's term as prime minister – relate to a time before Kosovo became an independent sovereign state. Haradinaj, a widely regarded war hero at home who continued to receive public support from some aspects of the international community's presence in Kosovo, enjoyed only 100 days in high office before submitting himself to the jurisdiction of the court in the Hague. The prosecution's case against him was so weak that he was acquitted of all charges in April 2008, although allegations that potential witnesses were too afraid to testify dogged the proceedings.[27]

UNIVERSAL JURISDICTION IN EUROPEAN COURTS

For more than a decade, courts in more than half a dozen European countries have permitted criminal prosecutions to proceed against perpetrators of abuses beyond their borders. In some cases, the courts gained jurisdiction because the defendant voluntarily entered the country. In others, the victims were nationals of the forum state. Spain and Belgium went the farthest and allowed prosecutions to proceed solely on the basis of universal jurisdiction, a legal principle holding that certain crimes are so heinous that those who commit them may be tried by any court, anywhere in the world, regardless of where the crimes occurred or the nationalities of the perpetrator or victims. Under Spanish law, Spain's courts have universal jurisdiction over genocide, crimes against humanity, and offenses that Spain is obliged to prosecute pursuant to its international treaty obligations.[28] On October 16, 1997, shortly after his arrival in the United Kingdom, a Spanish judge issued an international warrant for Chilean General Augusto Pinochet's arrest, and a London magistrate issued a warrant for his arrest under the U.K. extradition law. Pinochet was arrested the following day. The Pinochet case is documented in Chapter 4 of this volume.

Spain has since applied its universal jurisdiction provision to prosecute former Argentine military officer Alfredo Scilingo. He was convicted and sentenced to 640 years in prison for his role in throwing drugged political prisoners into the ocean from helicopters. Another Argentine, Ricardo Miguel Cavallo, was extradited from Mexico to Spain in 2003 to stand trial for genocide and terrorism as a result of his participation in kidnappings and torture. He was also charged with the kidnapping of sixteen babies who were stolen from their imprisoned mothers and given up for adoption during Argentina's dirty war. The trial was delayed to give the Spanish courts time to consider whether Cavallo should be extradited back to Argentina to stand trial. On March 31, 2008, the Spanish government extradited Cavallo to Argentina where he is being prosecuted for crimes against humanity. Other ongoing Spanish universal jurisdiction cases involve investigations into genocides in Tibet, Rwanda, and Guatemala, all of which implicate former or current heads of state.[29]

The more international human rights advocates and their clients pressed for justice in Spanish and Belgian courts, the more the governments of these countries questioned the wisdom of allowing their courts such wide latitude in trying foreign perpetrators with little or no connection to their courts. As Naomi Roht-Arriaza documents in her book *The Pinochet Effect*, several factors contributed to Spain's hesitation, including domestic legal concerns about bombings and assassinations carried out by the Basque separatist group ETA (Euskadi Ta Askatasuna; Basque for "Basque Homeland and Freedom") and the imminence of the establishment of the ICC. Pundits wondered whether Spain was becoming "a 'mini-ICC' that would solve all the world's problems except Spain's."[30] However, to the relief of victims and their supporters, Spain's highest court took a different view. In 1999, a case was filed by Nobel Prize winner Rigoberta Menchú against two former Guatemalan presidents, Romeo Lucas García and Efraín Ríos Montt, and eight other high-ranking officials, alleging that they were responsible for genocide, torture, and terrorism against the Guatemalan Mayan population in the 1980s. As part of these proceedings, in September 2005, Spain's Constitutional Court overturned a Supreme Court decision holding that cases could only be tried in Spanish courts if they contained some nexus to Spain. The Guatemalan case is now proceeding in the Spanish courts with interesting developments that are detailed in Chapter 3.

Belgium, which adopted legislation in 1993 permitting the exercise of universal jurisdiction for war crimes committed in both international and non-international armed conflicts, took a different route.[31] In 1999, the law was expanded to include genocide and crimes against humanity as defined in the Rome Statute of the newly created ICC and the Belgian criminal procedure code was amended to allow victims to bring criminal complaints on the basis of this universal jurisdiction.[32] These laws did not require that the victims or the perpetrators have ties to Belgium, and they provided that no one has immunity from prosecution, even sitting heads of state. By the beginning of 2003, some thirty complaints had been filed before Belgian investigating judges. They included complaints against Israeli prime minister Ariel Sharon, Cuban president Fidel Castro, Palestine Liberation Organization leader Yasir Arafat, and former Chadian president Hissène Habré.

One case, involving an arrest warrant issued for Yerodia Ndombasi, the incumbent minister for foreign affairs of the Democratic Republic of the Congo (DRC), provoked the DRC to turn to the International Court of Justice (ICJ) for a determination of whether the Belgian laws violated international customary law. The DRC alleged that the Belgian court's action violated the international law principle that senior government officials are immune from prosecution in the courts of other sovereign states. The ICJ agreed; it ruled that Belgium must dissolve the arrest warrant because Yerodia was immune from prosecution by virtue of his status as foreign minister.[33] In several separate opinions, the judges considered the validity of universal jurisdiction as a basis for prosecuting war crimes and crimes against humanity without reaching a clear consensus, although the narrowness of the ruling implied that except for the immunity enjoyed by heads of state and foreign ministers while they serve in office, states are free to prosecute perpetrators of serious violations of human rights and humanitarian law in their courts, even if the acts took place abroad.

After the ICJ issued its decision, a Belgian lower court decided that the case against Israeli president Ariel Sharon for alleged war crimes committed during Israel's war against Palestinians in Lebanon, particularly the 1982 destruction of the Sabra and Shatila refuge camps, could not proceed.[34] But on February 12, 2003, the Cour de Cassation (Belgium's Supreme Court) overturned the lower court decision, ruling that the case against Sharon could continue after he left office.[35]

Then, on March 18, 2003, seven Iraqi families filed criminal complaints in Belgium against former U.S. president George H. W. Bush, U.S. vice president Dick Cheney, U.S. secretary of state Colin Powell, and General Norman Schwarzkopf, the American commander of the first Gulf War, alleging that they were responsible for the 1991 bombing of a civilian air raid shelter in Baghdad that caused the deaths of their family members. In response, the United States reportedly threatened to pull NATO headquarters out of Brussels unless the law was changed.[36] This pressure was too much even for progressive Belgium, which regards itself as small country with a special moral role. A bill already before parliament that repealed the universal jurisdiction statute was quickly pushed through and adopted into law in April 2003. Ultimately, the universal jurisdiction provisions were withdrawn entirely in August 2003, and Belgian law now provides that the judiciary may reject complaints in which there are no victims of Belgian nationality or in which the plaintiffs have lived in Belgium for less than three years. In addition, the federal prosecutor is given considerable discretion to reject cases in which the accused person comes from a democratic country that could conduct its own trials. As a consequence, most of the complaints that were pending before the Belgian courts were declared invalid.[37]

One of a handful of cases over which the Belgian courts retained jurisdiction involved Hissène Habré. Habré ruled Chad from 1982 until 1990, when he was ousted and fled to exile in Senegal. His rule was marked by atrocities that included the targeting of the Sara, Hadjerai, Chadian Arab, and Zaghawa ethnic groups whenever he feared their leaders posed a threat to his political power. In 1992, a Chadian truth commission accused Habré's regime of some forty thousand murders, as well as systematic torture carried out by political police, the Documentation and Security Directorate, the leaders of which all came from Habré's Gorane ethnic group.[38] Habré's case survived the amendments to the Belgian law thanks to the concerted efforts of human rights nongovernmental organizations. Although Belgium was under intense political pressure to rescind its universal jurisdiction laws, legislators who were sympathetic to the justice efforts against Habré agreed to include loopholes in the new law that would allow the case to have a chance of continuing. Pending cases already in the system could still be investigated and judged as long as at least one of the initial plaintiffs was a Belgian citizen.[39] The Habré case was safe, because three of the twenty-one plaintiffs were Belgian nationals. In addition, the government of Chad confirmed that it waived any claim to immunity for Habré, which served to reassure the Belgian legislature that allowing the Habré case was not going to present the same political problems as many of the other more controversial cases.[40]

Although a group of victims had already launched proceedings against Habré in Senegal in 1999, which were hailed at the time as a landmark first instance of a former head of state being prosecuted by the state in which he lived in exile, the process had stalled after the Senegalese Cour de Cassation rejected the indictment on the basis that the crimes were outside Senegal's jurisdiction.[41] Belgian judge Daniel Fransen of the Brussels District Court and a team of investigators traveled to Chad in February and March 2002 to interview witnesses and government officials and gather other evidence. In September 2005, Judge Fransen issued an international arrest warrant for Habré and Belgium requested Habré's extradition from Senegal. On November 15, 2005, Senegalese authorities arrested Habré. Senegal's president, Abdoulaye Wade, evaded the politically sensitive decision about whether Senegal had a duty to try him or extradite him to Belgium by referring the question to the African Union.

The African Union set up a committee to review the Habré case at its January 2006 summit, but before that committee could render its opinion, the United Nations Committee against Torture weighed in, finding Senegal in violation of its obligations under the Convention against Torture for failing to try or extradite Habré.[42] At its July 2006 summit, the African Union called on Senegal to honor its obligations under the Torture Convention. President Wade agreed. In April 2008, Senegal amended its constitution to ensure that its courts could prosecute cases of genocide, crimes against humanity, war crimes, or torture, even if they were committed in the past and outside of Senegal.[43] Given that Judge Fransen spent four years accumulating evidence for a trial, the question now is whether Senegal's courts will make use of that evidence and hold a prompt trial. The European Union has offered to provide financial and technical assistance for the trial, which is expected to cost approximately 28 million Euros. However, there can be no doubt that Belgium's willingness to try Habré triggered a chain reaction that led Senegal to assume criminal jurisdiction over him.[44]

INDICTMENTS AND PROSECUTIONS OF EUROPEAN HEADS OF STATE ON CORRUPTION TRIALS

Although some countries in Europe, particularly the Scandinavian countries, have done a good job of insulating public officials from the temptations of corruption through the institutionalization of preventive measures, other countries' responses to head-of-state corruption can be characterized as a political-legal balancing act. As noted in the introduction to this volume, some governments, such as Germany, have opted for political sanctions rather than prosecution. Other countries have turned to the courts with varying degrees of success.

In Italy, Milanese prosecutors initiated the aggressive Mani Pulite campaign in response to more than four decades of institutionalized political corruption linked to the Catholic Church and the Mafia, popularly known as Tangentopoli. The campaign led to criminal charges against several prime ministers. One, Giulio Andreotti, who served several times during the Christian Democrat Party's forty-year post–World War II reign, was acquitted.[45] Socialist leader Bettino Craxi, whose extravagant lifestyle and arrogant insistence that corruption was something everybody did, fled to his private villa in Tunisia to avoid serving prison time for his conviction for accepting bribes. Tunisian dictator Ben Ali protected Craxi until his death in 2000.

The most notorious charges were brought against Italian prime minister Silvio Berlusconi. Berlusconi, a media magnate and one of the wealthiest men (if not the wealthiest man) in Italy, rode to political power in 1994 on a wave of anticorruption sentiment. Although his initial term in office was short-lived because of partisan politics, he was reelected in 2001 and served a full five-year term. In the interim, he was swept up in the Mani Pulite investigations that had brought down several of his predecessors. Over the years, charges against him have included perjury for lying in court about his affiliation with a Freemason lodge that was tainted by Tangentopoli; bribing a member of the financial police; illegally financing a political party through an illegal offshore banking account (two separate cases); false accounting; corrupting a judge; embezzlement, tax fraud, and false accounting in a business deal; false accounting for a secret 5 million Euro payment to a Torino soccer club so that it could buy professional player Luigi Lentini; accounting fraud regarding his media group Finivest; and corrupting a judge in connection with the privatization of a state-owned food company.[46]

So far, Berlusconi has managed to beat the charges in every case. In several he was found guilty by a trial court and sentenced to jail time. In these he was either acquitted on appeal or won motions to have the cases thrown out because the statute of limitations had run out (in Italy the statute continues running until all appeals are exhausted). To beat others, he had to take advantage of his position at the helm of Italian politics.

In June 2003, the Italian legislature passed a decree that offered immunity from criminal prosecution while in office to the prime minister, the president of state, the presidents of both chambers of Congress, and the president of the Constitutional Court. It was immediately apparent to many that the amnesty's purpose was to protect Berlusconi from international embarrassment on the eve of his assuming the presidency of the European Union. The law was repealed by the Italian Constitutional Court in January 2004.[47]

Other laws that have benefited Berlusconi have passed in record time and remain on the books. These include laws severely decreasing the statute of limitations for white-collar crimes, restricting the use of cross-border evidence, and amending the corporate corruption laws so that "cooking the books" is no longer a serious crime. Another bill, adopted by the legislature in 2002, allowed criminal defendants to request that their cases be annulled or moved if the defendant had a "legitimate suspicion" that a judge was biased against them. Other new laws have modified the rules for media monopolies in ways that fortified Berlusconi's control over the Italian media, even while in office.[48]

Neighboring France has similarly suffered corruption scandals that touch top government officials and, in November 2007, the political figure at whom the most fingers have pointed, former president Jacques Chirac, was placed under formal investigation for misusing Paris taxpayers' money to fund political allies and friends when he was mayor of Paris from 1977 to 1995.[49] Chirac has been implicated in numerous allegations of corruption, including listing fictitious employees on the staff of the Paris town hall when he was mayor and directing their salaries to staffers of his RPR (Rassemblement pour la République) political party; taking kickbacks for school-building contracts that were divided among the political parties in the Ile-de-France region of Paris; and using public funds to pay for costly trips for himself and his family. On January 30, 2004, Chirac's long-time deputy and former French prime minister Alain Juppé was convicted of diverting Paris taxpayers' money to bankroll political party jobs when Chirac was mayor of Paris and Juppé was general secretary and president of the RPR party. Other charges against Juppé, who at the time was mayor of Bordeaux, were dropped, and he was sentenced to an eighteen-month suspended sentence and loss of his right to hold or run for office for five years. Juppé immediately appealed. Meanwhile, commentators in the French press called Juppé "the fuse that blows to protect the main object," and "the fall guy for Jacques Chirac."[50]

Chirac managed to stay out of court on account of a 2001 French Cour de Cassation decision holding that a French president cannot be tried or even questioned in court proceedings for any offense short of high treason for the duration of his term.[51] In its ruling, the court explicitly recognized that compelling a head of state to testify in court could be a smokescreen for political attack and that presidential immunity was necessary for the cohesion of the nation and the image of France abroad.[52] However, Chirac's immunity ended with the election of Nicolas Sarkozy as France's president. Commentators following the Juppé case, as well as a subsequent trial of forty-seven other Chirac cronies for rigging public works contracts to pay for political party expenses in 2005, have long suggested that Chirac's interest in staying in power was motivated, at least in part, by his desire to stay out of court. Indeed, at one point, Chirac's supporters in parliament introduced legislation similar to that which long protected Augusto Pinochet of Chile, to make former presidents "senators for life" with the attendant immunity benefits. Chirac distanced himself from the measure, which failed. However, now that he is eligible to stand trial, it is not certain he will do so. He is now seventy-four and in poor health. While politically unpopular, he is still a fixture in the social circles of the country's top judges, including those who value France's image over the honesty of its politicians.

Elsewhere in Europe, corruption trials have proceeded against former heads of state in Belarus and Bosnia. In Belarus, Prime Minister Mikhail Chigir was appointed in 1994 but resigned in 1996 to protest a constitutional referendum orchestrated by President Alexander Lukashenko to dissolve parliament. Chigir was arrested in 1999 and charged with financial impropriety in relation to a position he held as head of a bank before he became prime minister. The proceedings were widely regarded as being a political move by President Lukashenko, and Chigir's trial was attended by representatives from various embassies in Minsk as well as from the Organization for Security and Co-operation in Europe. Chigir, who was named a "prisoner of conscience" by Amnesty International, was found guilty and sentenced to three years' imprisonment, which he avoided because of time served in pretrial detention and because two years of the three-year sentence were suspended. However, he also was fined $200,000 and banned from politics for five years.

Bosnia-Herzegovina co-president Dragan Čović, the ethnic Croat member of the tripartite presidency, was indicted for financial corruption along with the chief justice of Bosnia's constitutional court. Čović was convicted on November 17, 2006, and sentenced to five years in prison. He was released the following month after posting $2.1 million in bail and relinquishing his travel documents pending the completion of appellate proceedings. Although removed from the presidency by Paddy Ashdown, then the international community's high representative in charge of Bosnia's postwar administration, Čović recently was reelected as chairman of his political party, the Croat Democratic Union.

CONCLUSION

In concert with Europe's embrace of human rights, which are reinforced by regional institutions like the European Union, the Council of Europe, and the European Court of Human Rights, these cases show that Europe has embraced trials as the right and just response to serious human rights or financial crimes committed by top government officials. In some countries, there have been no trials because there has been no need for trials. Embedded political institutions such as successive democratic elections, separation of powers, the rule of law, and strong codes of professional ethical responsibility have done their work in preventing head-of-state misconduct.

In other countries, Europe's relatively free press, engaged civil society, and professional prosecutors and judges have uncovered misconduct at the pinnacles of political power, which has led to popular demand for accountability. This does not mean that heads of state will be prosecuted, however, or that if they are prosecuted, courts will be tough on them when they use legal maneuvers to run the statute of limitations or otherwise attempt to undermine justice. Nor does it mean that if they are convicted, they will spend time in prison. All of the branches of political power have an interest in mutual protection, shared social circles or common political and ethical frames of reference. Furthermore, there is the matter of weighing political capital in a region that is stable, democratic, and economically prosperous and that has a wide range of competing domestic, regional, and international concerns. These and other counterpressures combine to limit legitimate prosecutions of heads of state.

NOTES

1. See Manley O. Hudson, "The Proposed International Criminal Court," *American Journal of International Law* 32 (1938): 549.
2. *Convention for the Creation of an International Criminal Court,* opened for signature, November, 16, 1937, League of Nations O.J. Spec. Supp. 156 (1938); League of Nations Doc. C.547(I)M.384(I)1937V.
3. Telford Taylor, *The Anatomy of the Nuremberg Trials: A Personal Memoir,* Boston: Little, Brown & Co., 1993, 29.
4. One defendant, Robert Ley, committed suicide while awaiting trial; the case against another, Gustav Krupp (the industrial magnate who headed the Krupp family enterprises until 1940), was severed when it became clear that he was too old and infirm to stand trial. A third defendant, Martin Bormann (head of the Party Chancellery and private secretary to Adolf Hitler, who was uniformly despised not only by the Allies but also by his fellow German officers), was never arrested but was nonetheless tried and convicted in absentia.
5. Fritz Weinschenk, "Nazis before German Courts: The West German War Crimes Trials," *International Lawyer* 10, no. 3 (Summer 1976): 519–527. Reprinted in Neil J. Kritz, ed., *Transitional Justice: How Emerging Democracies Reckon with Former Regimes, Vol. II, Country Studies,* Washington, DC: United States Institute of Peace, 1995.
6. Ingo Muller, *Hitler's Justice: The Courts of the Third Reich,* Cambridge, MA: Harvard University Press, 1991, quoting Fritz Bauer, "Im Namen des Volkes," in *Zwanzig Jahre Danach,* Hammerschmidt, ed. (1965): 308, reprinted in Kritz, *Transitional Justice,* 16.
7. Kritz, *Transitional Justice,* 83–102, and articles cited therein.

8. Charles Williams, *Petain, How the Hero of France Became a Convicted Traitor and Changed the Course of History*, New York: Palgrave Macmillan, 2005, 3.

9. Ibid., 249.

10. Nicos C. Alivizatos and P. Nikiforos Diamandouros, "Politics and the Judiciary in the Greek Transition to Democracy," in *Transitional Justice and the Rule of Law in New Democracies*, A. James McAdams, ed., Notre Dame, IN: University of Notre Dame Press, 1997, 35.

11. Twenty-four were indicted, but three went into hiding and escaped arrest and a fourth was on trial at the same time for torture.

12. David Lauter, "Ceausescu, Wife Reported Executed; Secret Trial Condemned Dictator," *Los Angeles Times*, December 26, 1989, p. 1.

13. Helsinki Watch, "Decommunization in Bulgaria" (August 1993): 17, reprinted in Kritz, *Transitional Justice*, 710–711.

14. *Streletz, Kessler and Krenz v. Germany* (2001): E.C.H.R., judgment of 22 March 2001, app. nos. 34044/96, 35532/97 and 44801/98.

15. BBC World Monitoring, "Polish Court Orders Prosecutors to Revise Indictment against Communist Leader," *PAP News Agency*, Warsaw, May 14, 2008.

16. One defendant, John Demjanjuk, became a transcontinental ping-pong ball. Having obtained citizenship in the United States, he was extradited to Israel in 1986, where he was convicted of being a notorious concentration camp guard in Treblinka. The Israeli Supreme Court found the evidence against him wanting, and he returned to the United States. He was subsequently alleged to have been part of an SS unit that rounded up more than two million Polish Jews. Again the United States extradited him, this time to the Ukraine, to stand trial.

17. See, for example, "German Court Throws Out Conviction of Nazi SS Officer, Citing Age," *Agence France Presse*, June 25, 2004.

18. For more on the Klaus Barbie trial, see Guyora Binder, "Representing Nazism: Advocacy and Identity at the Trial of Klaus Barbie," *Yale Law Journal* 98 (May 1989): 1321; Alain Finkielkraut, *Remembering in Vain: The Klaus Barbie Trial and Crimes against Humanity*, New York: Colombia University Press, 1992.

19. For more on the Touvier case, see Michael Tiger et al., "Paul Touvier and the Crime against Humanity," *Texas International Law Journal* 30 (1995): 285.

20. Edith Coron, "Papon Verdict Rewrites the History Books," *Scotland on Sunday*, April 5, 1998.

21. Upon his conviction, Papon was stripped of his membership in the Legion of Honor and subsequently tried and fined for unlawfully wearing the Legion of Honor banner.

22. Papon brought an action against France in the European Court of Human Rights for the summary loss of his appeal on account of his flight. The European Court ruled in Papon's favor but did not award him damages or order France to provide him with a reprieve from his punishment.

23. George Jahn, "Ex-Austrian President Says CIA Files Vindicate Him," *Associated Press*, April 29, 2001.

24. S.C. Res. 827, May 25, 1993, U.N. Doc S/Res/1993/827. The subject matter jurisdiction of the ICTY is set out in Articles 1–5 of the Statute of the International Criminal Tribunal for the former Yugoslavia, which was appended to the resolution.

25. The International Tribunal for Rwanda was the first international court to indict a national government leader – former Rwandan prime minister Jean Kambanda, who was subsequently convicted of genocide.

26. *The Prosecutor against Ramush Haradinaj et al,* IT-04-84-I, Indictment, March 4, 2005.

27. Molly More, "Kosovo's Ex-Premier Acquitted of War Crimes against Serbs," *Washington Post,* April 4, 2008, p. A18.

28. Organic Law 6/1985 of the Judicial Power (*Ley Organica 6/1985, de 1 de Julio del Poder Judicial*), as amended by Ogranic Law 11/1999, art. 23.4 (a) and (g).

29. The Rwandan genocide case implicates current Rwandan president Paul Kagame who has immunity from prosecution; the Tibet case implicates former Chinese president Jiang Zemin, ex–Prime Minister Li Peng, and five military and security officials in Tibet.

30. Naomi Roht-Arriaza, *The Pinochet Effect: Transnational Justice in the Age of Human Rights,* Philadelphia: University of Pennsylvania Press, 2005, 376–377.

31. Act concerning Punishment for Grave Breaches of International Humanitarian Law, enacted 16 June 1993.

32. Code of Criminal Procedure of 1878, art. 7.

33. *Democratic Republic of the Congo v. Belgium,* Case Concerning the Arrest Warrant of 11 April 2000, ICJ, 14 February 2002, General List No. 121.

34. Roht-Arriaza, *The Pinochet Effect,* 409.

35. Bruce Zagaris, "Belgium Supreme Court Rules Sharon Must Face War Crimes Charge," *International Enforcement Law Reporter,* April 2003.

36. Paul Geitner, "Belgium Amends War Crimes Law; New Version Expected to Prevent Politically Motivated Indictments," *Associated Press,* August 2, 2003.

37. Marlise Simons, "Belgium Puts Limits on War Crimes Law," *International Herald Tribune,* April 7, 2003, p. 7; Richard Bernstein, "Belgium Rethinks Its Prosecutorial Zeal," *New York Times,* April 1, 2003, p. A8.

38. For further background on Habré's case, see Reed Brody, "The Prosecution of Hissène Habré: International Accountability, National Impunity," in *Transitional Justice in the Twenty-First Century: Beyond Truth versus Justice,* Naomi Roht-Arriaza and Javier Mariezcurrena, eds., Cambridge: Cambridge University Press, 2006, 278. See also Human Rights Watch, *The Trial of Hissène Habré: Time Is Running Out for the Victims,* January 2007.

39. Brody, "The Prosecution of Hissène Habré," 290.

40. Ibid.

41. Ibid., "The Prosecution of Hissène Habré," 288.

42. Decision of the Committee against Torture under article 22 of the Convention against Torture and Other Cruel, Inhuman or Degrading Treatment or Punishment – Thirty-sixth session, 19 May 2006, U.N. Doc CAT/C/36/D/181/2001.

43. "Senegal Passes Law to Put Chad's Habré on Trial," Reuters, April 9, 2008.

44. For more on the Habré case, see Human Rights Watch, *The Case against Hissène Habré, an African Pinochet,* May 2008.

45. Donatella della Porta, "A Judges' Revolution? Political Corruption and the Judiciary in Italy," *European Journal of Political Research* 39 (2001): 1–21.

46. Brianne Biggiani, "Designs for Immunity: A Comparison of the Criminal Prosecution of United States Presidents and Italian Prime Ministers," *Cardozo Journal of International and Comparative Law* 14 (Spring 2006): 209.

47. Ibid.
48. Ibid.
49. Marlise Simons, "Chirac under Investigation for Activities When Paris Mayor," *International Herald Tribune*, November 21, 2007, p. 8.
50. Antoine Lerougetel, "France: Former Prime Minister Juppé convicted on corruption charges," *World Socialist Web Site*, February 3, 2004, http://www.wsws.org/articles/2004/feb2004/jupp-f03.shtml.
51. *Arret No. 481*, Cour de Cassation, October 10, 2001.
52. Reported in Dean G. Falvy, "A Tale of Two Cases: Why France Said "Non" to the Logic of *Clinton v. Jones*," *FindLaw's Writ*, November 8, 2001.

3

Prosecutions of Heads of State in Latin America

Naomi Roht-Arriaza

When Augusto Pinochet, the former head of state of Chile, died in 2006, he left a dual legacy. There were the hundreds of criminal complaints filed against him, and thousands more cases of people dead and disappeared under his rule, for all of which he would never be tried or convicted. Yet Pinochet also was a symbol of a different legacy. His indictment by a Spanish court on human rights–related charges, the extradition proceedings in the United Kingdom establishing that former heads of state were not immune from extradition for torture, and the subsequent Chilean Supreme Court proceedings stripping him of his parliamentary immunity – all these events demonstrated that heads of state, at least in the Latin American context, were no longer beyond the reach of the courts.[1] In fact, Pinochet was one of at least eight Latin American heads of state then under investigation or on trial for human rights violations. Another dozen or so ex-presidents have been investigated, indicted, or convicted of corruption-related crimes. A couple of names appear on both human rights- and corruption-related lists.

This chapter looks at the increase in criminal investigations and prosecutions of heads of state and ex–heads of state in Latin America for both human rights and corruption crimes. Of those accused of human rights crimes, Pinochet was the most well known, but there were also attempted or pending prosecutions against Mexican ex-president Luis Echeverría, Argentina's Jorge Videla and Maria Isabel Martínez de Perón, Peru's Alberto Fujimori, Guatemala's ex-dictators Efraín Ríos Montt and Óscar Humberto Mejía Victores, Bolivia's ex-president Gonzalo Sánchez de Lozada, and Juan Bordaberry of Uruguay, as well as earlier proceedings against Bolivia's General Luis García Meza and Paraguay's Alfredo Stroessner.[2]

On the corruption side, investigations have been initiated or carried out against Argentina's Carlos Menem and Fernando de la Rúa; Venezuela's Carlos Andrés Pérez; Ecuador's Lucio Gutiérrez, Gustavo Noboa, and Abdalá

Burcaram; Paraguay's Luis González Macchi; Peru's Alejandro Toledo; Nicaragua's Arnoldo Alemán; Brazil's Fernando Collor de Mello; Colombia's Ernesto Samper; Guatemala's Alfonso Portillo; and three Costa Rican ex-presidents. Most of these investigations have gone nowhere, but a few ex-presidents have actually been tried and convicted. This chapter surveys the recent upsurge in such investigations and prosecutions in Latin America and concludes by considering why this has occurred now when both human rights violations and corruption have been endemic throughout the continent for decades.

Although each country and each case has its singularities, there is a process of regional diffusion of norms and strategies that justifies treating Latin America as a region. That process is not limited to trials of heads of state but extends to trials in the wake of massive repression and conflict more generally. Trials involving heads of state, however, tend to be high-profile test cases and to raise the largest number of difficult legal and political issues. The region also benefits as a whole from the influence and jurisprudence of the Inter-American human rights system, especially with regard to limits on amnesty laws, statutes of limitations, and other devices that perpetuate impunity. Its leaders, more than in any other region in the world, have been the subject of transnational litigation originating in Europe and the United States, and cases against heads of state in one country have influenced prosecutions against those in other countries. For example, the Spanish litigation involving both Pinochet and Guatemala's Ríos Montt and Mejía Victores was inspired by a case filed against the Argentine high command, which was itself inspired by a case in Italian courts against the same Argentine defendants. Finally, the region as a whole has been influenced by the efforts of international financial institutions including the World Bank and International Monetary Fund (IMF), and by bilateral efforts of donors to curb corruption and institute "good governance," often as a condition of further loans.

Clearly, the number of investigations, arrest orders, and prosecutions of heads of state in Latin America has surged over the past fifteen years or so. It is possible that these are merely the natural fallout from a period of extreme rights violations and economic uncertainty, but neither is new in the region. What does seem to be new is the impact of international justice ideas on the region.

Internationally, momentum has built for justice after massive crimes. Along with this has come the increasing development of international jurisprudence, particularly with respect to the legal definitions and requirements of crimes against humanity and genocide. A number of Latin American lawyers have assumed key positions in this international justice movement, including the election of Argentine Luis Moreno Ocampo as prosecutor of the International Criminal Court.

In Latin America, legal theories and ideas have been diffused by nongovernmental organization (NGO) networks and human rights lawyers as well as by judges with a particular interest in international law. This has strengthened and widened demands for justice, both generally and from family members of victims in particular. Thus, norms around statutes of limitation (limits on how long after a crime it may be prosecuted or litigated), the limits to amnesties, the characterization of enforced disappearances as continuing crimes, and the proper role of international law in national legal systems have all been the subject of jurisprudence that tends to be diffused from country to country and, indirectly, from court to court.

Moreover, the generation of leaders now coming to power in many Latin American countries lived through the worst period of repression and rights violations in the region and often bring a new commitment to making justice systems work. Setting themselves apart from the prior regimes entails a perceived commitment to letting justice take its course, no matter the status of the suspect.

A similar sort of norm diffusion process seems to be taking place with regard to corruption. Throughout the history of Latin America, high-level corruption, self-dealing, and influence peddling have been pervasive, but the result was typically either impunity or comfortable exile. Although in practice the outcome is largely the same, exile seems now to be the product of criminal investigations and arrest orders. A possible explanation for the change is the increasing international attention to corruption and its costs in lowered living standards and truncated development. The past few years have seen the adoption of United Nations (UN) and Organization of American States (OAS) treaties aimed at combating corruption, a strengthening of anti-money-laundering laws, and a weakening of the absolute nature of bank secrecy, albeit driven largely by antidrug and antiterrorist agendas. Transparency International, Publish What You Pay, and other NGO-generated initiatives have turned corruption from a perennial lament into a social policy issue.[3] Banks and governments have been pressured to adopt more stringent control measures through the creation of international networks of bank regulators and through bilateral aid mechanisms. The Millennium Challenge Account in the United States[4] and, above all, the increased rhetoric and attention to an anticorruption agenda in the World Bank and the IMF have set a tone in which corruption must be seen to be combated. This does not necessarily mean that the bank and the IMF have fundamentally changed their lending patterns to reflect a preference for less corrupt countries. Although loans to the world's most corrupt countries seem to have been curtailed, a preliminary perusal of lending patterns shows only a mild correlation between published indices of corruption and lending patterns in Latin America. Yet at both a political and project-oversight level, the perception that a country is not dealing with corruption by high government officials will bring unwanted scrutiny.[5]

In both human rights and corruption cases, transnational investigations and prosecutions have preceded or helped push forward domestic investigations. Thus, the Chilean, Argentine, and Guatemalan cases have their counterparts in Spanish investigations; there are also Belgian, French, German, Italian, Swedish, Swiss, and U.S. cases concerning these defendants. In Chile, the effect is clearest: although the first complaint against Pinochet predates his detention in London, a cascade of investigations followed it. The international legitimacy accorded the proceedings in Madrid and London clearly emboldened complainants and judges and put the government into a position in which, to argue against trial abroad, they needed to support trial at home.[6] Of course, this effect did not take place in a vacuum: judicial reform, changes in politics, and the existence of a strong Chilean diaspora all played a role. In Argentina, local human rights attorneys and groups combined domestic efforts to break open the local legal system with strategic use of extradition requests and arrest orders from abroad (as well as of Inter-American human rights bodies) to change the internal dynamics. In Guatemala, the effect on the domestic legal system has been minimal to date, but that may change as the proceedings move forward. No matter what the concrete outcome, the demonstration effect throughout the region was unmistakable.

Finally, structural changes within Latin America may have contributed to a temporary upsurge in prosecutions. The 1980s and 1990s were the decades of structural adjustment policies, including the downsizing of the public sector, an end to subsidies, and, above all, privatization. These policies created widespread hardship for the poor and middle classes and the perception that they widened economic inequality.[7] Privatization in particular was seen as a grab-fest in which corrupt politicians and their well-connected allies bought and sold state resources for enormous personal gain. In all the countries where prosecutions took place, there were privatizations of state utilities, including water, telecommunications, and electricity, as well as other enterprises. This created widespread resentment against the high-ranking government officials who implemented these policies, both from the middle and lower classes and from dominant sectors that lost out on privatization deals. Although not all the corruption cases can be tied to privatization scandals, the perception of widespread looting drove popular support for crusading prosecutors and judges.

At the same time, almost every country in Latin America engaged in a process of judicial reform. This included moves toward judicial independence as well as reform of criminal justice systems. The goal was to give less power to investigating magistrates and greater power to independent prosecutors' offices, switching from an inquisitorial to an adversarial system.[8] Hundreds of millions of dollars were spent on such judicial and prosecutorial modernization. Although in the human rights cases, the investigations and prosecutions were largely judge-driven (because the crimes were committed a long time ago, they fell under the pre-reform procedures), in the corruption cases the combination of widespread disgust with self-dealing privatizers and newly empowered prosecutors seeking to establish their bona fides seems to have increased the number of investigations. This would also explain why so many investigations were started but never followed through.

The next section of this chapter looks in greater detail at human rights–related investigations and prosecutions. The subsequent section looks at corruption-related cases, and the concluding section draws out some of the limitations and lessons of these regional tendencies in light of larger global trends.

LIONS IN WINTER: HUMAN RIGHTS CASES AGAINST HEADS OF STATE

Argentina initiated the modern Latin American spate of prosecutions of heads of state in 1985 when it tried the members of the three military juntas that ruled Argentina from 1976 through 1982. During this period more than nine thousand people disappeared into a sinister network of more than 350 secret detention camps, never to be seen again. Others were killed outright, tortured, arbitrarily imprisoned, or exiled. When President Raúl Alfonsín assumed office, he offered the military courts a chance to try their own for these crimes, but when those courts dragged their heels, he turned to the civilian federal courts. In 1985, the Buenos Aires Federal Court tried the nine junta members who had run the country since 1976, convicting five of them of being "necessary coconspirators" in a host of murders, kidnappings, torture, and other crimes under national law.[9] Those trials, which were extensively reported by the local media, spotlighted the range of the repression, raised the status of the judiciary, and created a valuable record.

Nonetheless, once victims and family members began bringing hundreds of cases against lower-ranking officers, military unrest convinced Alfonsín that it was better to back down. He passed "due obedience" and "full stop" or *punto final* laws that quickly ended all prosecutions of state agents for "dirty war" crimes. Alfonsín's successor, Carlos Menem, pardoned those who had been convicted in the junta trials as well as other high-ranking officers who might still have faced prosecution. For a period during the early 1990s, it looked as though Argentina's experiment in accountability at the top had been a failure. Nonetheless, over time, it had a profound influence elsewhere in the hemisphere. Indeed, in retrospect, Argentina was a pioneer in the international accountability movement, creating one of the first trials of heads of state since World War II, the first major truth commission, and some of the most comprehensive reparations since the German postwar program.[10]

In neighboring Bolivia, a coup in 1980 brought to power General Luís García Meza. García Meza imposed an extremely repressive regime, aided in part by Nazi war criminal Klaus Barbie (who spent years in Bolivia before being returned to France for trial in 1983). After García Meza left office a scant thirteen months later, the Bolivian congress – even before the Argentines – decided to begin a "trial of responsibilities" against García Meza and his close collaborators.[11] There were actually two separate proceedings: after a first set of hearings, the Bolivian National Congress in February 1986 accused García Meza, the Junta of Commanders, cabinet members, and security-force officers of a combination of political, human rights and economic crimes. These crimes included sedition (based on the 1980 coup), armed rebellion, deprivation of freedoms, attacks on press freedom, obtaining unlawful tax benefits in vehicle imports, violating university autonomy, the assassination of three union leaders, genocide and massacre of political opponents, creation of irregular armed groups, signing contracts unfavorable to the state, destruction of the national patrimony, illegal trafficking in minerals, embezzlement, undue influence, and corruption. Two years later, Congress added charges of undue enrichment stemming from the sale of the diary of Ernesto "Che" Guevara and other acts of self-dealing. A year later, García Meza went into hiding.

Although García Meza's absence slowed the process, on April 21, 1993, after hearing testimony from dozens of witnesses, the Bolivian Supreme Court found García Meza and his close collaborators guilty, in absentia, of genocide and all other charges.[12] The court rejected the "superior orders" defense for the lower-ranked defendants and found that all were either direct authors or complicit in the crimes. The Supreme Court also pointed out that genocide, including attempted genocide and conspiracy to commit genocide, is not subject to a statute of limitations. García Meza was sentenced to thirty years in prison, again in absentia.

After seven years in hiding, during which he apparently was protected by the militaries of Bolivia and Brazil, García Meza was captured in São Paulo, Brazil, in 1994. The Brazilian Supreme Court approved his extradition in 1995, and he was returned to Bolivia to serve his sentence.[13] Although he lost his army rank, he continued to draw a military pension.[14]

During the early 1990s, the prevailing wisdom in Latin America was that human rights trials of powerful figures were not viable because of amnesty decrees as well as political risks to weak new democracies. Even during this period, however, advocates and victims began searching for loopholes in the amnesty laws that would eventually reopen the cases against the surviving Argentine junta members. One of those loopholes concerned the kidnapping of the children of the disappeared. These children often had been given to military or police families to be raised free of the "taint of subversion." Several investigations into these cases followed. In July 1998, ex–junta leader Videla, along with ex-president Reynaldo Bignone, was ordered arrested on charges of child kidnapping and concealment, forgery of birth certificates, and suppression of the civil status of a minor. Videla objected on grounds that this was double jeopardy because he had already been tried in 1985 in the junta trials and on grounds that the statute of limitations had run. The judge replied that the court in the earlier trial specifically declined to rule on the existence of a systematic practice of child kidnapping, leaving the issue open. The judge also declared that baby-snatching and denial of identity were continuing crimes until the children were found and their identity restored, so the statute of limitations had not yet begun to run. Furthermore, the judge concluded that in the Argentine dirty war context, these were crimes against humanity that were not subject to statutes of limitations.[15] His order was upheld on appeal, and Videla spent thirty-eight days in prison before being transferred to house arrest on account of his age and health problems. In September 2006, Menem's pardons of the junta members convicted in 1985 were declared unconstitutional, setting the stage for a new trial. Bignone's case was set for trial in 2006, along with several other notorious operatives accused of kidnapping the children of the disappeared, but it was delayed by appeals. In January 2007, the Buenos Aires appeals court held that the baby-snatching charges against him could go forward because they were not barred by the statute of limitations.[16]

Videla was also accused of a large number of killings in a separate case brought against the heads of state of Argentina, Chile, Paraguay, and Bolivia, along with military leaders from those countries and Uruguay. The case concerned people who had been picked up and either taken across borders to be killed or disappeared by the security forces of one state based on allegations of "subversion" in another state. This six-nation coordinated effort in the 1970s was known as Operation Condor. The Argentine courts found they had jurisdiction over all the defendants because the crimes were either initiated or partially carried out in Argentina, as well as under a theory of universal jurisdiction.[17] The amnesty laws did not apply because the defendants either were not Argentines or were commanders and thus not covered.

In July 2001, an indictment was issued against Videla and the other defendants for forced disappearances (in violation of the Inter-American Convention on Forced Disappearances), illegal deprivation of liberty, and illicit association (conspiracy). The indictment also charged conspiracy to commit aggravated kidnapping, torture, homicide, and forced disappearance through the criminal use of each state's apparatus. On appeal, Videla again raised the double jeopardy and statute of limitations arguments, and again the Buenos Aires Court of Appeal rejected them on grounds that these were crimes against humanity. In addition, the court found that, in line with the legacy of the Nuremberg prosecutions, the charges of illicit association made each defendant potentially liable for the crimes committed by coconspirators.[18] The case was set for a full trial, and Videla's house arrest was continued.

The judge also asked for the extradition of the foreign defendants, but in each case it was denied. The Bolivian Supreme Court was set to consider the extradition of former Bolivian president Hugo Banzer when he died of cancer in 2002. The Chilean Supreme Court denied extradition for General Pinochet, although a domestic court did open an investigation into his role (and that of his deputies) in Operation Condor. Brazilian NGOs urged their government to extradite Paraguayan ex-president Alfredo Stroessner, who was then living in Brazil, but the government refused either to extradite or prosecute him despite requests from judges in both Argentina and Paraguay. Stroessner died in 2006 without facing justice but knowing he was a wanted man.

The Argentine amnesty laws were finally annulled in 2005, and several trials have reopened or moved forward as a result. Most spectacularly, in January 2007, María Isabel Martínez de Perón, who served as president for twenty months immediately before the military coup of 1976, was arrested in Spain in conjunction with extradition proceedings filed by two Argentine judges. The charges involved two cases of forced disappearance, characterized as crimes against humanity, as well as cooperating with the armed forces and ultra-right death squads in setting up the legal grounds for subsequent repressive campaigns. Martínez de Perón, the third wife of Juan Perón, was president during a period when some 1,500 people were killed by anti-Communist death squads allegedly linked to the state.[19] This is the first time that the legal proceedings in Argentina have reached beyond the period of military dictatorship into the origins of repression during a civilian government. However, on April 28, 2008, the Spanish federal trial court (Audiencia Nacional) denied the extradition request. In two parallel decisions, the trial court found that the

crimes had not been charged as crimes against humanity and were therefore barred by the statute of limitations, and that the cooperation charge did
not present sufficient indicators of Perón's responsibility and was moreover
barred because Argentine laws on jurisdiction over former presidents had not
been followed. The Spanish prosecutor's office vowed to appeal the results.[20]

By the late 1990s, the international climate had changed, making the idea
of trying former heads of state for human rights–related crimes more feasible.
The statutes for the International Criminal Tribunal for the Former Yugoslavia
(ICTY) and the International Criminal Tribunal for Rwanda (ICTR), both of
which were adopted by the United Nations Security Council, contain provisions that allow for heads of state to be held accountable.[21] The indictment of
Slobodan Milošević by the ICTY in 1999 for war crimes and crimes against
humanity showed that even a sitting head of state could be subject to criminal
prosecution. The Rome Statute of the International Criminal Court, completed in 1998, also made clear that there was no immunity for heads of state
before an international tribunal.[22] Latin American countries, for the most
part, strongly supported the nascent court. The jurisprudence of the international criminal tribunals developed and publicized the legal definitions and
requirements of crimes against humanity and genocide, including theories of
command and indirect responsibility.

On a regional level, the Inter-American human rights system insisted that
some of the traditional impediments to prosecutions for human rights–related
crimes constituted violations of the American Convention on Human Rights.
At first, the Inter-American Commission on Human Rights issued a series of
recommendations condemning amnesty or amnesty-like laws in El Salvador,
Uruguay, Argentina, and, later, Chile.[23] These were highly influential with
the Argentine courts, although much less so elsewhere. By 2001, the Inter-
American Court of Human Rights had agreed with the commission, finding
in a case involving a prison massacre in Peru that blanket amnesties violate the
rights of the victims and so are unlawful. In a later case, the court added that
statutes of limitations and other judicial impediments to prosecution also were
not allowed.[24] In addition, the court began handing down substantial damages
awards against governments for massive human rights violations.[25] Even for
governments that formally ignored or rejected these holdings, the moral and
political weight of the regional human rights system made a difference.

The wave of transnational prosecutions, involving the national courts of one
country investigating and prosecuting crimes committed in another, increased
the likelihood that Latin American heads of state would be held criminally
accountable. Cases against the Chilean and Argentine military high command

were opened in Spanish courts in 1996, a moment when domestic investigations seemed quixotic. The Spanish courts were chosen because Article 23.4 of the Spanish Organic Judicial Power Law allows for jurisdiction over certain heinous international crimes based solely on the nature of the crime regardless of whether the perpetrator or the victim had ties to Spain.[26] Spanish law also contains broad rules regarding victims' ability to initiate investigations, and Spain shared language and legal traditions with Latin American countries. Moreover, there were numerous Spanish victims of the repression in Latin America and thus much public sympathy, and there were large Latin American communities living in Spain.

By 1998, Spanish Judge Baltazar Garzón had issued arrest orders for Jorge Videla, Emilio Massera, and Leopoldo Galtieri, all former Argentine junta members. The Spanish Audiencia Nacional approved the orders. The court considered the status of amnesty laws in both Chile and Argentina but held that they did not impede Spanish prosecution because Spain does not allow a general amnesty and because an amnesty for the crimes charged is unlawful under international law.[27] Although the Spanish judge issued extradition requests, Argentine governments refused to honor them.

In September 1998, Judge Garzón issued an arrest order for Chile's Augusto Pinochet while Pinochet was visiting the United Kingdom. This led to extradition proceedings being brought against Pinochet in the United Kingdom and to his being held under house arrest there for more than a year and a half. Pinochet was eventually sent home by the United Kingdom on grounds that he was too infirm to be tried.[28] Upon returning home, however, his legal troubles intensified. That story is told in the next chapter.

After 1998, the pace of head-of-state investigations across Latin America picked up, although there were many more investigations than actual prosecutions. In Paraguay, for example, proceedings finally moved ahead in a 1991 case against ex-dictator Stroessner for the murder of Celestina Pérez, a teacher and the wife of well-known anti-Stroessner activist Martín Almada. Stroessner, who ruled Paraguay from 1954 to 1989, routinely killed, disappeared, and tortured political opponents. Stroessner was declared "in rebellion" after he did not appear before the court. However, the case stalled until it was reopened in 2000. Other investigations soon followed: in addition to the Argentine Operation Condor case discussed earlier, several Paraguayan judges opened new human-rights-related investigations or reopened old ones. In late 2000, Paraguayan judge Rubén Darío Frutos ordered Stroessner's arrest in the case involving the forced "disappearance" of Paraguayan doctor Agustín Goiburú in 1977. Goiburú, a political dissident who had escaped from detention in

Paraguay in 1970, was living in exile in Argentina at the time of his "disappearance." The judge asked Brazil to extradite Stroessner and eventually found him in contempt.[29] In 2003, a judge ordered the arrest of General Stroessner and his former interior minister, Sabino Montanaro (in exile in Honduras), for their alleged part in the killing of Celestina Pérez in 1974.[30] The Brazilian government consistently refused all attempts to extradite him, despite efforts in 2000 by the head of the Brazilian Chamber of Deputies' Human Rights Commission to strip him of his exile status. Stroessner died in 2006 in Brazil.

Guatemalans, who had suffered some of the worst violations in the hemisphere, also were encouraged by the cases from the Southern Cone (the southernmost region of South America) and the international trend favoring justice. During the Lucas García military regime, thousands of unionists, students, peasant leaders, priests, and political opponents were murdered or disappeared. When General Efraín Ríos Montt came to power in a coup in 1982, he unleashed a genocidal campaign against the country's rural Mayan indigenous population. He was soon succeeded by another military government, this one headed by Óscar Mejía Victores. According to the UN-sponsored Commission on Historical Clarification, some four hundred villages were obliterated as a result of the army's scorched earth campaign; from 1960 to 1996, some two hundred thousand people were killed, most during the early 1980s.[31]

In 2000, a complaint against Lucas García and his high command was filed in Guatemalan courts by victims from more than twenty communities, gathered under the rubric Association for Justice and Reconciliation and represented by the Center for Human Rights Action (CALDH). In June 2001, that complaint was broadened to cover defendants from the Ríos Montt period (1982–1983), including Ríos Montt and Mejía Víctores along with three other defendants. Although Lucas García had little political power left, Ríos Montt was a different story. He commanded a strong following and was a major political figure with support among military and paramilitary forces. The complaint charges genocide, incitement to genocide, and crimes against humanity, along with homicide, unlawful detention, and other charges under local law. The complaints were presented to a local investigating magistrate, who passed them on to the Public Prosecutors' office (Ministerio Público), which in turn appointed a prosecutor. Although the prosecutor took declarations from witnesses and gathered evidence based on exhumations of massacre victims, there has been little progress in the case in the past two years. Despite the lack of progress, there have been repeated death threats against CALDH lawyers.[32]

The major impediments to prosecution in Guatemala have been more a matter of lack of political will than legal constraints, although these existed as well. Blanket amnesties were passed during the late 1980s and early 1990s. In

1996, the Guatemala Congress passed a new Law of National Reconciliation (LRN) allowing defendants to claim amnesty, but as a result of international pressure, the law excluded forced disappearances, genocide, torture, and other crimes against humanity.[33] In addition, until June 2004 and again beginning in 2007 when he was elected to Congress, Ríos Montt had parliamentary immunity. Upon announcing his 2007 congressional candidacy, the former general bragged that he had outsmarted his accusers by gaining immunity from prosecution.[34]

Although the amnesty law has not been a large obstacle, other problems with the legal system have proved nearly fatal. The prosecutors' office suffers from frequent turnover, sluggishness, and the widespread perception that it is riddled with current or former intelligence officers. Prosecutors and judges often are threatened, and some have been killed or forced into exile for their work on high-profile investigations into human rights–related crimes. Defendants regularly file motions for *amparo* (relief for violation of their constitutional rights), and the courts entertain the same, or a slightly different motion, multiple times.[35]

Ríos Montt has been before the courts on two other occasions, one involving corruption and the other violent acts. In August 2000, Ríos Montt and twenty-three other parliamentary members of the Guatemalan Republican Front (FRG) political party were charged with abuse of authority, destroying evidence, and failure to carry out their duties for unlawfully altering a law taxing alcoholic beverages to favor powerful Guatemalan businesses. The Supreme Court agreed to lift their parliamentary immunity (at the time Ríos Montt was the president of Congress). Nonetheless, in April 2001, the trial court dismissed the charges amid a climate of threats against judges and lawyers.[36] Again in March 2004, he was charged with homicide (manslaughter), sedition, coercion, and threatening behavior. These charges stemmed from his role in instigating violent demonstrations in July 2003 against a court decision denying him the ability to stand as a presidential candidate. During those demonstrations, a journalist died from a heart attack while being chased by a mob of FRG supporters. A lower court judge ordered Ríos Montt confined to house arrest, but he was soon released on bail, and in February 2006 the charges were dropped for lack of evidence. The journalists' association protested that the prosecutors' office had not done a serious job of investigating.[37]

Most of the same defendants have also been the subject of transnational proceedings in Spain and Belgium. In 1999, Nobel Prize winner Rigoberta Menchú brought a complaint in Spain's Audiencia Nacional against Romeo Lucas García, Ríos Montt, and six other high-ranking officials, alleging genocide, terrorism, and torture against the Mayan population and others. An investigating magistrate initially accepted the complaint, but when the Spanish prosecutors' office appealed, it was dismissed on grounds that there had been no showing that the case could not be pursued in Guatemala. The Spanish Supreme Court, in an eight to seven vote, partially affirmed that decision, holding that cases brought under Spain's universal jurisdiction law required a link to Spain. They therefore ordered the case reopened only with respect to the Spanish citizens tortured in Guatemala. The Spanish Constitutional Court, in turn, ruled in September 2005 that no tie, either of nationality or interest, was required under universal jurisdiction. The nature of the crime was enough. They ordered the case fully reinstated.[38]

Spanish judge Santiago Pedraz visited Guatemala in July 2006, and although domestic legal maneuvering prevented him from taking the defendants' statements, he subsequently issued arrest warrants for the defendants, including Ríos Montt (Lucas García died in 2006). In November, he followed up with extradition requests. In November 2006, a Guatemalan trial court issued arrest warrants for several of the defendants, although not Ríos Montt. These were upheld by the appeals court, but on December 14, 2007, the Guatemalan Constitutional Court held that it would not recognize Spain's universal jurisdiction, that the extradition treaty between the two countries was inapplicable, and that in any case the crimes were political crimes because they occurred in the context of an internal armed conflict. Thus, they were not extraditable crimes.[39] The court ordered the arrest warrants quashed. Despite this outcome, the case has already had an impact in Guatemala, revitalizing calls for the defendants to be tried and prompting the new president, Álvaro Colom, to order the opening of military archives from the 1970s and 1980s.[40] Local attorneys and human rights groups are demanding that the defendants be tried at home, as required by Guatemala's obligations under the extradition treaty as well as the Genocide and Torture Conventions. A domestic judge took witness statements in response to a Spanish request for judicial cooperation and sent them to the prosecutor's office as well as to the Spanish judge.[41]

In Belgium, proceedings have also been underway against the same set of defendants for the killing of two Belgian priests during the Lucas García period. The case was one of a handful that were "grandfathered" when the Belgian universal jurisdiction law was amended in 2003.[42] Since then, the Belgian prosecutor has traveled to Guatemala to depose witnesses.

In Mexico, the end of seven decades of rule by the Partido Revolucionario Institucional paved the way for an investigation of ex-president Luis Echeverría. In 2000, President Vicente Fox came into office promising to deal with the misdeeds of the past. The Special Prosecutors' Office (SPO)[43] was created by presidential decree shortly after Fox took office. It had full power to name and gather evidence against the perpetrators of human rights violations, including the Tlatelolco massacre of 1968, the 1971 massacre of student protesters, and the cases related to the state-sponsored "dirty war," up to the recent past.[44] At its height, the SPO had more than a thousand cases under investigation.

In July 2004, Special Prosecutor Ignacio Carrillo Prieto charged former president Luis Echeverría, two of his former aides, three army generals, and a few other officials with genocide for the intent to destroy a national group during the massacre of at least twenty-five student protesters by government-sponsored paramilitaries on Corpus Christi Day in June 1971.[45] The evidence presented was voluminous – almost 10,000 pages of testimony and proof. It was immediately tossed out by a local judge on grounds that the statute of limitations had passed. Carrillo Prieto appealed to the Supreme Court, arguing that the genocide charges should stand because the PGR had investigated the case in 1982, interrupting the running of the statute of limitations.

In February 2005, the Supreme Court ruled that the International Convention on the Non-Applicability of Statutes of Limitation to War Crimes and Crimes against Humanity, which Mexico ratified in 2002, was not retroactive and so could not be used to overcome the statute of limitations problem. In June, however, the court held that the statute was tolled (suspended) for the time Echeverría was president and therefore did not begin to run until December 1, 1976, bringing the charges within the thirty-year statute of limitations. The Supreme Court returned the case to a lower court; a month later, a lower court judge found that there was insufficient evidence to hold the former president on the genocide charge, because there was no evidence of intent to destroy a national or ethnic group "as such."[46] Although there was ample evidence of homicide, the statute of limitations on that crime had long passed.

Undaunted, Carrillo filed new genocide and kidnapping charges against Echeverría and other officials for the Tlatelolco massacre and the 1969 disappearance of a student activist. In September 2005, a lower-court judge refused to issue arrest warrants, holding that these killings also failed to meet the definition of genocide and that there was not enough evidence tying Echeverría to the disappearance. The Supreme Court refused to overturn that decision, sending it to an appeals court. On June 30, 2006, appeals court judge José Ángel Mattar Oliva issued an arrest warrant for genocide, ruling that the students constituted a national group and that the statute of limitations had been tolled during Echeverría's presidency. He ordered the ex-president, now eighty-four years old and in poor health, confined to house arrest, a decision upheld on appeal in November 2006. In July 2007, the genocide charges were confirmed against lower-ranking defendants, but Echeverría was ordered released because the court found no evidence linking him to the crime.[47] By then, though, Carrillo was running out of time; the SPO mandate was nearly over, and President Felipe Calderón did not renew it. Civil society groups expressed disappointment with the results of the SPO, which only investigated a handful of disappearance cases, received no cooperation from the army and little from the rest of the government, and created little public awareness or support.

Since then, shootings of demonstrators have been the subject of new investigations in Bolivia. A trial of responsibilities is in process against ex-president Gonzalo Sánchez de Lozada. In October 2004, the Bolivian National Congress approved an investigation into his role in the killing of sixty-seven protesters in September and October 2003.[48] Again, the charge is genocide (in its "bloody massacre" variant under Bolivian law), along with economic crimes. Potential witnesses began providing testimony to the court in March 2005. On May 18, 2005, the prosecutor brought formal charges against nine ministers who live in Bolivia and asked Sánchez de Lozada and two other ministers who now reside outside the country to return to take their testimony and decide whether to proceed to the arrest/indictment stage. The prosecutor also asked the court to order military secrecy laws lifted, which it did, leading to subpoenas for several military officers.[49]

Sánchez de Lozada now lives in Maryland, United States, and has shown little inclination to return home. In April 2008, the prosecutors' office asked the Supreme Court to file extradition requests for him and two collaborators also living in the United States, but it is doubtful he will be extradited. The Bush administration has apparently refused even to forward the summons from the Bolivian prosecutor. There is a 1995 extradition treaty between the United States and Bolivia that allows extradition without regard to the exact wording of the charges, so long as the underlying conduct is criminal in both states; it does, however, have a political-offense exception that Sánchez de Lozada might invoke.[50]

Another new set of investigations is taking place in Uruguay, which long held out against the anti-impunity trends elsewhere in the Southern Cone. An amnesty law, ratified by a plebiscite in 1989, precludes prosecution of the military for human rights–related crimes, including disappearances and widespread torture. It does not cover civilians, however.[51] Previous civilian governments had defended the amnesty law and insisted that there was no evidence of government wrongdoing, but the official attitude changed with the election of the Broad Front center-left coalition government in 2005. In November 2006, an investigating magistrate ordered the arrest of former president Juan Bordaberry, who served as the civilian face of a twelve-year military dictatorship that began with a 1973 coup. Bordaberry was charged in several murders, including the assassinations of two prominent opposition politicians, Senator Zelmar Michelini and House Speaker Héctor Gutiérrez Ruíz, whose murders in Argentina in 1976 had long been emblematic of the dictatorship's crimes. The judge charged him and former foreign minister Juan Carlos Blanco with aggravated homicide, which, because the crimes were committed as part of Operation Condor, the judge characterized as a crime against humanity. In January 2007, Bordaberry was transferred to house arrest due to ill health.[52] He also is being investigated for other crimes, as is his ex–foreign minister.

Desi Bouterse, Suriname's former military dictator, encountered criminal prosecutions on both sides of the Atlantic. In 1999, a Netherlands court convicted Bouterse in absentia on cocaine-trafficking charges.[53] The international warrant issued pursuant to the conviction means that Bouterse cannot leave Suriname without threat of arrest, but the Netherlands has not asked to extradite Bouterse.

In another Dutch proceeding, relatives of fifteen political opponents executed on December 8, 1982, sought Bouterse's conviction for torture and crimes against humanity. The "December Murders" eliminated the opposition's leadership and consolidated Bouterse's grip on the nascent state.[54] At the pretrial stage, the lower court found it had jurisdiction to try Bouterse under the 1988 Torture Convention. It found that because torture was already a crime under customary international law as well as under Dutch law prohibiting assault, the convention could apply retroactively so as to provide extraterritorial jurisdiction. However, the Dutch Supreme Court reversed, holding that the Torture Act did not apply retroactively to these human rights violations and that the prosecution was barred by the statute of limitations.[55]

In November 2007, domestic proceedings finally began in Suriname for Bouterse's role in the December Murders. Filed by former relatives just before the expiration of the applicable statute of limitations, Bouterse is one of twenty-five defendants now facing prosecution for murder. Because most of the accused were military personnel, the prosecutor determined that the defendants will be tried by court martial. Human rights groups denounced the procedural maneuver, citing conflict with the International Covenant on Civil and Political Rights.[56] Bouterse's murder trial has not concluded.

THE CORRUPTION CASES

There are more corruption-related investigations than human rights investigations in Latin America. Augusto Pinochet in Chile and Gonzalo Sánchez de Lozada in Bolivia as well as Alberto Fujimori in Peru face (or faced) both human rights and corruption charges. In the Pinochet and Sánchez de Lozada cases, human rights charges came first, and the economic charges were added later.

In one of the earliest of the current crop of corruption cases, Brazilian President Fernando Collor de Mello was impeached in 1992 after a congressional investigation into corruption charges. He resigned in December 1992, on the day his trial in Congress began, but the Supreme Court held that the resignation did not bar the trial proceedings. He was charged with illegally profiting from an alleged billion-dollar scheme headed by his former campaign treasurer, but the charges were thrown out because of technical problems in the prosecution's case. The widespread view in Brazil was that Collor and his associates, many of whom were convicted on related charges but never spent time in jail, manipulated the legal system to their advantage. Collor did, however, spend several years outside Brazil, and his political rights were suspended until 2006. The same year his rights were reinstated, Collor won a seat in the Brazilian Senate.[57]

Another early corruption case involved Carlos Andrés Pérez, ex-president of Venezuela, who has the distinction of being accused of corruption not once, but twice. The first time followed his second term as president (1989–1993), when he was impeached for embezzling $17 million in public funds, tried, and sentenced to two years and four months under house arrest plus payment of a fine. He served his time at his farm. In 1998, he was accused of illegal enrichment for hiding between $50,000 and $900,000 in U.S. banks, but before trial, he won election to a Senate seat and so gained parliamentary immunity. His immunity was short-lived, however, because Congress was dissolved in August 1999. He and his wife were ordered detained in 2001 on the illegal-enrichment charges, and they fled to the Dominican Republic. Although the Supreme Court approved extradition requests to both the Dominican Republic and the United States (where Pérez resides part of the time), neither has been successful. They are less likely to be so now, after Venezuelan President Hugo Chávez – no friend of the United States – accused Pérez of backing a failed 2002 attempt to depose him.[58]

Pérez's predecessor, Jaime Lusinchi (1985–1989), was also implicated in several corruption cases, including stealing funds from the National Horseracing Institute. He was indicted and ordered not to leave the country but promptly did so, settling in Costa Rica. In 1994 and again in 1997, the Superior Court ordered the charges against him thrown out on grounds that the statute of limitations had expired. The Supreme Court ordered the charges, along with other corruption charges, reinstated in 1999, but there appears to have been no movement in the case nor attempt at extradition since then.[59]

Next door in Colombia, former president Ernesto Samper was accused in 1994, in the so-called Case 8000, of accepting $3.7 million from the drug traffickers of the Cali cartel to fund his election campaign. In prison, Fernando Botero, who ran the campaign, admitted that Samper obtained money in exchange for a promise not to extradite the drug lords to the United States. Brought before Congress, Samper was acquitted on December 15, 1995, amid allegations that his business cronies had used money from privatization schemes to pay off his congressional accusers.[60]

The pace of investigations in Latin America picked up after 2000, but again, there were many more investigations than trials or convictions. Carlos Menem, often blamed for Argentina's economic collapse in 2001, was the subject of several unsuccessful investigations. In June 2001, Menem was ordered to remain under house arrest as a result of a six-hundred-page indictment charging him with being the head of an illicit organization and, as such, authorizing illegal arms shipments worth more than $100 million to Croatia and Ecuador in violation of a UN embargo. The charges could have resulted in a five- to ten-year prison sentence. He was cleared by the Supreme Court (a court in which his adherents held an "automatic majority") for lack of evidence in November 2001.[61] In June 2005, the case was reopened and his former brother-in-law, Emir Yoma, was reindicted.[62] So far, Menem has avoided reindictment, but as the case moves forward under the now less pliant Supreme Court, that may change.

In October 2001, Swiss authorities froze two accounts connected to Menem as part of a money-laundering investigation. In addition to the Croatian and Ecuadorian arms deals, the Argentine authorities asked for judicial cooperation in investigating whether any of the money in those accounts was related to supposed payments from Iran to a Menem-controlled account in connection with the 1994 bombing of the Jewish Asociación Mutual Israelita Argentina (AMIA) center in Buenos Aires, in which eighty-six people died. A third criminal investigation into the Swiss accounts, which started in 2002, involved crimes of undue influence, embezzlement, and bribery in the construction of two prisons, as well as tax evasion. Menem managed to avoid prosecution by fleeing to Chile, where he successfully fought extradition. A Chilean judge in May 2004 denied extradition on the grounds that although the Argentine authorities wanted to question him, his refusal to answer questions without any arrest order against him was not an extraditable crime.[63] Eventually two judges agreed to cancel the arrest warrants while leaving the investigations open and Menem promptly returned to Argentina, where he ran for office, and lost, in 2007. Shortly thereafter, yet another accusation, this time of hiding assets and forging documents, led to his house arrest. That case was scheduled to go to trial in October 2008; Menem faces a possible twelve-year sentence.[64]

President Fernando de la Rúa, also of Argentina, who resigned at the height of Argentina's economic crisis, was indicted for corruption in 2008 based on the testimony of former senate secretary Mario Pontaquarto, who claims that he personally delivered $5 million to senators on behalf of President de la Rúa in 2000 in connection with the passage of a labor law.[65]

The post-2000 wave of corruption investigations has even reached Costa Rica. That country, which had been considered a model of probity and good governance in Latin America, has been rocked by corruption indictments against three ex-presidents over the last several years. Miguel Ángel Rodríguez (1998–2002) was arrested and put under house arrest in 2004 on corruption charges stemming from kickbacks to Alcatel, a French telecom company that won a telecommunications contract in 2001. He also was expelled from his political party and forced to resign as OAS secretary general. As of 2008, that case remained under investigation.[66] Rafael Ángel Calderón Jr. (1990–1994) was arrested in 2004 for taking a "commission" to steer contracts for medical equipment for the social security system to a Finnish company. He too was jailed and then put under house arrest.[67] José María Figueres (1994–1998) is accused of taking $900,000 in payments from Alcatel; he lives outside the country.[68] Further, a parliamentary inquiry into the provenance of 2002 election campaign funds was opened against Abel Pacheco.[69] All have declared their innocence and argued that the charges are politically motivated.

Like Costa Rica, most of Ecuador's recent ex-presidents have been indicted for corruption. Unlike Costa Rica, the charges seem much harder to pin down. Congress ousted ex-president Abdalá Bucaram (1996–1997) after six months in office on grounds of "mental incapacity" and corruption. He faced multiple charges, including the misuse of national-reserve funds and embezzlement of between $100 million and $300 million from the state, as well as treason and influence peddling.[70] The interim president appointed to succeed Bucaram, Fabián Alarcón, was himself removed for participating in a scheme to pad congressional rolls with thousands of phantom employees. The scheme was discovered by an anticorruption commission created by Alarcón himself. He was briefly jailed.[71] Next came Jamil Mahuad, who governed from 1998 to 2000. He was overthrown after political demonstrations and fled the country amid accusations of illegal campaign contributions and maladministration of public funds.[72]

The next president, Gustavo Noboa (2000–2003), faced investigation on allegations of financial impropriety in debt negotiations and misuse of discretionary funds, but he sought refuge in the embassy of the Dominican

Republic and was granted safe passage to that country. Supreme Court Chief Judge Guillermo Castro annulled the charges against him, and he returned to Ecuador.[73] Chief Judge Castro also annulled the charges against Bucaram on the grounds that prosecutors had opened criminal investigations without congressional authorization. The annulments were widely perceived as the result of a deal with then-President Lucio Gutiérrez. In part because of his politicization of the Supreme Court, President Gutiérrez was chased out of office in April 2005. He took refuge in the Brazilian Embassy after Chief Prosecutor Cecilia Armas de Tobar ordered him arrested and placed in preventive detention for the crime of "ordering members of the military and police to repress the population of the capital."[74] After several months in exile (including in the United States, Brazil, Peru, and Colombia), Gutiérrez decided to return home to clear his name. Meanwhile, a new prosecutor filed more charges against him in July 2005, this time for inciting rebellion and crimes against national security, based on declarations Gutiérrez made to the press while in exile. He was imprisoned, together with his brother and a third person, until the Supreme Court could rule. He was finally cleared of the charges in March 2006.

Unlike most of the cases considered here, Arnoldo Alemán, president of Nicaragua from 1997 to 2002, is one of the few heads of state who was actually convicted and sentenced to prison on corruption charges. Several related cases involve diverting more than $1 million from the state television company, large-scale money laundering ($96.7 million, according to *The Economist*[75]), opening secret bank accounts abroad with some of the looted money, using government credit cards to run up millions of dollars in personal expenses, donating state properties to his family, and the like. As a result of a pact with Daniel Ortega, then leader of a Sandinista faction in the Congress, at the end of his presidential period, Alemán was given an automatic seat in the National Assembly. Before trial could take place, Alemán's parliamentary immunity had to be removed. He finally lost his immunity for the television and large-scale money-laundering cases in December 2002 and was immediately arrested.[76] Alemán was found guilty in these cases and sentenced to twenty years' imprisonment but until recently was allowed to serve out his sentence mostly under house arrest at his family farm. In 2006, even those restrictions were lifted, and he took an active role in political campaigning for his party. With the election of Daniel Ortega in 2007, it seemed that Alemán would be the beneficiary of a deal changing the definition of his crimes. However, in December 2007, an appeals court decided that Alemán should return to prison and that prison authorities should determine whether he was eligible for house arrest. In January 2008, Alemán's house arrest was reinstated, but the terms of the "confinement" allow the prisoner to move freely within the entirety of Nicaragua.[77]

In 2006, prosecutors in Miami opened investigations into the provenance of $700,000 that Alemán had deposited in Miami banks; if it is found to be the fruits of embezzlement, he will forfeit the money and may be subject to criminal trial in the United States.[78] Panama also opened a case against him for money laundering in Panamanian banks in March 2006 and issued orders for his arrest.[79] The media speculate that another deal between Alemán's party and that of President Daniel Ortega will lead to Alemán being pardoned.[80] Ortega, for his part, has faced his own legal troubles. In March 1998, his stepdaughter Zoilamérica Narvaez accused Ortega of sexual abuse and rape, but her criminal complaint met numerous legal obstacles. The Nicaraguan Supreme Court dismissed it in 2003, and Narvaez has complained of the dismissal to the Inter-American Commission on Human Rights.[81]

Elsewhere in Central America, corruption allegations have been leveled against ex-president Mireya Moscoso in Panama[82] and Fernando Flores in El Salvador,[83] but little seems to have come of them. In Guatemala, former president Alfonso Portillo is under investigation for corruption and money laundering during his term as president (2000–2004); he fled to Mexico days after leaving office. Meanwhile, the judge who ordered his arrest in Guatemala in July 2005 reported in sick two days later and was promptly replaced by a judge who found the arrest order unlawful because of procedural irregularities. Several other challenges by Portillo and his associates are pending at various levels of the Guatemalan justice system, up to and including the Constitutional Court. While legal maneuvers continued, he remained free on bond in Mexico. The Mexican foreign minister, Luis Ernesto Derbez, authorized Portillo's extradition to face embezzlement charges on October 31, 2006, and ordered immigration authorities not to let him leave the country. On November 3, however, a federal court provisionally suspended the extradition while Portillo's appeal was heard.[84] In January 2008, Mexico's Supreme Court determined that Portillo could be extradited back to Guatemala and he was eventually transferred on October 8, 2008.[85]

In the Dominican Republic, former president Salvador Jorge Blanco (1982–1986) was accused of corruption and fraud. He fled to the Venezuelan embassy and was allowed to leave the country on grounds of ill health, but was eventually sentenced to twenty years in prison and payment of a large fine. In 1989, that sentence was annulled, but he was retried and resentenced to the same term, although with a smaller fine. He spent only a couple of months in jail, however, before the incoming president dismissed all charges against him.[86]

Paraguay as well has seen multiple investigations and prosecutions of recent heads of state. A succession of traditional Colorado Party members followed the ouster of long-time dictator Alfredo Stroessner. Juan Carlos Wasmosy, who governed from 1993 to 1998, was convicted in April 2002 and sentenced to four years in prison for fraud, stemming, in part, from the irregular privatization of the state shipping line and other resources. An appeals court absolved him in September. Raúl Cubas, who succeeded him until 1999, also was denounced for the misuse of public funds after he was forced to step down by social unrest in the wake of the assassination of Vice President Luis María Argaña and the killings of seven young protesters in March 1999. Cubas fled to Brazil but returned to Paraguay in 2002, where he was subject to house arrest until 2003, when apparently charges were dropped.[87]

Following a failed impeachment attempt in 2001 on grounds of corruption, ex-president Luis González Macchi left office in 2003. He was convicted in 2006 of embezzlement on charges that he diverted $16 million from two failing government banks to private accounts in the United States. He was sentenced to six years in prison.[88]

OBSTACLES TO PROSECUTIONS

Despite the breadth of head-of-state prosecutions, there are sizeable boulders in the path of prosecutions. Obstacles seem to be of two kinds: legal and structural/political. In terms of legal doctrine, the most salient problems are immunities, statutes of limitations, retroactivity, and lack of adequate domestic definition of international crimes. Parliamentary immunity creates a need for a preliminary proceeding to remove it, but to date has not proved much of a problem, because the standard of proof is lower than for a full-fledged criminal trial. It does, however, create significant delays, which, given the age and health of defendants, can mean that justice is effectively denied. Other immunities have not arisen at the domestic level.

The single biggest legal obstacle is the statute of limitations. Especially in human rights cases, it can take a long time to muster the requisite political will to try ex–heads of state. Meanwhile, most Latin American countries have a statute of limitations for murder and other serious crimes, often a relatively short one. The Echeverría case and the Chilean and Argentine prosecutions came up against this limit. In response, prosecutors made two arguments: that no statute of limitations applies to crimes against humanity and that the statute is tolled during the time it is impossible to bring a criminal complaint against the defendant on account of immunities or other causes.

Related to the statute of limitations problems are definitional and retroactivity problems. International crimes, especially forced disappearances or other crimes against humanity, often were not incorporated into domestic penal codes until well after the crimes took place. This has led to strained characterizations of criminal acts (i.e., genocide for the killing of student or union leaders in Mexico or Bolivia), as well as arguments over the retrospective application of treaties or of newly incorporated definitions in criminal procedure codes. Courts sometimes have overcome these problems by noting that although the treaty obligation or legal characterization may be new, the underlying conduct has long been prohibited under customary international law, the domestic law (i.e., as kidnapping or assault, even if not as forced disappearance or torture), or both.[89]

Interestingly, other legal problems that commonly occur in international criminal prosecutions have not arisen in domestic cases. Command responsibility, for example, has not been an issue in the human rights prosecutions to date because in all the cases the defendants are accused of ordering, or specifically condoning, the criminal acts; in no case is prosecution based on their command position.[90] Nor have any of the defendants raised former-head-of-state immunity in the domestic prosecutions, although they have raised current parliamentary immunity. The amnesty issue, although raised in the Pinochet case, has been sidestepped for now on grounds that the amnesty can only be applied after investigation and trial. In any case, there is ample jurisprudence in Chilean courts stating that forced disappearances are not subject to the amnesty, and the amnesty law may be legislatively annulled.

The structural and political obstacles have been more difficult, and more salient, than the legal ones. First, the independence of the judiciary has been a serious problem. In some cases, such as Guatemala, cases against heads of state and other powerful figures have in the past been difficult to pursue because of threats and pressures against judges, prosecutors, and lawyers, which leads them to abandon the case, leave the country, or suddenly find themselves in poor health. The politicized nature of specific courts, such as the Constitutional Court in Guatemala or the Supreme Court in Ecuador, has also been problematic. Particularly in the corruption cases, prosecutorial legitimacy has been undermined by the perception that the judiciary is responding to the political agenda of the executive branch by starting or stopping prosecutions on cue depending on the political interests of the moment. It has also meant that although there are many investigations, there are far fewer cases carried through to trial and conviction.

Related to this, incoming governments are necessarily tempted to use investigation and prosecution of their predecessor as a convenient explanation for the dismal state of the economy and their own failures to meet expectations quickly. Thus, arrests and even trials take place but rarely reach conclusion. Several successive prosecutions of this ilk, even if based in fact, can give rise to the suspicion that prosecutions are not a legitimate exercise of justice but merely a routine and cynical variant of politics. In some cases the charges second-guessed economic or political choices rather than statutory crimes, and prosecutions were merely politics by other means.

Second, international cooperation has been lacking. Despite the advances described earlier, in many cases accused heads of state have been able to comfortably retire abroad despite calls for their extradition. In part this reflects a long tradition in Latin America of granting asylum to deposed or disgraced leaders, no doubt with the expectation of reciprocity. However, it also reflects the rudimentary state of judicial cooperation and extradition regimes. Bilateral extradition treaties do not exist between many countries, and judicial cooperation, often routed through diplomatic channels, is slow and cumbersome. Ex-leaders often raise political offense and other bars to extradition. Criminal charges are sometimes so vague that double criminality requirements may pose bars to extradition. Although some inroads have been made, bank secrecy and noncooperation in financial investigations is still a significant hurdle. The United States, in particular, perhaps out of a concern for possible negative precedents, has been unresponsive to requests to extradite, or even question, ex-presidents who have sought refuge on U.S. soil. Brazil has been similarly unresponsive.

Third, because of ex-leaders' age or health, there has been a marked reluctance to send them to prison. This, in part, reflects the amount of time it takes to muster political and other resources to investigate the powerful, who are often already of middle age or older when they assume power. Laws in many countries allow those over the age of seventy to avoid prison altogether and subject them instead to house arrest. Laws also forbid the trial and imprisonment of those with serious mental or physical health problems. Although these laws no doubt were intended to serve humanitarian interests, in practice what the population sees is men (except for Isabel Peron, all defendants have been men) who, even when caught, are still powerful enough to mock justice by serving their detention in their mansions or on their farms, going on shopping sprees, holding parties, and even campaigning, while claiming age- or health-related disabilities. Again, this de-legitimizes the process.

CONCLUSION

Latin American is experiencing a limited "justice cascade" in which many more cases are initiated but few are carried through to conclusion. Although obstacles abound, the trend is toward greater numbers of investigations and prosecutions, especially on corruption charges. The massive human rights violations on the scale of the 1970s and 1980s are a thing of the past, and large-scale privatization seems also to be waning as more and more countries reject neo-liberal formulas. Given these changes, one might expect a downturn in the number of investigations and prosecutions after the current crop plays itself out. Excessive use of force against demonstrators and the like continues, however, and there is no reason to expect corruption to disappear. The test will be whether the increased level of prosecutions and investigations continues over the next few years. If it does, it will be due in large part to changed regional and international expectations that countries should try their leaders, and others, who commit human rights and corruption crimes.

NOTES

1. The various prosecutions of Augusto Pinochet are discussed in Chapter 4 of this volume.
2. The chapter does not consider the extradition proceedings and domestic prosecution of Peru's Alberto Fujimori and other Peruvian cases, which are discussed in Ronald Gamarra's contribution to this volume (Chapter 5).
3. Transparency International uses existing statistics to compile annual corruption ratings for countries. See www.transparency.org. Publish What You Pay is a coalition of more than three hundred NGOs that calls for the mandatory disclosure of the payments made by oil, gas, and mining companies to all governments for the extraction of natural resources, and for resource-rich developing country governments to publish full details on revenues. See www.publishwhatyoupay.org.
4. The MCA, according to the U.S. Government, is "a new compact for global development, defined by new accountability for both rich and poor nations alike. Greater contributions from developed nations must be linked to greater responsibility from developing nations." The President pledged that the United States would lead by example and increase its core development assistance by 50 percent over the next three years, resulting in an annual increase of $5 billion by FY 2006. Available at http://www.whitehouse.gov/infocus/developingnations/millennium.html.
5. Comparing Transparency International's Corruption Perceptions Index (CPI) with the overall trend in World Bank lending in Latin America yields the following results: the ten most corrupt countries, in order, are (with comments regarding the growth or decline of World Bank loans in parentheses): Haiti (slow increase), Venezuela (frozen since approximately 1996), Ecuador (increasing, but more slowly since 2000), Paraguay (steadily increasing), Honduras (tremendous growth up to 2005, then sharp deceleration), Nicaragua (steadily increasing with a big jump between 1996 and 2000, probably Hurricane Mitch related), Guyana (steadily increasing, then deceleration in 2006 and no new loans in 2007), Guatemala (steady increase with a recent surge), Bolivia (very little initially, massive growth to 2005, then nothing new in the last two years), Argentina (fast growth, with no new loans in 2005, then resumed increasing loans in 2007). In contrast, loans to the world's ten most corrupt countries declined sharply, but many of these countries were also in the midst of armed conflict or political upheaval, so lending and corruption may be unrelated. See generally Transparency International, Corruption Perceptions Index 2007; the World Bank, World Bank Annual Reports 1996–2007.

6. For a full discussion of this dynamic, see Roht-Arriaza, *The Pinochet Effect: Transnational Justice in the Age of Human Rights*, Philadelphia: University of Pennsylvania Press, 2005.

7. See John Nellis, Rachel Menezes, and Sarah Lucas, *Privatization in Latin America: The Rapid Rise, Recent Fall, and Continuing Puzzle of a Contentious Economic Policy*, Center for Global Development, Policy Brief, January 2004.

8. See, for example, Linn A. Hammergren, *Donor Supported Criminal Justice Reform – Topic Brief*, The World Bank; Luz Estella Nagle, "The Cinderella Government: Judicial Reform in Latin America," *California Western International Law Journal* 30 (2000): 101.

9. *Causa 13*, Corte Suprema de la Nación, 30 December 1986, Revista de Jurisprudencia Argentina, no. 5513, April 29, 1987.

10. For more on Argentina's role, see Kathryn Sikkink and Carrie Walling, "Argentina's Contribution to Global Trends in Transitional Justice," in *Transitional Justice in the Twenty-First Century: Beyond Truth vs. Justice*, eds. Naomi Roht-Arriaza and Javier Mariezcurrena, Cambridge: Cambridge University Press, 2005, 306–307.

11. Under Bolivian law, Congress is responsible for bringing criminal charges against presidents and ministers of government under an impeachment-type proceeding known as a "trial of responsibilities."

12. The definition of genocide under Bolivian law does not strictly parallel the 1948 UN Convention on the Prevention and Punishment of the Crime of Genocide definition. García Meza was convicted of "the destruction of a group of politicians and intellectuals" as a crime against humanity as interpreted by national law.

13. Luís García Meza, "Condenado y extraditado, el ultimo dictador está tras rejas," *La Razón*, October 10, 2007. Available at http://www.la-razon.com/versiones/20071010_006055/nota_244_491476.htm.

14. Antonio Peredo Leigue, "Las deudas que aún no se pagan," *América Latina en Movimiento*, July 17, 2006. Available at http://alainet.org/active/12389&lang=es.

15. The Supreme Court had previously held that no statute of limitations applied to crimes against humanity in a case involving extradition from Italy of a Nazi war criminal. Priebke, Erich s/solicitud de extradicción, Corte Suprema, November 2, 1995.

16. Marcela Valente, "Justicia ordenó arresto del ex dictador Reynaldo Bignone," *Alterinfo*, March 12, 2007. Available at http://www.alterinfos.org/spip.php?article1010.

17. Lourdes Heredia, "Operación Condor: Videla procesado," *BBC Mundo*, September 27, 2001. Available at http://news.bbc.co.uk/hi/spanish/latin_america/newsid_1567000/1567495.stm.

18. Federal Criminal Court of Appeals of Buenos Aires, First Chamber, Judges Cavallo, Vigliani, and Riva Aramayo. Registry 489. Decision of May 23, 2002. In the case "Videla, Jorge R. s/procesamiento." Number 33714 of the Federal Investigative Judge No. 7, Secretariat No. 14.

19. "Bringing Bigwigs to Justice," *The Economist*, January 10, 2008, International. Available at http://www.economist.com/displaystory.cfm?story_id=10498849&fsrc=RSS.

20. "Espana negó la extradición de Isabelita a la Argentina," *Página 12*, Buenos Aires, April 28, 2008. Available at http://www.pagina12.com.ar/diario/ultimas/20-103226-

2008-04-28.html; Juan Carlos Algañaraz, "Espana no extraditará a Isabel Perón en la causa por delitos de la Triple A," *Clarín*, Buenos Aires, April 29, 2008. Available at http://www.clarin.com/diario/2008/04/29/elpais/p-01001.htm.

21. Article 7 (2) of the statute for the ICTY, for example provides:

> The official position of any accused person, whether as head of state or government or as a responsible government official, shall not relieve such person of criminal responsibility nor mitigate punishment.

22. Article 27, titled "The Irrelevance of Official Capacity," provides:

> 1. This statute shall apply equally to all persons without any distinction based on official capacity. In particular, official capacity as a head of state or government, a member of a government or parliament, an elected representative or a government official shall in no case exempt a person from criminal responsibility under this statute, nor shall it, in and of itself, constitute a ground for reduction of sentence.
> 2. Immunities or special procedural rules which may attach to the official capacity of a person, whether under national or international law, shall not bar the court from exercising its jurisdiction over such a person.

23. The commission is composed of seven experts elected by the OAS members and is charged with monitoring human rights in the Americas. Among other tasks, it responds to individual complaints that states have violated the American Convention on Human Rights, issuing nonbinding recommendations that nonetheless have substantial weight. It can also refer cases to the Inter-American Court on Human Rights, which holds public hearings and issues binding judgments.

24. *Barrios Altos* case, Judgment of March 14, 2001, Inter-Am Ct. H.R. Series C, No. 75 [2001]; for a range of views on the impact of the Inter-American system, see Due Process of Law Foundation, *Victims Unsilenced: The Inter-American Human Rights System and Transitional Justice in Latin America*, July 2007. Available at http://www.dplf.org/uploads/1190403828.pdf.

25. For example, in the *Plan de Sánchez* case, the Guatemalan government was ordered to pay nearly $8 million to 268 victims of a massacre in 1982. *Massacre of Plan de Sánchez v. Guatemala*, Reparations Judgment of November 19, 2004, Inter-Am Ct. H.R. Series C, No. 116 [2004].

26. Ley Orgánica 6/1985, del Poder Judicial, Noticias Juridicas. Available at http://noticias.juridicas.com/base_datos/Admin/lo6-1985.l1t1.html.

27. See Audiencia Nacional, Decision (Auto) of the Full Penal Chamber Confirming Spanish Jurisdiction over the Crimes of Genocide and Terrorism Committed during the Argentine Dictatorship, Appeal No. 84-98, 3rd Section, File 19/97 from Judicial Chamber 5, November 4, 1998. Available at http://www.derechos.org/nizkor/arg/espana/audi.html; Decision (Auto) of the Full Penal Chamber Confirming Spanish Jurisdiction to Investigate Genocide in Chile, Appeal No. 173/98, 1st Section, File 1/98 from Judicial Chamber 6, November 5, 1998. Available at http://www.derechos.org/nizkor/chile/juicio/audi.html.

28. See Roht-Arriaza, *The Pinochet Effect*, at pp. 44–66.

29. Amnesty International, *Amnesty International Report 2003 – Paraguay*, POL 10/003/2003.

30. "Piden la captura de Stroessner," *BBC Mundo*, October 17, 2003. Available at http://news.bbc.co.uk/hi/spanish/latin_america/newsid_3199000/3199408.stm.

31. Guatemalan Commission for Historical Clarification, *Guatemala Memory of Silence: Report of the Commission for Historical Clarification Conclusions, and Recommendations*, February 1999. Available at, http://shr.aaas.org/guatemala/ceh/report/english/toc.html.

32. "Antigenocide Activists in Guatemala Kidnapped, Threatened," *San Diego Independent Media Center*, February 24, 2007. Available at http://sandiego.indymedia.org/en/2007/02/125160.shtml.

33. *Ley de Reconciliación Nacional*, Decrete numero 145-1996.

34. Martín Rodríguez and Wendy Ruano, "Ríos Montt se jacta de inmunidad," *Prensa Libre*, May 23, 2007. Available at http://www.prensalibre.com/pl/2007/mayo/23/171857.html.

35. For a fuller description of some of these problems, see Roht-Arriaza, "Making the State Do Justice: Transnational Prosecutions and International Support for Criminal Investigations in Post-Conflict Guatemala," *Chicago Journal of International Law*, forthcoming (2008).

36. Conié Reynoso, "Ríos Montt queda fuera del caso jueves negro," *Prensa Libre*, January 31, 2006. Available at http://www.prensalibre.com/pl/2006/enero/31/133557.html.

37. *Condenan Resolución a Favor de Ríos Montt*, Organización Católica Latinoamericana y Caribeña de Comunicación, February 8, 2006. Available at http://www.oclacc.org/index.php?id_seccion=41&id_noticia=1368.

38. "España reafirma jurisdicción universal de la Justicia," *El Litoral*, October 6, 2005. Available at http://www.ellitoral.com/index.php/diarios/2005/10/06/internacionales/INTE-02.html.

39. "Guatemala anula el proceso de España contra los militares acusados de genocidio," *Madrid Press*, December 19, 2007. Available at http://www.madridpress.com/noticia.asp?ref=68148.

40. Luisa F. Rodríguez and Hugo Alvarado, "Álvaro Colom ofrece abrir archivos militares," *Prensa Libre*, February 26, 2008. Available at http://www.prensalibre.com/pl/2008/febrero/26/222553.html.

41. Roht-Arriaza, *Making the State Do Justice*.

42. See Roht-Arriaza, *The Pinochet Effect*, 189–191.

43. This was formally named The Special Prosecutors' Office for the Attention of Matters Allegedly Related to Federal Crimes Committed Directly or Indirectly by Public Servants Against Persons Linked to Social or Political Movements of the Past.

44. This description of the SPO is taken from Mariclaire Acosta and Esa Esselin, "The 'Mexican Solution' to Transitional Justice," in *Transitional Justice in the Twenty-First Century: Beyond Truth vs. Justice*, edited by Naomi Roht-Arriaza and Javier Mariezcurrena, Cambridge: Cambridge University Press, 2005.

45. Kevin Sullivan, "Mexico Prepares to Charge Ex-President," *Washington Post*, July 24, 2004, p. A1.

46. Article 149 *bis* of the Mexican Penal Code defines genocide as a series of acts carried out "with the purpose of destroying, in whole or in part, one or more national groups or those of an ethnic, racial, or religious character." The slight

variation in wording from the 1948 convention definition may have allowed the judge some leeway, as has the Spanish Audiencia Nacional's gloss on the definition of a national group to allow for group-based claims not related to ethnicity, race, or religion. See Roht-Arriaza, *The Pinochet Effect*, 46; see also Alfredo Mendez Ortiz, "Carpetazo al 10 de junio; Exoneran a Luis Echeverría y Mario Moya," *La Jornada*, July 27, 2005. Available at http://www.jornada.unam.mx/2005/07/27/003n1pol. php.

47. "Rechaza al Suprema Corte intervenir en caso Echeverría," *El Siglo de Torreón*, December 6, 2007. Available at http://www.elsiglodetorreon.com.mx/noticia/ 316187.rechaza-la-suprema-corte-intervenir-en-caso-e.html.

48. Human Rights Watch, *Bolivia: Strengthen Investigation into Protest Deaths*, December 22, 2003.

49. "Fiscal general acuso formalmente a Goni y sus ministros por genocidio," *Indymedia Bolivia*, October 17, 2007. Available at http://bolivia.indymedia.org/ node/1857.

50. Jean Friedman-Rudovsky, "Bolivia Calls Ex-President to Court," *Time*, February 6, 2007. Available at http://www.time.com/time/world/article/0,8599,1586707,00. html.

51. See Raul O. Garces, "Uruguay: Denuncian violaciónes a ley de amnistía," *Yahoo! Noticias España*, June 9, 2008.

52. "La Justicia Uruguaya confirma el procesamiento del ex presidente Bordaberry," *Deia.com*, June 3, 2007. Available at http://www.deia.com/es/impresa/2007/ 06/03/bizkaia/mundua/370277.php.

53. Mike Corder, "Former Suriname Leader Convicted," *AP Online*, July 16, 1999.

54. Simon Romero, "Long Memories May Ensnare a Dictator," *New York Times*, April 13, 2008, p. 7.

55. See Roht-Arriaza, *The Pinochet Effect*, 180.

56. Amnesty International, *Suriname: After 25 Years, a Chance for Accountability and Justice for the Families and Victims of the December 1982 Extrajudicial Killings*, November 29, 2007.

57. "Brazil's Disgraced Former President Wins Senate Seat," *International Herald Tribune*, October 2, 2006. Available at http://www.iht.com/articles/ap/2006/ 10/02/america/LA_POL_Brazil_Collor_Elected.php.

58. Centro de Investigación de Relaciones Internacionales y Desarrollo, *Biografías Líderes Políticos – Carlos Andrés Pérez Rodríguez*. Available at http://www.cidob. org.

59. Ibid. See also "World Briefing," *New York Times*, October 22, 1999, p. 6.

60. Maurice Lemoine, "Fishing for Gold in Colombia," *Le Monde Diplomatique*, February 2000. Available at http://mondediplo.com/2000/02/11lemoine.

61. Silvania Boschi, "La corte deja libre a Emir y le abre la puerta a Menem," *FMM Educación*, November 20, 2001. Available at http://www.fmmeducacion. com.ar/Historia/Cacerolazos/035libertadmenem.htm.

62. "Emir Yoma perdió otro rondo en la causa armas," *Diario de Cuyo*, June 28, 2005. Available at http://www.diariodecuyo.com.ar/home/new_noticia.php?noticia_id= 103646.

63. "Chile Declines to Hand Over Menem," *BBC News Online*, June 9, 2004. Available at http://news.bbc.co.uk/2/hi/americas/3789059.stm.

64. "Argentina trying Menem in arms scandal" *Prensa Latina*, October 13, 2008. Available at http://www.plenglish.com/article.asp?ID={5DBD60C3-A4EA-4112-9F51-DBBE60AA66A1}&language=EN.
65. "Pontaquarto y el procesamiento de De la Rúa: 'Se comprobó lo que yo venía diciendo'," *Clarín.com*, February 26, 2008. Available at http://www.clarin.com/diario/2008/02/26/um/m-01615809.htm.
66. "Costa Rica: Partido Social Cristiano quiere que regresen expresidentes corruptos," *Radio La Primerísima*, May 17, 2007. Available at http://www.radiolaprimerisima.com/noticias/13852.
67. "Dan arresto domiciliario a ex presidente costarricense," *El Siglo de Torreón*, March 24, 2005. Available at http://www.elsiglodetorreon.com.mx/noticia/139953.dan-arresto-domiciliario-a-ex-presidente-cost.html; see also Transparency International, *Informe Global de la Corrupción 2006*, 57.
68. "Costa Rica Financial Row Deepens," *BBC News online*, October 27, 2004. Available at http://news.bbc.co.uk/2/hi/americas/3960267.stm.
69. Freedom House, *Freedom in the World – Costa Rica (2006)*, 2006 Edition.
70. See CIDOB Foundation. Available at http://www.cidob.org.
71. Ibid.
72. Ibid.
73. At the same time, the judge also annulled corruption charges against ex–vice president Alberto Dahik Garzoni (1992–1995). See Eduardo Tamayo G., "Convulsión tras Perdón a ex Mandatorios Prófugos," *América Latina en Movimiento*, April 5, 2005.
74. See CIDOB Foundation, http://www.cidob.org/es/documentacion/biografias_lideres_politicos/america_del_sur/ecuador/lucio_gutierrez_borbua.
75. "Waiting for the Fat Man to Sing," *The Economist*, August 24, 2002, US Edition, The Americas.
76. "Nicaragua: detienen a Arnoldo Alemán," *BBC Mundo*, December 13, 2002. Available at http://news.bbc.co.uk/hi/spanish/latin_america/newsid_2571000/2571557.stm.
77. "Arnoldo Alemán tendrá a Nicaragua por cárcel," *Nacion.com*, January 12, 2008. Available at http://www.nacion.com/ln_ee/2008/enero/12/mundo1381805.html.
78. "Arnoldo Alemán apelará en Atlanta confiscación fondos familiares," *Terra*, December 26, 2006. Available at http://noticias.terra.com/articulo/html/act692751.htm.
79. "Panamá ordenará juicio a Arnoldo Alemán," *El Nuevo Diario*, July 6, 2007. Available at http://impreso.elnuevodiario.com.ni/2007/07/06/nacionales/53145.
80. Tim Rogers, "Why Nicaragua's Caged Bird Sings," *Time*, May 2, 2007. Available at http://www.time.com/time/world/article/0,8599,1616952,00.html.
81. Case 12,230. The case was settled in March 2002. Available at http://www.envio.org.ni/articulo/1130.
82. "Vinculan ex presidenta Mireya Moscoso en escándolo." *La Plana*, August 15, 2007. Available at http://www.laplana.com.do/?module=displaystory&story_id=12874&format=html.
83. Carlos Martínez, "Ex presidente Flores y funcionarios de su gabinete señalados por "irregularidades" en enriquecimiento," *El Faro*, August 29, 2005. Available at http://www.elfaro.net/secciones/noticias/20050829/noticias1_20050829.asp.

84. "Jueza mexicana frena extradición a Guatemala de Alfonso Portillo," *Diario Co Latino*, November 3, 2006. Available at http://www.diariocolatino.com/es/20061103/internacionales/internacionales_20061103_10241.

85. "Mexico Court Clears Portillo Move," *BBC News Online*, January 31, 2008. Available at http://news.bbc.co.uk/2/hi/americas/7219766.stm.

86. David Tamez Mancillas, "Ex Presidentes a Juicio, Segunda Parte," *El Milenio*, November 8, 2007. Available at http://reportajesdepolitica.blogspot.com/2007/11/ex-presidentes-juicio-primera-parte.html.

87. Ibid.

88. "El ex presidente paraguayo González Macchi, condenado a seis años de cárcel por corrupción," *El Mundo Es*, June 6, 2006. Available at http://www.elmundo.es/elmundo/2006/06/06/internacional/1149560547.html

89. See, for example, the Argentine jurisprudence, including the decision of Judge Cavallo invalidating the amnesty law. *Simon, Julio, Del Cerro, Juan Antonio, sustracción de menores de 10 años*, causa 8686/2000, Juzgado Crim y Correc Fed no. 4, March 6, 2001.

90. For further discussion, see Chapter 5, this volume, in which one of the key issues in Fujimori's trial is the nature of his responsibility.

4

The Multiple Prosecutions of Augusto Pinochet

Naomi Roht-Arriaza

General Augusto Pinochet of Chile thought it would be a short trip. His plan had been to shop a bit in Paris, then go look into some arms sales in the United Kingdom, one of his favorite countries. He also needed back surgery, and surgeons at a prestigious private London clinic had agreed to perform it. He thought he would soon be back in Chile, the country he had led for seventeen years as dictator and later as appointed president, and where he was now an appointed senator-for-life. He turned out to be wrong. It would be 502 days before he would see Chile again; when he did, it would be a changed country, and he would have a changed position in it.

Pinochet was the poster child for the dictatorships that swept across Latin America during the 1970s. On September 11, 1973, he overthrew Chile's elected president, Salvador Allende, and installed himself at the head of a military junta. Over the next months and years, former government officials, leaders of unions or student groups, or anyone suspected of antiregime political activity would be rounded up, imprisoned, tortured, and killed. In more than one thousand cases, the bodies were never found, and the families never knew the fate of their loved ones. Congress was dissolved, unions and political parties banned, and the courts tamed. In 1978, the military passed a law giving itself amnesty for the crimes committed up until that time.

Eventually, Pinochet felt secure enough in his power, and in a new custom-made constitution, that he called a plebiscite on his rule. To his surprise, he lost. By the time civilian government was reinstated in 1990, more than four thousand people had been killed or disappeared, and some fifty thousand

Author's Note: The material in this chapter is based on my book *The Pinochet Effect: Transitional Justice in the Age of Human Rights*, Philadelphia: University of Pennsylvania Press, 2005. Readers interested in a more in-depth treatment, and in specific references, should consult the book, especially chapters 1–3.

had been imprisoned and tortured; more than a half million were in exile. Pinochet retained his post as head of the army.

The new civilian government, headed by Patricio Aylwin, tried to strike a balance between pressures for justice and fear of a military backlash. Aylwin commissioned a group of well-known figures with a broad spectrum of political views, known as the Rettig Commission, to investigate and report on abuses during the military regime. The commission took testimony from victims and their relatives and published a report along with extensive recommendations for reform. The report outlined the broad trends of the repression and named most of the victims, but it was prohibited from naming individual perpetrators. In accepting their report, President Aylwin apologized to the victims in the name of the Chilean state. The legislature approved reparations to victims of executions and disappearances and their families, including medical and educational services as well as pensions. The report and subsequent legislation had limits: although torture was well documented in the Rettig report, individual torture survivors were not named, and they received no monetary reparations. Despite the continued protests of organizations of family members and of a handful of human rights lawyers, a broad consensus existed among the Chilean elite that the past had been dealt with and it was time to move on.

On the legal front, very little was done. The Rettig Commission report had detailed the list of victims but could shed little light on who killed them, how, or why. To the extent the report gathered information on perpetrators, the information was turned over to the courts, which by and large did nothing with it. The Supreme Court not only had upheld the 1978 amnesty law against domestic and international law-based challenges but had said it precluded all investigation into acts that potentially fell under its sway. The one notable exception, the trial and sentencing in 1993 (to seven and six years of imprisonment, respectively) of former general Manuel Contreras and former brigadier Pedro Espinoza of the secret police (known by its Spanish initials as DINA) for the killing of Allende's former foreign minister Orlando Letelier in Washington, D.C., resulted from U.S. government pressure. Even those cases that fell outside the purview of the amnesty law remained stalled in the courts. Most of them were eventually turned over to military justice tribunals made up of a majority of active-service officers. Those courts promptly archived the cases.

THE SPANISH CASE

Half a world away in Spain, in April 1996, members of the Spanish Union of Progressive Prosecutors filed a complaint in the Spanish federal court (the

Audiencia Nacional) accusing members of the Argentine military junta of genocide, terrorism, and other crimes regarding the detention and subsequent disappearance during the 1970s of a number of Spanish citizens and Argentine citizens of Spanish descent. That case was accepted by Judge Baltazar Garzón, who was already well known in Spain because of his daring investigations into ETA (Euskadi Ta Askatasuna, the Basque separatist group) terrorism and Spanish government death squads.

Three months later, Spanish lawyer Joan Garcés filed a similar complaint against Pinochet and a number of his high-ranking military and civilian officials. Garcés had been a young academic when he arrived in Santiago in 1970, enchanted by Chile's vibrant democracy. Through a twist of fate, he met Salvador Allende, then chairman of the Senate. When in 1970 Allende became Chile's new socialist president, Garcés became Allende's political advisor, working in La Moneda, Chile's presidential palace, directly with the president. When the coup came, he was one of the last to leave the embattled president's side. He only left the palace minutes before it was bombed and Allende died. The president told him to escape because "someone has to tell the world what happened here."[1] After hiding in Santiago for two days, he made it to the Spanish ambassador's residence and eventually returned to Europe, where he became a professor of political science and, later, started his own law practice in Madrid.

The Chilean complaint alleged genocide, terrorism, torture, and illegal detention followed by disappearance, all between 1973 and 1990. Spanish law is peculiarly well suited for pursuing criminal complaints brought by ordinary citizens. In the United States and many other countries, criminal charges must be brought by a government prosecutor, who can decide whether to bring charges regardless of the wishes of the victim of the crime. If a prosecutor decides not to press charges, there is little the victim can do. In Spain, not only can victims bring a complaint directly to an investigating judge and ask him or her to pursue it, but the victim then becomes a party to the case and can propose witnesses, evidence, or theories of the case. Spain also has broad rules allowing people who are not directly connected to an alleged crime to file complaints. These "popular accusers" must be reputable nongovernmental groups concerned with the public interest. Even if the public prosecutor disagrees, if the victim can convince the investigating magistrate that there is a valid case, it will go forward. After the criminal phase is complete, plaintiffs can pursue civil damages.

Article 23.4 of the Spanish Judicial Law allows prosecution of non-Spanish citizens for some crimes committed outside Spain, among them genocide, terrorism, and other crimes under international law contained in treaties ratified by Spain.[2] Under this type of universal jurisdiction, the connection to the prosecuting state is not made through any particular link between the state and the criminal event, such as the nationality of the victims or perpetrators or the site of events, but rather results from the nature of the crime itself. Certain crimes are so universally agreed to be heinous, so potentially disruptive of international peace, and so difficult for states to adequately prosecute on account of potential links to state officials or other powerful people that all states have the right to try anyone accused of them. Many states (more than 125 according to Amnesty International) have some variant of these universal jurisdiction laws, but few actually use them.[3]

The Chilean investigation proceeded apace before Judge Manuel García-Castellón, who accepted the complaint in July 1996. One of the lawyers' first tasks was to create lines of communication to Chile. "We heard from Garcés, who some people knew had managed to escape after the *coup* through the Spanish Embassy," recounts Verónica Reyna of the legal aid organization FASIC. "We thought it was a bit crazy, when he started sending us lists of things he needed, among them things that were impossible to find. The Family Members of the Disappeared Group were the first to believe in him. They began going to the Spanish embassy in Santiago to give their statements for transmission to Madrid."[4] Witnesses began making the trek across the Atlantic. There was no money for witness travel, so many came at their own expense.

The Chilean government at first paid little attention, although the local press had mentioned the case and in December 1996 even published interviews with some of the lawyers involved. A turning point came in 1997 when García-Castellón asked the U.S. government for the results of official investigations into the Letelier case and other documents related to Chile. The U.S. investigators in the Letelier/Moffitt murder had testified in Madrid, and as a result of their testimony, García-Castellón sent off a request to the United States for cooperation. This made the Chilean government take notice; an inquiry into U.S. support for their military could potentially be explosive.

On March 13, 1998, the lawyers asked Judge García-Castellón to issue arrest warrants for thirty-nine military and civilian officials of the ex-dictatorship, including Pinochet, Contreras, and the leadership of the DINA. Among those accused were the operatives believed to be responsible for the deaths and disappearances of Spanish citizen and United Nations official Carmelo Soria, several Spanish priests, and a number of other Spanish citizens.

Witnesses produced evidence of the tight chain of command of Pinochet's armed forces. Air force general Sergio Poblete testified about his own arrest and torture as well as about Pinochet's role in designing the military's policies. Others sent copies of declarations they had made in local investigations of

Pinochet's control over the Caravana de la Muerta (Caravan of Death), a series of visits to military bases around Chile shortly after the coup by a group of handpicked military men led by General Arellano Stark. The group would land at a base, pull out a group of prisoners, and kill them. In some cases, the bodies of the victims were never found. Witnesses also testified about military decrees establishing that "only the President of the Junta [that is, Pinochet] can arrest people and detain them in places that are not recognized as prisons."

Meanwhile, a parallel inquiry in Argentina began hearing evidence of a larger conspiracy: the Chilean DINA had conspired to commit terrorist acts in Spain, France, Italy, Portugal, the United States, Mexico, Costa Rica and elsewhere, with Pinochet's knowledge and participation. Documentation from the Letelier investigation also indicated Pinochet's involvement in the murder of Argentine General Carlos Prats and other crimes. These crimes were part of an effort in the 1970s, known as Operation Condor, in which the military intelligence services of Chile, Argentina, Uruguay, Paraguay, Bolivia, and Brazil, alarmed by the continental spread of revolutionary groups, decided to form a counterrevolutionary alliance of their own. Starting in 1973, they agreed to share information, exchange captives, and coordinate their activities both bilaterally and on a regional level. This expanded the scope of Garzón's investigation from Argentina to the entire region.

Why, knowing of the Spanish arrest warrants, did Pinochet decide to travel? Although we'll never know for sure, a likely explanation is that he thought the Spanish case would soon be dismissed. Upon hearing of the Spanish arrest warrants, Pinochet dispatched his personal advisor and the army's auditor general, General Fernando Torres Silva, to Spain to investigate. Torres Silva contacted Judge García-Castellón, who courteously but firmly advised him that if he wanted to provide information, he was free to appear before the judge and present his testimony like anyone else. Torres Silva did so on October 3. He apparently intended to defend Pinochet's record, but more important, from the point of view of the Chilean press, by appearing before the judge he had validated the Spanish court's jurisdiction over the affair. Nonetheless, Torres Silva returned home and apparently advised Pinochet that the threat of the Spanish case was remote and should not interfere with any European travel plans.

THE EXTRADITION PROCEEDINGS – *PINOCHET I*

In October 1998, when Pinochet decided to make his short trip to Paris and London, Amnesty International, alerted to his travel plans, got in touch with Joan Garcés. Garcés joined forces with a colleague from the Argentine investigation, and they filed motions asking for an arrest warrant for Pinochet on grounds of crimes in Chile and, through Operation Condor, crimes being investigated by Judge Garzón. Although García-Castellón declined, Judge Garzón decided to ask the London police to hold Pinochet until he could be questioned on Operation Condor.[5]

On October 16, Judge Garzón received an urgent fax back from the U.K. police. The police could not guarantee Pinochet's presence for any interrogation. Pinochet was free to go whenever he wished and in fact, according to police information from his entourage, was planning to leave the next day. The only way to stop him, the police helpfully added, was to issue an arrest order. Under the European Convention on Extradition, if the Spanish arrest warrant was valid, the British authorities would have little choice but to arrest Pinochet in London.[6]

It was a Friday afternoon, and Garzón, like the rest of the court's staff, was about to leave town for the weekend. Garzón sat down and formulated an arrest order for Augusto Pinochet, accused of genocide and terrorism, based on the facts of Operation Condor. Garzón asked the British authorities to execute the international arrest order. It was by then evening, but the police were still able to get in touch with Nicholas Evans, a stipendiary magistrate of the Bow Street Courts, who could approve an arrest warrant. Magistrate Evans called the Home Office to ask whether the subject of the warrant had diplomatic immunity, and was informed that as far as the British government was concerned, he did not. Late that evening, Magistrate Evans, acting from his home, issued a warrant for the arrest of one Augusto Pinochet, Chilean. Police served the warrant on the general in his hospital bed.

Pinochet quickly hired a high-priced legal team and later rented a luxury villa in Surrey, where he remained under house arrest. His lawyers quickly attacked the warrant on the grounds that it did not describe extraditable offenses in the United Kingdom. In response, Garzón sent a second, revised warrant, which was quickly approved. Pinochet's lawyers challenged both warrants in the High Court, arguing among other things that their client was immune from prosecution as a former head of state. The Divisional Court of the Queen's Bench Division convened five days later, on October 28. A three-judge panel found that under U.K. law, Pinochet, as a former head of state, would have immunity only for his official functions.[7] However, could the crimes alleged be considered "official functions"? The court found that they could. After all, if a head of state was clearly entitled to immunity for *some* criminal acts carried out as part of his official functions (which was uncontested), then there was no logical way to distinguish the most serious criminal acts, like torture, from less serious ones. To the argument that such heinous crimes could never be carried out as official functions, Justice Collins replied:

> Unfortunately, history shows that it has indeed on occasions been state policy to exterminate or to oppress particular groups. One does not have to look very far back in history to see examples of that sort of thing having happened. There is in my judgment no justification for reading any limitation based on the nature of the crimes committed into the immunity which exists.[8]

The only recourse for the prosecution was to appeal to the House of Lords, Britain's final legal authority. A panel of five lords met to consider the arguments over several days. On the morning of November 25, the lords announced their decision to a packed chamber, before the assembled journalists and television cameras.[9] Argument focused on the question of Pinochet's immunity as a former head of state.

The first two lords to speak argued in favor of immunity. For Lord Slynn, a former judge at the European Court of Justice, there was nothing in international law to preclude crimes from being official functions.[10] Rather, immunity for any and all official acts of a former head of state was a matter of customary international law. Subsequent international treaties on genocide, torture, hostage-taking, and the like did not change the rule because they did not explicitly address the issue of immunity. Lord Lloyd of Berwick went through a similar chain of argument. He found first that the distinction was between private and official acts and that the acts at issue were clearly official.[11] He then asked whether there was some exception to immunity in customary international law for particularly horrendous acts, and found that there was not; immunity could be waived or overridden by an international tribunal, but not otherwise.[12] In any case, the issue was not one for the courts.

Lord Nicholls went over much the same ground until he got to the question of whether the acts charged against Pinochet could be considered done "in the exercise of his functions" as head of state, as required by statute. Here he departed from the previous opinions. In his view:

> It hardly needs saying that torture of his own subjects, or of aliens, would not be regarded by international law as a function of a head of state.... International law recognizes, of course, that the functions of a head of state may include activities which are wrongful, even illegal, by the law of his own state or by the laws of other states. But international law has made plain that certain types of conduct, including torture and hostage-taking, are not acceptable conduct on the part of anyone. This applies as much to heads of state, or even more so, as it does to everyone else; the contrary conclusion would make a mockery of international law.[13]

Lord Steyn agreed that horrific crimes condemned by international law could not be official functions. He concluded with a list of reasons why the act of state doctrine did not apply.[14]

With the lords thus split two-two, Lord Hoffman, a well-known commercial lawyer, cast the deciding vote. Hoffman's speech was one sentence long. "My lords, I have had the advantage of reading in draft the speech of my noble and learned friend Lord Nicholls of Birkenhead and for the reasons he gives I too would allow this appeal."[15] The gallery, where the Chilean exile community sat, erupted into cheers. Crowds celebrated on the streets of Santiago and Madrid. Pinochet was not immune from extradition. The judgment was handed down on Pinochet's eighty-third birthday; it must have been a rather glum celebration for him.

PINOCHET'S LAWYERS STRIKE BACK – *PINOCHET II*

The euphoria was short-lived. Pinochet's lawyers soon filed an application with the House of Lords arguing that Lord Hoffman should have been recused because he had ties to an Amnesty International affiliate, and Amnesty had intervened in the case. The lords agreed that there was a possible appearance of impropriety and set the case for reargument before a different panel of judges.[16] Meanwhile, Pinochet remained under house arrest.

With more time to prepare, all sides reevaluated their strategy over the December holiday period. The major issue in *Pinochet I* had been Pinochet's immunity as a former head of state. Pinochet's defenders had focused on immunity because it was a threshold issue: if there was immunity, there was no need to consider anything else about the crimes in the extradition request. The House of Lord's decision of November 25, 1998, by a bare majority, that torture could not constitute the kind of official act protected by the doctrine of state immunity, now presented a problem. It was possible to convince a new panel of judges to go the other way, but not likely. The judges would be influenced by the institutional imperative to maintain uniformity between different panels of the same court, to avoid appearing arbitrary. With this in mind, the defense team began looking for other possible arguments. They focused on the question of double criminality. That question, which asks whether the acts in question were criminalized in both countries, had been raised earlier, and easily dismissed. Now it took center stage.

THE SPANISH PROCEEDINGS CONTINUE

Meanwhile, the Spanish courts considered the case as well. The opposition of Spain's public prosecutor to the jurisdiction of the Spanish courts over crimes occurring elsewhere led to an appeal before the full Audiencia Nacional. On November 5, 1998, the court affirmed its jurisdiction over the Chilean and Argentine cases, with a ringing defense of universal jurisdiction.[17] The decision turned on three main issues: the definition of the crimes involved under international and Spanish law, the applicability of the current universal jurisdiction and torture provisions to events that took place before the laws were enacted, and the effect in Spain of the local amnesty laws that shielded the defendants from prosecution at home.

At the time, crimes against humanity had not yet been defined as part of Spanish domestic law, so the best characterization of what had happened in Chile as an international crime was unavailable. Garzón was left only with genocide, terrorism, and torture (the U.K. case focused on torture because neither genocide nor terrorism existed as such in British law and so the double criminality requirement for extradition was not met). Genocide, under the 1948 Convention definition,[18] requires the intent to destroy an ethnical, national, racial, or religious group, in whole or in part; as such, Garzón argued that a kind of autogenocide had been committed in both Chile and Argentina. The "national" group required under the definition as the target of a genocidal attack was simply a subset of the national population singled out on the basis of some common, defining characteristic. In this case, the common characteristic was active or even passive opposition to the new vision of a "nation" and a "national project" espoused by the military governments. As the Audiencia Nacional put it in approving Garzón's assertion of jurisdiction, the victims of the regime were against "the understanding of national identity and national values supported by the new government."[19]

The court then turned to the question of whether it would violate the defendant's rights to investigate crimes that happened before all the current definitions of the law were in place. A cardinal maxim of international criminal law states that there should be no crime (or punishment) unless there is already a law in place criminalizing the relevant acts at the time they were committed, otherwise known by the Latin maxim *nullum crimen sine lege*.[20] The public prosecutor argued that the Spanish court could not hear the cases because the current law allowing the court jurisdiction dated from 1985, well after the bulk of the events at issue in both Chile and Argentina. The court found that the behavior to be punished had clearly been criminal by the 1970s. The 1985 law had not created new crimes or penalties nor had it punished anyone or restricted anyone's rights; it had merely created the jurisdictional scheme under which trial could take place. That was a procedural, not a substantive, norm, and as such applying it retroactively violated no due process rights.

Finally, the Audiencia Nacional touched on the issue of the Chilean amnesty laws. The court found that, independent of whether the laws violated treaty norms, they could not be seen as an acquittal or pardon that would preclude retrial in Spain because they decriminalized the acts before judicial proceedings had even begun and thus were neither acquittals nor pardons and so were irrelevant to the proceedings.

STATE IMMUNITY AND DOUBLE CRIMINALITY – *PINOCHET III*

Back in London, on March 24, 1999, the new panel of seven law lords announced their decision to a packed chamber.[21] In the English tradition, each judge gave his own opinion, and it was up to the spectators to add up the votes and offer an interpretation on what the opinions, taken together, meant. It was not easy to do in this case. Several things were clear: by a vote of six to one, the lords decided that Pinochet had committed extraditable crimes and that his immunity as a former head of state did not extend to these crimes. Torture could be prosecuted, even if the person ordering it was once a high-ranking official. What is more, under the Convention Against Torture and Other Cruel, Inhuman or Degrading Treatment or Punishment (Torture Convention), states have an obligation, not just an option, to act against allegations of torture.[22] These findings represented major steps forward in international criminal law.

Beyond that, however, the judgments took various paths. What is common to most of them is that they rely on the intricacies of U.K. law, not international law. To the extent international law comes into play, a majority of the lords looked to treaty law – in this case, the Torture Convention – rather than to the more nebulous (and harder, for judges, to apply) customary international law. Only Lord Millet looked to customary law as the basis of his discussion.[23] In terms of the development of international law, this decision was far more conservative than that of the first panel. Wherever the judges could choose, they took the more limited route.

The judgment focused on two points: the "double criminality" issue and the immunity of an ex–head of state. The judges found that the conduct at issue had to have been a crime under U.K. law on the date that it happened, rather than on the date extradition was requested.[24] The result was that five judges decided to limit Pinochet's extraditable crimes to those that occurred after 1988.

On the immunity question, a majority of the lords found that although a sitting head of state has personal immunity, a former head of state's immunity was limited to his official acts. Three of the lords then found that torture and conspiracy to torture could not be part of a head of state's official functions. Lord Browne-Wilkinson grounded this rule on the Torture Convention,[25] Lord

Hutton on customary law that made torture an international crime, and Lord Phillips on a rule that said former heads of state never have immunity.[26] Lords Hope and Saville thought that there was immunity under international law but that Chile had waived that immunity by ratifying the Torture Convention.[27] Lord Goff thought that although immunity could be waived, it had to be done explicitly and not by implication through ratifying the treaty; thus, for Lord Goff alone, Pinochet still had immunity.[28] Lord Millet was the only judge to find that torture had been a crime under customary international law long before 1988, and so there was no immunity for any of the charges.[29] In this, his explanation more closely matched that of the majority in *Pinochet I*, which had relied much more on broad principles of international law.

Two weeks after the House of Lords decision, Home Secretary Jack Straw approved the extradition, and after yet another hearing, Deputy Chief Stipendiary Magistrate Ronald Bartle decided that Pinochet was in fact extraditable.[30] However, by this time, the Chilean government, which opposed Pinochet's extradition to Spain, was insisting that the general's health had deteriorated sharply and that he was unfit to stand trial. The British government ordered medical tests, which bore out the Chilean government's assertions. On March 2, 2000, Jack Straw issued a final decision not to continue with the extradition proceedings on the basis of the general's poor health.[31] After a few final legal skirmishes, Pinochet flew back to Chile. But at home, things had changed.

THE CASE AT HOME

Litigation against Pinochet in Chile began before his detention in London, when, in January 1998, Gladys Marín of the Chilean Communist Party filed the first complaint against him for the forced disappearance of her husband and his colleagues. The immediate impetus for the timing of the complaint was that Pinochet had resigned as commander-in-chief of the army and immediately become a senator-for-life, thus giving himself limited immunity from criminal process. According to Marín's lawyer, Eduardo Contreras, this created a "moment of national indignation" that overcame, at least for him, the perception of invincibility Pinochet still enjoyed.[32] Once the general returned from London, other complaints alleging his participation or complicity in killings and disappearances quickly followed. Pinochet was also added as an alleged defendant to existing complaints naming lower-ranked officials.

There were a number of potential impediments to prosecution of Pinochet in the Chilean courts. The first obstacle was Pinochet's official position and immunity. The procedural device used in Chile when high-ranking figures with politically generated immunity are accused of crime is two-fold. First, rather than go to a local investigating judge, the case must go to a designated (by lottery) Santiago Appeals Court judge to investigate. That judge then centralizes all the complaints that name the defendant, even if they also name others. Thus, the claim that the case should go to military jurisdiction, which had been used to stymie other cases involving the military, did not arise. The judge chosen for the Pinochet prosecution, Juan Guzmán Tapia, proved tireless and determined to bring the cases he investigated to trial; this was a major factor in keeping them alive through innumerable obstacles.

Second, to remove Pinochet's senatorial immunity and allow his arrest, Chilean law requires a pre-hearing and a showing that there is probable cause (*sospechas fundadas*) to believe he participated in, or covered up, crimes. The purpose of the immunity law is to make sure legislators are not routinely bothered by frivolous or politically motivated complaints. Judge Guzmán first invoked the procedure, called *desafuero*, in the notorious Caravan of Death killings. There was evidence that Pinochet had personally covered up, and probably approved, the killings. Some of the bodies were never recovered, making those cases aggravated kidnappings, not homicides, under Chilean law.

The next hurdle was posed by the 1978 amnesty law. Decree-Law 2191 of April 18, 1978, as noted above, had shielded the security forces for almost any crime committed during the worst period of repression.[33] Until 1998, the courts overwhelmingly had held that the amnesty meant that when the facts implicated the armed forces, no investigation should even be opened. Judge Guzmán found that the amnesty law did not apply in cases where no body had ever been found. These were continuing crimes until the victim, or their remains, were found. Because it was not clear whether the victim was still alive in 1978, Guzmán argued the amnesty law could not apply.

On May 23, 2000, the Santiago Appeals Court decided to strip Pinochet of his parliamentary immunity, opening the way for his trial.[34] The Supreme Court affirmed this decision in August 2000.[35] The majority vote of fourteen judges held that because this was a preliminary proceeding, no definitive showing of guilt was needed, and a fuller investigation of the facts could follow. The court ratified aggravated kidnapping, homicide, illegal association, and illegal exhumation charges against Pinochet. They limited the reach of the 1978 amnesty law for murder as well as forced disappearance. They also rejected the defense's argument that the statute of limitations had run, holding that these defenses could only be considered at the end of the trial stage, when it was clear which defendants had committed which crimes. Although Judge Guzmán had charged only crimes under national law, a concurring opinion went on to suggest that the underlying crimes were also violations of the Geneva Conventions and that those Conventions also forbade amnesty for such crimes. With Pinochet's immunity lifted, he was indicted for the Caravan of Death crimes in January 2001. Other complaints piled up, more than two hundred in all. The courts ruled that a new *desafuero* procedure would be necessary for each one.

The government and military realized that the issue of the military's crimes had not just gone away, nor would it disappear with the passage of time. They created a "dialogue roundtable" in which a group of human rights lawyers, military officials, and representatives of civil society met over the course of several months to hammer out an agreement. The human rights lawyers and civil society wanted an apology and a commitment to turn over the military's information on the disappeared; the military wanted trials and investigations to end. The roundtable resulted in limited military recognition that their agents had carried out unacceptable crimes, and a commitment to search for the bodies of the disappeared. In early 2001, the military presented its report, which, as expected, contained limited and contradictory information on a fraction of the cases. As military barracks were dug up and offshore sites investigated, more bodies began to appear.

Prosecutions of other military officers continued. President Ricardo Lagos in 2001 appointed a number of judges whose main task was to accelerate investigations into disappearance cases. These judges, many of them women, pushed ahead, and by mid-decade, dozens of cases were at the conviction stage.

Meanwhile, Pinochet's defense team used every fresh opportunity to raise anew an issue that they had lost in the Caravan of Death case: Pinochet's failing health. Defense lawyers argued that it was a due process violation to try an old man with mental and physical health problems that made it impossible for him to communicate adequately with his lawyers. Judge Guzmán had ordered medical and psychological tests before indicting Pinochet in the Caravan of Death case, and those exams had found a "light to moderate" degree of dementia, insufficient to keep him from exercising his rights and directing his defense, and in any case insufficient to meet the legal standard of "crazy or demented" for excusing a defendant from trial. By July 2002, the Supreme Court reversed, permanently closing the case against Pinochet for the Caravan of Death crimes on the basis of a new finding that he suffered from a "subcortical dementia."[36] Twice more during 2003, Judge Guzmán tried to strip Pinochet of immunity, in the murder of Carlos Prats and his wife and in the Calle Conferencia (Gladys Marín's) case, but both times the appeals courts denied the request on health grounds.[37]

Two events reversed this panorama. A few months after the second decision to close an investigation, Pinochet gave an interview to a Miami television station in which he called himself an "angel" of democracy who had done nothing wrong. Judge Guzmán pounced on the footage as evidence that the general was fit for trial and soon after indicted him for twenty disappearances in conjunction with Operation Condor. On August 26, 2004, the Supreme Court agreed to strip him of his immunity for that case, and he subsequently lost immunity in several other cases.[38]

The other factor that changed the political and legal landscape was the discovery of a large number of secret bank accounts belonging to Pinochet and his family at Riggs Bank in Washington, D.C. According to a U.S. Senate inquiry, the bank had skirted federal banking laws to help Pinochet open offshore accounts containing at least $27 million, impossible to amass on a military salary. Politically, this was a devastating blow: the substantial minority of Chileans who still supported Pinochet had always argued that he might have been harsh but at least he was honest. Now it seemed he was not. The right wing parties abandoned him. Soon a new judicial inquiry was looking into charges of money laundering and income tax evasion. In November 2005, Pinochet lost his immunity from prosecution in the financial wrongdoing case. In April 2006, the Santiago Court of Appeals upheld charges of tax evasion and falsifying passports.[39] The Riggs Bank scandal had a further consequence. The Spanish court had earlier issued an order freezing Pinochet's assets, which Riggs had obviously disregarded. Joan Garcés and his associates worked out a deal: in exchange for the Spanish court dropping charges, Riggs agreed to pay $8 million into a fund for victims of Pinochet, and two of the bank's directors agreed to personally contribute another $1 million.

At the moment of his death on December 10, 2006 (ironically, International Human Rights Day), Pinochet faced two separate inquiries into his financial dealings and human rights–related crimes. Cases against other military and police defendants continue apace, with the appeals courts upholding convictions despite the amnesty laws. In 2007, spurred by a ruling from the Inter-American Court of Human Rights condemning the law as a violation of its international obligations,[40] the Chilean Congress began debating permanently annulling the law or interpreting it to not apply to crimes under international law.

CONCLUSIONS

Once the Spanish cases were underway, it became a matter of national pride within Chile to argue that Pinochet could be tried at home. Judges took it as an affront that a foreign judge was leading an investigation into events that had occurred in their country: several became much more active in investigations that had been pending for years. Judges admitted that they had been too passive and began acting assertively.

The Spanish (and other European) cases put the Christian Democrat–Socialist coalition government in Chile into something of a bind: to argue for Pinochet's release, it had to affirm that he could be fairly tried at home. Once he returned, they were under political pressure to show that it was true. It became fashionable for politicians to call for domestic trials, and even the right wing was forced to go along. This deepened Pinochet's isolation and made the military more eager to find a political solution. A new generation of military officers began to see the old general as a liability, not an asset.

Pinochet's position as a former head of state created difficulties, but none were insurmountable. In the extradition proceedings, it forced the U.K. courts to confront the issue of official immunity. They responded by drawing a distinction between official and unofficial acts and by finding that crimes under international law cannot constitute official acts. They agreed, and subsequent cases in other courts have affirmed, that a sitting head of state or minister cannot be tried, except by an international tribunal. With regard to past heads of state – or other top government officials – they may be tried under at least some circumstances.[41] On a national level, the *desafuero* pre-proceeding, created to protect high-level suspects, ended up allowing ventilation of a good part of the evidence against Pinochet in a number of proceedings, making that evidence public and putting it into the official record despite the lack of an actual trial. It also led to a finding – given Pinochet's death the only official finding – that there was good reason to believe he was involved in the crimes charged against him.

As this case shows, transnational judicial processes based outside a country can have a profound impact on changing internal political dynamics. In the Pinochet case, they revitalized anti-impunity movements and gave the judiciary new incentives to push forward. Far from destabilizing democracy, the main effect was to improve the chances for justice at home.

This does not mean that there is not also potential for conflict between domestic and transnational processes. If, as occurred in the Spanish cases concerning Chile and Argentina, the predicate for Spanish courts to act is the inability to bring the cases in domestic courts, then the opening caused by a transnational prosecution may lead a foreign court to prematurely assess the viability of a domestic prosecution and dismiss the foreign action, even though there is no guarantee of trial at home. Further, even if trial at home is a real possibility, it may be inadvisable for reasons of judicial economy – so much evidence may have already been gathered (not to mention time and money spent) that it may still make sense to complete a case where it started. Alternatively, a conviction for lesser offenses may cause one court to abstain because the other has already acted. These problems did not arise in the Pinochet case, however.[42] A careful strategy as to defendants and charges, involving a high degree of cooperation and coordination among private complainants across several jurisdictions, minimized (but did not completely avoid) these potential problems.

Transnational civil society plays a key role in both pushing forward these transnational prosecutions and translating them into catalysts of domestic change. In the Chilean cases, human rights groups within the country were deeply involved in the preparation of the European as well as the domestic legal cases. They provided most of the evidence and access to victims and witnesses. The role of long-term exiles and people with long connections to Chile within Europe was particularly important in understanding both the local and home-country legal systems and politics. These networks also had to mediate potential conflicts between the legal strategies of domestic groups and those working on transnational prosecutions. These transnational networks are continuing to play a key role in combining legal and political strategies.

The Pinochet case was a landmark in international law, reaffirming that international crimes are not subject to immunity (except for sitting heads of state), and breathing new life into the legitimacy and validity of universal jurisdiction. Since then, the Spanish courts have become trailblazers in the use of universal jurisdiction. Other courts have followed: there have been prosecutions for torture or genocide committed in another country in the United Kingdom, the Netherlands, Germany, France, and even the United States.[43]

The Chilean case would seem to refute those who argue that transnational prosecutions, especially those carried out on the basis of universal jurisdiction, necessarily interfere with domestic processes. It is true that the advances on the legal front in Chile would probably have happened, to some extent, anyway – they just would have taken longer.[44] However, the amount of initiative, work, and money that it took to sustain the Spanish and other investigations over a number of years, with few paid staff and no institutional infrastructure, provides some guarantee that such endeavors will not be embarked on lightly. They provide a potent reminder of the potential of law, combined with the power of transnational social movements, to create positive social and political change.

NOTES

1. Roht-Arriaza, *The Pinochet Effect*, 4.
2. Organic Law 6/1985, of July 1, of the Judicial Power (*Ley Organica 6/1985, de 1 de julio, del Poder Judicial*), as amended by Organic Law 11/1999, Article 23.4 (a) and (g). A Spanish version of the relevant article is available at http://www.juridicas. com/base_datos/Admin/lo6-1985.l1t1.html.

3. Amnesty International, "Universal Jurisdiction: The Scope of Civil Universal Jurisdiction," July 1, 2007.

4. Roht-Arriaza, *The Pinochet Effect*, 25.

5. Eventually, in November 1998, the Argentine and Chilean cases were combined under Judge Garzón's control.

6. European Convention on Extradition. December 13, 1957, Eur. T.S. No. 24.

7. See *In re Augusto Pinochet Ugarte*, 38 I.L.M. 68, 79 (Q.B. Div'l Ct. 1998).

8. Ibid., per Lord Collins.

9. *R v. Bow Street Metropolitan Stipendiary Magistrate, ex parte Pinochet Ugarte (Pinochet I)*, [1998] 37 I.L.M. 1302.

10. Ibid., per Lord Slynn, 1308–1309.

11. Ibid., per Lord Lloyd of Berwick, 1320.

12. Ibid., 1321.

13. Ibid., per Lord Nicholls, 1333.

14. Ibid., per Lord Steyn, 1335.

15. Ibid., per Lord Hoffman, 1339.

16. *R v. Bow Street Metropolitan Stipendiary Magistrate, ex parte Pinochet Ugarte (Pinochet II)* [2000] A.C. 119.

17. *Auto de la Sala de lo Penal de la Audiencia Nacional confirmando la jurisdiccion de Espana para conocer de los crimenes de genocidio y terrorismo cometidos durante la dictadura chilena* [Order of the Criminal Chamber of the Spanish Audencia Nacional affirming Spain's Jurisdiction to Try Crimes of Genocide and Terrorism Committed during the Chilean Dictatorship], SAN, November 5, 1998 (Appeal No. 173/98, Criminal Investigation No. 1/98).

18. Convention on the Prevention and Punishment of the Crime of Genocide, December 9, 1948, 78 U.N.T.S 277, Article 2.

19. *Auto de la Sala de lo Penal de la Audiencia Nacional*, section 6.

20. *Nullum poena sine lege* – "no punishment without a law authorizing it," *Black's Law Dictionary*, 7th abridged edition, s.v. "nullum poena sine lege."

21. *R v. Bow Street Metropolitan Stipendiary Magistrate, ex parte Pinochet Ugarte (Pinochet III)*, [2000] A.C. 147.

22. December 10, 1984, S. TREATY Doc. No. 100–20, 1465 U.N.T.S. 85 [hereinafter Torture Convention].

23. *Pinochet III*, per Lord Millett, 268.

24. *Pinochet III*, per Lord Browne-Wilkinson, 188; per Lord Goff, 206; per Lord Hope, 224; per Lord Hutton, 249; per Lord Saville, 265 (agreeing with reasoning and conclusions of Lord Browne-Wilkinson on this issue); per Lord Millett, 268 (agreeing with reasoning and conclusions of Lord Browne-Wilkinson except with respect to certain aspects of his analysis on immunity issue); per Lord Phillips, 279 (accepting conclusions of Lord Browne-Wilkinson with respect to application of double-criminality rule).

25. *Pinochet III*, per Lord Browne-Wilkinson, 201.

26. *Pinochet III*, per Lord Phillips, 280.

27. *Pinochet III*, per Lord Hope, 240; per Lord Saville, 264.

28. *Pinochet III*, per Lord Goff, 210.

29. *Pinochet III*, per Lord Millet, 278.

30. *The Kingdom of Spain v. Augusto Pinochet Ugarte*, U.K. Bow Street Magistrate Court October 8, 1999.

31. See Clifford Krauss, "Freed by Britain, Pinochet Is Facing a Battle at Home," *New York Times*, March 3, 2000, p. A1.

32. Roht-Arriaza, *The Pinochet Effect*, 68.

33. See Jorge Mera, "Chile: Truth and Justice under the Democratic Government," in *Impunity and Human Rights in International Law and Practice*, Naomi Roht-Arriaza, ed., Oxford: Oxford University Press, 1995, 171, 179 (describing Decree Law 2191 of April 18, 1978).

34. See Clifford Krauss, "Ruling on Immunity Puts Chile Closer to Trial of Pinochet," *New York Times*, May 25, 2000, p. A4.

35. The Chilean Supreme Court upheld this ruling in August 2000. See Clifford Krauss, "Pinochet Ruled No Longer Immune from Prosecution," *New York Times*, August 9, 2000, p. A3.

36. See "Chile Drops Pinochet Trial," *BBC World Edition*, July 1, 2002.

37. See "Chile: Court Bars Pinochet Rights Trial," *Reuters*, August 28, 2003.

38. See "Chile Strips Pinochet of Immunity," *BBC World Edition*, August 26, 2004.

39. See "Court Win for Chile's Ex-Leader," *BBC World Edition*, April 7, 2006.

40. *Almonacid-Arellano et al. v. Chile*, Judgment, Series C No. 154 [2006] IACHR (September 26, 2006) para. 110.

41. See the discussion of the case before the International Court of Justice between the Democratic Republic of the Congo and Belgium in Chapter 1 of this volume.

42. Some of these problems have, in contrast, arisen in the prosecution of the alleged Argentine torturer Miguel Cavallo in Spain, both before and after the annulment of Argentina's amnesty law in 2005.

43. For example, Chuckie Taylor, the son of the former Liberian president Charles Taylor, was indicted under 18 USC §§ 2340A and 2441, the U.S. Federal Anti-Torture Statute, which makes it a crime prosecutable in the United States for a U.S. citizen to commit torture and war crimes abroad. He is currently being prosecuted in Miami, Florida, on federal torture charges that he allegedly committed in Liberia. See the U.S. Attorney General's Office press release, December 6, 2006. Available at http://www.usdoj.gov/opa/pr/2006/December/06_crm_813.html. For a survey of recent developments in universal jurisdiction laws, see Amnesty International, Supra n 3.

44. For example, Chile engaged in substantial efforts at judicial reform during the 1990s, which clearly had an effect on the attitude of the judges. See Roht-Arriaza, *The Pinochet Effect*, chapter 3.

5

A Leader Takes Flight: The Indictment of Alberto Fujimori

Ronald Gamarra

THE ANTECEDENTS

Peru's internal armed conflict between 1980 and 2000 was the most intense and prolonged period of violence in the republic's history. The most reliable fatality estimate is the Peruvian Truth and Reconciliation Commission's (TRC) figure of 69,280. Of the victims, 79 percent lived in rural areas, 75 percent spoke either Quechua or another indigenous language as their mother tongue, and 56 percent worked in agriculture.[1]

The violence was initiated by armed acts against the state by Sendero Luminoso (the Shining Path), an ideologically communist, fundamentalist, totalitarian organization, with terrorist and genocidal tendencies. The Shining Path was responsible for carrying out crimes against humanity, as well as grave breaches of international humanitarian law. Its militants were responsible for 54 percent of the deaths and disappearances reported to the TRC. The Tupac Amaru Revolutionary Movement (MRTA), a smaller contemporaneous revolutionary movement, was responsible for 1.5 percent of the fatalities registered by the TRC.[2]

Successive democratic governments adopted military responses to deal with these terrorist groups that aggravated the situation. At first, the armed forces carried out indiscriminate repression against those they suspected of belonging to or collaborating with the Shining Path. Later they became more selective in their practices, which nonetheless led to forced disappearances, extrajudicial executions, rape, and torture. According to the TRC, the security forces were responsible for 37 percent of all deaths and disappearances, but that figure does not include the deaths and disappearances attributed to local self-defense committees in rural areas that the military used as an auxiliary corps in their counter-subversive campaign.[3]

According to the TRC, the government of Fernando Belaúnde (1980–1985) ignored denunciations of human rights violations with the "expectation of ending the subversion quickly, without considering the cost in human lives." Following prison massacres in June 1986, the government of Alan García (1985–1990) showed itself incapable of confronting the autonomy of the armed forces in their fight against the terrorists. However, it was the government of Alberto Fujimori (1990–2000) that embraced and expanded the counter-subversive strategies of the armed forces.

A series of attacks by the Shining Path in Lima between 1989 and 1992 swelled the antiterrorist outrage of Peru's urban elite, which until then had been largely spared the violence that was wreaking havoc in Peru's country-side. This provoked the country's security forces and police to reformulate their counter-insurgency strategies. On April 5, 1992, Fujimori carried out a self-coup, which he claimed was necessary to address the terrorist issue. He temporarily dissolved the Congress, reorganized the judicial branch, and established his Government of National Emergency and Reconstruction to selectively eliminate the subversive groups. He also approved the actions of a secret death squad within the armed forces known as the Colina Group. Meanwhile, the National Intelligence Service (Servicio de Inteligencia Nacional, or SIN) and the police were closing in on Abimael Guzmán, the Shining Path's leader, who was arrested in Lima in September 1992. The arrests of many intermediate-level leaders followed, weakening the Shining Path's internal organization.[4] By 1997, the last major Shining Path leader had been captured and, like Guzmán, sentenced to life imprisonment.[5]

None of the governing regimes between 1980 and 2000 permitted serious, impartial inquiries aimed at discovering the truth and imposing sanctions on military or police personnel responsible for human rights violations. Those who committed them and the senior officials who were their intellectual authors were protected by a variety of complex impunity strategies. All attempts by the Congress to investigate specific cases were blocked. The Ministerio Publico (the approximate equivalent of a U.S. Office of the Attorney General) investigated a few high-ranking military officials but nearly always concluded that there was no basis for bringing criminal charges. When the judiciary tried to bring criminal cases forward, the military immediately took them over, despite the fact that, by law, the cases fell outside military jurisdiction. The military proceedings that followed often involved fraudulent legal tactics, dismissals, or the imposition of minor sentences. In 1995, with the support of the Congress, Fujimori's administration expedited amnesty laws aimed at protecting any member of the military, police, and civilian authorities who had masterminded or participated in human rights violations committed between May 1980 and June 14, 1995.

THE ACCUSED

Alberto Fujimori, a descendant of Japanese immigrants, was a political unknown until 1989, when he formed the political group Cambio 90 to contest Peru's general elections. A mathematician, agricultural engineer, and university professor, he was the rector of the National Agrarian University from 1984 until 1989. Fujimori prevailed over writer and neo-liberal candidate Mario Vargas Llosa in the second round of voting, largely because of his populist platform and his opposition to traumatic readjustment of the economy. Once in power he quickly rid himself of some of his Cambio 90 partners, adopted a liberal economic plan, called on the armed forces to adopt an aggressive response to armed terrorist organizations, and formed a personal alliance with Vladimiro Montesinos, whose shady past included removal from the army, a stint in prison, and a second career as a lawyer.[6] From his initial post as head of Peru's antidrug and antiterrorist units, Fujimori named Montesinos as his principal advisor, and he became the de facto leader of the National Intelligence Service. Yet despite winning a clear majority in the election, Fujimori was saddled with a parliament in which he could count on only a minority of the representatives to support his agenda.

Fujimori's 1992 self-coup was accepted by Peruvians as a means to ridding the country of terrorists, but it cost him legitimacy in the eyes of the international community. To repair relations with other American and European states, Fujimori called for presidential elections in 1995, under the parameters of a new constitution that was approved by popular referendum in 1993. Fujimori won these elections with 64 percent of the votes and obtained 52 percent of the congressional vote.

Furthermore, from 1996 he set his sights on reelection, notwithstanding his ineligibility to do so because of term limits established in his own 1993 constitution. This brought him into conflict with Peru's democratic institutions. To prevent them from impeding his authoritarian pretensions, Fujimori intervened to undermine the authority of the judiciary (1996) and the Ministerio Publico (1997); undermined Peru's constitutional tribunal (1997); cut back the functions of the National Council of the Judiciary (1998); and in other ways limited the means for electoral organizations to declare his new candidacy illegal (1999). These acts produced a strong negative reaction from the public and weakened the internal legitimacy of his regime.[7]

Fujimori governed at the edges of institutional restrictions, without any checks or balances to his power. As one commentator put it, Fujimori "like[d] to govern in small circles, within the clan, the ethnic group, the family, without having to explain or seek consensus. In his opinion, parliamentary life [was] parasitic, useless, a democratic façade which must be maintained because of foreign pressures. Political parties [made] him uncomfortable; [to him they were] only acronyms, blurred references, paperwork in order to obtain power. Alliances and rules [existed] only for short periods. When they became a burden, they [were] modified."[8] Although his regime was authoritarian, vertically integrated, and personality-based, he cared about its legitimacy, which he sought to earn through populist practices.[9] His success was due, among other factors, to his policy of favoritism as well as taking a firm hand to stop the terrorism and the economic hyperinflation that plagued Peru at the time. He also benefited from a fragmented and weak opposition.[10]

In addition to his notoriety for consolidating power through illegal means and for committing human rights crimes, Fujimori was also responsible for establishing one of the greatest systems of organized corruption Peru has ever known. The magnitude of the corruption was revealed in a series of videos showing various public personalities selling their jobs or their consciences to Montesinos in exchange for public money or influence. Through these leaked videos, Peru's citizens learned that Fujimori and Montesinos had used the state's money to perpetuate their power and enrich themselves by diverting funds from the armed forces to the SIN, among other things. They also learned that Fujimori and Montesinos had their own income stream from arms sales and that Montesinos had hidden part of his illicit gains in offshore banks. Fujimori had removed his fortune from Peru to Japan through dozens of trips by family members with diplomatic passports. No one knows precisely how much money was stolen from the Peruvian state during Fujimori's decade in power, although some calculate it as high as $1.5 billion.[11]

THE FLIGHT TO JAPAN

Four months after winning his third term in office, Fujimori was facing embarrassment on account of the corruption scandal, a collapsing regime, and an opposition that refused to negotiate a package of legal reforms. On November 14, 2000, he traveled to Brunei to attend the Eighth Asia-Pacific Economic Cooperation Summit. Four days later, he was scheduled to be in Panama to take part in the Tenth Ibero-American Summit. Instead, without waiting for the final paper to be presented at the Brunei meeting, he flew to Japan. On November 19, 2000, he sent a letter of resignation to the president of Peru's congress, Valentín Paniagua. Peruvian authorities immediately declared Fujimori "morally incapacitated" and removed him from office. On December 15, the Japanese government announced that Fujimori had Japanese citizenship and would not be forcibly returned to Peru. News of the flight and of his Japanese citizenship caused a wave of outrage in Peru.

THE NEW OFFICIAL POLICY CONCERNING HUMAN RIGHTS

Valentín Paniagua's democratic transition government immediately changed course on human rights policy. It reaccepted the compulsory jurisdiction of the Inter-American Court of Human Rights, which Fujimori had withdrawn, entered into agreements or "friendly solutions" with the Inter-American Commission on Human Rights and the Inter-American Court, which were investigating specific human rights violations, and set in motion domestic investigations into these cases. Paniagua's government also supported the creation of the TRC in 2001 to investigate the human rights violations that occurred between 1980 and 2000. The TRC completed its work and published its final report in 2003. It found Fujimori responsible for human rights abuses and named him in some of the forty-three cases that it sent to the Ministerio Publico with a recommendation that they be prosecuted. The government supported the report's findings, recognizing that doing so could help avoid the repetition of human rights crimes and internal armed conflict in the future.

Similarly, once the scope of Fujimori's corruption came to light, public indignation was so great that one of the transitional government's first acts was a series of measures to investigate the facts and determine who was responsible. Unsurprisingly, it soon became clear that many of those charged with corruption had also been involved in human rights violations. The link between corruption and human rights violations destroyed any opposition to investigating Fujimori and the members of the Colina Group, the most notorious armed forces unit involved in human rights crimes.

The investigations and trials of Fujimori, Montesinos, and the members of the Colina Group began with indictments for corruption in Peru's anticorruption courts even before the TRC was established. Following the publication of the TRC's report, which relied in part on information obtained from the corruption cases, the judiciary decided to continue the trials for human rights violations within this subsystem.

THE ACTS ATTRIBUTED TO ALBERTO FUJIMORI

Fujimori was investigated and indicted for extensive financial crimes, including leading a criminal organization to defraud the state; issuing emergency decrees to use funds from privatized sectors of the economy to inflate the budgets of the Ministry of Defense and the Ministry of the Interior; and entering into contracts to acquire arms and supplies for which illegal commissions were paid. He also was alleged to have diverted public funds from the armed forces and the National Police to the SIN, which was controlled by Montesinos, to benefit himself and others; paid opposition congressmen to gain parliamentary majorities to pass his own party's initiatives; maintained a secret list of civil servants to whom he passed money in exchange for obtaining judicial or electoral results that were favorable to the regime; and to have given public money to news media magnates to control what they published. To control military officers, he was alleged to have offered promotions in exchange for undated requests for retirement that could be used whenever they failed to support the administration or Montesinos's illicit organization. In addition, he was alleged to have paid Montesinos $15 million out of public funds as compensation for his years of service and to fund his escape to Panama in September 2000 to keep him out of the hands of the justice system, which wanted to try him as part of a web of government corruption. In conjunction with this, he was charged with abuse of authority for ordering an illegal search of Montesinos's wife's home and seizing and destroying videotapes that allegedly would have incriminated him. Finally, Fujimori was accused of abandoning his position as president, revealing national secrets, using foreign donations for his own benefit, and falsifying income to justify excessive expenses.

Fujimori also was indicted for human rights violations. He was accused of applying torture to a journalist to obtain information about the people who had given the journalist videos showing compromising acts of corruption within the regime. He was also charged with using the basement of the Army Intelligence Service to torture those imprisoned for terrorism; for assassinating a union leader; for the extrajudicial execution of forty-two internees in the Miguel Castro Castro maximum security penitentiary; for intercepting telephone conversations by political opponents and independent journalists; and for two massacres carried out in Lima in 1991 and 1992 by the Colina Group known as "Barrios Altos" and "La Cantuta."

THE DEFINING CASES: BARRIOS ALTOS AND LA CANTUTA

The Barrios Altos and La Cantuta cases are perhaps the best-known nationally and internationally and have come to symbolize the worst of the human rights crimes carried out during Fujimori's administration. In the Barrios Altos case, on November 3, 1991, six members of the Colina Group, masked and heavily armed, barged into a social gathering in Lima's Barrios Altos neighborhood. After forcing those present to lie on the ground, the intruders fired their submachine guns for about two minutes, killing fifteen people and seriously injuring four. In the La Cantuta case, members of the Army Intelligence Service and the Army Intelligence Directorate burst into the student residences of the Enrique Guzmán and Valle National University, more commonly known as La Cantuta. After forcing the students to lie in fetal positions on the floor, the soldiers detained nine students. They then went to the home of Professor Hugo Muñoz Sánchez and took him captive. Following their abduction, the ten victims disappeared, but the remains of their bodies, and of a macabre attempt to cover up the massacre, were uncovered in 1993 by the magazine *Sí*.

These two cases not only provoked a huge public outcry in Lima but were brought to the Inter-American Commission on Human Rights and later the Inter-American Court of Human Rights. The applicants challenged the Fujimori government's amnesty law that made it impossible for the victims of these crimes to learn the full truth or seek justice or redress in Peru's courts. The Inter-American Court found that the amnesty laws violated Peru's obligations under the American Convention on Human Rights and ordered Peru to "determine the identity of those responsible for the human rights violations referred to in this judgment, and also publish the results of this investigation and punish those responsible."[12]

After the Ministerio Publico filed charges and the judiciary began to investigate, written and oral proof linking Fujimori with these crimes mounted. Evidence showed that he had designed a scheme to centralize political and military power and to change the state's counter-subversive strategy. These changes included the passing of a new normative framework (1991–1992) regarding relations between the commanders of the armed forces and his office; the concentration of military decisions about counter-subversion within a new political-military structure that he controlled; and the redefinition of the role of the intelligence apparatus, especially the SIN, which he also controlled. The Colina Group's crimes corresponded directly to Fujimori's new political-military structure. Given the political and military complexity and the magnitude of the operations executed by the Colina Group,[13] it is unimaginable that Fujimori remained ignorant of them. A poll taken in Peru at the end of 2005 found that 69 percent of Lima's inhabitants believed the ex-president to be guilty of human rights violations and acts of corruption.[14]

Witnesses who gave evidence during the judicial investigation corroborated that Fujimori was aware of, and authorized, the military and intelligence activities of the Colina Group. Furthermore, the witnesses confirmed that the action at La Cantuta was a political decision in response to an attack by the Shining Path, which had placed a car bomb in Lima. The testimony was all the more damning because the witnesses not only formed part of the nucleus of power closest to Fujimori, including an ex-general commander of the army, but were also members of the Colina Group and the intelligence apparatus within the army responsible for executing the orders. Other witnesses included high-ranking officers who were aware of the existence of the Colina Group, and independent journalists who had direct contact with some of its members, and who carried out in-depth investigations of their actions. Documentary evidence gathered during the proceedings went to Fujimori's position of leadership and the decision-making authority in relation to the crimes perpetrated by military operatives who were members of the army's intelligence unit. It also demonstrated the existence of a criminal agreement following the events.

Among the documentary evidence was the TRC's Final Report, which concluded that "During the two governing periods of Alberto Fujimori . . . a functional relationship existed between political power and criminal behavior. Intentionally, and progressively, the government organized a state structure that controlled the state's powers, as well as other key dependents, and used formal/legal procedures in order to assure impunity; first for human rights violations, and later for corruption."[15] The report also stated that "President Alberto Fujimori, his advisor Montesinos, and high-ranking members of the SIN were criminally responsible for the assassinations, forced disappearances, and massacres perpetrated by the death squad known as Colina."[16] In addition, there were memoranda from 1991 in which Fujimori recognized and recommended the promotion of different officers and subofficers of the army, among them four members of the Colina Group, for their work in intelligence. There also was a video recorded in the SIN, in which Montesinos makes it understood that Fujimori was the one who gave the orders in the cases of Barrios Altos and La Cantuta. In addition, the amnesty laws pushed by Fujimori directly benefited members of the Colina Group.

In March 2004, the public prosecutor requested a sentence of thirty years' imprisonment, probation for the same number of years, and payment of approximately $30 million in civil reparations. In accordance with Peruvian law, the magistrates ordered Fujimori's detention, although they could not carry it out because he was in Japan.

EXTRADITION

Following Fujimori's flight from the country and his quasi-asylum in Japan, the Peruvian state twice requested his extradition. On the first occasion, in July 2003, the request was in relation to the crimes at Barrios Altos and La Cantuta; the second request, in October 2004, was for illegally giving $15 million of public money to Montesinos. The Japanese government said it needed more information about the facts, the evidence, and about Peruvian legislation before it could make a decision. When this information was provided, it invented various other excuses to win time and indefinitely postpone a response.

In November 2005, Fujimori surprisingly left his golden refuge in Japan and traveled to Chile, where he hoped to influence the outcome of Peru's 2006 presidential elections or even continue on to Peru to run in those elections. Notwithstanding the international warrant for his capture, the ex-president passed through police checks and immigration controls without being detained. He was arrested shortly thereafter at a hotel and detained at a prison service training academy. His decision to go to Chile came at a particularly tense moment in political relations between the two countries, which were then wrangling over their maritime border. His arrest, however, contributed to an improvement in those political relations.

Based on the extradition treaty between the two countries, Peru petitioned Chile's Supreme Court, through its Ministry of the Exterior, to provisionally detain and extradite Fujimori. The Chilean Supreme Court reacted quickly. A warrant of preventive arrest was granted by Instructing Minister Orlando Alvarez, and was carried out on November 7, 2005.

As Fujimori was likely well aware before leaving Japan, Chile rarely accedes to requests for extradition. It refused to do so in the cases of Argentine ex-president Carlos Menem, who was wanted to stand trial in Argentina for crimes including embezzlement, bribery, and tax evasion. Chile had similarly refused to extradite its senior secret police officials Manuel Contreras and Raúl Iturriaga to Italy and Argentina, where they were wanted for political violence committed during the Pinochet regime.

Although Peru could have included all the crimes Fujimori was charged with, it limited its extradition request to the gravest accusations and to those with the greatest quantity of proof, including Barrios Altos and La Cantuta. In January 2006, Peru requested the extradition of Fujimori for twelve cases, three of which were for human rights violations, and the others for acts of corruption or abuse of authority.

In May 2006, arguing that his release would not constitute a danger to society nor hinder the extradition proceedings, the Second Chamber of the Chilean Supreme Court gave Fujimori provisional freedom, ordering only the payment of bail and that he remain in Chile. Thus, while the final decision on extradition was pending, Fujimori enjoyed his liberty in Chile. Given past events, Peru called on Chile to take extreme measures to prevent Fujimori from once again seeking the protection of Japan.

Throughout 2006, Fujimori managed to keep the extradition proceedings moving at a snail's pace. The former president overwhelmed the investigative process with offers of proof including witnesses and numerous documents (many of which were irrelevant), as well as petitions seeking information from Peru (most of which were equally irrelevant). In strictly legal terms, these strategies bought nothing but time, but they gave him a five-month advantage to position himself politically. During that period, Fujimori's Alliance for the Future made gains in the Peruvian parliament and had other political successes. He also harmonized his political positions with the interests of Chile's governing party. His ex-lawyer, who subsequently became the president of the Peruvian Congress' Foreign Relations Commission, met with Chilean president Michelle Bachelet, although his lobbying did not stop her from supporting Fujimori's extradition to Peru.

In a historic decision, on September 21, 2007, the Second Criminal Chamber of the Supreme Court of Chile, basing its decision on the existence of "well-founded presumptions of responsibility," approved Fujimori's extradition for seven cases linked to his presumed responsibility for violations of human rights, acts of corruption, and abuse of authority: the Barrios Altos and La Cantuta massacres, using the basements of the Army Intelligence Service as a torture chamber, paying $15 million to Montesinos, bribing members of Congress, making illegal payments to the news media, tapping the telephones of political opponents, and breaking and entering Montesinos's wife's home.[17]

The unanimous judgment, which overturned a lower court's decision to refuse extradition, was a critical turning point in Latin America, and the world, with respect to holding former political leaders accountable for their presumed participation in human rights crimes and, as such, marks a milestone in the development of international law. The Supreme Court's decision, which the Bachelet administration promptly implemented, revived extradition as a mechanism of cooperation between states in judicial matters, particularly those involving human rights violations. It stands as a warning to former heads of state who seek the protection of other countries that their attempts to escape justice will be frustrated and they will be extradited and tried. The Supreme Court correctly rejected Fujimori's invocation of former head of state immunity on the grounds that human rights crimes do not constitute functions of a head of state and therefore cannot be attributed to the state to circumvent personal criminal responsibility of the president.[18] In other words, nobody, not even an ex-president, can avoid responsibility for violations of human rights.

THE ACCUSED AND THE CRIMINAL PROCESS

Beginning with the earliest judicial investigations into his alleged crimes, Fujimori decried the authority and competence of the Peruvian courts to try him, claiming that he was the object of political persecution. Initially he refused to appoint a lawyer for his defense, then changed his mind in April 2005, and appointed a lawyer to demonstrate his defenselessness, destroy the charges, and create the political conditions that would enable him to return to Peru to run in the 2006 presidential elections. Through his lawyer's astuteness, he raised a variety of due process challenges, such as the fact the court had not appointed an attorney for him at the outset of the proceedings, that his declaration of absence from the country had been omitted, and that when a court-appointed attorney was named, that lawyer did not undertake a proper defense. At the same time, Fujimori counted on his sympathizers to create a corresponding political uproar to sustain his claims of abuse and political prosecution. Although he lost these legal challenges, one strategy did work. By aggressively fighting his extradition from Chile to Peru, he managed to stall those phases of the proceedings that could not proceed without him present. It also bought time for his children and followers to build political momentum and penetrate Peru's political institutions. His daughter Keiko was elected to congress in 2006 with the most individual party votes of any candidate, and she and her brother Kenji formed a new political party, Fuerza 2011, the principal platform of which was to win their father's freedom and enable him to reenter Peruvian politics.[19]

Despite these efforts, the rule of law prevailed over legal and political manipulation. Alberto Fujimori was extradited to Peru on September 22, 2007. He was taken directly to the headquarters of the Special Operations Directorate of the National Police, where a special detention center and headquarters for the judicial process were created for his trial.

In keeping with the idea of a fair, transparent, and expeditious trial, the executive council of Peru's judiciary authorized the Special Criminal Chamber, presided over by César San Martín Castro, to dedicate itself exclusively to the seven cases against the ex-president. The tribunal aggregated the actions into three categories: human rights cases, corruption cases, and an abuse of authority case. It scheduled continuous hearings three times a week and agreed to the transmission of the proceedings via mass media, especially television.[20]

The first case heard against Fujimori – the abuse of authority case involving the raid and videotape theft at the home of Montesinos's wife – was wrapped up quickly with a conviction on December 11, 2007, and the imposition of a prison sentence of six years and a $155,000 fine. Fujimori did not deny ordering the search. Instead he argued that he did so as part of his manhunt for Montesinos and that it was necessary because of Swiss allegations of money-laundering against Montesinos. He subsequently appealed, but his conviction and sentence were affirmed.

On December 10, 2007, the trial against Alberto Fujimori for the Barrios Altos and La Cantuta cases began. The tribunal, composed of three prestigious magistrates who also are well-known law professors, made it known in a declaration read at the opening of the public hearing that this was a criminal trial and not a political one; that the court would use as its "performance criteria the objective parameters offered by the law"; that it "recognizes that the prerequisite for a decision that is legally in line with the law is judicial independence and impartiality"; that it "reaffirms its independence before any constituted or factual power whatsoever, that would be respected at all times and in all circumstances"; and that "it would take care that the probative proceedings take place with meticulousness and that they permit the full elucidation of the facts."[21]

Like other leaders whose trials are described in this volume, Fujimori tried to use the trial's opening as a public platform to proclaim his innocence, insisting that he developed a counter-subversive campaign based on respect for human rights; that the training and utilization of death squads, such as the Colina Group, were incompatible with his orders as president; that he had no knowledge of the existence of the Colina Group; and that he only found out about the events of Barrios Altos and La Cantuta after the fact by means of the press. He then played to the media by shouting, "I received Peru in 1990 in a state of collapse, with hyperinflation, international isolation, and widespread terrorism. . . . Peru is progressing today because there were reforms in the context of respect for human rights. . . . I totally reject the charges. I am innocent."[22] His further attempts to deliver a political proclamation at the opening of the trial were cut off by the president of the tribunal.

Substantial evidence has been presented against him since the start of the trial. At one point the mounting evidence appeared to get to him. In an outburst just before Christmas 2007, Fujimori, while denying that he had knowledge of military death squad murders, asked forgiveness from all the victims, saying that their suffering "hurt my soul."[23] More recently, however, prosecutors have complained that Fujimori sleeps, laughs, and plots his party's political comeback instead of paying attention to the testimony against him.[24] That testimony includes many members of the Colina Group who face their own trials for the crimes committed by their unit. Montesinos, who has already been convicted of corruption in more than twenty cases, appeared as a witness. In a previous election fraud case, Montesinos testified that he "did not make any decisions on his own, always taking orders from Fujimori."[25]

THE POLITICAL AND POPULAR RESPONSE
TO THE JUDICIAL PROCEEDINGS

The victims and family members of the Barrios Altos and La Cantuta cases have shown their satisfaction with the criminal proceedings against Fujimori and with the charges laid against him. They have taken part in the criminal proceedings, given evidence to the judges appointed to the case, intervened in a series of judicial matters, and respected the limits imposed by the extradition decision. In Lima and in Santiago, the victims and family members supported the extradition request, pointing out that Fujimori should be judged by the Peruvian justice system. More recently, they have participated in the criminal trial against him. When Fujimori sought their "forgiveness," they reacted angrily. Gisela Ortiz, sister of La Cantuta victim Luis Enrique Ortiz, exclaimed, "He's had fifteen years to ask for forgiveness but instead he rewarded the murders with an amnesty law. . . . Now he only offers apologies."[26]

Human rights organizations also welcomed the initiation of the criminal proceedings against Fujimori and the members of the Colina Group for the Barrios Altos and La Cantuta crimes, proclaiming them a necessary step to overcoming impunity and a contribution to consolidating the rule of law in Peru. These nongovernmental organizations are now monitoring the criminal trials, as are lawyers who represent the victims in the hearings. Some write articles and legal commentary about the advance of judicialization, the defense strategies of the ex-president and the members of the Colina Group, and the decisions put out by the tribunal. Although overall they have expressed satisfaction with the process, some have complained of slowness and lack of diligence.

Both the Ministerio Publico and the ad hoc attorney general have said they consider the proceedings against the ex-president to have been correctly undertaken and in strict accordance with international norms with respect to the rights of the accused. The government of President Alejandro Toledo, which spurred the justice system to investigate and try Fujimori, called for greater speed from the judiciary. President Alan Garcia's subsequent administration has opted for silence, saying that it does not want to intervene or politicize the matter, although politics may also be influencing this silence: Garcia's first vice president was very close to Fujimori's government, and because his party lacks a majority in the congress, he needs the support of Fujimori's supporters in the congress to carry out his agenda. It also cannot be forgotten that grave violations of international human rights and humanitarian law occurred during Garcia's first administration, a fact to which he probably does not want attention drawn.

CONCLUSION

Fujimori's trial would have been unthinkable at any other time in Peru's history. The country has long suffered a reputation of having a weak judiciary that was susceptible to corruption and easily controlled by strong executives. The Fujimori proceedings and the many associated human rights and corruption trials of lower-level officials, in contrast, have so far been models of impartiality and fairness, notwithstanding the efforts of the accused and his supporters to politicize and derail them.

As was the case of many other heads of state in this volume, Peru's political will to try Fujimori for human rights crimes followed the exposure of his self-enrichment, corruption, bribery, and other financial and power-consolidating crimes. However, once the political will to try him for human rights crimes took hold, there was no turning back.

Although a minority of Peruvians feel that the trials are more than a man who rid the country of subversion and calmed devastating inflation deserves, the majority appreciate that Fujimori's trial is a necessary part of the institutionalization of the rule of law and an independent judiciary that Peru has long suffered without. Indeed, for many Peruvians, Fujimori's worst crime was using his status as a democratically elected official to consolidate his personal power and wealth at the expense of the legitimacy of Peru's democratic institutions. Instead of being a national hero, he turned out to be a ruthless dictator, and a coward to boot, and he is now where he deserves to be – in jail and facing justice in a court of law.

This book will go to print before the final outcomes of the criminal proceedings against Fujimori are known. Although the conduct of the court trying him has been exemplary, it has faced competition from Fujimori's countercampaign in the media, where he still enjoys a following among the conservative press. Fujimori is certain to appeal whatever judgments are handed down against him, and while he now is detained, he also is approaching seventy years of age. Under Peruvian law, if convicted he may be eligible to apply for a presidential commutation of any sentence imposed on him on humanitarian grounds.[27] Thus, whether he will actually face prison time remains to be seen.

One victory is already apparent, however: the newly found independence and vigor of at least some sections of Peru's judiciary. After years of subordination, the courts in general – and the Special Criminal Chamber in particular – now appear to be doing their job independently, impartially, expeditiously, and with dignity. They are setting the standard for a new attitude toward the rule of law in Peru that could prevent crimes like those Fujimori conducted in the past from occurring in the future.

NOTES

1. Truth and Reconciliation Commission, Peru, *Final Report*. Lima, 2003.
2. Ibid., *Conclusions*, para. 13,34.
3. Truth and Reconciliation Commission, Peru.
4. Carlos Reyna Izaguirre, "Shining Path in the 21st Century," NACLA *Report on the Americas* 30, no. 1 (July/August 1996): 37–38. Available at http://www.hartford-hwp.com/archives/42a/016.html.
5. All the terrorism judgments against Shining Path leaders were declared null and void after the decision of the Inter-American Court on Human Rights (see n. 14 and accompanying text) by Peru's Constitutional Court. Their current convictions and sentences were handed down in 2003.
6. Luis Jochamowitz, *Vladimiro: Vida y tiempo de un corruptor*, Lima: El Comercio, 2002. See also Nick Caistor, "Who Is Vladimiro Montesinos?" *BBC News*, November 2000.
7. Martín Tanaka, "Perú: Elecciones 2000 y los conflictos poselectorales," *Nueva Sociedad*, no. 169 (September–October 2000).
8. Abelardo Sánchez León, "The Fujimorists Are Not Ashamed to Be So," *Revista Quehacer*, no. 156 (September–October 2005).
9. Tanaka, "Perú: Elecciones 2000."
10. Ibid.
11. Juan Carlos Ruíz Molleda, "Campaign: 'Corruption Is Still Stealing from You: Break the Chain of Impunity'," *Justicia Viva Mail*, no. 161 (December 2004).
12. *Barrios Altos Case*, Judgment of March 14, 2001, Inter-Am Ct. H.R. Ser. C, No. 75 (2001).
13. The Colina Group is also known as the "Colina detachment" or "Colina detach."
14. "Los peruanos opinan que el gobierno de Japón colaboró para que Fujimori viaje a Chile," *El Diario Exterior*, November 15, 2005.
15. Truth and Reconciliation Commission, Peru, *Final Report*. Lima, 2003.
16. TRC, *Final Report, Conclusions*, para. 100.
17. Fujimori Extradition ruling, Second Chamber of the Supreme Court of Chile, September 21, 2007, pp. 177–179. See http://www.poderjudicial.cl/noticias/File/fallos_fujimori.pdf.
18. Ibid.
19. Jo-Marie Burt, "Fujimori on Trial," NACLA *Report on the Americas*, May/June 2008.
20. Ronald Gamarra, "Fujimori: El juicio final," *Desco/Revista Quehacer* no. 168 (September–December, 2007).
21. Gamarra, "Fujimori: El juicio final."
22. Lucien Chavin, "Fujimori Outburst Sets Tone for Peru Human Rights Trials," *Christian Science Monitor*, December 12, 2007, p. 7.
23. "Peru's Fujimori Apologizes for Death Squad Massacres; 'It hurt my soul,' Former President Says," *Grand Rapids Press*, December 22, 2007 , p. 9.
24. "Peru: Trial Proceedings Fail to Faze Former President," *Ottawa Citizen*, May 10, 2008, p. 14.

25. Chavin, "Fujimori Outburst."

26. Burt, "Fujimori on Trial."

27. See Article 22 of the Reglamento Interno de la Comisión de Indulto y Derecho de Gracia por Razones Humanitarias y Conmutación de la Pena (Resolución Ministerio 193-2007-Jus).

6

Charm and Punishment: How the Philippines' Leading Man Became Its Most Famous Prisoner

Abby Wood

On July 1, 1998, after appearing in almost 150 movies and spending almost thirty years in public service, actor and politician Joseph "Erap" Ejercito Estrada was elected president of the Philippines.[1] Once in office, he not only continued living like a movie star but used government funds to enrich himself, his mistresses, and his cronies. Just three years after his landslide victory, Estrada was ousted in a popular uprising. In a country besieged by generations of political corruption, Estrada's crimes and lifestyle proved the perfect lightning rod for the country's first attempt to hold a head of state accountable for crimes committed while in office.

During Estrada's trial, many worried that the Philippine antigraft court, the Sandiganbayan, would be unable to muster sufficient institutional independence to convict Estrada. In addition, they suspected that Estrada's lenient treatment and the frequent trial delays were a response to President Gloria Macapagal Arroyo's political fragility. Yet to the amazement of many, Estrada's trial demonstrated that the Philippine judiciary could deliver justice.

But old habits die hard. After Estrada's conviction, President Arroyo, then looking for a way to divert attention from one of her own corruption scandals, delivered a pardon so swift that the result now feels like a return to corrupt politics as usual.

Author's Note: This chapter is the result of thirty-three interviews conducted in Manila with people having close knowledge of the trial. My interviewees included members of the prosecution and defense teams, former judges, a former Supreme Court justice, members of prominent Manila law firms, current and past officials from two government ministries, current and past legislators, a high-ranking Catholic official, journalists involved in breaking the story of Estrada's ill-gotten wealth, members of the international development community who had observed the trial, professors, university administrators, and members of the nongovernmental organization community. Because of the politically sensitive nature of the interviews, many interviewees requested anonymity. Where interviewees allowed me to use their names, I have done so. I am grateful to Alexsia Chan and Karoun Demirjian for helpful comments.

This chapter details the political, historical, and institutional context in which Estrada was prosecuted, his crimes and the acts that led to his impeachment and subsequent trial, and the complex interrelationship between the different branches of government in the Philippines still consolidating democracy. Despite political intrusions from both the president and the opposition that eventually led to his pardon, the Estrada trial is cause for optimism that the Philippines is building ever-stronger institutions of governance able to withstand the worst political pressures and fulfill their responsibilities to their citizenry.

POLITICAL AND HISTORICAL CONTEXT

Estrada's tale must be understood against the backdrop of a socioeconomic structure produced by 375 years of Spanish and U.S. colonial rule. It also must be seen in relation to recent decades of impunity for political leaders, especially Ferdinand Marcos, who controlled – and pillaged – the Philippines from 1965 to 1986, an era from which Philippine government institutions are still recovering.

One of the remnants of colonialism is an entrenched class of socially and economically prominent families who were privileged by the colonial powers. To this day, these families cycle in and out of political power, with the occasional outsider like Estrada, a Marcos crony and mayor of San Juan during the Marcos era, gaining office. The Marcos regime disrupted the political and economic hierarchy of these families, because Marcos "used his martial-law powers to punish enemies among the old oligarchy."[2] A mix of Marcos's cronies and the traditional postcolonial oligarchic families comprise the current oligarchy.[3]

Corruption in government goes back at least as far back as the Spanish colonial period[4] and reached new heights during Marcos's "crony capitalism."[5] Assassinated Marcos opponent Ninoy Aquino once said that "[n]o recent president has actually *done* anything – other than corruption. Every president tried to prove that they were not corrupt and they fell. Marcos no longer tries to prove that."[6] Every president since Marcos has had at least one corruption scandal during her or his tenure.[7] Since independence, the ubiquitous "pork barrel" has received almost constant criticism, and election fraud is decried as standard procedure.

The Marcos regime's impunity casts a shadow over much of current-day Philippine politics. It is estimated that during his two decades in power, Marcos stole approximately $10 billion from government coffers. When his successor, Corazon Aquino, the widow of Ninoy Aquino, came to power, she established the Presidential Commission on Good Government (PCGG), which investigated the stolen funds but recovered only a small portion. Now, twenty years after Marcos's ouster, the occasional crony or junior member of his administration has been found guilty in lower courts but has either successfully appealed or delayed being sentenced. As a result, "not one of the Marcos family or the Marcos cronies have spent a day in jail. This is because they have employed an army of the country's most brilliant lawyers, first, to hide the ill-gotten wealth and, later, to flood the courts with motions that delay trial."[8] To complicate matters, the PCGG is chronically understaffed, and the court system is notoriously slow.

In addition to impunity for financial crimes, Marcos and his cronies escaped domestic prosecution for human rights abuses. His administration violated the human rights of thousands of Philippine citizens who were imprisoned, tortured, killed, and disappeared. Victims of human rights abuses living in the United States brought civil cases under the Alien Tort Claims Act (ATCA) in Hawaii and California shortly after Marcos arrived in the United States,[9] and won. The money awarded to the victims is in a Swiss bank account, collecting interest. The estimated amount is $680 million. None of the human rights victims has seen any of the money, and the PCGG has made little progress on either the corruption cases or human rights cases in the intervening years.[10]

Ferdinand Marcos's wife, Imelda, was elected to congress in 1995 and ran for president against Estrada and nine others in 1998, backing out before the election to support Estrada. Two of her children, Imee and Ferdinand Jr., have held elected government positions, Imee as a congressional representative, and Ferdinand Jr. as governor of Ilicos Sur and as a congressional representative. Imelda has had ten graft cases pending against her for more than a decade. In 1999, she was convicted by a panel of the Supreme Court in one of the cases, but the conviction did not stick. Her then-lawyer, Marcos's Solicitor General and Minister of Justice Estelito Mendoza, succeeded in having the case re-heard *en banc*, and the decision was reversed.

The lack of closure on the Marcos cases complicates efforts to stop current-day political corruption. As the prosecution in the Estrada trial put it, the lesson learned from Marcos's impunity is that "if you are going to steal, steal big," so that you can afford the top lawyers to delay the trial endlessly. With that kind of precedent and an anticorruption court of questionable independence, the fight against corruption in the Philippines has been, and promises to continue to be, a long one.

The same weak institutions that permit the continued impunity of the Marcos regime also contribute to the fragility of Philippine democracy. In the past two decades, Filipinos have ousted two presidents extra-constitutionally, through so-called People Power movements. Weak institutionalization is not unexpected in a young democracy ruled by political clientelism. Lacking the ability to make credible promises to most voters, politicians underprovide public goods, overspend on transfers to narrow groups, and engage in significant rent seeking.[11] Yet as this chapter illustrates, weak institutionalization throughout the political system failed to prevent Estrada's corruption trial.

THE INSTITUTIONAL FRAMEWORK

The Philippine judiciary consists of a single national system, with most courts having general jurisdiction over a municipality or metropolitan area. Cases are appealed to intermediate appellate courts, and then to the Supreme Court, which has discretionary review on appeal and original jurisdiction in a narrowly defined class of cases. The judicial system also contains specialized courts.[12] The Sandiganbayan, the specialized antigraft court in which Estrada's case was heard, is ranked on par with an appellate court, and it decides questions of both fact and law. A "special division" of the Sandiganbayan was created to hear Estrada's case to avoid frequent turnover in justices due to retirements and other disruptions. Although Estrada initially requested that the special division be created, he later opposed it on equal protection grounds.[13]

The Sandiganbayan was established by the 1973 constitution ushered in by the Marcos regime[14] but was retained by President Aquino after Marcos fell and martial law ended.[15] Today serving as a justice at the Sandiganbayan is often a stepping stone to a seat on the Supreme Court. Indeed, Justice Teresita de Castro, the lead justice of the special division of the Sandiganbayan assembled to conduct Estrada's trial, was appointed to the Supreme Court mere weeks after handing down Estrada's guilty verdict.[16]

It is unclear whether Filipinos trust the judiciary. Answers to a survey of lawyers and judges indicated corruption remains a major problem among lawyers and judges.[17] Attorney Rene Saguisag, Estrada's lead counsel, explained that "Marcos destroyed the institutions, and we have not recovered . . . [Lawyers] tried to know the law in our time; today they try to know the judge."[18]

The Philippines has had only fourteen presidents, most of who have struggled to maintain power. Incumbent President Arroyo, Estrada's successor, faced at least two coup attempts and has spent much of her presidency mired in corruption scandals. The most important corruption scandals concern allegations of election tampering in the 2004 elections and receiving kickbacks in a telecommunications deal.

The ups and downs of Estrada's trial were seen by many Filipinos as a reflection of Arroyo's political troubles. Throughout the trial, the more Arroyo's position was threatened, the more likely the Sandiganbayan was to grant Estrada's motions, leading to accusations that Arroyo was interfering with the independence of the judiciary. This seemed especially true during the summer of 2005 when Arroyo was threatened with impeachment over allegations that she had interfered with election returns. The Sandiganbayan permitted Estrada to attend a televised prayer rally (where most of the attendees were poor – Estrada's most loyal followers). Arroyo was scheduled to appear at the rally as well, and television commentators expressed hope that they would appear together as a sign of reconciliation. (They did not. Estrada arrived hours after Arroyo departed.) While at the rally, Estrada made a speech and sang a song, in direct violation of the order permitting him to attend, which forbade him from addressing the crowd. He suffered no sanctions for violating the order.

The Philippines has a bicameral legislature and a formal separation of powers system, based on the United States' system of government. The legislative roster contains members of almost all of the prominent families, with spouses, children, and siblings regularly passing seats from one to another. For example, in the 2007 elections, Ferdinand Marcos's daughter Imee retired, and her brother Ferdinand Jr. won the seat. Before Estrada's impeachment, the Philippine legislature had never conducted an impeachment trial.

From a constitutional perspective, the Philippines has the strongest ombudsman's office in the world. The Philippine ombudsman is a fourth branch of government and has independent powers of investigation and prosecution of members of the other branches of government for graft. Weak checks on the appointment process, however, can result in appointees being political allies of the president. The capacity of the ombudsman shifts from one appointment to the next, and the two ombudsmen who were key to Estrada's trial, Aniano Desierto and Simeon Marcelo, had drastically different track records. Desierto, a notoriously bad ombudsman who was appointed by President Fidel Ramos, was the target of three impeachment complaints – one in 1996 and two in 2001. Marcelo, in contrast, who was appointed by Arroyo after she took office, and was generally thought to have done an excellent job, increased conviction rates from around 6 percent under Desierto to above 40 percent.

The main weakness of the Philippine ombudsman's office is its lack of funding from Congress, the members of which have little interest in an effective ombudsman. Because of the difficulties of securing congressional funding, Marcelo sought – and received – funding from the international community and bilateral donors.

Philippine civil society is highly engaged. In the battle against corruption, and the Estrada corruption scandal in particular, the Makati Business Club (MBC), the Catholic and Evangelical churches, and the media were major players. Makati is the financial and business district of Manila, and MBC members include domestic corporate conglomerates and multinational corporations. The MBC, which lobbies on behalf of these business interests, believes that reducing corruption in government will help promote business, and to that end it formed a group called Transparent and Accountable Government (TAG). The MBC and TAG rarely lead the anticorruption charge, but once enough evidence or political momentum has mounted, they jump in.

Civil society organized to monitor Estrada's trial, but by the time the prosecution rested its case, civil society interest had dwindled. The main organization, called PlunderWatch, stopped watching because the political left wanted to forge a tactical alliance with the poor, who form the core of Estrada's supporters, to oppose Arroyo's 2004 election.[19]

Investigative journalism in the Philippines is highly developed and powerful. The Philippine Center for Investigative Journalism (PCIJ) played a large role in gathering the evidence that led to Estrada's impeachment. The PCIJ receives funding from international donors, like the Asia Foundation, the Ford Foundation, the World Bank, and various UN agencies.[20]

Media coverage of Estrada's impeachment and the early phases of his criminal trial was incessant. As the months passed, however, media interest waned. When Arroyo's political troubles spiked in 2005, Estrada again made news, but his trial was of secondary importance to speculation about political reconciliation.

When Estrada took the stand on his own behalf in March 2006, media interest resurfaced, but even the best-known investigative journalist in the country, Sheila Coronel, seemed sympathetic to the defense's argument that the government had lost the moral high ground from which to pursue Estrada. She wrote, "In this climate of moral ambiguity, the charges against Estrada seem to have lost their zing, with the public made weary, rather than angry, by the accusations and the realization that the more things change, the more they remain the same."[21]

The Philippine Roman Catholic Church, which claims 83 percent of the population as members, can make or break presidents. Cardinal Jaime Sin, who died in July 2005, is commonly thought of as the mobilizing force behind the People Power movements that ousted Marcos and Estrada. Because the Catholic Church has such immense political power, Philippine presidents are aware of the ramifications of challenging its authority, and government policies are often influenced by Catholic philosophy. Arroyo, a practicing Catholic, abolished the death penalty in 2006.[22] This pleased the Catholic Bishops Conference, but it also had the side-benefit of reducing Estrada's possible sentence from death to life in prison.

Seeing Estrada through the lens of the Catholic Church, it is astounding that he was ever elected president. For decades, Estrada had been notorious for his partying lifestyle and infidelity to his wife – he has eleven children by six women. He spun the existence of his several families by explaining that he is a good father to all of the children by all of the women. His previous career as a movie star probably granted him leeway to live like one: "The president does not deny his sins; he merely cracks jokes about them . . . That is why the Catholic Church and the other vanguards of public morals do not know how to react. How do you deal with a sinner who makes you laugh? Who confesses to his sins with devastating nonchalance?"[23] The Church supported Estrada for a while – and indeed, some bishops still do – but it was easy for the Church to distance itself from him once his drinking and late-night gambling came to be "too much." Archbishop Oscar V. Cruz once said that Estrada "tried to enrich himself too fast. He needed money to finance the women, children, drinking sprees, vices. It was offensive."[24]

Iglesia ni Cristo, a fundamentalist Christian group to which an estimated three million Filipinos belong, and El Shaddai, an evangelical Catholic group, are popular among the poor, the vast majority of whom supported Estrada in the choice between him and Arroyo. Iglesia ni Cristo supporters made up an estimated 75 percent of the crowd that violently protested Estrada's arrest, and they are an increasingly important political force in the Philippines.[25]

It was in the context of weak governmental institutions, the ongoing impunity of the Marcos regime, the pervasive church presence, and the increasingly strong media in the Philippines that Joseph Estrada entered politics.

THE ESTRADA STORY

Estrada, who came from a middle-class (nonoligarchy) family, initially achieved fame as an actor. He appeared in 148 movies,[26] often playing a tough "Robin Hood" character and fighting for the underdog. His movie persona followed him into his political career, helping him to convince the country's impoverished majority that he was one of them.

Estrada's political career spanned more than thirty years. In the early years of his tenure as mayor of San Juan, Estrada was considered an effective public official.[27] Many of the projects that he implemented during the martial law era were attributable to Marcos's political and financial support, for which Estrada was publicly grateful.[28] When Marcos was pushed from power in 1986, Aquino dismissed Estrada as mayor. Estrada then won a seat in the senate, where he was best known for his desire to close the U.S. military bases in the Philippines, even making a movie called *In the Claws of the Eagle* to advocate their removal. He also voted for the Plunder Law under which he was eventually convicted.[29] Later, as vice president to Fidel Ramos, Estrada bided his time, although the sharp contrast between his and the ex-general Ramos's working styles were widely noted.[30]

Estrada's pro-poor platform in his presidential campaign fit his movie persona. He successfully presented himself as a "simple man with a simple message . . . Erap for the poor."[31] Supporters from the private sector and academia believed he would head a "reform-oriented government."[32] His vast popularity assured him victory long before the election took place. He won handily, garnering almost 40 percent of the vote in a field of eleven candidates.

Estrada appointed two cabinets. The official one was strong and capable,[33] but its independence was threatened by a duplicative body known as the "midnight cabinet" made up of Estrada's closest cronies who flaunted their positions and interfered in policies and programs.[34] The midnight cabinet was notorious for its late-night drinking and mahjong playing. A former member reported, "We discussed who should get appointed and who should get promoted. We talked about contracts. But most of the time, we talked about girls . . . The president always want[ed] to win [at mahjong]. We never stopped playing until he won . . . Once, when we were playing at his mother's house, he won 45 million."[35] In addition to making the president too tired (or possibly too hungover) for the next day's appointments and meetings, the midnight cabinet exercised influence over the president in a way that blurred the line between the official cabinet and those to whom Estrada owed political debts. "At the nocturnal gatherings . . . participants routinely advised Estrada on official matters, not so subtly promoting their own business interests, sometimes leading the president to awaken real cabinet members with his cellular phone to amend government policy."[36]

As one former cabinet member who requested anonymity put it, "Any talk of governance left him stiff. Basically, he wanted everyone to acknowledge him as president. He attended cabinet meetings for ten to fifteen minutes and would read a prepared statement. . . . Then he would wander off, saying 'I need to smoke' and would not return." After a while, the cabinet started holding meetings without him, "so that he wouldn't feel obliged to attend."

Estrada's accumulated wealth and his lack of interest in governance contributed to Philippine society's lack of willingness to overlook his sins. Within months of his taking office, media reports of corruption in the presidential palace, Malacañang, began to surface. By late 1998, the PCIJ began a series of investigations into the number of political debts that the president seemed to be repaying with choice appointments, and "fancy mansions being built for presidential mistresses and of Estrada taking cuts from various business deals."[37]

In addition to his corruption and poor governance, Estrada presided over an "all-out war" against Muslim insurgents in the southernmost major island in the Philippines, Mindanao. Mindanao and the surrounding southern islands have been home to militant Muslim separatist groups, most famously Abu Sayyaf and the Moro Islamic Liberation Front (MILF), for decades. Indeed, the underlying conflict is one of the oldest in the world.[38] A cease-fire was put in place in 1997, but in response to several bombings attributed to (but denied by) the MILF, the Armed Forces of the Philippines attacked MILF camps, including Camp Omar and Camp Abubakar.[39] Less than three months into the conflict, "independent observers estimated that 200 combatants had died and more than 100,000 civilians had been displaced by the Mindanao fighting."[40] Government troops celebrated after the fall of Camp Abubakar by eating roasted pig and drinking beer next to a mosque.[41]

The cynical critique of the Estrada regime's anti-insurgent campaign was that it was a "wag the dog" strategy to divert the media from the ever-mounting list of corruption accusations against Estrada. Indeed, the president's approval rating, which had fallen as a result of the corruption allegations, rose during the war. Shortly after the war ended in October 2000, however, Governor Luis "Chavit" Singson, a long-time friend and member of Estrada's midnight cabinet, turned the table on him. He held a press conference in which he accused Estrada of receiving millions of pesos in "protection money" from jueteng, an illegal gambling game.[42] The next day, a member of the opposition requested a Senate investigation into the allegations.[43]

IMPEACHMENT

A 150-page impeachment complaint was filed on October 18, 2000. It accuses Estrada of bribery,[44] graft and corrupt practices,[45] betraying the public trust,[46] and culpably violating the constitution. Making an airtight case was less important than the timing of the allegations, according to a representative of the Public Interest Law Center (PILC), which represented civil society in the compliant. For the PILC, filing the impeachment complaint was not about the constitutional impeachment process, because many behind the complaint lacked faith in that process. Instead, they saw it as a low-risk means to expose

Estrada and a possible means to replace him with his vice president, Gloria Arroyo, whom they saw as a more professional, better prepared, less corrupt alternative to Estrada.

The impeachment trial began on November 20, 2000. Estrada's coalition held the majority in the Senate. The case against him was prosecuted by members of the House of Representatives and a team of "private prosecutors," lawyers from private law firms whose firms – which had political connections – volunteered their time. Two of the country's most prominent legal figures, Attorney Estelito Mendoza, Marcos's solicitor general, and former supreme court chief justice Andres Narvasa, defended Estrada. Chief Justice Hilario Davide, Jr., an Estrada appointee with a reputation for being independent-minded and capable presided. Because this was the first impeachment trial in Philippine history, the senator-judges hotly debated most procedural questions.

The country paid rapt attention to the impeachment, and as each piece of evidence against Estrada came to light, public clamor for his removal from office increased. Crippled by the impeachment proceedings, on January 6, 2001, Estrada ceded sweeping presidential powers to his executive secretary.

The turning point in the impeachment trial came on January 16, 2001, when the senator-judges voted not to open an incriminating piece of evidence, the contents of which would have linked Estrada to an account in the name of "Jose Velarde" containing 500 million Philippine pesos. After the last vote was cast, members of the prosecution walked out. The next day, the Senate adjourned until the House of Representatives acted on the prosecutors' walkout.[47]

Between the time of the walkout and the decision to adjourn indefinitely, the streets were full of activity. Notified by mobile phone text messages to "go to EDSA" (the place where the People Power movement that ousted the Marcos regime rallied) and "wear black for the death of democracy," people gathered throughout the night at the EDSA shrine. Participants at what was called "EDSA II" were mostly middle-class residents of metro Manila. By the time the military withdrew its support for Estrada's government on January 19, 2001, the crowd's numbers were estimated at around 700,000.[48] On Saturday, January 20, just minutes after Estrada left the palace, Gloria Macapagal Arroyo was sworn in as president. Estrada challenged the swearing-in before the Supreme Court, claiming that he had not resigned. The court upheld the swearing-in.[49]

ARREST

Estrada and his son, San Juan Mayor Jinggoy Estrada, were arrested on April 25, 2001, on a warrant issued by the Sandiganbayan. Both were charged with plunder, which was a nonbailable offense that was, at the time, punishable by death. The officers who tried to serve the warrant were confronted by an unruly crowd of Estrada supporters. The Estradas eventually were taken to be photographed and fingerprinted and were placed in jail for four days. Images of the mug shots and jail cell were broadcast both domestically and internationally, to the outrage of Estrada's supporters, who thought he should not have been treated like a "common criminal."[50]

A call went out for "EDSA III," and this time thousands of Estrada's supporters gathered at the EDSA shrine. They were almost all urban poor, many of them were paid or offered free meals in order to attend, and a large percentage were members of Iglesia ni Cristo. Encouraged by Estrada's political allies, their numbers swelled to an estimated 270,000 by the second day. On May 1, an estimated 40,000 to 50,000 Estrada supporters started down the road to Malacañang. It took twelve hours for the police and military to beat them back from the gates. Four people died, 113 people were injured, and property damage was valued at 1 million Philippine pesos.

TRIAL

In April 2001, eight cases were filed against Estrada by Ombudsman Aniano Desierto, but his deputy almost lost the case before it started.[51] Alarmed, the private prosecutors wrote to Arroyo, pointing out Desierto's and his lawyers' bungling.[52] Presumably under pressure from Arroyo, Desierto appointed Special Prosecutor Dennis Villa-Ignacio, who remained on the case until it ended. Estrada's defense was conducted by an all-star team of lawyers and consultants. Eight major law firms, former cabinet officials, and former Supreme Court justices took part. The main defense attorneys, Jose Flaminiano and Rene Saguisag, strategized brilliantly. Flaminiano's legal creativity before the court and Saguisag's charisma before the media worked in Estrada's favor. The defense team was instrumental in helping Estrada maintain political power throughout the trial by keeping him in the public eye despite waning media attention that resulted from their delay tactics. Had Estrada not remained politically strong, his trial might have ended much sooner, and he might not have received a pardon.

Because of logistical difficulties, the case was heard one day a week, which nonetheless satisfied the country's speedy trial rules. By Philippine standards, where the average case before the Sandiganbayan lasts 6.6 years, and many graft cases against political elites have been in the system for more than twenty years,[53] the six-and-a-half-year trial was speedy for a case of this magnitude. Estrada received lenient treatment by the Sandiganbayan throughout the trial. Although the prosecution estimated that the trial could have gone much faster had defense delay tactics not been tolerated, the justices of the special division seemed to consider each concession they made to Estrada one less issue he could raise on appeal. Although he was treated far better than the average Philippine prisoner, the defense constantly protested the conditions of Estrada's confinement and filed motions seeking his release. As Attorney Saguisag explained, "It really will bring down the tension if he is treated better, because there is a hidden social cost in being perceived as oppressing someone, who, according to reports, rates much higher than Gloria [Arroyo]."[54] The court allowed the former president to seek medical treatment in Hong Kong; attend an El Shaddai prayer rally; attend his mother's 100th birthday celebration and his brother's wake; and spend both Christmas and New Year's with his mother. A major concession on the part of the Sandiganbayan was to move Estrada to his luxurious "rest house" in July 2004, after imprisoning him briefly in jail and then in a hospital. During his time under house arrest, he stayed busy constructing buildings on his compound, including an "Erap Museum" complete with a movie theater, and his tomb.[55]

The main thrust of the defense's *political* argument was that Estrada was wrongfully removed from office. The main thrust of its *legal* argument concerned due process violations and allegations of selective prosecution, as well as his immunity from prosecution as a head of state. In an attempt to wait for a political solution, the defense dragged out its case, presenting dozens of largely irrelevant, but sometimes sympathetic, character witnesses. The hoped-for political solution did not occur during the 2004 election. In 2005, after election-tampering allegations surfaced against Arroyo, the defense saw another opening for "reconciliation" and their political solution.

Among the "nonelite" Filipinos with whom I discussed the trial in 2005, opinion seemed split as to whether Estrada would be convicted or acquitted, although most thought he was guilty. Nonetheless, most people believed that Arroyo controlled the process. They told me about how "she" would let him go or how "she" would keep him in jail. Even when I asked what they thought the court would do, suggesting a separation between the judiciary and the executive, the response remained the same: Arroyo was in charge. The corollary to this was that if Estrada's close friend Fernando Poe, Jr., had won the 2004 presidential election, Estrada would now be free.

With impeachment complaints pending against her in 2005, headlines said that Arroyo was open to "reconciliation," even as articles quoted her as denying involvement in the Sandiganbayan's decisions. Her press secretary affirmed that "the Sandiganbayan, as we all know, is an independent judicial body."[56] Arroyo's administration reminded reporters of the separation of powers: "The law is clear that [Estrada's] crime is against the people of the Philippines, and the President cannot enter into a compromise with him in a criminal case."[57]

FROM CONVICTION TO PARDON IN FORTY-THREE DAYS

Estrada's defense rested its case in June 2007, and the Sandiganbayan handed down its decision three months later on September 12. It found Estrada guilty of plunder and acquitted him of perjury.[58] He was sentenced to *reclusion perpetua*, or life imprisonment not to exceed forty years, and forfeiture of his illegally obtained assets.

Instead of being taken to prison upon his conviction, Estrada was allowed to return to his rest house to await further orders.[59] Commentators seemed impressed that the Sandiganbayan could deliver a conviction,[60] but, after at least two years of talk of political reconciliation, Filipinos probably suspected a pardon could not be far off. The business community responded to the conviction by "pushing Philippine stock prices to a dramatic high and strengthening the Philippine peso against the United States dollar."[61]

Estrada's lawyers filed an appeal soon after the conviction and entered into negotiations with Malacañang. Estrada never admitted to his crimes and was vocal about not being willing to accept a pardon that was not on his terms. Nonetheless, the desired pardon came sooner than the public anticipated. On October 25, just six weeks after his conviction and two days after his attorneys withdrew his appeal, Arroyo granted Estrada executive clemency, restoring his civil and political rights in exchange for his agreement not to run for public office. She noted that he had already spent almost six and a half years under arrest and that she has a policy of releasing *reclusion perpetua* prisoners once they turn seventy years old, Estrada's age at the time.[62]

Public response to the pardon was mixed. There were no protests, although when Estrada returned to San Juan, where his son Jinggoy still governed, he was welcomed by a crowd of supporters. Some commentators expressed hope for national political unification.[63] Others expressed suspicion that a pardon would distract the country from corruption in Malacañang. At the time of the pardon, Arroyo was under suspicion of kickbacks in a telecommunications deal[64] and some in the Catholic Church had been calling for her to step down.[65] A recurring theme in the news media was that the pardon came too soon and undermined Arroyo's legitimacy.[66] At least one commentator noted that Arroyo might have more to gain than Estrada by showing generous clemency to her predecessor. "She may indeed lose whatever remaining support she still enjoys among the . . . middle classes, but that is a small price to pay for throwing the opposition [into] disarray and defanging its most militant segment – the mass followers of Estrada."[67]

Estrada is now enjoying his freedom. The news media covers his social endeavors, which have included visiting his ailing 102-year-old mother and attending various family weddings, debuts, and parties. He has said that he will continue to oppose Arroyo, but that he also wants to live as a "plain citizen."[68] The MBC has pointed out that because Estrada's civil and political rights were restored by executive clemency, the only thing keeping him from running for office is his promise not to do so, and if he breaks that promise, there is no formal penalty.[69]

CONCLUSION

The Estrada case provides insight into head of state prosecutions that are almost entirely domestic matters and highlights the importance of institutional capacity to try a head of state in domestic courts. Whereas some trials of heads of state have direct international involvement in the form of international tribunals, bilateral or international pressure to prosecute, or extraditions, the international community was largely absent in Estrada's trial. The only international influence came from international anticorruption programs, whose funds made it easier for investigative journalists to uncover Estrada's graft and made prosecution easier for the underfunded ombudsman's office.

Estrada, like some of the other heads of state examined in this volume, commanded substantial political support during his trial, but his popularity did not prevent the proceedings from taking place. The evidence against him was aired publicly during the congressional impeachment trial that preceded his ouster. This, in turn, fueled pressure to prosecute him once he left office. But his political support also worked for him. It ensured his lenient treatment and fueled regular talk of political reconciliation throughout the six-and-a-half year proceedings, and ultimately it contributed to his pardon.

Although it would be easy to compare Estrada to Marcos or to view Estrada's prosecution as a proxy for the prosecution of the former dictator, the trial made clear that Estrada's conviction and Marcos's escape from justice were unconnected. Estrada was tried because he had committed graft and other crimes during his presidency. The Philippines tried Estrada and not Marcos, who plundered hundreds of times more from the country, because government institutions in 2001 were much stronger than they were 1987. The prosecution was able to meet a powerful defense team head-on in a court of law, and the justices of the Sandiganbayan were able to hold the line against political pressures. Although they were lenient enough to pacify everyone except the prosecution, in the end, the justices handed down a decision that was supported by the evidence and accepted by the public. This would have been impossible in the 1980s after Marcos, who was much more powerful than Estrada, had left government institutions in shambles.

In some trials of senior government officials corruption charges are seen as a second-best alternative to prosecution for human rights violations; this was not the case in the Estrada trial. Although his administration engaged in a violent assault against an insurgent force that left two hundred dead and thousands displaced, it was popularly deemed as a necessary action to halt terrorism. Even the victims have not raised an outcry about violations of their human rights by Estrada's regime – and no one compares Estrada's human rights record to that of Ferdinand Marcos. Moreover, Estrada's financial crimes had no connection to the counter-insurgency war or alleged human rights abuses. Rather, they were committed to line the pockets of his family, mistresses, and cronies. Estrada is seen as a good-natured, although bumbling, social figure who enjoyed parties and gambling more than governing, not as a perpetrator of human rights abuses.

Although the Philippine judiciary is still not yet free from executive inter- ference, it is far more independent than it was in the post-Marcos era. The Sandiganbayan's ability to convict a still-powerful political actor, and the fact that no civil unrest followed, suggests that the judiciary is far more institution- alized than the public had given it credit for being. Estrada's pardon and the almost immediate appointment of Justice de Castro to the Supreme Court provided fodder for the opposition to accuse the executive of interference with the judiciary, but that has since died down. Furthermore, no one disputes that since the Marcos era, the institutionalization and effectiveness of the judiciary and other government bodies has improved dramatically. What remains to be seen is whether that positive momentum will continue, and whether President Arroyo's alleged efforts to interfere in judicial independence will undermine her legitimacy in the long run.

NOTES

1. Erap, Estrada's nickname, is the reverse spelling of the word *pare*, which means "friend" in Filipino.
2. Alfred McCoy, "An Anarchy of Families," in *An Anarchy of Families, State and Family in the Philippines,* Alfred W. McCoy, ed., Madison: University of Wisconsin Press, 1994, 17.
3. Sheila Coronel et al., *The Rulemakers: How the Wealthy and Well-Born Dominate Congress,* Manila: Philippine Center for Investigative Journalism, 2004.

4. Patricio N. Abinales and Donna J. Amoroso, *State and Society in the Philippines*, New York: Rowman and Littlefield, 2005, 71.
5. David C. Kang, *Crony Capitalism*, Cambridge: Cambridge University Press, 2002.
6. James Hamilton-Paterson, *America's Boy: The Marcoses and the Philippines*, London: Granta Books, 1998, 251–252, quoting Ninoy Aquino as cited in *Horizons*, De La Salle College's student magazine, 1969.
7. Aquino is accused more of her refusal to go after corrupt relatives than her own abuse of power (Robert L. Youngblood, "Review: Corazon Aquino and the Brush-fire Revolution," *Journal of Asian Studies* 56, no. 2 [1997] 565–566. Fidel V. Ramos was accused of patronage bargaining (Abinales and Amoroso, p. 3); Estrada's scandal is the subject of this chapter; and current President Gloria Macapagal Arroyo has been accused of interfering with election returns (Juliet Labog-Javellana, "Interim Report: Senate Finds Massive Cheating in '04 Election," *Philippine Inquirer*, June 15, 2006, p. A1).
8. Ruben Carranza, "The Meaning of Plunder Past and Present," paper presented at University of the Philippines Third World Studies Center, May 10, 2001, p. 3.
9. See, for example, *Trajano v. Marcos*, No. 86-0207 (D. Haw. July 18, 1986); *Hilao v. Marcos*, No. 86-0390 (D.Haw. 1989); *Sison v. Marcos*, No. 86-0225 (S.D. Cal. filed June 30, 1986), and *Marcos v. Hilao et al.*, 25 F.3d 1467 (1994); cert. denied, 513 U.S. 1136 (1995). The Alien Tort Claims Act of 1789 grants jurisdiction to U.S. Federal Courts over "any civil action by an alien for a tort only, committed in violation of the law of nations or a treaty of the United States," 28 USC §1350.
10. The PCGG between 1986 and 2000 recovered approximately 88 billion Philippine pesos, which in 2006 U.S. dollars was almost $1.8 billion, almost all of which through litigation in U.S. courts. Carranza, "The Meaning of Plunder Past and Present," p. 3.
11. Philip Keefer, "*Democratization and Clientelism: Why Are Young Democracies Badly Governed?* World Bank Policy Research Working Paper 3594 (May 2005): 2.
12. Chan Robles Virtual Law Library, "Judicial Hierarchy." Available at http://www.chanrobles.com/philippinejudicialsystem.htm.
13. *Resolution, Re: Request of Accused through Counsel for Creation of a Special Division to Try the Plunder* Case (SB Crim. Case No. 26558 and Related Cases), Adm. Matter No. 02-1-07-SC. January 21, 2002. Available at http://www.supremecourt.gov.ph/jurisprudence/2002/jan2002/am_02_1_07_sc.htm.
14. Art. XIII, §5, 1973 Constitution.
15. Art XI, §4, 1987 Constitution.
16. Annie Rose A. Laborte, "Sandiganbayan Presiding Justice De Castro Is New SC Justice," *Court News Flash*, December 3, 2007. Available at http://www.supremecourt.gov.ph/news/courtnews%20flash/index.php.
17. Linda Luz Guerrero, Mahar Mangahas, and Marlon Manuel, "New SWS Study of the Judiciary and the Legal Profession Sees Some Improvements, but Also Recurring Problems," *Social Weather Station* (January 25, 2005). Available at http://www.sws.org.ph.
18. Rene Saguisag, PCIJ Podcast. Available at http://www.pcij.org.
19. "Interview with Glenda Gloria," *Newsbreak*, August 17, 2005.

20. "Interview with Malou Mangahas," August 25, 2005. Ms. Mangahas hastened to add that the editors retain full editorial control of content.
21. Ibid.
22. Sarah Toms, "Philippines' Death Penalty Debate," *BBC News*, June 26, 2006.
23. Sheila Coronel, "The Pare Principle," *Public Eye* IV, no. 4 (October–December 1998).
24. Interview with Archbishop Cruz, August 24, 2005.
25. Abinales and Amoroso, *State and Society in the Philippines*, 12.
26. Internet Movie Database, "Joseph Estrada." Available at http://www.imdb.com/name/nm0261825/.
27. Aprodicio A. Laquian and Elanor R. Laquian, *The Erap Tragedy: Tales from the Snake Pit*, Manila: Anvil Publishing, 2003, 121. The Laquians advised Estrada's run for president, and Aprodicio was fired from the cabinet after he revealed to the press that he was the only sober person in the room by 4:00 A.M.
28. Randolf S. David, "Erap: A Diary of Disenchantment," in *Between Fires: Fifteen Perspectives on the Estrada Crisis*, Amando Doronila, ed., Manila: Anvil Publishing, 2001, 148, 152.
29. *An Act Defining and Penalizing the Crime of Plunder*, R.A. 7080.
30. Laquian and Laquian, *The Erap Tragedy*, 6. A Voice of America editorial roundup was less diplomatic: "Where Mr. Ramos was a workaholic, Mr. Estrada is reputedly lazy." Andrew N. Guthrie, "Monday's Editorials," *Voice of America*, June 1, 1998.
31. David, *Diary of Disenchantment*, 149.
32. Karina Constantino-David, "Surviving Erap," in *Between Fires: Fifteen Perspectives on the Estrada Crisis*, Amando Doronila, ed., Manila: Anvil Publishing, 2001, 148, 152.
33. Ibid.
34. Ibid., *Surviving Erap*, 212–215.
35. Rajiv Chandrasekaran, "Living the High Life in Manila; Associates Say Estrada Prefers Parties to Policy," *Washington Post*, December 4, 2000, p. A1. In 2000, 45 million Philippine pesos was about $1 million.
36. Ibid.
37. Sheila Coronel, "Investigating the President," in *Investigating Estrada: Millions, Mansions and Mistresses*, Sheila Coronel, ed., Manila: Philippine Center for Investigative Journalism, 2000, vii, ix.
38. Salvatore Schiavo-Campo and Mary Judd, *The Mindanao Conflict in the Philippines: Roots, Costs, and Potential Peace Dividend*, World Bank Social Development Papers: Conflict Prevention & Reconstruction, Paper No. 24 (February 2005): 1.
39. Antonio Lopez, "Meeting Force with Force: Estrada Strikes Back – Hard – at the MILF," *Asia Week*, March 10, 2000. Available at http://www-cgi.cnn.com/ASIANOW/asiaweek/magazine/2000/0310/nat.phil.mindanao.html.
40. Anthony Davis, "The Descent into War: Army Clashes with the Moro Islamic Liberation Front Are Escalating into Full-Scale Warfare," *Asia Week*, May 19, 2000. Available at http://www-cgi.cnn.com/ASIANOW/asiaweek/magazine/2000/0519/nat.phil2.html.
41. Ibid.
42. Singson turned on Estrada because Estrada had been trying to legalize jueteng by creating a similar game that a government corporation would run, called "Bingo 2

Ball," and had chosen another crony, Charlie Ang, to administer the new legalized game over Singson. Raul V. Fabella, "What Happens When Institutions Do Not Work: *Jueteng*, Crises of Presidential Legitimacy, and Electoral Failures in the Philippines" Asian Economic Papers 5:3, Fall 2006, pp. 111–112.

43. Francisco Tatad, *A Nation on Fire: The Unmaking of Joseph Ejercito Estrada and the Remaking of Democracy in the Philippines*, Manila: Icon Press, 2002, 41–42.

44. Complaint for Impeachment against President Joseph Ejercito Estrada. Main text, without exhibits, available at http://www.chanrobles.com/legal11impeachment-complaint.htm (hereinafter "Complaint"). The bribery referred to is of jueteng lords.

45. Ibid. The graft allegation was for taking money from the tobacco excise tax, and the corruption allegation was for participating directly in a real estate purchase and by perjuring himself on a statement of assets and liabilities, stating that his family had business interests in three corporations, when the PCIJ revealed the number was closer to sixty-six.

46. Ibid. The allegation of betraying the public trust was for allegedly intervening in an investigation by the Securities and Exchange Commission on behalf of a crony, intervening when his relatives broke the law, appointing relatives to government posts, and engaging in conflicts of interest.

47. Tatad, *A Nation on Fire*, 488.

48. "People Power Redux," *Time*, January 29, 2001. Available at http://www.time.com/time/asia/magazine/2001/0129/cover1.html.

49. *Estrada vs. Desierto*, 353 SCRA 452 (March 2, 2001).

50. Doronila, *Fall*, 222.

51. Malou C. Mangahas, "Trial of the Century May Take Ages to Finish: The Estrada Plunder Case, Year 1," *Philippines Center for Investigative Journalism Report*, January 16–18, 2002.

52. Ibid.

53. Karen Tiongson-Mayrina, "Guilty! But Special Concessions for Accused Show Flawed System." *Philippines Center for Investigative Journalism Report*, September 12, 2007. Available at http://www.pcij.org/i-report/2007/verdict.html.

54. Interview with Rene Saguisag, August 24, 2005.

55. Volt Contreras, "Detained, Estrada Free to make history, build legacy" *Philippine Inquirer*, September 9, 2007. Available at http://archive.inquirer.net/view.php?db=1&story_id=87466.

56. E. T. Suarez, "Open to Reconciliation – GMA," *Manila Bulletin*, August 21, 2005, p. 16.

57. Ibid., quoting House Majority Leader Prospero Nograles.

58. *Decision for Criminal Case No. 26558 for Plunder*, September 12, 2007. Available at http://www.chanrobles.com/cralawsandiganbayandecisionconvictionofestrada forplunder2007.html. *Decision for Decision for Criminal Case No. 26905 for perjury*, September 12, 2007. Available at http://www.chanrobles.com/cralawsandiganbayan decisiononestradaperjurycase2007.html.

59. Tiongson-Mayrina, "Guilty!"

60. Randy David, "Making Sense of the Arroyo-Estrada Deal," *Philippine Inquirer*, November 3, 2007. Available at http://archive.inquirer.net/view.php?db=1&story_ id=98525.

61. Jurado, "Economic Analysis."
62. For the full text, see Lira Dalangin-Fernandez, "(Update 3) Arroyo grants pardon to Estrada," *Philippine Inquirer*, October 25, 2007. Available at http://archive.inquirer. net/view.php?db=1&story_id=96730.
63. Archbishop Angel N. Lagdameo, "The Bigger Picture in the Presidential Pardon," *Catholic Bishops Conference Press Release*, October 26, 2007. Some Catholic Bishops came out against the decision.
64. Makati Business Club, "Makati Business Club Statement on the Pardon of Joseph Ejercito Estrada," October 26, 2007. Available at http://www.mbc.com.ph/ pressStatements/2007_26%20Oct.htm?StoryId=87046.
65. "Catholic Bishops Call on Philippines' Arroyo to Quit," *Reuters News Service*, October 19, 2007.
66. Carlos H. Conde, "Estrada Pardon Weakens Arroyo's Opposition in Philippines," *International Herald Tribune*, October 28, 2007, quoting *Philippine Star* Editorial dated October 28, 2007. Available at www.iht.com/articles/2007/10/28/asia/ phils.php.
67. David, "Making Sense of the Arroyo-Estrada Deal."
68. "Ex-Philippine Leader Estrada Free," *BBC News*, October 26, 2007.
69. MBC, Statement on Pardon.

7

Shifting Legitimacy: The Trials of Frederick Chiluba

Paul Lewis

The Principal Resident Magistrate Court in Zambia's capital, Lusaka, is an unimpressive building. A tinned roof caps a dusty set of rooms, fake-mahogany panels peel off the walls, and discarded brooms lay hunched in an unruly pile. Smoke from mounds of burning grass outside infiltrates the courtroom, filling it with a woody haze. And everything, from the gate to the witness box to the judge's chair, creaks. Yet this humble setting forms the backdrop to a continent-wide precedent in judicial accountability. On a morning in early May 2005, Zambia's former president, Frederick Chiluba, arrived at court in an ad hoc motorcade of white Toyota pickup trucks. As usual, he was adorned in a dazzlingly sharp suit, as if audaciously exhibiting the evidence of his infamous shopping trips to Geneva. Chiluba took his seat wedged next to a window latticed with iron bars – the first African former head of state ever to be tried for serious crimes in a free and fair domestic court process.[1]

This chapter concerns the numerous trials of Frederick Chiluba on charges of large-scale corruption under ordinary criminal law and gives an analytical focus to the changing levels of international involvement in the process. In doing so, the chapter distinguishes between two phases in Chiluba's trials. The first (Phase I) involves the events leading up to the removal of Chiluba's presidential immunity and his eventual arrest, which were the outcome of a Zambian political movement free from outside assistance. In contrast, since the commencement of Chiluba's trials (Phase II), Zambian investigators and prosecutors have relied on multifaceted forms of support provided by

Author's Note: The author conducted interviews in May 2005 with ordinary Zambians, government ministers, former judges, lawyers, diplomats, civil servants, opposition politicians, civil society leaders, academics, journalists, investigators, prosecutors, the Task Force Against Corruption's Chief Prosecutor and Execution Chairman, various officials from the Anti-Corruption Commission, the Director of Public Prosecutions, and two of Zambia's former presidents: Kenneth Kaunda (1964–1991) and the defendant himself, Frederick Chiluba (1991–2001).

international facilitators. This pattern informs a second point: that changing levels of international involvement prompted, to some degree, a corresponding shift in sources of legitimacy. Whereas Chiluba's trials may not have been *caused* by an internationally influenced normative change, they may well be *affecting* one.

ZAMBIA AND CORRUPTION

A former British colony, the Republic of Zambia achieved independence in 1964. Although an ostensible constitutional democracy, with a de jure separation of executive, legislative, and judicial branches, a bill of rights, and a recent upturn in the national economy, Zambia remains one of the poorest countries in the world.[2] The nation's first president, Kenneth Kaunda, governed from 1964 to 1991 according to the prescriptions of his own brand of socialistic philosophy, which he called humanism. It was, for the most part, a relatively benign one-party state. By 1991, following a disastrous economic decline and political unrest, Kaunda ceded to calls for the reintroduction of contested elections and scheduled multiparty elections for later that year. His main electoral rival, the leader of the newly formed Movement for Multi-Party Democracy (MMD), was an unlikely contender: a five-foot tall bus conductor-cum-trade union leader by the name of Frederick Jacob Titus Chiluba.

Chiluba was born in the Luapula province of Zambia in 1943, the son of a miner. In 1974, he was elected general secretary of the Zambia Congress of Trade Unions. It was in this capacity that throughout the 1980s Chiluba gained notoriety as the foremost spokesman for Zambian workers, spending several months in detention for allegedly inciting Zambians to unrest and revolution. By 1991, Chiluba's demands for political pluralism and economic deregulation were striking a popular chord, inspired by Eastern Europe's citizen-driven campaign for democratic reform.[3] Mass rallies of support ensued, and on October 31, 1991, Chiluba won Zambia's national elections with 80 percent of the popular vote.[4] After gaining power, Chiluba's MMD government pursued its promise of economic deregulation vigorously by adopting a package of privatization and structural adjustment advocated by the IMF and donors.

Corruption has abounded in every sector in Zambia since colonial rule.[5] Under Kaunda's reign, corruption took the form of patronage and influence peddling within clientelist party networks. With Chiluba's hasty economic changes in the 1990s, however, came lucrative new avenues for corruption. As Szeftel explains, "Liberalization and structural reform created new opportunities for accumulation. Privatization and deregulation opened up possibilities for using political office to acquire state assets and make personal fortunes."[6]

The impact on Zambia's economy was catastrophic: an estimated $500 million of national wealth was allegedly stolen or diverted during Chiluba's ten years in office (1991–2001).[7]

Meanwhile, Zambia's accountability infrastructure was unable to prevent or punish senior figures guilty of financial corruption. The Anti-Corruption Commission (ACC), like all other law enforcement agencies in Zambia, had been chronically underresourced and subject to political interference from its inception.[8] Legislative mechanisms of accountability similarly failed to constrain the executive branch.[9] Zambia's English common-law judiciary is also much weaker and less adequately resourced than judicial systems in the region's other evolving democracies. In neighboring Tanzania, the judiciary has historically been more willing to pursue cases involving breaches of authority.[10] Zambia's judiciary, in contrast, is noted for its timidity and, with only two exceptions, an almost total reluctance to give rulings that challenge the sitting government.[11] Finally, the only precedent for the arrest of a former head of state in Zambia was disastrous. On Christmas Day in 1997, Chiluba arrested Kaunda for alleged involvement in a botched coup. The arrest was politically motivated – designed to humiliate Kaunda rather than place him in any real danger – and prompted international condemnation. In keeping with the Zambia government's tendency to recoil from overt human rights violations, he was soon released.[12]

International frameworks for accountability were not a feature of Zambian politics. Although the country had a good record of ratifying human rights treaties, including the International Criminal Court statute, rates of incorporation of international law into domestic law have been low, and international law has a low profile in Zambian legal discourse.[13] Flagrant violations of civil and political rights are rare. The country displays a good, if stunted, performance on human rights indicators such as arbitrary arrest, freedom of movement, and political persecution. Since the country became a democracy, there have been criticisms over freedom of the press, although state-sponsored repression of free speech is rare and ineffectual.[14] When Chiluba left office, Zambia had not signed or ratified any international corruption treaty. Until his indictment, the country's former president appeared cloaked in impunity.

PHASE I – PRELUDE TO THE TRIALS

Given the country's poor legal history, Zambia was an unlikely setting for the trial of a former president for serious crimes. Chiluba was the president of an impoverished, evolving democracy with neither the judicial resources nor the historical precedents to try a member of the political elite. If that was not enough, Chiluba was protected from prosecution – even after leaving office – by a constitutional immunity clause.[15] Repealing presidential immunity in Zambia requires the consent of Parliament, which in turn requires the support of the executive branch and, under normal circumstances, that means the dominant party in government – in Chiluba's case, his own MMD party.[16] However, a succession of key events throughout Chiluba's last year in office and during his successor's first months in power culminated in the annulment of his constitutional protection from prosecution.

The process was spurred by a successful civil uprising against Chiluba's bid to extend his presidency. This victory was compounded by the discovery of evidence – ironically, evidence obtained in a defamation trial initiated at Chiluba's request – that implicated the former president and his associates in corruption. Finally, the perceived illegitimacy of Chiluba's chosen presidential successor, Levy Mwanawasa, left him beholden to an anticorruption drive as the sole guarantor of his political credibility. Phase I of Chiluba trials was therefore a wholly Zambian affair; international and transnational actors had next to no impact on the process.

Chiluba's Third-Term Bid

Throughout his presidency, Chiluba maintained that he would not seek to outstay his constitutionally determined two-term limit in office. By January 2001, however, it was clear that he intended to amend both his country's and his party's constitutions to enable him to run for a third term. It was a move viewed by many in Zambia as highly regressive. Concerns were confounded when rumors spread that Chiluba was distributing "brown paper bag bribes" to persuade politicians to back his bid for an extended presidency.[17] Questions were also raised in political circles as to why Chiluba was so resistant to leaving office. Was it, many asked, because he had something to hide? Rumors in the country's elite classes, which contained many alleged beneficiaries of diverted government funds, suggested he had presided over a corrupt administration. But there was no proof.

The reaction to Chiluba's ambition for an extended presidency was robust: church leaders, the legal fraternity, civil society groups, political rebels, independent journalists, and ordinary Zambians joined forces in a movement to prevent constitutional reform that would allow for a third term. The Oasis Forum, an umbrella collaboration of various civil and religious groups, spearheaded the campaign, which was funded in part by a $120,000 donation from the Danish Embassy.[18] By April 2001, the campaign against Chiluba's third term had developed real momentum. Protesters against Chiluba took to the streets each Friday at 5 P.M., and rebel members of parliament employed more surreptitious methods to escape government intimidation. A church gathering led by Bishop Mosusu on April 7 conspicuously named "a day of reflection," for example, enabled an anti-Chiluba petition to be distributed among the aisles of parliamentarians in between hymns. In the meantime, Zambia's fiercely independent daily newspaper, *The Post*, was instrumental in garnering support from the public with reports of Oasis activities and editorial condemnations of Chiluba's third-term aspiration. Not since the campaign for democratic pluralism in the early 1990s had Zambians – a people renowned for their peaceful demeanor and distaste for militancy – been so thoroughly mobilized by a political campaign.

The Oasis Forum also discovered a new political tool: the law. In May 2001, Oasis lawyers successfully obtained a court injunction to stall Chiluba's attempts to expel awkward parliamentarians from the MMD party, which Chiluba had hoped might reduce the number of votes against his proposed amendments. Two days later, rebel parliamentarians filed another legal petition: this time for Chiluba's impeachment, citing alleged misconduct. This legal move was not expected to succeed, campaigners now admit, but was viewed as a high-profile instrument with which to apply additional pressure to the now-vulnerable president.[19] The following day, May 4, 2001, Chiluba wilted, announcing the end of his third-term ambition in a televised address to the nation. The defeat of Chiluba's attempt to nudge Zambia back toward autocracy had set two lasting precedents: first, the notion of presidential impunity had been decisively undermined; second, campaigners had learned how the law could be legitimately used to political ends.

The defeat of Chiluba's third-term ambitions, and the critical events that followed, resulted from the working collaboration of a spectrum of interest groups. It was in the crystallization of a campaigning relationship between three key players, however, that the Oasis Forum really functioned as a precursor to Chiluba's later downfall. Mark Chona, then the chairman of the Oasis Forum but formerly foreign representative and political advisor to Kaunda, provided the social glue the Oasis movement needed to bind together diverse factions. Chona would later become executive chairman of the organization tasked with investigating and prosecuting Chiluba and would use his networking abilities to bring international facilitators on board. Fred M'membe, long-time editor of *The Post*, who had been Chiluba's thorniest critic during his decade in power, valiantly published documentary evidence incriminating Chiluba and his associates and called for trials. A young commercial lawyer named Mutembo Nchito, at the time just thirty-two, along with his partner and brother Nchima Nchito, first provided pro bono legal advice and representation in cases against Chiluba and his associates. This young attorney was the bridge between Chona and M'membe and was to become Chiluba's most prominent legal adversary, serving, eventually, as chief prosecutor in his trials. First, however, Nchito had to put his legal skills to the test as defense counsel in a fascinating defamation trial, known popularly as the "Chiluba Is a Thief" trial – a trial, ironically, initiated by Chiluba himself.

"Chiluba Is a Thief"

The "Chiluba is a thief" case was in some ways a product of the Oasis movement's ongoing momentum. Chiluba's Oasis opponents had been emboldened by the defeat of his third-term bid. Their resolve was further strengthened by the findings of a quasi-judicial tribunal that two of Chiluba's ministers had diverted $460,000 of government money to fund their party convention.[20] As rumors of Chiluba's corruption spread, *The Post* made a bold journalistic move: in articles reporting the anti-Chiluba speeches of two rebel members of parliament, the newspaper declared, unflinchingly, that "Chiluba is a thief."[21] *The Post*'s publication was an intrepid step in a country where defaming or insulting the president is an offense punishable by imprisonment.[22]

Chiluba reacted furiously and ordered the arrest of the journalist who wrote the story, his editor (M'membe), and the two members of parliament reported to have made the comments. On August 21, 2001, after a manhunt that momentarily froze parts of Zambia's capital with road blocks and took police officers into the bush, the four surrendered themselves to police and were arrested on charges of defaming the president. M'membe, *The Post*'s editor, refused to back down. The following day, the newspaper continued its campaign and devoted six pages to the publication of the names of more than two thousand petitioners who agreed with M'membe by signing the statement: "Chiluba is undoubtedly a thief."

Mutembo Nchito, now lead defense counsel to the accused in the Chiluba Is a Thief trial, had two defense strategies available to him. First, he could seek an acquittal of his clients on the basis that their comments had been misinterpreted. Alternatively, Nchito could accept the premise of the charges – that his clients had accused Chiluba of theft – but prove that the substance of their allegations was, in fact, true. After discussions with his defendants and encouragement from M'membe, Nchito chose the latter; the defense case would rest on the contention that Chiluba had indeed stolen. So it was that a trial initiated by Chiluba to silence his political adversaries was transformed, de facto, into a trial in which his own claims to innocence would be adjudicated. Bestowed with, as he put it, "the biggest legal fish hook in the country," Nchito begun subpoenaing witnesses to testify in court, including Chiluba himself. In April 2002, by which time Chiluba had left office, it was obvious that the trial was backfiring, and Chiluba tried, unsuccessfully, to halt the proceedings. It was too late; the trial had gained a momentum of its own, and Chiluba was no longer in a position to stop it.

The real breakthrough came a month later, in May 2002. Tipped off by intelligence sources of money laundering via an intelligence service account in the Zambia Commercial National Bank, Nchito obtained a court order to inspect the bank's books. In particular, he asked to see documentation from an intelligence account based in London called Zamtrop. It quickly became clear that Nchito had just unveiled the epicenter of a vast network of fraudulent payments. Zamtrop, which was administered by the head of Zambia Intelligence Services, would later turn out to be just one of numerous mechanisms for embezzling state funds. The sheer scope of this account, and the simplicity with which it incriminated scores of collaborators in Chiluba's administration by simply listing them as recipients, was breathtaking. Payments in excess of $1.1 million had been made to Zambia's ambassador in Washington. A Reuters journalist had received $20,000. Chiluba's "institute" was the recipient of more than $36,000, his youngest son $10,000, his daughter $90,000. The chief justice, previously renowned for his independent and progressive judgments, had received over $168,000 in payments from the account. Chiluba's tailors had received in excess of $1.1 million. Even an official at the World Bank was reportedly an accomplice to Chiluba's enrichment.[23] The list went on and on, with additional millions channeled into accounts belonging to ministers, jewelers, civil servants, and banks in offshore tax havens. This was the turning point in Chiluba's fortunes: here was hard documentary evidence, obtained by a court of law and divulged to the nation via the pages of *The Post* in an exposé the newspaper coined "Chiluba's matrix of plunder." "Will [President] Mwanawasa finally help lift Chiluba's immunity and prosecute him and others?" *The Post* demanded to know.[24] It was a question Zambians were not about to let their newly elected president ignore.

The Turn of President Mwanawasa

In the middle of a night in late August 2001, Levy Patrick Mwanawasa awoke to a phone call from his president. Chiluba informed him that he was to be his chosen MMD candidate for the forthcoming presidential elections. No one had predicted he would receive a nomination from Chiluba; in 1994, Mwanawasa had resigned from Chiluba's cabinet, taking out a full-page advertisement in two daily newspapers complaining of corruption among his MMD colleagues.[25] Ever since, he had taken a backseat in politics and concentrated on his professional career as a distinguished lawyer.[26] Perhaps it was Mwanawasa's reputation for integrity that compelled Chiluba to select him as his successor candidate; the intended message behind the nomination being that Chiluba had nothing to fear. Alternatively, or dually, in a political system dominated by patronage, Chiluba may have presumed it unthinkable that Mwanawasa could be so ungrateful as to harm the man who plucked him from political obscurity and promoted him to the front runner in the elections for the country's presidency. Either way, Chiluba could have been forgiven for thinking he made the right decision because Mwanawasa's initial instinct in the ensuing election campaign was to defend Chiluba's record in office.[27] As the campaign progressed, however, it became clear that a tough line on corruption – by then, the hottest political topic in Zambia – was a prerequisite for any successful candidacy. Mwanawasa began to promise zero tolerance for corruption under what he said would be a "New Deal" government but stopped short of criticizing Chiluba directly.[28] The 2001 elections were the closest presidential and parliamentary elections in Zambia's history. Mwanawasa prevailed over his closest rival, the United Party for National Development's Anderson Mazoka, by just 34,000 votes. In parliamentary elections, he was not so lucky: the MMD party achieved insufficient seats to form a ruling government. For the first time ever, no single party had a stranglehold on Zambia's political system.[29]

Mwanawasa's greatest concern, however, was that the validity of the results in his election was coming under intense scrutiny. It was alleged that the new president was the beneficiary of corrupt campaign financing and vote rigging by his party. Official European Union observers noted poll irregularities, expressed serious concerns over the conduct of the Electoral Commission of Zambia, and refused to accept the declared results as valid.[30] A raft of other domestic and international election monitors concurred that the elections had failed to meet democratic standards of transparency and fairness.[31] Most worryingly for Mwanawasa, opposition parties successfully lodged a Presidential Petition in the courts to dispute his victory.[32] By mid-2002, Mwanawasa may have secured a tentative grasp over the executive wing of government, but he lacked the credibility to rule. Zambia's third president was getting desperate.

When in June 2002, the "Chiluba Is a Thief" defamation trial uncovered the Zamtrop account evidence, President Mwanawasa was provided with a much-needed opportunity to restore his political fortunes. The demand from the Zambian people and civil society lobbyists – including the Oasis Forum – was unequivocal: Chiluba's immunity should be lifted, and he should be tried for his alleged crimes. With one fell swoop, Mwanawasa was able to assert his independence over his predecessor, regain the trust of the Zambian people, and maintain a hold over his unstable government. His supporters maintain that Mwanawasa turned on his predecessor because he was an astute legal eagle with a proven record of integrity, whom Chiluba blindly underestimated. When he discovered the full extent of his predecessor's plunder, they argue, Mwanawasa's legal inclinations left him with no choice but to choose a legal recourse to accountability. Most likely, though, Mwanawasa foresaw the chance to restore the legitimacy of his presidency and save his political career in the process.

Either way, on July 11, 2002, at a special session of parliament, President Mwanawasa made a landmark speech in which he gave his support to the removal of Chiluba's immunity from prosecution.[33] Like a lawyer arguing a case in court, he presented documentary evidence to Parliament to substantiate a plethora of suspected transgressions committed during Chiluba's administration. Mwanawasa chronicled how the government had given a $20.5 million deposit through a Congolese businessman in a dubious arms deal; how payments were made into a suspect consultancy firm in London; how sixty-seven fully paid-for fuel tankers simply disappeared; how a so-called Presidential Housing Initiative had been misused; and how national leaders had "built huge mansions which their known incomes could not support."[34] The crux of his presentation, however, rested on the very evidence uncovered by the Chiluba Is a Thief trial: the Zamtrop account. Zamtrop payments, Mwanawasa said, presented a "prima facie case that funds were embezzled." He dramatically read out the names of recipients of Zamtrop money, including his own minister for foreign affairs. The message was clear and stated plainly in Mwanawasa's concluding remarks: "Mr. Speaker, the demand from the people is that they want accountability. This demand is perfectly legitimate." The next day, the defendants-turned-accusers in the Chiluba Is a Thief defamation trial were acquitted. Four days after that, on July 16, 2002, while thousands of protestors heeded *The Post*'s calls and demonstrated outside Parliament demanding accountability, parliamentarians voted unanimously in favor of repealing Chiluba's immunity.

The efforts that culminated in the removal of Chiluba's immunity were distinctly Zambian. They stemmed from three decisive events – Chiluba's third-term bid, the Chiluba Is a Thief defamation trial, and the election of Mwanawasa – without which he may never have faced prosecution. Any suggestion that Chiluba's demise was the result of a backfire of his own decisions belies the agency of the Zambian people.

In truth, it was the combined efforts of thousands of tireless campaigners and *The Post* that ultimately opened the gate to Chiluba's prosecution. The momentum created by the Oasis movement proved unstoppable. It delivered a humiliating blow to Chiluba, underscored his vulnerability, and encouraged campaigners to delve deeper into his past. With the courageous efforts of *The Post*'s editor, M'membe, and Chiluba's newfound legal nemesis, Nchito, the remarkable reach of Chiluba's administration's plunder was laid bare. Mwanawasa might, of course, have ignored clamoring calls for the removal of Chiluba's immunity, but the fragility of his own electoral mandate left him desperately in need of his own political legitimization, and he probably would not have survived politically without prosecuting his MMD colleagues – Chiluba included.

International influence throughout this process was minimal.[35] Concerned about the precedent that the trial of a former head of state could set for their own countries, Zambia's neighbors remained quiet. International Monetary Fund and World Bank representatives, enthusiasts for Chiluba's neo-liberal reforms, were reportedly unhappy with the removal of Chiluba's immunity.[36] Despite the importance donors to Zambia generally attach to good governance, no promises of expanded aid assistance were made contingent on Chiluba's trials. Further, although closed-door assurances given by diplomats that they would support an anticorruption drive may have given Mwanawasa some encouragement, the traction of donors was much reduced by the decline in diplomatic relations following Mwanawasa's controversial election.[37] When Chiluba first appeared in court in early 2003, his trial boasted the kind of legitimacy that only a national movement can confer.[38]

PHASE II – THE TRIALS: A LITTLE HELP FROM OUR FRIENDS

With Chiluba's immunity from prosecution gone, expectations among Zambia's public for swift and efficient justice were sky high. Mwanawasa hastily established an ad hoc investigative and prosecutorial institution, the Task Force against Corruption (commonly known as the Task Force), with jurisdiction over those financial crimes suspected to have taken place during Chiluba's decade in office.[39] On February 24, 2003, four days after the Supreme Court upheld Parliament's decision to remove Chiluba's immunity,[40] Task Force officers arrested him along with six codefendants, on multiple charges of theft by a public servant totaling some $4 million. Six months later, on August 4, 2003, Chiluba was arrested again, this time along with four codefendants for theft of $40 million. On both occasions, all of the accused pleaded not guilty and were released on bail.

Despite the public's high hopes of a quick conviction, the Chiluba case met with difficulties from the outset. A slow judicial system allowed protracted

adjournments and appeals, and many began to question the competence of
Zambia's courts and law enforcement institutions to deal with crimes of such
magnitude. Popular support for the trial waned as the two cases initiated
in 2003 struggled to make any significant progress because of prosecutorial
mismanagement. By September 2004, after a succession of judicial setbacks
and acquittals, nearly all of the charges against Chiluba had been dropped.
However, he was rearrested on September 14, 2004, along with two directors of
an allegedly complicit company, Access Financial Services, on much-reduced
charges of theft of $500,000. Three years later, at the end of 2007, beset by delays
brought on by Chiluba's declining health, the continuation of his trial hung
in the balance. While the previous section (Phase I) gave a diachronic view of
the evolution of events resulting in Chiluba's trials, this section (Phase II) takes
a synchronic snapshot of the trials themselves. As we will see, wide-ranging
international facilitation provided political, practical, and legal support to
Zambia in its quest to bring Chiluba to justice.

Political Support

Civil society organizations that were originally at the forefront of calls for
Chiluba's prosecution had, by 2005, become frustrated by the absence of tan-
gible results. Four years after Chiluba's third-term bid had been defeated, the
former president seemed insignificant, even pitiful, and civil society interests shifted elsewhere. The most prominent civil society groups concentrated
instead on lobbying for constitutional reform. Some civil society organizations
even suggested that the judicial route to accountability was misguided and that
a quasi-judicial tribunal or truth commission would have been more efficient.
In private, many in the law fraternity also began to bemoan the mismanagement of the Chiluba trials and complain about the increased wages of Task
Force attorneys. Others complained that the Task Force was not a constitutional body and appeared, therefore, to be more susceptible to interference.
Further, Mwanawasa's alleged embrace of "soft" or nepotistic corruption made
his anticorruption drive appear hypocritical. Although *The Post* remained committed to the anticorruption cause, public support further declined. Phrases
such as "we cannot eat anticorruption" became commonplace on Zambia's
shantytown buses. Sensing a change in mood, opposition politicians began
to condemn what they declared was Mwanawasa's botched and politically
selective anticorruption drive.

As well as voicing declining support for the trials, some politicians also
attempted to interfere in the work of Task Force prosecutors. Mwanawasa
repeatedly suggested that he would pardon Chiluba if he returned 75 percent

of the laundered money to the government. These remarks elicited the censure of the magistrate in Chiluba's trial on the grounds that they preemptively presumed his guilt.[41] Of even greater concern for legal practitioners, however, was what prosecutors confide were direct attempts by government officials to influence prosecutions by suggesting that plea bargains or acquittals for favorable individuals be offered.[42] Suspicions that prosecutions might be politically influenced in turn exacerbated public discontent.

Partly because there was insufficient domestic support for Chiluba's trials, international facilitators began to advocate on the Task Force's behalf. A cluster of six diplomatic missions – the United Kingdom, the United States, Denmark, the Netherlands, Sweden, and Norway – provided varying types of support to the Task Force (including technical and financial assistance). Ambassadors from the group made frequent speeches, which were reported in *The Post* and elsewhere, hailing Zambia's anticorruption fight and encouraging Zambians to show patience.[43] Most lobbying, however, took place behind closed doors in discussions with Zambian government ministers and occasionally with President Mwanawasa. Meetings between the "cluster of six" and government officials were, at times, tense and awkward but strengthened, diplomats say, by the unified stance the cluster usually took. By mid-2005, these six diplomatic missions were actively calling on government representatives to give a renewed declaration of commitment to the anticorruption fight, to halt political interference in the work of prosecutors, and to enhance the security arrangements for Task Force staff. When they met resistance, strong diplomatic hints were dropped that investments might be terminated. The members of the diplomatic cluster of six were, of course, not the only ones making these demands: *The Post* and those Zambians still committed to the process were equally adamant. However, the sustained political pressure of this diplomatic core – directed at powerful officials often inaccessible to Zambians themselves – was no less important.[44] One mission, for example, threatened to withdraw all direct budgetary investments and possibly close its embassy in Zambia if government officials did not cease their attempts to meddle in the judicial process. Using their leverage collectively, these diplomats became what Keck and Sikkink have termed "advocates beyond borders."[45]

Financial and Technical Assistance

Declining political support to one side, the Task Force was mainly impeded by its own organizational incapacity and that of its constituent institutions.[46] Task Force and other law enforcement officers were, at the start of the trials, underqualified, underpaid, underresourced, and too small in number to

manage the enormous workload. In the office of the Director of Public Prosecutions – the authority responsible for authorizing all Task Force prosecutions – only fifteen out of forty-nine public prosecutor positions were filled.
More to the point, overburdened law enforcement institutions were drowned
in the complexity and reach of Chiluba's suspected criminal activities. More
than 450 companies, 270 fixed assets, and 170 individuals across the world were
estimated to be involved in fraudulent activities linked to Chiluba's administration. Proceeds and assets from Zambian corruption were thought to reside
in the United Kingdom, Southeast Asia, the United States, Switzerland, South
Africa, the Bahamas, Belgium, and the Channel Islands. The Task Force was
therefore responsible for investigating the disappearance of an estimated $500
million, allegedly laundered through a complex web of worldwide financial
criminality, all with a staff of just twenty untried investigators who had neither
the technical knowledge nor the manpower to uncover evidence. Indeed, the
professional expertise to deal with complicated money laundering crimes did
not exist anywhere in Zambia.[47] Hiring expensive private investigative assistance was well beyond the financial capacity of Zambian law enforcement
institutions without additional funding. As Chona recalls, "Everyone was a
student: investigators, prosecutors, magistrates – even the defense counsel."[48]

Hence, international help was sought in the nascent stages of the Task
Force's investigations. Weeks after Chiluba's immunity was lifted, and while
his appeals against Parliament's decisions were still before the High and
Supreme Courts, a delegation of investigators and prosecutors traveled to London, Washington, D.C., and New York. Officially, this delegation was seeking
international backing for Zambia's incipient anticorruption campaign; in reality, they were in search of invaluable advice and support, and they succeeded
in establishing professional relationships that would last well into the future.[49]
What Zambian investigators really needed, however, was hands-on help in
Zambia. The U.S. Embassy in Lusaka therefore arranged for veteran prosecutors with experience in American fraud trials to be flown into Lusaka to provide
advice. That technical assistance, investigators said, was indispensable to their
work. Zambian investigators' capitalizing on foreign expert assistance in these
economic crimes was similar to Argentinean officials' well documented use
of foreign forensic experts during investigations into human rights crimes
committed by junta leaders in the late 1970s.[50] In both cases, foreign experts
bolstered the otherwise impossible work of underresourced and inexperienced
investigators.

Technical advice helped to guide prosecutions as well. Partly as a result
of their inexperience with these kinds of crimes, prosecuting authorities mis-
managed cases by bundling together all of the suspected crimes committed

by a raft of codefendants in gargantuan lists of indictments.[51] Not only did this overzealousness overburden the magistrate courts, but it portended trials that would take years to reach judgment. Worse still, it resulted in damaging splits between prosecuting authorities.[52] In mid-2004, prosecutors suffered another blow when two of Chiluba's codefendants – the former ambassador to the United States, Attan Shansonga, and the chief of intelligence services, Xavier Chungu – escaped from Zambia. Authorities did not have the resources or the know-how to find and seek the extradition of these fugitives. Given the prosecution's controversial strategy of amalgamating codefendant's cases to form one grand prosecution, the loss of two key defendants was a severe setback; it seemed that the entire prosecution might collapse. However, with help from fraud prosecution specialists from the United States and the United Kingdom, the cases against Chiluba were reorganized, resulting, eventually, in the more focused case that is currently before the courts. This prosecutorial advice did not at any point infringe on the autonomy of Zambian officials; rather, it functioned in a framework of assistance provided at Zambia's behest.

International facilitators also provided financial support to remedy the Task Force's budgetary shortfalls. Five northern European donors – the United Kingdom, Denmark, the Netherlands, Norway, and Sweden – provided almost $4 million to the Task Force by the end of 2004.[53] By mid-2005, donors had agreed to an expanded package of financial support amounting to $10 million.[54] Although international donor financing was essential to the Task Force's survival, these financial arrangements are controversial; an ad hoc law enforcement agency responsible for the prosecution of a former president is, to say the least, an unconventional destination for development aid.[55] Certainly, for most of the donors involved, this type of aid had never before been tried anywhere in the world. Some even referred to their involvement as a "test" – an experiment in direct involvement in a democratizing country's judicial process.[56]

Legal Support

The most intriguing dimension to the international facilitation lies in the legal process itself. Chiluba's trials have generally upheld international standards of judicial due process. On two counts, however, Zambia's judicial system has struggled with the highest-profile trials in its forty-year history. First, the legal process failed to inspire sufficient levels of confidence from Zambia's public. Magistrates, not all of whom have received adequate legal training, are paid so little they must ferry between shanty towns and courts in dilapidated minibuses. Moreover, as Gloppen et al. explain, "That high-level economic crimes and corruption cases, often involving government officials, are tried by magistrates who lack specialized knowledge and relevant case material, detracts from the judiciary's accountability performance."[57] Judicial strikes, unfilled vacancies, and inefficiencies slowed down the judiciary, causing lengthy backlogs.[58] Low pay also fuels widespread suspicion of corruption among magistrate judges.[59] According to *Afrobarometer*, 56 percent of Zambians distrust the judiciary.[60] Chiluba's first prosecution took nearly six months to move from his arrest to the commencement of his trial and was almost immediately criticized for its slow pace. Yet much of the slow pace was the result of what appeared to be a deliberate strategy by his lawyers to frustrate the courts with obstructive legal maneuvers that prompted procedural impediments, adjournments, and lengthy appeals.

The second shortcoming in the judiciary's management of Chiluba's trials is, in some ways, a corollary of the first. It seemed unlikely that Zambian courts would either have license to consider financial transactions committed outside of Zambia's borders or muster the juridical muscle necessary to compel foreign banks to relinquish fraudulently obtained investments and assets. Given the transnational nature of Chiluba's alleged crimes and the increasing importance that the Zambian public was placing on asset recovery, this constituted a real hindrance for the Task Force.

By late 2004, however, the Task Force had developed an innovative legal strategy to overcome both problems. On October 4, 2004, British attorneys representing Zambia filed a civil case in the British High Court to recover fraudulently obtained assets belonging to, among others, Frederick Chiluba.[61] The trial opened in October 2006, and the judge visited Lusaka to hear testimony from defendants subject to a travel ban because of simultaneous criminal proceedings in Zambia, although they refused to participate. Chiluba and his Zambia-based codefendants declared the trial an imposition from a former colonial power and an "infringement of Zambia's sovereign rights."[62] In order not to prejudice the Zambian criminal trial, hearings were held in private, and a special order was made to prevent the release of court materials, including evidence.

The reasons behind the British civil case were manifold. First and foremost, the case offered the Task Force an enhanced prospect of asset recovery. Many of the assets recovered as a result of the civil action may not have been returned at the instruction of a Zambian judge. In addition, prosecutors hoped that the civil action would yield a conclusion more rapidly than was expected in the snail-paced Zambian criminal courts, thereby providing an early, symbolically important, judicial success. At the time the civil case commenced, Task Force officials expected the trial to lend political legitimacy to criminal proceedings in Zambia. They hoped that the reputed probity of the British judicial system would influence perceptions of Zambian criminal proceedings by association. At a time of declining support for Chiluba's trials, the legitimacy-bolstering impact of international presence was especially important. Chiluba himself requested international observers from the African Union, Commonwealth, or Southern African Development Community to monitor his criminal trials, thereby acknowledging the legitimizing presence of international figures.[63]

Both in juridical and legitimacy terms, then, the British civil action augmented the criminal proceedings in Zambia. It provided, in some senses, a band-aid for the shortcomings in Zambia's judicial system. The sovereignty of both jurisdictions remained intact and uncompromised in this process by the ostensible separateness of the concurrent cases. Importantly, too, the Zambian Task Force (the client in the British proceedings) was responsible for both processes. In the end, the British action proved not just to be an early victory in the campaign against Chiluba but may indeed turn out to be the only one. In late 2006, a Zambian court declared Chiluba medically unfit for trial because of heart complaints. After months of delays, the trial was suspended while Chiluba sought a heart transplant in South Africa. In early 2008, when Chiluba returned to Zambia, the prospects for his faltering trial seemingly bleak. In contrast, in May 2007, the civil case in the United Kingdom came to an end when a British High Court found Frederick Chiluba liable for stealing $46 million of public money.[64] In Zambia, where the judgment was dramatically broadcast via video link to Lusaka's High Court, the conclusion of the trial was received as a verdict of guilt. The wording of Justice Peter Smith's judgment compounded the view that this was proxy justice. He singled out Chiluba's fraudulently acquired wardrobe as "the most telling example of corruption." "This was at a time when the vast majority of Zambians were struggling to live on $1 a day and many could not afford more than one meal a day," the judgment stated. "The people of Zambia should know that whenever he appears in public wearing some of these clothes he acquired them with money stolen from them."[65]

CONCLUSION: SHIFTING LEGITIMACY?

This case shows the different levels of international involvement in two separate phases of the trials of Zambia's former president. In Phase I, Zambian actors exclusively drove the all-important prelude to the trials. In three critical developments – the defeat of Chiluba's third-term bid, the disclosure of evidence in the Chiluba Is a Thief defamation trial, and Mwanawasa's surrender to public calls for the removal of Chiluba's immunity – Zambians acted alone, and prevailed.

In Phase II, a framework of international facilitation provided by a cluster of six diplomatic missions at Zambia's request provided political, practical, and legal support to the Zambian trials and a parallel civil trial in the United Kingdom. The conclusion of the foreign civil case proved critical for perceptions of Chiluba's criminal trial in Zambia. The Chiluba corruption trials were neither a proxy for broader crimes nor were they politically controlled. Instead, they are testament to a complex project of democratic consolidation. They were as reliant on the careful navigation through popular outrage and adherence to due process as upon external facilitation.

It is too early to assess the impact of this landmark prosecution on the region and the continent. Much is likely to depend on the outcome of the remaining trial. Already, however, there is some indication that Chiluba's trials have prompted an incipient shift in judicial accountability in the neighboring countries. In July 2006, two years after Malawi's Bakili Muluzi stood down as president, he was arrested and charged with forty-two counts of corruption, fraud, and theft after an inquiry by the country's anticorruption bureau. Although the charges were dropped within days, the parallel with the Chiluba prosecution prompted much debate about the relationship between the two. Like Chiluba, Muluzi was the victim of an anticorruption drive launched by the presidential successor whom he handpicked, Bingu Mutharika. This may, however, represent a special case rather than a normative nudge; it is of note, for example, that President Mutharika worked for the Zambian administration under Kaunda in the 1970s and is likely to have strong ties with the country.

Back in Zambia, however, international involvement legitimated Chiluba's trials. The exclusively Zambian prelude to the trials gave them a source of national legitimacy, but political support wavered, causing that legitimacy to be questioned. Then, for purely practical reasons, investigators and prosecutors sought assistance from abroad, and fresh legitimacy resulted from the interaction of the Zambian judicial process with international facilitators. This normative shift – in part a result of the influence of a former colonial judiciary – may prove controversial for a country in which memories of imperialism are still ripe. Indeed Chiluba has cast himself as the victim of "colonial" interference.[66] The truth is, however, that international facilitation has kept credibility for Chiluba's faltering trial alive. As Chiluba himself declared while still in office, "Zambia is now part of a modern, global village, where changes are happening and affecting everyone at every turn."[67] Everyone – including, it seems, former presidents.

NOTES

1. Other head of state or government indictments in Africa since 1990 were sponsored either by the United Nations or a foreign state (Jean Kambanda, Rwanda,
1997; Hissène Habré, Chad, 1999; Charles Taylor, Liberia, 2003), did not conform
to international standards of due judicial process (Moussa Traore, Mali, 1993;
Mengistu Haile Mariam, Ethiopia, 1994; Olusegun Obasanjo, Nigeria, 1995; Hastings Kamuzu Banda, Malawi, 1995/1997; Pascal Lissouba, Congo-Brazzaville, 1998;
Bernard Kolelas, Congo-Brazzaville, 2000; Didier Ratsiraka, Madagascar, 2003),
or were related to nonserious crimes (Canaan Banana, Zimbabwe, 1997).

2. In April 2005, Zambia met its completion point for Highly Indebted Poor Country
(HIPC) status, thereby qualifying for $3.9 billion debt relief; Poverty Line Data:
World Bank (1998), 2994ff.

3. Craig Clancy and Steven Chan, *Zambia and the Decline of Kaunda 1984–1998*,
Craig Clancy, ed., New York: The Edwin Mellen Press, 2000.

4. Ibid.

5. Munyae M. Mulinge and Gwen N. Lesetedi, "The Genesis and Entrenchment
of Corruption in Sub-Saharan Africa: A Historical and International Contextu-
alisation," in *Corruption, Democracy and Good Governance in Africa: Essays on
Accountability and Ethical Behaviour*, Kwame Frimpong and Gloria Jacques, eds.,
Gaborone, Botswana: Lightbooks, 1997; *Nchekelako: An Afronet Reader on Corruption in Zambia*, Lusaka: Zambia: Afronet, 2002.

6. Morris Szeftel, "'Eat with Us: Managing Corruption and Patronage under Zambia's
Three Republics, 1964–99." *Journal of Contemporary African Studies* 18, no. 2
(2000): 207–224.

7. Interview with Mark Chona.

8. Michelo Hansungule, "The Underlying Causes of Corruption In Zambian Society," in *Promoting and Protecting Integrity in Public Life in Zambia* 1, Sibalawa
Mwaanga, ed., Lusaka: Anti-Corruption Commission Zambia, 2001.

9. Peter Burnell, "Legislative-Executive Relations in Zambia: Parliamentary Reform
on the Agenda." *Journal of Contemporary African Studies* 21, no. 1 (2003):
47–68.

10. Siri Gloppen, Roberto Gargarella, and Elin Skaar, eds. *Democratization and the
Judiciary: The Accountability Function of Courts in New Democracies*, London:
Frank Cass, 2004.

11. Ibid.

12. Interview with the former president Kenneth Kaunda.

13. Interview with Professor Alfred Chanda (Transparency International Zambia).

14. The editor of Zambia's independent national newspaper, *The Post*, was harassed
and arrested after publishing articles critical of the Chiluba administration.

15. Constitution of the Republic of Zambia: Part IV, Article 43, Subsection 3.

16. Opposition parties include the Forum for Democracy and Development (FDD),
Heritage Party, Patriotic Front, United National Independence Party (UNIP), and
United Party for National Development (UPND).

17. Interviews, multiple and confidential.

18. The Oasis Forum was founded on February 21, 2001, and named after the dilapidated restaurant that hosted its first meeting. Member organizations included

the Law Association of Zambia, the NGO Coordinating Committee, the Zambia Episcopal Conference, the Christian Council of Zambia, and the Evangelical Fellowship of Zambia. The donation by the Danish Embassy was disclosed in an interview with diplomats.

19. Interview with attorneys who instigated the proceedings.
20. Gloppen et al., *Democratization*. Summary of tribunal findings.
21. *The Post*, July 10–15, 2001.
22. An estate agent was jailed for two years for calling president Chiluba "stupid." *The Post*, October 21, 2001.
23. *The Post*, June 25, 2002.
24. Ibid.
25. Clancy and Chan, *Zambia*.
26. Mwanawasa was the first Zambian lawyer to be appointed advocate and solicitor of the Supreme Court of England and Wales.
27. *The Post*, August 27, 2001.
28. *The Post*, November 13, 2001.
29. Mwanawasa, 29.16 percent; Mazoka, 27.15 percent. For full election analysis, see Lise Rakner and Lars Svåsand: "From Dominant to Competitive Party System: The Zambian Experiences 1991–2001." *Party Politics* 10, no. 1 (2004): 49–68.
30. Michael Meadowcroft, *The European Union Election Observation Mission, Final Statement on the Zambian Elections*, 2001, Lusaka: February 5, 2001.
31. The Carter Center, *Post-election Statement on Zambia Elections*, January 31, 2002; the Foundation for Democratic Process, *Zambia's 2001 Tripartite Elections: Report*, 2002; "Press Release," Non-Governmental Organizations Coordinating Committee, January 1, 2002.
32. *Anderson Kambela Mazoka and Others v. Levy Patrick Mwanawasa and Others*, SCZ/EP/01/02/03/2002. The Mwanawasa Presidential Petition, the Supreme Court of Zambia.
33. Full Speech by President Mr. Levy Patrick Mwanawasa, Zambia Government Archives, SC, the special meeting of Parliament on July 11, 2002.
34. Ibid.
35. The single exception is the Danish Embassy's investment in the Oasis Forum. The Danish ambassador at the time, Mads Sandau-Jensen, reputed to be a "progressive risk taker," took an atypical interest in Zambian civil society movements.
36. Interviews with prosecutors and investigators.
37. Interviews with investigator and diplomats.
38. Mark Osiel, *Mass Atrocity, Collective Memory and the Law*, New Brunswick, NJ: Transaction Publications, 1997.
39. The Task Force was set up by government decree, or "gazette," as a substitute for the ACC. It consists of Zambia Police, the ACC, the Drug Enforcement Commission, Zambia Revenue Authority, and the Zambia Intelligence Authorities. It is legally empowered to investigate and prosecute financial crimes to have taken place between 1991 and 2001.
40. *Frederick Titus Jacob Chiluba v. the Attorney General*, Supreme Court of Zambia (Case: 2002/HP/063).
41. *The Post*, August 20, 2004.

42. The Minister for Justice and Attorney General at that time, George Kunda, is accused by investigators of taking an inappropriate interest in the workings of the trials. (Sources: interviews with diplomats, prosecutors, and investigators.)

43. *The Post*, December 5, 2002; January 30, February 22, February 26, March 8, June 15, July 11, and December 8, 2003; May 11 and August 6, 2004.

44. Court reports, "Dr. Bulaya Case," *The Post*, May and June 2005.

45. Margaret Keck and Kathryn Sikkink, *Activists beyond Borders*, Ithaca: Cornell University Press, 1998.

46. Prosecuting attorneys say they were at one point expected to volunteer pro bono legal advice to the state.

47. Interview with Mark Chona.

48. Ibid.

49. In the United States, they met with representatives from the Justice Department, Treasury, World Bank, International Monetary Fund, State Department, National Security Council, USAID, and Financial Intelligence Unit.

50. Alison Brysk, *The Politics of Human Rights in Argentina: Protest, Change, and Democratization*, Stanford: Stanford University Press, 1994.

51. In one single case read out in court, there was a list of 169 separate indictments involving seven codefendants. *The Post*, August 6, 2003.

52. In early 2004, after heated disagreements with Task Force prosecutors, the Director of Public Prosecutions was removed from office in circumstances that appeared to contravene due process. *The Post*, January, 2004; interviews with prosecutors.

53. Ireland and Canada were initially involved in anticorruption assistance but later backed out. The United States did not provide financial assistance, although according to comments by the U.S. deputy chief, the cost of technical assistance to investigators amounted to $3 million. *The Post*, March 6, 2004. Investments were made in installments: 1) December 2002–November 2003: $1,862,000; 2) June–August 2004: $840,000; 3) September–December 2004: $1,000,000. (Source: Confidential documents.)

54. Missions pledged $2 million each.

55. Interviews with diplomats.

56. Ibid.

57. Gloppen et al., *Democratization*.

58. Ibid.

59. Ibid.

60. Ibid.

61. The next month, the High Court granted an injunction to freeze the worldwide assets of Chiluba and four others, amounting to a total of $13 million.

62. *Zambia v. Meer Care and Desai*, High Court Judgment (2007) EWHC 925 (Executive Summary).

63. *The Post*, April 28, 2004. Chiluba's requests were not granted.

64. *Zambia v. Meer Care & Desai*, High Court Case: (2007) EWHC 925 (Executive Summary).

65. Ibid.

66. When asked his thoughts on the civil action, Chiluba responded: "It is absurd. If our courts are lacking in capacity we should strengthen the capacity of our

8

A Justice "Trickle-Down": Rwanda's First Postgenocide President on Trial

Lars Waldorf

During the fifth commemoration of the 1994 Rwandan genocide, then-president Pasteur Bizimungu startled the audience by accusing one of the assembled dignitaries, Bishop Augustin Misago, of genocide. Three years later, the new president, Paul Kagame, used the genocide ceremony in turn to denounce Bizimungu for ethnic "divisionism." Whereas Bishop Misago was acquitted, Bizimungu was convicted and sentenced to fifteen years (ironically, he spent almost five years in Bishop Misago's old prison quarters before being pardoned). All told, Bizimungu can consider himself lucky, having fared better than any of his predecessors in office: Gregoire Kayibanda was starved to death in prison after being overthrown in a military coup in 1973, Juvenal Habyarimana was killed in April 1994 when his plane was shot down, and Theodore Sindukwabo died of cholera in exile after having presided over the genocide.

Bizimungu's trial offers a revealing glimpse of Rwanda's post-genocide transition, which is so often obscured by Western shame and Rwandan spin: an increasingly authoritarian, one-party state has instrumentalized ethnicity and the genocide to silence political opponents and independent civil society organizations. The 2004 trial itself had all the drama of a badly staged show trial: political machinations, ludicrous accusations, recanted confessions, and a predictable ending. Furthermore, like every show trial, it unwittingly showed up the gap between power and legitimacy, between the ruler and the rule of law.

Four years later, Bizimungu's trial was suddenly subject to renewed scrutiny in a London magistrate's court as four Rwandans battled extradition back to Rwanda to stand trial on genocide charges. The Rwandans argued they could not get a fair trial in Rwanda. Their witnesses repeatedly invoked the

The author is deeply indebted to Allison Des Forges, Chris Huggins, and Sarah Wells for sharing their observations of the Bizimungu trial.

Bizimungu trial not only as an example of an unfair trial, but also to make the point that the presence of international observers would not deter the government from staging further show trials. Their most well-known witness, Paul Rusesabagina, the former Rwandan hotel manager whose story was made into the film *Hotel Rwanda*, testified that Bizimungu was accused "because he was speaking a different language from the RPF [Rwandan Patriotic Front].... Witnesses are created and false charges are created and invented."[1]

This chapter begins with a brief sketch of Rwandan history, focusing on the genocide and the postgenocide political transition, which provide the backdrop for Bizimungu's dramatic rise and fall. It then provides an overview of Rwanda's highly politicized judicial system, which pursues accountability for the genocide while ensuring impunity for the current regime's war crimes. The chapter continues by discussing the Bizimungu case in some detail. It concludes with some reflections on the trial's implications for the theory of a "justice cascade" in Central Africa.

HISTORICAL BACKGROUND

Bizimungu's personal and political journey is intertwined with the tragic history of ethnic politics between the majority Hutu and minority Tutsi in Rwanda. Hutu and Tutsi are socially constructed ethnic identities: both groups speak the same language, share the same culture, practice the same religion, live in integrated communities, and often intermarry.[2] Bizimungu was born in 1950 to a Hutu father and Tutsi mother, but in Rwanda's patrilineal society he is considered Hutu.

Hutu and Tutsi were somewhat fluid sociopolitical categories in precolonial times. The Belgian colonialists, however, fixed Hutu and Tutsi as immutable racial identities and viewed the Tutsi as racially superior "Hamites" who had supposedly come from Ethiopia. The Belgians imposed a system of ethnic identity cards and favored the Tutsi elite who had governed the precolonial kingdom. In 1959, three years before independence, the Belgians suddenly switched allegiance from the Tutsi elite to the Hutu majority and condoned the ensuing anti-Tutsi violence. Approximately 120,000 Tutsi fled the violence and became refugees in neighboring countries.[3]

Gregoire Kayibanda's First Republic (1962–1973) engaged in periodic pogroms against Tutsi, often in response to incursions from Tutsi guerrillas, who sought to reinstate the Tutsi monarchy. Major Juvenal Habyarimana toppled Kayibanda in a military coup in 1973, shifting power and patronage from Hutu in central Rwanda to those in the northwest. Although Habyarimana halted violence against Tutsi, he instituted discriminatory quotas in education and hiring. In the late 1980s, the Rwandan economy, which was built on coffee and tea exports, declined sharply due to falling commodity prices and structural adjustment. International donors also began pressuring Habyarimana to replace one-party rule with multiparty democracy.

Bizimungu's Rise

Bizimungu first rose to prominence in 1990 when Habyarimana unexpectedly appointed him to be director general of Electrogaz, the energy parastatal corporation. Although Bizimungu was from the same northwest province as the president, he was not a member of the president's inner circle, and his brother, an army colonel, had recently been assassinated.[4] At the end of August 1990, Bizimungu fled to Uganda along with his close friend Valens Kajeguhakwa, a wealthy Tutsi businessman, and joined the Rwandan Patriotic Front, a rebel movement consisting predominantly of Tutsi exiles in Uganda, which demanded the right of return for all Tutsi refugees.[5] As Bizimungu later explained, "At that time [1990], the Tutsi were considered pariahs, so that's why I went to fight on their side."[6]

In October 1990, the RPF invaded Rwanda, setting off a civil war that lasted almost four years. Bizimungu quickly became the public face of the RPF, which was anxious to appeal to the Hutu majority inside the country. He became one of the RPF's principal negotiators during the drawn-out peace talks, which finally resulted in a shaky agreement in 1993. Despite the peace accords, both sides continued to prepare for war. On April 6, 1994, unknown assailants shot down Habyarimana's plane, killing all on board.[7] Hutu extremists seized control of the state and launched an extermination campaign against the Tutsi. They incited genocide by deploying racist stereotypes of Tutsi as "Ethiopians" who wanted to reimpose a feudal monarchy and dispossess the Hutu majority. They also broadcast hate propaganda over the radio that portrayed Tutsi civilians as a "fifth column" of the RPF. By the time the genocide ended in July 1994, with the RPF's military victory, at least half a million Tutsi, as well as thousands of Hutu, had been killed.[8]

Bizimungu became president of a new "national unity" government in July 1994, but real power lay with the military commander of the RPF, Paul Kagame, who became vice president and defense minister. Notably, Kagame did not swear allegiance to the new president.[9] Within a year, Prime Minister Faustin Twagiramungu and Interior Minister Seth Sendashonga, both Hutu, fled into exile, where they denounced the RPF for monopolizing power and killing Hutu civilians. Several other high-ranking Hutu officials also left the government, and sometimes the country. As the most prominent Hutu

member left in the RPF, Bizimungu came across as a convincing inter-
locutor to sympathetic foreign journalists like the *New Yorker's* Philip
Gourevitch:

> It annoyed Kagame and his RPF colleagues that Rwanda's new government
> was routinely described in the international press as his government and
> labeled "Tutsi-dominated" or, more pointedly, "minority-dominated." ... As
> President Pasteur Bizimungu, who was Hutu, told me, to speak of Tutsi dom-
> ination echoed "the slogans or the way of portraying things of the extremists,"
> when for the first time in the hundred years since colonization, "there are
> authorities in this country, Hutu and Tutsi, who are putting in place policy so
> that people may share the same fundamental rights and obligations irrespec-
> tive of their ethnic background – and the extremists don't feel happy about
> that."[10]

It is not without irony, then, that Kagame later portrayed Bizimungu as an
anti-Tutsi extremist for having criticized Tutsi domination of the government.

The defining public moments of Bizimungu's presidency both took place
at Kibeho in southwestern Rwanda. In April 1995, RPF soldiers killed an
estimated two thousand Hutu civilians as they forcibly dismantled a camp
for internally displaced persons. Arriving on the scene afterward, Bizimungu
ordered exhumations for the benefit of the international community and at
the end of the day declared, "It is 338 corpses. If you pretend there are more,
tell me where they are, show them to me!"[11] Four years later, Bizimungu
went back to Kibeho for that year's genocide commemoration. He made
no apologies for the 1995 killings; rather, he claimed that the Interahamwe
(genocidal militia) "provoked an incident that the international community
decried, saying this was carried out against innocent civilians when in reality
these were Interahamwe who were killed."[12] In that same speech, Bizimungu
accused Bishop Misago of genocide and called for his prosecution.[13] A week
after Bizimungu's speech, the authorities arrested Misago on genocide charges.
This was a troubling reminder of the RPF's "accusatory practices" and its
influence over the judicial sector.[14]

It is tempting to dismiss Bizimungu as an opportunistic politician who
kowtowed to Tutsi hardliners within the RPF. One Rwanda expert clearly saw
Bizimungu in these terms: "It became quickly obvious that the RPF had no
intentions of sharing real power. Sharing the trappings, yes – and President
Pasteur Bizimungu soon became adept at ingratiating himself with the new real
power structure."[15] The quasi-independent journal *Umuseso* offered a similarly
harsh appraisal: "In truth, Bizimungu never had any power ... Bizimungu has
[always] been used as a cover for unity and reconciliation."[16] A former member

of the RPF's inner circle (and an Anglophone Tutsi) remembered Bizimungu quite differently, telling this author that Bizimungu had been a powerful and charismatic player. Indeed, Bizimungu largely engineered the RPF's shift to a policy of "national unity and reconciliation" through a series of consultations with political and business elites in 1998 and 1999.[17] For example, in late 1998, Bizimungu created a commission to explore how to speed up trials for the nearly 100,000 genocide suspects then in detention. That commission proposed what later became known as *gacaca* – an ambitious scheme involving thousands of community courts using lay judges.[18]

Bizimungu's Fall

In early 2000, the RPF successfully marginalized Tutsi critics, who, unlike Hutu opponents, could not be tarred as *génocidaires*. Francophone Tutsi survivors and their political allies had challenged the RPF's integration of suspected *génocidaires* into government ranks, the absence of reparations, and the concentration of power and wealth in the hands of the RPF's Anglophone Tutsi leadership. The RPF forced the speaker of Parliament, Joseph Sebarenzi, to resign in January 2000 over corruption allegations. When the RPF next accused Sebarenzi of plotting to reinstall the Tutsi king, he fled Rwanda. Two prominent Tutsi journalists followed him into exile after the government banned their newspaper for exposing the RPF's role in Sebarenzi's removal. The RPF also arrested Jean Mbanda, a survivor and parliamentarian, on corruption charges after he publicly criticized the government.

On February 28, the RPF forced the resignation of the Hutu prime minister, Pierre-Celestin Rwigyema, accusing him of corruption. After he fled to the United States, the Rwandan government added him to the list of top genocide suspects and unsuccessfully sought his extradition. On March 3, Bizimungu handed in a one-sentence letter to Parliament, resigning the presidency for "personal reasons."[19] In a subsequent interview, Bizimungu elaborated on the reasons behind his resignation:

> The first break [with President Kagame] dates from September 1999, when the RPF members in Parliament wrote Kagame to demand the dismissal of two Hutu ministers from the Socialist Party without consulting me. They accused them of corruption. I telephoned Kagame. He responded that these people could not hide themselves behind their ethnicity to gain impunity ... The problem was repeated two days later for six other Hutus in the government. I did not want to intervene officially to avoid criticism that I only intervene in favor of Hutu. I chose to defend Patrick Mazimpaka, the presidential aide, for he is Tutsi ... We spent months bickering. When I understood they were going to get rid of me, I took the initiative.[20]

At the time, however, "Senior [RPF] party members said Mr. Bizimungu was playing the ethnic card in defending a fellow Hutu, to try to deflect accusations of corruption which he himself was facing."[21]

Two days after Bizimungu's resignation, his aide, Assiel Kabera, was assassinated. Kabera, a prominent Tutsi survivor, had also been close to Sebarenzi. The subsequent flight of Kabera's two brothers ended the independence of the survivors' organizations: One brother was vice president of IBUKA, the main survivors' association, and the other was head of the survivors' assistance fund.[22] Bizimungu's old comrade, Kajeguhakwa, who had served as an RPF parliamentarian from 1994 to 1999, also fled after being accused of defrauding the bank he managed.

Bizimungu eventually launched a new political party called PDR-Ubuyanja (Party for Democracy and Renewal) on May 30, 2001. Five individuals signed the founding statutes: Bizimungu, Charles Ntakirutinka (the Social Democratic Party's representative at the Arusha peace talks and then a minister after the genocide), Major Sam Bigabiro (an RPF officer), Eugene Rwibasira (a former RPF member and deputy governor after the war), and Denis Ntakirutimana (a former prosecutor before the Kigali Appeals Court). Both Bigabiro and Rwibasira are Tutsi.

PDR-Ubuyanja's statutes called for "a system of governance where the participation of all ethnic groups must be arranged in a fashion to reassure all Rwandans, to stabilize society, and, at the same time, to permit democracy."[23] That seemingly anodyne statement represented a radical departure from RPF orthodoxy: it proposed a multiethnic system in place of a nonethnic system.[24] According to PDR-Ubuyanja, the RPF had monopolized power for itself and a small group of Tutsi under the pretense of creating a nonethnic system: "The real desire of the group taking the reins of power is to rely on a Tutsi grouping in all the sectors."[25] PDR-Ubuyanja's founders also criticized the RPF in harsh terms:

> The incapacity of the judicial system to render justice to survivors and suspects of the genocide and massacres, the use of the genocide by the government for its own political ends, the increasingly marked isolation of Rwanda in the concert of nations . . . the tensions and wars with our neighbors, the silence on certain crimes committed (i.e., by the RPF), all that denotes the lack of the rule of law . . . The aspirations for democracy are all smothered, as are the fundamental freedoms, while the RPF multiplies maneuvers for ensuring the monopolizing of power.[26]

The party's criticism of the "silence" surrounding RPF crimes made its inclusion of Major Bigabiro all the more peculiar. Bigabiro is the highest-ranking

RPF soldier convicted of massacring Hutu civilians (although his conviction was overturned on appeal).[27]

The cabinet banned PDR-Ubuyanja the same day Bizimungu announced its formation, claiming that no new political parties could be formed during the postgenocide transition period. In fact, the cabinet's action contravened the procedures for registering and suspending political parties set forth in the 1991 law on political parties and the 1993 Arusha Peace Accords, which were still in effect at the time.[28] Security forces broke up Bizimungu's press conference, detained him briefly, expelled diplomatic observers, and confiscated Bizimungu's recorded interviews from British Broadcast Company (BBC) and Voice of America (VOA) journalists. The following day, May 31, President Kagame cancelled all the privileges accrued to Bizimungu as a former president. In compliance with the cabinet's decision, Bizimungu and his colleagues called off PDR-Ubuyanja's constituent assembly, which had been scheduled for June 1. On June 3, high-ranking government officials held a press conference where they denounced PDR-Ubuyanja as divisionist.[29] Two days later, PDR-Ubuyanja's five principals sent an open letter to President Kagame denying the accusations of divisionism and arguing that the laws did not prohibit the creation of PDR-Ubuyanja.[30]

Not long after the banning of PDR, Bizimungu gave an interview to *Jeune Afrique L'intelligent*, which the government later used as evidence against him:

> We thought that with the RPF things would change, but we have been disappointed. We fought the Hutu regime of Juvenal Habyarimana, which controlled the institutions, the police, the banks, etc., but now, it is exactly the same thing. . . .
>
> We are convinced that if things continue, the Hutu will prepare for battle and in 10, 15, or 20 years they are going to chase[31] the Tutsi, with the consequences that one can imagine. It is necessary to arrange the mechanisms so that each community really participates in power. That will create a national identity that transcends the Hutu-Tutsi cleavage. Furthermore, here as in Burundi, the army is mono-ethnic. One cannot govern Rwanda with an army that is 100 percent Tutsi when 85 percent of the population is Hutu![32]

Bizimungu also criticized the RPF for turning Hutu into "second-class citizens."[33] He warned that, "If there is no change, the only option is violence. The war of 1990 is not finished."[34] Bizimungu ended the interview stating his willingness to pay the highest price. He did not have to wait long.

Authorities harassed Bizimungu and other PDR supporters over the next several months. In August 2001, Bizimungu and Ntakirutinka were attacked by street gangs, placed under brief house arrest, and had some of their property

searched and seized by police. Bizimungu's planned memoir was confiscated
in November before it could be printed. More seriously, a member of PDR-
Ubuyanja, Gratien Munyarubuga, was murdered at midday in the capital
in late December 2001. Another PDR-Ubuyanja member was arrested the
same month and released a few weeks later without charge. In January 2002,
authorities briefly detained the founders of Association Modeste et Innocent, a
religiously inspired nongovernmental organization (NGO) dedicated to conflict resolution, and charged them with attacking state security because they
had used the word *ubuyanja* in their journal's masthead.[35] In early 2002, the
government placed Bizimungu and Ntakirutinka under virtual house arrest,
although it allowed them to visit various Western embassies, where they pled
their cause. In a March 2002 open letter to the prime minister, Bizimungu and
Ntakirutinka complained that the government had violated their freedoms of
speech, religion, movement, and association.[36] Bizimungu also alleged that
he had been prohibited from attending Mass.

President Kagame attacked Bizimungu for the *Jeune Afrique* interview in
his April 7, 2002 speech commemorating the genocide:

> There are also some Rwandans who have learned nothing from the recent
> history of our country, like this person who predicts another genocide in five
> years...The height of tragedy is that he is received in embassies...where
> he makes politics over tea. What politics?...It is the politics that have killed
> these people...When our patience reaches its limits and we decide to hold
> them to account, no one will be able to save them.[37]

In this passage, Kagame skillfully linked Bizimungu's reception at foreign
embassies to the international community's failure to halt the 1994 genocide,
while reminding his audience that only the RPF could save the country from
a recurrence of genocide.[38]

Three weeks after Kagame's speech, Bizimungu and Ntakirutinka were
arrested on charges of endangering state security, fostering ethnic divisions,
and engaging in illegal political activities. The prosecutor subsequently modified the charges to plotting to overthrow the government, inciting rebellion, and forming a criminal association. That shifted the focus away from
PDR-Ubuyanja. Over the next several weeks, approximately twenty people
were arrested for allegedly supporting PDR-Ubuyanja.[39] Although most were
released after short periods in detention, six residents of Bizimungu's neighborhood were joined to the case against Bizumungu and Ntakirutinka. The
coaccused included a plumber who worked at the U.S. Embassy and the
treasurer of Ligue Rwandaise pour la Promotion et la Defense des Droits
de l'Homme (LIPRODHOR), the most independent Rwandan human rights
NGO at the time.[40]

The two-year pretrial detention of Bizimungu, Ntakirutinka, and their six alleged coconspirators coincided with important political developments that further tightened the RPF's grip on power. In early 2003, in advance of presidential and parliamentary elections (the first since the genocide), the government essentially banned the main opposition party, the Mouvement Democratic Republicain (MDR), by accusing it of promoting "ethnic divisionism" and "genocidal ideology." Several persons linked to MDR fled the country (including the former minister of defense), and five others disappeared (including an MDR parliamentarian and the former Supreme Court vice president). Not surprisingly, the 2003 elections consolidated the RPF's domination: President Kagame won 95 percent of the popular vote and the RPF garnered 74 percent amid credible reports of widespread fraud and intimidation.[41] In addition, a new constitution concentrated power in the presidency, limited judicial review of legislation abridging civil liberties, reduced political pluralism, and criminalized "any" form of division.[42] After the elections, the RPF stepped up its repression of independent civil society organizations and the press, going so far as to accuse Care International, BBC, and VOA, among others, of propagating "genocidal ideology."[43]

Rather than using his trial as a platform for denouncing the RPF during the 2003 election year, Bizimungu adopted a highly legalistic strategy that unsuccessfully challenged his pretrial detention on procedural grounds. He argued that the prosecutor should not have been permitted to modify the charges and therefore he should be tried for PDR-Ubuyanja's political activities (the charges in the arrest warrant) or released.[44] That argument kept the case tied up in pretrial motions, hearings, and appeals for the better part of two years.[45] By and large, Bizimungu shied away from political rhetoric, and he never directly criticized President Kagame. That approach not only appeared to legitimize the proceedings, but it also limited media coverage and popular interest.

RWANDA'S JUSTICE SYSTEM

To fully understand Bizimungu's trial, one must first understand Rwanda's national judicial system and its relationship with international criminal justice efforts.

National Justice

Rwanda inherited its civil law system from Belgium, its colonial master. Up until the 1994 genocide, "The Rwandan legal system had never been more than a corrupt caricature of justice."[46] Those who incited and perpetrated massacres against Tutsi civilians before 1994 were rarely, if ever, prosecuted and punished. The 1994 genocide devastated the judicial infrastructure and left the country with few lawyers and judges.

Following the genocide, the RPF arrested thousands of genocide suspects, often on the basis of unsubstantiated denunciations. By 2000, approximately 120,000 alleged *génocidaires* were crammed into Rwanda's prisons and communal jails.[47] From December 1996 to December 2006, the courts managed to try approximately ten thousand suspects.[48] To speed up trials and reduce the prison population, the government created an ambitious system of eleven thousand local community courts for lower-level genocide suspects. These courts were named for *gacaca*, a largely moribund "traditional" dispute-resolution mechanism. *Gacaca*, which started as a pilot project in 2002, has led to accusations against approximately eight hundred thousand people.

The quality of justice in national courts has been generally poor due to inadequate defense representation, lack of resources, and especially political interference.[49] The clearest examples of executive interference were the executive branch's wholesale removal of the Supreme Court in 1999 and its removal of six Supreme Court judges in 2002. On occasion, prosecutors and police rearrested genocide suspects after they had been acquitted. The government also brought genocide or corruption charges against some Hutu judges and prosecutors who refused to convict or arrest people for genocide.[50] Furthermore, no one has been arrested, let alone tried, for the assassinations and disappearances of the RPF's perceived political opponents.

Despite the RPF's pledge to end the impunity that characterized Rwanda from 1962 to 1994, it refuses to allow nonmilitary courts to hear allegations of war crimes and crimes against humanity committed by its soldiers. Military courts have tried only a few RPF soldiers for such crimes, and most received light sentences.[51]

The 2003 constitution and 2004 judicial reforms introduced elements of common law, which were more familiar to Anglophone Tutsi who had grown up in exile in Uganda and Tanzania and who now dominate the judicial sector. Parliament passed a series of laws in 2004 to streamline the judicial sector, strengthen judicial independence, increase professionalism, and reduce endemic corruption. Such ambitious law reform had a major, unintended consequence. Most judicial-sector activity was placed on hold in 2003 and 2004 as key government actors jockeyed for power and judicial-sector personnel worried about losing their jobs or authority. Courts stopped functioning for most of 2004, and no new genocide trials were heard that year. Numerous judicial-sector employees were fired, including some who met the new educational requirements.[52] That raised concerns about judicial independence, due process, and discrimination. Lower courts were forced to halt all activity in early 2006 as ambitious reforms were made throughout Rwanda's administrative structures.

International Justice

In the aftermath of the Rwandan genocide, the United Nations Security Council created the International Criminal Tribunal for Rwanda (ICTR), modeled on the International Criminal Tribunal for the Former Yugoslavia (ICTY) in the Hague. The ICTR has been dogged by corruption, mismanagement, and incompetence. The sluggish pace of genocide trials – just twenty-three full trials (involving twenty-nine accused) as of March 2008 – has been due to the absence of a clear prosecutorial strategy, poor case management and courtroom control by the judges, and a largely incompetent administration.[53] Nevertheless, the tribunal has apprehended most of the presumed genocidal leadership, and it is the first international tribunal to have convicted a former head of state (Prime Minister Jean Kambanda) of genocide.

The Rwandan government has taken a largely antagonistic attitude toward the ICTR.[54] Although Rwanda originally pushed for the tribunal's creation, it was the only country to vote against the Security Council resolution because it objected to the tribunal's location (in Tanzania rather than Rwanda), limited temporal jurisdiction (covering only 1994), primacy over Rwandan national courts, exclusion of civil parties, and refusal to apply the death penalty. Since then, Rwanda has roundly criticized the ICTR's poor performance. However, the main bone of contention between Rwanda and ICTR concerns the tribunal's jurisdiction over RPF war crimes. To date, Rwanda has succeeded in preventing the ICTR from investigating and indicting RPF soldiers for such crimes by threatening to end all cooperation with the tribunal.[55]

Rwanda has cooperated with several national judicial systems that have tried Rwandans for crimes linked to the 1994 genocide.[56] Since 2006, the Rwandan government has demanded that European jurisdictions and the ICTR transfer or extradite genocide suspects to Rwanda to stand trial there. To encourage such transfers, the Rwandan government abolished the death penalty in 2007. That same year, the U.K. government began extradition proceedings against four accused Rwandans.

Bizimungu's Trial

Bizimungu's trial finally began in earnest on March 31, 2004, almost two years after his arrest. By then, the RPF had already accomplished its main goal of preventing Bizimungu and his supporters from challenging its hold on power in the 2003 parliamentary and presidential elections. So why go ahead with the trial itself? And why a trial on political charges rather than one solely focused on corruption charges? After all, trials of deposed political figures can be risky affairs. As Saddam Hussein and Slobodan Milošević have shown, former heads of state may use their trials as public platforms to denounce their successors.

Like many other political show trials, Bizimungu's trial served as a spectacle of power and an instrument of pedagogy. The trial was meant to demonstrate that political dissent would not be tolerated and that ethnic discourse would be criminalized. The trial further showed that the international community would not, and could not, protect political dissidents (like Bizimungu), human rights defenders (like LIPRODHOR's treasurer), or even its own Rwandan staff (like the U.S. Embassy's plumber). In that sense, it complemented the parliamentary report (released the same month as the Bizimungu verdict) that leveled accusations of genocidal ideology against internationally funded Rwandan civil society organizations (such as LIPRODHOR), international civil society organizations (such as CARE International), and embassy personnel (a named Rwandan employee of the Dutch Embassy).[57]

The trial took place before a three-judge panel of Kigali City's Tribunal de Première Instance in a small, shabby courtroom that could not accommodate all the family members, diplomats, human rights observers, journalists, and curious onlookers. The trial spanned two months, although there were only twelve days of actual hearings. Significantly, the trial was held during the anniversary period for the Rwanda genocide.

At the outset, the prosecutor charged Bizimungu, Ntakirutinka, and their six coaccused with plotting to overthrow the government,[58] inciting rebellion through false rumors,[59] and creating a criminal association[60] from May 2001 (the date of PDR-Ubuyanja's founding) until Bizimungu's arrest on April 19, 2002. He also separately accused Bizimungu with the embezzlement of public funds, illegal possession of a firearm, and forgery. In his opening statement, the prosecutor claimed that Bizimungu "hid himself behind a so-called political party PDR-Ubuyanja . . . simply to camouflage the expression of his hate towards Tutsi that he has had for a long time, hate shown . . . in the statements he gave to the journalist at *Jeune Afrique l'Intelligent*."[61]

The trial got off to a sputtering start for the prosecution. The first prosecution witness dramatically recanted his earlier statement to the police, saying he had given it out of fear after being arrested in April 2002 as an alleged PDR-Ubuyanja supporter.[62] He was quickly hustled out of the courtroom. When the defense later tried to recall him to give testimony for the accused, he could not be found. The second witness claimed she and the first witness were members of PDR-Ubuyanja and that they had held several party meetings at the parish church in Murambi near where Bizimungu lived. Bizimungu pointed out there was no parish church at that location. When he asked the witness if she had heard any messages in those alleged meetings to trouble security, she replied no. The third witness, another supposed PDR member, contradicted the accounts of meetings given by the second witness. Under cross-examination from Bizimungu, he admitted that he did not know any of the accused. The fourth witness, Theogene Bugingo, spun a fabulist tale that involved efforts to recruit street children for armed insurrection, blow up an electric power station in the capital, assassinate high-ranking security officials, and terrorize genocide survivors. He was the only witness who inculpated the six coaccused, but his testimony was riddled with contradictions.[63]

The prosecution's case largely rested on the testimony of four witnesses who had been involved in PDR-Ubuyanja's founding. Major Bigabiro testified that Bizimungu and Ntakirutinka had advocated a fifty-fifty division of government and army posts between Hutu and Tutsi in conversations with him. According to him, they also claimed the RPF had killed Hutu civilians. Ntakirutinka later responded by reminding Bigabiro he had been imprisoned for such killings. A second PDR-Ubuyanja member asserted that Bizimungu had given him money to distribute a critique by a former RPF major living in exile in Uganda. According to the third party member, Bizimungu expressed the desire that each ethnic group should have equal representation in the army. However, he also acknowledged that Bizimungu had rejected the idea of forming a terrorist unit, thus contradicting Bugingo's earlier testimony. Finally, the fourth member testified that Bizimungu had said they would overturn the existing government.

When his turn came, Bizimungu made several arguments in his own defense.[64] First, he repeated his procedural argument that the prosecution should have been based on the laws governing political parties.[65] He argued that the government acted illegally in banning PDR-Ubuyanja but that he had nonetheless respected that decision by ceasing PDR-Ubuyanja's activities. He contended that the party opposed genocidal ideology:

> The statutes of PDR-Ubuyanja say it is necessary to put in place a special tribunal for the genocide and other crimes against humanity and to severely punish the planners. Our statutes also state that true reconciliation is to see the wrong the Hutu have done to the Tutsi and Twa, but also to see the wrong that the Tutsi have done to the Hutu and Twa so corrections can be made to avoid falling into the same error again. . . . In the statutes, it says that each Rwandan citizen has human dignity no matter what his ethnic appearance. Also, we underlined the brotherhood and solidarity between Rwandans.

Throughout his testimony, Bizimungu sought to underscore his commitment to ethnic harmony in Rwanda, while implicitly accusing the RPF of favoring the Tutsi:

> I never incited the Hutu to hate against the Tutsi because I added [in the *Jeune Afrique* interview] that it is necessary to set up mechanisms so that each community really participates in power.... The idea of violence is not ours because I have equally stated ... that we are going to create a party and we fight with peaceful means.

Finally, Bizimungu referred to his and Ntakirutinka's personal history to refute the charges that they were divisionists:

> I had a Tutsi friend, Valens Kajeguhakwa, who, in 1990, was under police surveillance. Seeing my friend's situation, which was caused by his ethnic appearance, I sacrificed myself for him.... We went together into exile leaving behind me a very lucrative job, my brothers and sisters, my friends, my colleagues from work and lots of others. And everyone perished. Arriving in Uganda, I met other people who had the same idea as me: the unity and reconciliation of Rwandans and the struggle against injustice founded on nepotism.... We did enormous work at risk to ourselves. For example, my colleague Charles Ntakirutinka lost 16 close members of his family, of which the majority were intellectual elites. That is why I say to you that I have never had divisionist ideas.

When the presiding judge questioned Bizimungu about the *Jeune Afrique* interview, he responded: "More than six times, I have talked about each ethnic group having effective participation in power so that each ethnic group will be reassured and will engage in peaceful debates."

Bizimungu and Ntakirutinka had no witnesses willing to testify in their defense.[66] Consequently, Bizimungu had to make do with pointing out inconsistencies in the testimonies of the prosecution witnesses. In particular, he emphasized how other prosecution witnesses contradicted Bugingo's testimony that Bizimungu had created a guerrilla force comprising soldiers and street children. Bizimungu also stated that none of the six coaccused were PDR-Ubuyanja members.[67]

During the case, the presiding judge displayed bias against the lead defendants. At one point, the judge asked Bizimungu how he could distinguish Hutu from Tutsi. The judge then selected four people in the courtroom to come forward and asked Bizimungu to identify them as Hutu or Tutsi. Bizimungu sidestepped the judge's efforts to have him incriminate himself as a divisionist. On the third day of trial, the judge refused to allow Ntakirutinka to follow up on Bizimungu's questioning of a prosecution witness. When the defense lawyer intervened to remind the judge of a defendant's right to examine the witnesses against him, the judge ordered the lawyer immediately imprisoned for forty-eight hours for contempt[68] and then tried to continue the trial in the lawyer's absence.

In closing argument, the prosecutor stated that Bizimungu's interview in *Jeune Afrique* formed the basis for the charge that he had incited rebellion through false rumors. He also implausibly claimed the interview was linked to attacks by Interahamwe in northern Rwanda in mid-2001.[69] The prosecutor demanded the maximum possible sentences for all the accused: life sentences for plotting violence against the government, twenty years for forming a criminal association, and ten years for inciting the population with false rumors.[70]

On June 7, 2004, the trial court convicted Bizimungu of spreading rumors to incite rebellion, creating a criminal association, and embezzling state funds, and sentenced him to five years on each count. The judges sentenced Ntakirutinka to ten years for spreading rumors to incite rebellion and creating a criminal association. All six coaccused were sentenced to five years for belonging to a criminal association. The court found the prosecution had not proved its case that the accused had plotted violence against the government.

Although lengthy, the decision mostly summarized witness testimony and the parties' arguments and examinations. The court presented its findings of facts and conclusions of law in a conclusory manner. It gave the following grounds for convicting Bizimungu and Ntakirutinka of spreading rumors to incite rebellion:

> In a document they called "party statutes"...they published...that the Rwandan administration within all the [government] institutions...are composed of a sole ethnic group, the Tutsi; that the RPF has scorned human rights...and the government exploited the genocide and genocide survivors for its own political ends...Witness testimonies...all affirm that in the meetings directed by Pasteur Bizimungu and Charles Ntakirutinka they said that the RPF had massacred the people they had come to liberate, that all the posts within all government organs are in the hands of Tutsi only (the army, the police, as well as others), that the Hutu have been maltreated.[71]

The court convicted the six coaccused of forming a criminal association based on the uncorroborated (and indeed contradicted) testimony of a single witness, Bugingo. The court justified its reliance on Bugingo's testimony by citing two treatises on evidence and the ICTR's *Musema* judgment: "As it has been said in the trial of Alfred Musema, a sole witness when questioned often can sometimes contradict himself. That does not prevent the court from giving weight to the statements of a single witness who seems inconsistent in his statements."

All the parties appealed the trial court's decision. The High Court declined to hear the appeal, citing jurisdictional constraints. After Bizimungu and Ntakirutinka litigated and lost that issue, five Supreme Court judges (with the Supreme Court president presiding) finally heard the appeal over the course of four days between November 25 and December 2, 2005.

On appeal, Bizimungu and his codefendants argued that the trial court failed to apply the correct standard of proof, particularly with respect to Bugingo's uncorroborated and controverted testimony. They cited article 153 of the Code of Criminal Procedure (2005), which provides that "[a]ny doubt should be resolved in favor of the accused." They further argued that the court should have found the testimony of the prosecution witnesses either inadmissible or unreliable because they had not been prosecuted for the crimes to which they had confessed.[72] Bizimungu also sought to appeal directly to the professional pride of the Supreme Court judges:

> Our judicial system has recently known a reform, the goal of which was to combat corruption, ignorance, and interference. Thus, we say "Hurrah! Viva justice! Life is beautiful!" Rwandans are finally going to get the equitable justice they have been waiting for. I hope that this Supreme Court, which was instituted after that reform, will redress the wrongs done to us by the prosecutor and the trial court which went so far as to knowingly violate the law... [and] that this Supreme Court will install a justice by law and not a justice without law.

The Supreme Court issued its decision on February 17, 2006. Finding the testimony of Bugingo inadmissible and not credible under the Code of Criminal Procedure, it overturned the convictions of the six coaccused and ordered their immediate release. At that point, the six had served almost four years of their original five-year sentences. By contrast, the Supreme Court upheld the convictions of Bizimungu and Ntakirutinka for criminal association and inciting rebellion. It also overturned their acquittal for plotting against the government and gave them ten-year sentences to be served concurrently with their existing sentences.

In early April 2006, Bizimungu sent a short letter to President Kagame requesting clemency on the basis of his poor health. Bizimungu stopped short of making an apology in his letter: "In my trial, which has ended, I have been guided by my conscience, which has shown me that I never had the intention to sin, do wrong, or break the law."[73] A year later, on April 6, 2007 (the day before the thirteenth genocide commemoration ceremony), President Kagame unexpectedly announced an official pardon for Bizimungu. That pardon broadly prohibits Bizimungu from doing "any thing, in word, deed, or writing, which could result [in] the public disorder or public disquiet and to avoid any action whatsoever that could lead to recidivism."[74] Not surprisingly, Bizimungu has largely maintained a discreet silence since his release. Some Rwanda experts attributed the pardon to subtle pressure from international donors, particularly the United States.[75] Perhaps, but its timing and manner seemed designed to convey that President Kagame had outlasted international pressure and finally acted out of clemency. As of March 2008, Bizimungu's codefendant, Ntakirutinka, was still languishing inside Kigali's red-brick, crenellated prison, hoping perhaps for the day when Amnesty International might draw attention to his case.

International donors and human rights organizations were publicly critical of the initial trial.[76] The European Union declared that it "appears to have fallen short of international standards of fairness and impartiality."[77] In its 2005 human rights report, the U.S. State Department criticized the trial:

> The trial...was marred by a lack of corroborating evidence against the defense and was characterized by many international observers as having fallen short of international standards of fairness and impartiality. During the course of the trial, Bizimungu's attorney was detained for 24 hours for contempt of court, the judge prevented the defense from fully cross-examining the prosecution's witnesses, and the defense was only allowed to present a limited number of witnesses.[78]

In 2004, Amnesty International labeled Bizimungu a "political prisoner" and "possible prisoner of conscience," whose arrest, detention, and trial "fell far short of international standards of fairness." Amnesty concluded that the verdict and sentences are "further proof of the government's willingness to subvert the [Rwandan] criminal justice system in an attempt to eliminate all potential political opposition."[79] LIPRODHOR, the Rwandan human rights NGO whose treasurer was one of the six coaccused, did not issue any statement. A year and half later, it noted that all "the [Rwandan] human rights collectives and associations have observed a prudent silence on this case."[80] That spoke volumes about the emasculation of Rwanda's human rights community.

The official government newspaper, *Imvaho*, focused its coverage of the verdict on Bizimungu's conviction for embezzling public funds that had been allocated for genocide orphans and for reburying genocide victims. By contrast, the quasi-independent journal, *Umuseso*, emphasized the international community's criticism of Bizimungu's trial and called on President Kagame to pardon Bizimungu.[81] What made *Umuseso*'s stance courageous – by Rwandan standards – is that the editor of another journal was expelled in mid-2002, shortly after he published an editorial calling for Bizimungu's release.[82]

CONCLUSION

At first glance, Rwanda appears to be an example of an international justice cascade in sub-Saharan Africa, a region long dominated by impunity for gross human rights abuses.[83] After all, the Rwandan government has shown a vigorous commitment to prosecuting and punishing large numbers of *génocidaires* (including many former government officials) through national courts and community courts (*gacaca*). Rwanda has also worked with the ICTR and foreign jurisdictions to prosecute genocide suspects. Furthermore, international donors have spent hundreds of millions of dollars to increase judicial capacity and improve the rule of law. At the same time, however, the government has successfully resisted international pressure to try its own soldiers for war crimes committed in Rwanda and the Democratic Republic of Congo.[84]

Bizimungu's trial represents a throwback to an earlier generation of political show trials designed to destroy or disgrace political opponents. Yet for all its flaws, the trial did reveal something of a "trickle-down effect" of justice norms. First, unlike President Kayibanda, who died in pretrial detention, Bizimungu did get a public trial. Second, the trial and appeal conformed to some of the minimum due process standards guaranteed by the Rwandan Constitution and the international human rights covenants ratified by Rwanda. Third, the trial court invoked international criminal jurisprudence (the ICTR's *Musema* judgment) to support its most controversial evidentiary decision. Finally, the Supreme Court did overturn the unjust convictions of the six coaccused. These aspects probably resulted from a mix of political calculation and internalized justice norms on the part of various Rwandan elites. The RPF leadership was willing to defy the international community by arresting and detaining Bizimungu, but it still felt enough international pressure and concern for its own legitimacy to put on a political show trial that had the semblance of a fair trial. In the end, then, Bizimungu's trial points up the need to do a better job of explaining the (halfhearted) realization of transitional justice norms by successor regimes that are not transitioning toward democracy.

NOTES

1. Author's notes from hearings in *Republic of Rwanda v. Emmanuel Ntezilyayo*, Westminster Magistrates Court, April 3, 2008.
2. Hutu are thought to comprise about 85 percent, Tutsi 14 percent, and the indigenous Twa forest people less than 1 percent of Rwanda's 9 million people, although for political reasons the 2002 census did not consider ethnicity. National Census Service, *A Synthesis of the Analyses of the 2002 Census of Rwanda*, Kigali: Republic of Rwanda, 2005, 3. Out of convention, Hutu and Tutsi are described here as ethnic

groups. There is a contentious debate about the origins and content of differences between Hutu and Tutsi. Catherine Newbury, *The Cohesion of Oppression: Clientship and Ethnicity in Rwanda, 1860–1960*, New York: Columbia University Press, 1988, 10–16; Johan Pottier, *Re-imagining Rwanda: Conflict, Survival and Disinformation in the Late Twentieth Century*, Cambridge: Cambridge University Press, 2002, 109–123.

3. Gerard Prunier, *The Rwanda Crisis: History of a Genocide*, New York: Columbia University Press, 1999, 53 n. 19.

4. Valens Kajeguhakwa, *Rwanda: De la terre de paix à la terre de sang et apres?*, Paris: Fayard, 2001, 234–235; Colin M. Waugh, *Paul Kagame and Rwanda: Power, Genocide, and the Rwandan Patriotic Front*, London: McFarland, 2004, 120, 152.

5. For an account of Bizimungu's flight, see Kajeguhakwa, *Rwanda*, 260–264. The RPF's early history is recounted by Gerard Prunier, *The Rwanda Crisis*, 126–133, and Waugh, *Paul Kagame*, 36–45.

6. Pasteur Bizimungu, "Je suis prêt a payer le prix fort" (interview with Valerie Thorin), *Jeune Afrique/L'Intelligent* No. 2112 (July 3–9, 2001): 27. Also, Bizimungu's wife is Tutsi.

7. In November 2006, a French investigating magistrate charged the RPF leadership, including President Kagame, with downing Habyarimana's plane. Jen-Louis Bruguiere, "Délivrance de mandats d'arret internationaux," *Le Monde*, November 17, 2006. Available at www.medias.lemonde.fr/mmpub/edt/doc/20061127/838957_rwanda-rapport-bruguiere.pdf.

8. The best single account of the Rwandan genocide, which examines it from local, national, and international perspectives, is by Allison Des Forges, *Leave None to Tell the Story: Genocide in Rwanda*, New York: Human Rights Watch, 1999. A superb account of the genocide's local-level dynamics is offered in Scott Straus, *The Order of Genocide: Race, Power, and War in Rwanda*, Ithaca: Cornell University Press, 2006.

9. Waugh, *Paul Kagame*, 152.

10. Philip Gourevitch, *We Wish to Inform You That Tomorrow We Will Be Killed with Our Families*, New York: Farrar, Strauss & Giroux, 1998, 222.

11. Pottier, *Re-imagining Rwanda*, 161.

12. Pasteur Bizimungu, "Allocution du President Pasteur Bizimungu prononcée à Kibeho a l'occasion de la commemoration du cinquieme anniversaire du genocide," April 7, 1999 (unpublished).

13. Ibid.

14. On the accusations against Misago, see Gourevitch, *We Wish to Inform You*, 136–140. The RPF elite hold the Catholic Church partly responsible for the genocide. See, for example, Tom Ndahiro, "The Church's Blind Eye to Genocide in Rwanda," in *Genocide in Rwanda: Complicity of the Churches?*, Carol Rittner et al., eds., St. Paul, MN: Paragon House, 2004. The factors behind Misago's acquittal remain murky, and the government prosecutor subsequently fled the country. A 2004 parliamentary commission report repeated the allegations against Misago as if he had never been acquitted and criticized various Catholic churches for spreading genocidal ideology. Front Line, *Front Line Rwanda: Disappearances, Arrests, Threats, Intimidation and Co-option of Human Rights Defenders, 2001–2004*,

Dublin: Front Line, 2005, 25–28. Available at http://www.frontlinedefenders.org/files/en/FrontLineRwandaReport.pdf.

15. Prunier, *The Rwanda Crisis*, 367.

16. Emmanuel Niyonteze, "Ma vérité: Bizimungu a été utilisé comme un trèfle de l'unité et de la réconciliation," *Umuseso*, No. 249 (March 19–25): 2005.

17. That shift was made possible by the government's successful (although often brutal) counterinsurgency campaign in northwest Rwanda and eastern Congo, which significantly reduced the threat posed by the former genocidal forces.

18. For more details on the role of Bizimungu and the commission in formulating *gacaca*, see Alice Karekezi, "Juridictions gacaca: Lutte contre l'impunitie et promotion de la reconciliation nationale," *Cahiers du Centre de Gestion des Conflits* 1 (2000): 17–18.

19. Pasteur Bizimungu, March 23, 2000, Resignation Letter, *Official Gazette Special Issue* (March 28, 2000): 10.

20. Bizimungu, "Je suis prêt," 26.

21. "Analysis: Why Bizimungu Mattered," *BBC News*, March 23, 2000.

22. Human Rights Watch, *The Search for Security and Human Rights Abuses*, 2000, 10–11; see also Filip Reyntjens, "Rwanda, Ten Years On: From Genocide to Dictatorship," *African Affairs* 103, no. 441 (2004): 181. The RPF installed a member of its central committee as IBUKA's new president. International Crisis Group, *Rwanda at the End of the Transition: A Necessary Political Liberalization*, 2002, 13. Available at http://www.icg.org/library/documents/report_archive/A400817_13112002.pdf.

23. PDR-Ubuyanja, Statutes, 2001, Article 5 (unpublished).

24. The top RPF leadership helped bring Yoweri Museveni's National Resistance Movement (NRM) to power in Uganda in 1985. Like the NRM, the RPF preaches non-ethnic politics and practices a de facto one-party state. Human Rights Watch, *Preparing for Elections: Tightening Control in the Name of Unity*, 2003. The RPF's position was succinctly expressed by the prosecutor during Bizimungu's appeal proceedings before the Supreme Court: "Neither Tutsi, nor Hutu, they don't exist. Only Rwandan citizens exist."

25. PDR-Ubuyanja, "Exposé des motifs," 2001, 38 (unpublished).

26. Ibid., 38.

27. Des Forges, *Leave None*, 709 & 733.

28. Protocol of Agreement between the Government of the Republic of Rwanda and the Rwandese Patriotic Front on Power-Sharing within the Framework of a Broad-Based Transitional Government (Arusha, January 9, 1993), in William A. Schabas and Martin Imbleau, *Introduction to Rwandan Law*, Quebec: Les Editions Yvon Blais, 1997; Republic of Rwanda, Law on Political Parties, Law No. 28/91 of 18/06/91.

29. In early 2002, the government passed a criminal law punishing "divisionism," which it broadly defined as any "speech, written statement, or action that causes conflict that causes an uprising that may degenerate into strife among people." Law No. 47/2001 of 18/12/2001, Instituting Punishment for Offences of Discrimination and Sectarianism, Article 1, *Official Gazette*, No. 4 of February 15, 2002. Since 2002, prosecutors, police, and government officials have used vague charges of "divisionism" and "genocidal ideology" to criminalize and suppress perceived

political dissent, human rights defenders, and independent journals. Front Line, *Disappearances*, 7–30, 45–80; Human Rights Watch, *Preparing for Elections*, 4–7.

30. PDR-Ubuyanja, Demande, 2001.

31. The original French text uses the word *chasse*, which is normally translated as "chase" for people and "hunt" for animals.

32. Bizimungu, "Je suis prêt," 26–27.

33. Ibid., 27.

34. Ibid., 28.

35. For more on these events, see Human Rights Watch, *Preparing for Elections*, 13; Front Line, *Disappearances*, 10–12.

36. Pasteur Bizimungu and Charles Ntakirutinka, Letter to the Prime Minister, March 27, 2002 (unpublished).

37. Paul Kagame, "Discours prononce par le President Kagame a l'ocassion du huitieme anniversaire du genocide," April 7, 2002 (unpublished).

38. Kagame also likened PDR-Ubuyanja to ALIR, a rebel movement in the Democratic Republic of Congo, whose leadership contained former *genocidaires* and which had been placed on the United States' list of terrorist organizations. Kagame, "Discours."

39. Ligue Rwandaise pour la Promotion et la Defense des Droits de l'Homme (LIPRODHOR), "Communique," 2002.

40. For a description of the government's repeated attacks on LIPRODHOR, see Front Line, *Disappearances*, 45–56.

41. European Union, *Rapport final: election présidentielles et legislatives*, European Union, 2004. Available at http://ec.europa.eu/external_relations/human_rights/eu_election_ass_observ/rwanda/moe_ue_final_2003.pdf.

42. Republic of Rwanda, Constitution, 2003.

43. Front Line, *Disappearances*, 19–30.

44. The courts sided with the prosecutor's arguments that the prosecutor can modify the legal characterization of the facts presented in an arrest warrant.

45. The two-year delay also partly resulted from sweeping judicial reforms, which saw most court activity grind to a halt for various periods.

46. William A. Schabas, "Justice, Democracy, and Impunity in Post-Genocide Rwanda: Searching for Solutions to Impossible Problems," *Criminal Law Forum* 7, no. 3 (October 1996).

47. Filip Reyntjens and Stef Vandeginste, "Rwanda: An Atypical Transition," in *Roads to Reconciliation*, Elin Skaar et al., eds., Lanham, MD: Lexington Books, 2005, 110. For a fascinating account of Rwanda's genocide detainees, see Carina Tertsakian, *Le Château: The Lives of Prisoners in Rwanda*, London: Arves, 2008.

48. Human Rights Watch, *Struggling to Survive: Barriers to Justice for Rape Victims in Rwanda*, 2004, 18.

49. Nonetheless, the fairness of genocide trials has improved over the years: the acquittal rate rose from 6 percent to 27 percent, and the percentage of death sentences fell from 45 percent to 4 percent. Human Rights Watch, *World Report 2002: Rwanda*, 2003; International Crisis Group, *Five Years After the Genocide: Justice in Question*,1999, 13, available at http://www.crisisgroup.org/home/index.cfm?

id=1412&l=1. No executions have occurred since April 1998, when twenty-two people were killed by firing squads in public stadiums around the country.

50. Human Rights Watch, *World Report 2002: Rwanda*; Eugene Habiyambere, "Le tournant critique du process Anaclet Nkundimfura et ses coaccuse," *Le Verdict* no. 34 (January 2003): 3–4.

51. Federation internationale des ligues des droits de l'homme (FIDH), *Victims in the Balance: Challenges Ahead for the International Criminal Tribunal for Rwanda*, 2002, 16–17. Available at http://www.fidh.org/article.php3?id_article=1321.

52. U.S. State Department, *Country Reports on Human Rights Practices 2004: Rwanda*, 2005. Available at http://www.state.gov/g/drl/rls/hrrpt/2004/41621.htm.

53. Thierry Cruvellier, *Le tribunal des Vaincus*, Paris: Calmann-Levy, 2006.

54. Rwanda's hostility to international justice also extends to the International Criminal Court (ICC). It has not signed the ICC treaty (the Rome Statute), and it has supported American efforts to weaken the ICC. In 2003, Rwanda signed a so-called Article 98 agreement with the United States, pledging that it would never hand over American nationals to the ICC. Presidential Order No. 17/01 of 08/07/2003, Ratifying the Agreement between the Government of the Republic of Rwanda and the Government of the United States of America regarding the Surrender of Persons to International Tribunal Signed at Washington on March 4, 2003. *Official Gazette*, Special Issue of July 11, 2003, Republic of Rwanda, 2003.

55. After Carla del Ponte, then the ICTR prosecutor, precipitously announced that she would bring war crimes indictments against the RPF, the Rwandan government imposed travel restrictions on prosecution witnesses, which caused three genocide trials to be suspended for lack of witnesses. FIDH, *Victims in the Balance*, 47–52. Del Ponte then suspended her RPF investigations and informed the Security Council that the Rwandan government was pressuring her to halt those investigations. The Security Council eventually issued a tepid statement reminding Rwanda of its legal obligation to comply with the tribunal. Del Ponte then made an oral agreement to give over Rwanda primacy RPF investigations, but she reneged on the deal at the last moment. Cruvellier, *Le tribunal des Vaincus*, 241–244. This infuriated the Rwandans, who successfully lobbied for a new ICTR prosecutor. So far, the new prosecutor, Hassan Jallow, has not had any greater success in pursuing the RPF investigations: as of March 2008, he had not issued any RPF indictments. In February 2008, a Spanish judge indicted forty Rwandan army officers – including President Kagame – for crimes against humanity committed after the genocide. Tracy Wilkinson, "Spanish Judge Indicts Rwanda Officers," *Los Angeles Times*, February 7, 2008.

56. Belgian courts handed down criminal convictions against six Rwandans (two nuns, three businessmen, and an educator), whereas a Swiss military tribunal sentenced a former mayor. The Canadian Supreme Court ordered the deportation of a Rwandan who incited the killing of Tutsi two years before the genocide. A U.S. federal court sanctioned a Hutu extremist *in absentia* in a case brought under the Alien Tort Claims Act. For an overview of genocide proceedings at the national and international level, see Allison Des Forges and Timothy Longman, "Legal Responses to Genocide in Rwanda," in *My Neighbor, My Enemy: Justice and Community in the Aftermath of Mass Atrocity*, Eric Stover and Harvey Weinstein, eds., New York: Cambridge University Press, 2004.

57. Front Line, *Disappearances*. In late 2007, the Rwandan Parliament issued a third report on genocidal ideology, which it defined very broadly. That same year, the police handled 187 cases of divisionism and 460 cases of genocidal ideology. U.S. State Department. *Country Reports on Human Rights Practices 2007: Rwanda*, 2008, available at http://www.state.gov/g/drl/rls/hrrpt/2007/100499.htm.

58. Articles 164 and 165 of the Rwandan Penal Code punish plots that resort to terrorism, armed force, or any other violence with a view to attacking the government. If any act has been committed to further the plot, the sentence is life imprisonment; otherwise, the sentence ranges from five to ten years.

59. Article 166 of the Penal Code reads in part: "Whoever. . . . knowingly spreads false rumors to incite or attempt to incite the population against the government, to rouse or attempt to provoke persons against one another, to alarm people and cause troubles on Rwandan territory, will be punished by imprisonment for two to ten years."

60. Under Article 281 of the Penal Code "Any association formed . . . with the goal of attacking persons or property is a crime which exists by virtue of the fact that the group was organized." Article 282 imposes a prison sentence of five to twenty years.

61. There is no official transcript of the trial and appeal. The author relies on notes taken by various trial observers whom he has reason to trust. All quotations from the proceedings are approximate as they were translated from Kinyarwanda into French by the observers, and then from French into English by this author.

62. Another prosecution witness, who never took the stand, interrupted the trial to announce he had been arrested, beaten, and detained for two years to get him to testify against Bizimungu. He subsequently fled the country. Human Rights Watch, *Rwanda: Historic Ruling Expected for Former President and Seven Others*, 2006.

63. Bizimungu and Ntakirutinka also pointed out that they could not have participated in some of the meetings described by Bugingo because they were under police surveillance at the time.

64. In his initial appearances immediately after his arrest, Bizimungu had appeared in the pink uniforms worn by all Rwandan detainees. He was subsequently afforded the privilege of appearing in a suit and tie.

65. In his closing argument, the prosecutor responded by saying, "PDR-Ubuyanja was a phantom; that's why the prosecutor's office prosecuted these people for common crimes." The court agreed with that reasoning and rightly pointed out that membership in a political party does not exempt one from prosecution for ordinary crimes.

66. This was not surprising, because any potential defense witness would have had to weigh the possibility of being charged as a member of their supposed criminal association.

67. Following Bizimungu, Ntakirutinka and the six co-accused presented their defense. Arguing that PDR-Ubuyanja was not divisionist, Ntakirutinka reminded the judges that Major Bigabiro had testified that Bizimungu commissioned Bigabiro to find other *Tutsi* soldiers to join PDR-Ubuyanja. Ntakirutinka concluded his defense with a personal statement: "This accusation of being divisionist is an insult for me. I have always worked for the unity of Rwandans. I represented the PSD [Social Democratic Party] at Arusha in the peace negotiations. It is not me who can take the

initiative in fighting this unity." The six co-accused called nine defense witnesses who contradicted the testimony of Bugingo, the sole prosecution witness against them. Two of the co-accused, including the U.S. Embassy employee, testified that they could not have threatened genocide survivors, as Bugingo alleged, because they themselves were genocide survivors. LIPRODHOR's treasurer argued that LIPRODHOR's football team was not a front for PDR-Ubuyanja, that the police who searched his house never found any documents linking him to PDR-Ubuyanja, and that Bizimungu had testified he was not a party member.

68. There is some discrepancy between the court's judgment, which says the defense lawyer was sentenced to forty-eight hours, and the reports of various observers, which state that the penalty was twenty-four hours.

69. The prosecutor never made any showing that members of the Interahamwe had actually read Bizimungu's interview in *Jeune Afrique*.

70. The prosecutor also asked that Bizimungu be sentenced to twenty years for embezzlement of public funds, ten years for fraud, and one year for illegally carrying a weapon.

71. All quotes from the judgment are the author's translations of a French translation of the official Kinyarwandan version.

72. Article 59 of the Code of Criminal Procedure seems to preclude prosecutors from calling accomplices or accessories as prosecution witnesses: "Persons against whom the prosecution has evidence to suspect that they were involved in the commission of an offence cannot be heard as witnesses." Under Article 121, however, the court itself can summon accomplices and accessories as witnesses: "In the course of trial, a court can order the prosecution to bring in the trial accomplices or accessories of the principal authors when it discovers that there is strong evidence against them. If it appears to the court that the prosecution does not want to prosecute them, it may summon them and the court proceedings continue."

73. A trusted Rwandan colleague gave me a French translation of the first part of Bizimungu's letter, a copy of which he saw himself.

74. Presidential Order No. 10/01 of 16/04/2007 Granting Pardon, Article 2(3), *Official Journal*, Special Issue of May 2, 2007: 19–21.

75. Fondation Hirondelle, "Bizimungu's Freedom, a Political Decision According to Experts," April 17, 2007. Available at http://www.hirondellenews.com/content/view/322/26/.

76. It is impossible to gauge public opinion about Bizimungu, his trial, and his conviction given that any support for Bizimungu can be interpreted as "divisionism" in Rwanda's repressive political climate. Ordinary Rwandans are generally reluctant to express themselves publicly on politically sensitive issues. This author's interviews among a small sample of Rwandans revealed a range of opinions about Bizimungu and his trial.

77. European Union, "Declaration by the Presidency on Behalf of the European Union on the Case of Pasteur Bizimungu," July 9, 2004.

78. U.S. State Department, *Country Reports on Human Rights Practices 2004: Rwanda*. By contrast, the Supreme Court's judgment elicited no criticism from the international community, which appeared satisfied with the release of the six coaccused.

79. Amnesty International, *Rwanda: Government Slams Door on Political Life and Civil Society*, June 9, 2004.

80. LIPRODHOR, *Situation des droits de la personne au Rwanda: Rapport 2003–2004,* 2005, 120.
81. See, for example, Joseline Fannethe, "Bizimungu ne peut pas bénéficier la libération conditionnelle!" *Umuseso,* no. 249, March 19–25, 2005.
82. Front Line, *Disappearances,* 69.
83. Ellen Lutz and Kathryn Sikkink have defined a "justice cascade" as a rapid shift toward accomplishing compliance with human rights norms. In common with the transition paradigm, the justice cascade makes teleological assumptions about the steady increase of liberal democratic principles. Ellen Lutz and Kathryn Sikkink, "The Justice Cascade: The Evolution and Impact of Foreign Human Rights Trials in Latin America," *Chicago Journal of International Law* 2, no. 1 (2001): 1–34. Yet, as Thomas Carothers has powerfully argued, the actual situation of most "third-wave" states calls those assumptions into question. Thomas Carothers, "The End of the Transition Paradigm," *Journal of Democracy* 13, no. 1 (2002): 5–21.
84. Kathryn Sikkink has argued that the threat of international or foreign trials pushed democratic (or democratizing) Latin American states to hold domestic trials for perpetrators of past human rights abuses. Kathryn Sikkink, "Memo for SSRC International Law and International Relations Project: Workshop on International Criminal Accountability: Washington, D.C. Nov. 6–7, 2003," pp. 8–9 (unpublished). Such a threat has clearly proved insufficient in Rwanda's case: investigations of RPF killings by the ICTR and French and Spanish magistrates have not spurred domestic trials.

9

Justice Squandered? The Trial of Slobodan Milošević

Emir Suljagić

The death of Slobodan Milošević, the first head of state to be tried before an international tribunal, only ten working days before the end of the grueling trial, was for some the defining moment of the International Criminal Tribunal for the former Yugoslavia (ICTY or the tribunal). Although that may be the case, what defined the trial was not its end but rather its conduct. Despite prosecution assertions to the contrary, the trial was perhaps inevitably going to be perceived, at least symbolically, as about prosecuting a regime and an ideology.[1] To this extent, it should have been acknowledged as a political trial. In this regard, as Gary Bass eloquently argues in his "qualified defense" of "victor's justice," it was a choice between imperfect justice and no justice at all.[2] The attempt by ICTY prosecutors to isolate the trial from its political context undermined the historical mission of the ICTY and caused many of its intended beneficiaries – the victims of Milošević's campaigns in Croatia, Bosnia and Herzegovina, and Kosovo – to lose confidence in it.[3] A further result of this attempted depoliticization, along with other political developments – such as decisions of the United Nations Security Council, from which it was paradoxically impossible to isolate the ICTY – strengthened the rule of impunity in the former Yugoslavia, a condition that the tribunal had aimed to end.[4]

The trial itself was a triumph for international justice, regardless of its outcome. Yet it produced little in terms of consequent national prosecutions of middle- and lower-ranking officials from the apparatus of terror that Milošević had created over the years. Those individuals who committed atrocities in Croatia, Bosnia and Herzegovina, and Kosovo did so in some kind of official capacity. Orders to commit crimes came from heads of some form of government, local or regional. They were executed through their military or police apparatus (or both) and carried out in conjunction with elements of the Yugoslav National Army (JNA), and later the Croatian Serb force Srpska Vojska Krajine (SVK) and the Bosnian Serb Army (VRS), as well as paramilitary groups which were recruited, equipped, and sanctioned by Milošević's Secret Service (Resor Državne Bezbednosti, RDB). The systematic and protracted campaign against non-Serbs did not allow for any "private initiative," even though different governments and organizations in the former Yugoslavia continue to portray the genocidal campaign in such terms.

Substantial parts of the structure that Milošević put in place and relied on in his campaigns in Croatia, Bosnia and Herzegovina, and Kosovo have outlived him. This chapter briefly outlines the breakup of the Socialist Federal Republic of Yugoslavia and the rise and fall of Slobodan Milošević. It also touches on his campaigns in Croatia, Bosnia and Herzegovina, and Kosovo. It then deals with the events surrounding his fall, arrest, and extradition to the Hague to face trial. It continues with the account of the trial and its interplay with events that have shaped the legacy of the trial in the region. Although there is no shortage of commentary about the international significance of Milošević's trial, this analysis focuses on how the trial filtered through to Bosnia and Herzegovina and Serbia.[5] Finally, it offers conclusions on what the implications and the direct results of the trial have been in the former Yugoslavia.

THE RISE

In April 1987, in a speech in Kosovo Polje, a suburb of Kosovo's capital Priština, Slobodan Milošević began cementing his personal power within the Communist establishment in Serbia and opening the door for the breakup of the Socialist Federal Republic of Yugoslavia. This carefully staged event was shown by Belgrade Television, by then already under control of Milošević's close friend and ally Dušan Mitević, as a spontaneous outpouring of justified frustration of the long wronged Serbian people.[6] Although there is evidence that whereas the protest may have been staged, Milošević's speech was in fact a spontaneous reaction to what he perceived as the predicament of Kosovo Serbs.[7] It could be described as the final act in the process that began in September 1986, when an infamous Memorandum of the Serbian Academy of Science and Arts (SANU) was leaked to a Belgrade newspaper. However, the memorandum did not call for the dissolution of Yugoslavia; it sought to rearrange the Yugoslav federation on the basis of what the authors believed to be Serbian national interest, breaking one of the strongest taboos in Yugoslav public life. Although the memorandum was heavily criticized in other Yugoslav republics and even in Serbia – at the urging of the Serbian Communist Party, the Serbian Academy halfheartedly recanted the memorandum – it apparently did have some backers. Milošević, the head of the party, kept silent about the memorandum at the time it was leaked; yet when he spoke in Kosovo

Polje, he did so to legitimize the nationalist discourse expounded in the memorandum.[8]

Between September 1987 and January 1990, Milošević took over the reins of the Serbian Communist Party, engineered a virtual coup d'état in Montenegro, abolished the autonomy of the provinces of Kosovo and Vojvodina, and, most important, seized control of the key Yugoslav institutions: the Yugoslav People's Army (JNA) and the Yugoslav presidency. More to the point, Milošević kidnapped the Yugoslav cause through what some authors have described as a "central secession." As Daniele Conversi observes,

> By seizing the central state, the secessionists do not necessarily develop a secessionist vocabulary, and therefore can act from a secure under-the-table position. With this face-saving gimmick, their 'impunity' is granted. In the case of Yugoslavia, Belgrade's rhetoric throughout the conflict remained eminently 'unitarian.'[9]

Milošević thus became the driving force behind the creation of the Federal Republic of Yugoslavia (FRY) from Serbia and Montenegro after the Republics of Slovenia, Croatia, and Bosnia and Herzegovina each declared their independence in 1991 and 1992. He declared it to be the sole state-successor to the Socialist Federative Republic of Yugoslavia.

Following an embarrassing ten-day war in June 1991, the JNA pulled out of Slovenia. As the army abandoned the mission of preserving both Yugoslavia and socialism – and eventually lost both – Milošević focused his attention on Croatia and Bosnia and Herzegovina.[10] He began arming the Serb communities in these two republics, relying primarily on a powerful network of the Serb Democratic Party from those republics together with Serbia's State Security Service and a number of officers from the JNA loyal to the Serb cause and to Milošević personally.[11] A simultaneous media campaign by state-owned Serbian media, such as the newspaper *Politika* and television stations in Belgrade and Novi Sad, sought to draw the line between Serbs in Croatia and Bosnia and Herzegovina and their non-Serb neighbors. By August 1991, war in Croatia had begun. In Bosnia and Herzegovina, by November 1991, the Serb Democratic Party of Radovan Karadžić had established control over significant parts of the country in the form of Serb Autonomous Areas (Srpska Autonomna Oblast). In March 1992, following a referendum on Bosnia and Herzegovina's independence, the Serb Democratic Party, with the aid of the JNA, blockaded Sarajevo, setting the scene for the subsequent three-and-a-half year siege of that city and a war that engulfed the republic. Although estimates of numbers vary, the combined devastation of the Croatian and Bosnian wars probably resulted in well over one hundred thousand deaths and the expulsion of up to 2.5 million people.[12] Hundreds, perhaps thousands, of cultural and religious objects were destroyed as a result of thorough ethnic recomposition of the region.

The Serbian campaigns in Croatia and Bosnia and Herzegovina were marked by brutality unseen in Europe since World War II. The shelling of Dubrovnik and the carnage of Vukovar, the siege of Sarajevo, and the camps in western Bosnia all, however, failed to prompt the international community to act. Although the conflict was not over, in May 1993 the United Nations (UN) Security Council established an international tribunal to prosecute the crimes committed in the former Yugoslavia. In establishing the ICTY, the authorizing Security Council Resolution declared that it was

> for the sole purpose of prosecuting persons responsible for serious violations of international humanitarian law committed in the territory of the former Yugoslavia between 1 January 1991 and a date determined by the Security Council upon the restoration of peace.[13]

To many observers it was a token gesture aimed at showing moral concern in light of the international community's reluctance to engage in military intervention to stop the mass atrocities.[14] The existence of the tribunal failed, however, to act as a deterrent: in July 1995, the Bosnian Serb Army massacred almost the entire male population of the UN-declared safe area of Srebrenica. Six months later, Milošević was instrumental in bringing about the Dayton Peace Accords, which finally brought an end to the war in Bosnia and Herzegovina. He was seen by the West as an "indispensable diplomatic partner."[15]

In early 1999, Milošević turned to Kosovo. He repeated the same policies of ethnic cleansing that characterized the Bosnian and Croatian wars in Kosovo. Eight hundred fifty thousand Kosovar Albanians were driven from their homes as a result of intense fighting between the JNA and the Kosovo Liberation Army.[16] After the peace negotiations in Rambouillet, France, collapsed, NATO intervened militarily despite the absence of prior UN approval. Milošević used the NATO air campaign to intensify violence against ethnic Albanians, and within a fortnight, hundreds of thousands of Kosovo Albanians were deported to neighboring Albania and Macedonia. It took seventy-eight days of bombardment for the Yugoslav Army and troops of the Ministry of the Interior to pull out of Kosovo, a defeat that seems to have spelled the end for Milošević.

AND FALL...

All the while, between December 1990 and September 2000, Milošević maintained his legitimacy in Serbia. He won three consecutive presidential elections, and his Socialist Party of Serbia, either on its own or in coalition with other smaller parties, retained some form of majority in both the Serbian Parliament and the Parliament of the Federal Republic of Yugoslavia.[17] In the first elections after the Kosovo war, scheduled for September 24, 2000, Milošević lost to Vojislav Koštunica, the candidate of the Democratic Opposition of Serbia, a coalition of eighteen parties, ranging from center-left to center-right. Initially, he refused to acknowledge the results and repeatedly ordered the police and the army to quash the massive popular demonstrations that had arisen across the country. On October 6, after the Yugoslav Constitutional Court ruled in favor of the Democratic Opposition, Milošević finally withdrew from office.[18]

Almost a year and a half earlier, on May 27, 1999, when the Kosovo war was at its peak, the ICTY announced that the prosecutor had indicted Slobodan Milošević.[19] Along with four senior civilian, police, and military officials of the Federal Republic of Yugoslavia and Serbia, Milošević was the first head of state to be charged "during an on-going armed conflict with the commission of serious violations of international humanitarian law."[20] At a press conference in the Hague, the chief prosecutor, Louise Arbour, was the first to say what everyone seemed to know: Milošević was responsible for the deportation and murder of Kosovo Albanians.[21] The indictment seemed to mirror priorities of Western democracies in that there was no word in it about Bosnia and Herzegovina or Croatia.[22] Although this may have seemed to be an indication of the politicized nature of the case from the outset, Milošević was first charged with what was a relatively straightforward case: crimes related to and allegedly committed by the Yugoslav Army and police in Kosovo, of which he was formally commander-in-chief. On the other hand, he waged his campaigns in Croatia and Bosnia and Herzegovina by proxy, through a network that involved hundreds, perhaps even thousands, of individuals. Those individuals also were implicated to some extent in the perpetration of atrocities and were therefore less willing to testify in any investigation or trial. As limited as it initially was, the indictment was seen as an obstacle to peace by some European officials and, unexpectedly, in some parts of the opposition in Belgrade.[23]

Six months after the indictment was issued, Milošević was ousted from power. Despite international pressure, the new Yugoslav president, Vojislav Koštunica, refused to recognize the primacy of the tribunal over national law and worked to prevent the extradition of Yugoslav nationals.[24] Koštunica believed that if Milošević was to be tried, the trial should be in Belgrade and for what Milošević did to Serbia and its citizens: ruining the economy, terrorizing political opponents, and stealing elections.[25]

Eventually Milošević was preliminarily charged with abuse of power and embezzlement by the Belgrade Office of the Prosecutor, and an investigation opened.[26] An arrest operation conducted on April 3, 2001, was ill coordinated and possibly sabotaged by elements of the Yugoslav Army, resulting in an embarrassment for the government of Serbia.[27] A group of Milošević supporters maintained a vigil in front of his house, preventing an efficient police action and showing that the former strongman still enjoyed if not sizeable then certainly fervent support in some corners in Serbia. After protracted negotiations, Milošević agreed to go to jail. However, he did so only after receiving a written guarantee that the action was not "in response to the demand of ICTY" and that he would "not be handed over to any judicial or other institution outside the country." The guarantee was signed by Yugoslav president Koštunica, Serbian president Milan Milutinović – himself indicted by the ICTY – and Serbian prime minister Zoran Đinđić.[28]

The new Koštunica government wanted to try Milošević in Belgrade on abuse of power and corruption charges precisely to avoid what would take place in the Hague: a trial, transparent and widely covered by the media that would reveal the role of Serbia and various branches of its government, media, and ordinary citizens in some of the most heinous crimes committed during Milošević's campaigns in Croatia, Bosnia and Herzegovina, and Kosovo. Moreover, Croatia and Bosnia and Herzegovina had sued the Federal Republic of Yugoslavia for violating the Convention on the Prevention and Punishment of the Crime of Genocide at the International Court of Justice, and any public evidence used in an international proceeding against Milošević could seriously undermine Serbia's case.[29]

Outside Serbia, charges against Milošević and his subsequent arrest were seen as a farce, another attempt on the part of the new government to avoid coming to terms with its role in the violent breakup of Yugoslavia. Furthermore, although many cheered Milošević's arrest, it was obvious that unless the government was forced to deliver him to the tribunal, Milošević was unlikely to be called to account for other notorious crimes such as those committed at Vukovar and Dubrovnik, during the siege of Sarajevo, at the Prijedor concentration camps, or the massacres in Srebrenica, Izbice, and Račak.

Following Milošević's arrest, however, there was increased international pressure on the Yugoslav and Serbian government for Milošević to be handed over to the ICTY, which as a creation of the UN Security Council exercising its powers under Chapter VII of the UN Charter compelled all UN member states to comply with its orders.[30] On June 22, 2001, the federal government passed a decree "on extraditing the accused to the Hague Tribunal" with the obvious intent to create a legal basis for delivering Milošević to the ICTY.[31] Almost immediately, Milošević's Socialist Party of Serbia and its allies, as well as a group of fifty-one professors from Belgrade Law Faculty, filed a motion with the

Federal Supreme Court challenging the legality of the decree.[32] Predictably, the Supreme Court, presided over by judges still loyal to Milošević, ordered a temporary suspension of the decree on June 28, 2001.[33] In a dramatic turn of events, the government of Serbia held a session the same day and overruled the Supreme Court: it gave primacy to the ICTY Statute over domestic legislation as part of its cooperation with the tribunal. It also made a decision to hand over Milošević immediately to the ICTY.[34] By the end of the day, Milošević was transferred from the Belgrade Central Prison to the Netherlands and placed in the custody of the tribunal.

The decision marked a definitive split in the weak ruling coalition. Yugoslav President Koštunica issued a press release claiming that he was unaware of the decision; he went even further and called it "precipitate and humiliating" in one of his first interviews following the transfer.[35]

When the handover finally took place, the pro-Hague block, headed by Serbian prime minister Đinđić, chose to offer the Serbian public an "economic" rationale for the transfer,[36] obviously motivated by a donors conference scheduled for the next day in Brussels.[37] Đinđić aimed to present Milošević as an obstacle between Serbia's ordinary citizens and their better future: his arrest was the price to be paid for Serbia's reentry into international community rather than the result of the gravity of charges against Milošević.

Even though most Western leaders welcomed the news of Milošević's extradition, they legitimized Đinđić's reasons, with only a few exceptions.[38] In fact, the international community sent mixed signals throughout the affair, with some, such as the U.K. Foreign Secretary Robin Cook, saying that Milošević could be dealt with by the Yugoslav judiciary first and then be handed over to the Hague.[39] Others, such as EU Foreign Policy and Security Chief Javier Solana, praised the new government and refused to exert any pressure on Đinđić.[40]

Although the Serbian judicial system was far from capable of trying such a high-profile case, it is likely that Milošević would have been found guilty of abuse of power if he had been tried in Belgrade. In an atmosphere in which he was seen by many in Serbia as the reason for the misery that had befallen them, a domestic trial would have made him a perfect scapegoat for the woes of the country, including international isolation, high inflation, and rampant corruption and organized crime. How that would have affected the possibility of a war crimes trial at the Hague is a matter of speculation, but it is highly improbable that any Yugoslav or Serbian government would have entertained the idea of delivering him to the Hague once he was behind bars. Similarly, had Milošević remained in Serbia, he would most likely have faced trial for his role in the assassination of his former mentor and fellow ex-president of Serbia

Ivan Stambolić, who was killed by an elite paramilitary unit shortly before he was due to challenge Milošević in the 2000 presidential election. Although Milošević was indicted by Serbian prosecutors in 2003, the indictment against him was unable to proceed because by that time he was already in the Hague. A domestic trial would have had an another important effect that the trial in the Hague Tribunal failed to achieve: it would have deeply compromised him in the eyes of ordinary Serbs and, in all probability would have put an end to his political legacy in Serbia.[41]

THE TRIAL

A Free Reign for Milošević

In the five months after Milošević's arrest, the ICTY prosecutor issued further indictments against him for crimes committed in Bosnia and Herzegovina and Croatia. He was indicted under Articles 7 (1) and 7(3) of the ICTY statute for genocide, crimes against humanity, and grave breaches of the Geneva Conventions and violations of the laws or customs of war.[42] Although the Trial Chamber initially opted to proceed with a separate trial on the Kosovo charges, it was overruled by the Appeals Chamber, which allowed the prosecution's request to join the three indictments. As a result, the Trial Chamber commenced trial on February 12, 2002 with a single indictment that contained sixty-six charges spanning almost a decade and three conflicts.[43]

To the extent that a trial is a platform for stagecraft, it became clear from the start that Milošević played the lead. By deciding that Milošević had the right to self-representation, the Trial Chamber allowed Milošević to act as his own counsel and, according to author Michael Scharf, regularly "treat the witnesses, prosecutors, and judges in a manner that would earn ordinary defense counsel a citation or incarceration for contempt of court." He demonstrated his refusal to recognize the tribunal's legitimacy by remaining seated while speaking in court and refusing to address the judges by their judicial titles.[44] Although the right to represent oneself is part of many adversarial legal systems, it was unfamiliar to trial observers from European inquisitorial criminal justice systems including the countries of the former Yugoslavia. The Trial Chamber appointed amici curiae or "friends of the court" to help defend Milošević's legal interests, but ultimately the accused knew his case better than anyone and skillfully used the role to further his own interests.

Before long Milošević succeeded, in the words of David Rieff, "in making many impartial observers lose respect for the proceedings."[45] In an attempt to ensure a fair trial, the Trial Chamber allowed Milošević not only to use the trial as a podium to present his own version of the recent history of Yugoslavia but to discredit the trial itself. Furthermore, the Trial Chamber imposed numerous restrictions and deadlines on the prosecution in order to manage the size of the case.[46] As a result, the prosecution opted to prove genocide in only seven municipalities in Bosnia and Herzegovina as opposed to the initial number of thirty-three.

Strict adversarial rules of procedure may also have lessened the impact of the trial in the former Yugoslav republics. Although the flexible rules of evidence were broadly derived from Continental legal models, the presentation of evidence by each party and the process of cross-examination were unfamiliar to many observers in the region, as was the right to self-representation. A better blend of the two systems might have contributed to regional comprehension of what was taking place in the courtroom.

As it was, the majority of the "crime base" witness testimony – the kind that is perhaps the most repetitive and even tiresome in terms of reporting but that provides essential legitimacy to these kinds of trials by presenting what happened to the victims of the crimes – was introduced in writing. This seriously undermined the transparency of the trial and, in turn, made it possible for Milošević to pin stereotypes on prosecution witnesses that resonated with his regional audience.[47] Once again Milošević succeeded in hijacking the Serb cause; he presented himself as the greatest defender of the Serb nation, and now, in the courtroom, as the personification of the persecuted Serb people. In the process, he helped further reinforce anti-tribunal attitudes in Serbia. The polls taken during the first year of the trial showed that some 70 percent of Serb citizens did not trust the tribunal to render justice.[48] A similar regional poll taken in the early stages of Milošević trial showed that more than 50 percent of the citizens of Bosnia and Herzegovina and 83 percent of Kosovar Albanians trusted the ICTY.[49] Furthermore, the Serbian government's failure to confront Serb crimes from the war did nothing to dispel the perception that the trial was causing Milošević's popularity to grow in Serbia, where he continued to enjoy significant support until his death. The government decision to allow his funeral in Serbia threatened to jeopardize the country's already-fragile democracy: the funeral turned into a show of force for his Socialist Party and the nationalist Radical Party.[50]

MAPPING OUT GENOCIDE

Despite its missteps, the prosecution scored a number of important points during its case, both in terms of establishing a clear historical record of events in the former Yugoslavia and in the judicial process. In relation to Kosovo, the trial showed that Albanians were expelled en masse and that expulsion and murder were carried out in an organized fashion, following an almost identical pattern across the province.[51] In addition, testimony by personnel of the Army of Yugoslavia (formerly the Yugoslav People's Army) left no doubt that the Serbian police force was integrated into the army chain of command and that so-called paramilitaries were in fact highly equipped and trained troops acting on orders from top officials of the police and the army.[52] In the same vein, a number of witnesses testified that Milošević was aware of the events in Kosovo but chose to disregard serious violations of international humanitarian law.[53] One of the witnesses, a German general, Klaus Naumaan, who at the time was head of NATO's Military Committee, recounted a meeting in October 1998, in which Milošević summed up the solution for the Albanians of Kosovo: "We do the same [that] we did in Drenica in '45 or "46. . . . We got them together and we shot them."[54] The prosecution also submitted evidence that there was systematic destruction of evidence, which Milošević had ordered during a meeting of top police, military, and civilian officials in March 1999. The campaign to cover up evidence of atrocities came to light after a truck full of corpses was found in the Danube River, on the border between Serbia and Romania.[55]

Whereas the Kosovo allegations against Milošević were factually and temporally distinct, the Croatian and Bosnian charges were more closely related, both in terms of timeframe and modus operandi. As the prosecution presented its case, it became clear that in addition to the Yugoslav People's Army Milošević had relied on Serbia's Security Service (the RDB) in equipping and controlling the Serb leadership in neighboring republics. The late Croatian Serb leader Milan Babić – perhaps the single most important witness in the trial – testified that the military and police of the Croatian Serbs were under the control of the Army of Yugoslavia and the Security Service, a situation that also ensured its control over their political leadership. Most important, Babić mapped out the command-and-control structure.[56] One line of command stemmed from what remained of the Yugoslav presidency and included the Yugoslav National Army and the civilian or paramilitary structure known as the Territorial Defense.[57] The other line came from the State Security Service, which ran through parallel structures and reached down to local police and volunteer formations.[58] According to the prosecution evidence, the Security Service recruited, armed, and trained the bulk of the paramilitary forces that committed the most heinous atrocities in Croatia and Bosnia and Herzegovina. They took orders directly from the Security Service Chief, Jovica Stanišić, or his underlings, and thus were controlled by Serbia's Ministry of Interior Affairs.[59] An identical pattern was employed in Bosnia and Herzegovina.

The intercepts of conversations between the Bosnian Serb leadership and Milošević and other Serbian and Yugoslav officials left little doubt about the identity of the real "boss."[60] An expert witness explained how the money trail demonstrated the complete dependency of Croatian and Bosnian Serb entities on monetary support from Serbia, so much so that without it they would not have been able to remain afloat, let alone carry out a war.[61] In the later stages of the war, Milošević went so far as to integrate their military structures into the Army of Yugoslavia in terms of finance, logistics, and military planning.[62]

Perhaps the single most important revelation of the trial was that Serbian police units, for which Milošević was constitutionally responsible, took part in the mass-murder operation in Srebrenica. According to witness testimony and documentary evidence presented by the prosecution, it was possible to link Milošević directly to the massacre. A document introduced into evidence during the testimony of a Montenegrin police expert Budimir Babović indicated that a Serbian police unit took part in the operation in Srebrenica.[63] When a film of the execution of a group of men and boys from Srebrenica was later introduced as evidence, it left no doubt that the unit had participated in the massacre. In addition, British General Sir Rupert Smith, a former commander of UN forces in Bosnia and Herzegovina, testified that Milošević was aware of the outcome of the attack on Srebrenica yet chose not to act.[64] American General Wesley Clark testified that not only did Milošević know of the outcome, but he was also aware of the planning of the operation at the time.[65]

The best indication of what the possible outcome of the trial might have been is contained in the Decision on Motion for Judgment of Acquittal issued by the Trial Chamber in mid-June 2004 at the end of the presentation of the prosecution's case. The judges unanimously decided that there was sufficient "evidence on which a Trial Chamber could be satisfied beyond reasonable doubt" of the guilt of the accused.[66] The decision also specified that there were sufficient grounds for finding Milošević to be a member of a joint criminal enterprise formed with the intent to commit genocide (although one of the judges dissented regarding the possession of intent).[67]

THE LONG AND VISIBLE HAND OF SERBIA

In addition to the Trial Chamber's liberal interpretation of the right to self-representation, another crucial factor that discredited the trial and, for some, the tribunal itself, was the ICTY's inability to prevent Milošević from receiving assistance from his supporters in the Yugoslav Army and the Security Service in the conduct of his case. A Commission on Cooperation with the ICTY was formed within the Yugoslav Army General's staff office to facilitate Milošević's defense.[68]

This support stemmed from an alliance between the new Yugoslav president, Koštunica, and elements within the former federal and Serbian military and police. The "anti-Hague" lobby, as it came to be known in Serbia and the region, had sought an alliance with the new government at the time of Milošević's arrest. The lobby's representative, the chief of the Security Service, who had offered evidence of Milošević's corruption and involvement in political assassinations in Serbia, first approached Đinđić. The chief reportedly asked for assurances from Đinđić that he and others would not be transferred to the Hague if the time came, but he was turned down and instead he turned to Koštunica, who apparently accepted the offer.[69]

Given the difficulty of obtaining insider witness testimony, the prosecution had to rely on documents originating from the Serbian and Yugoslav executive branches, military, and police to paint the complete picture of Milošević's involvement in the crimes alleged in the indictment. The Yugoslav government opposed or obstructed numerous requests by the prosecution to obtain documents pertaining to the case from the official archives.[70] The prosecution then asked the Trial Chamber to compel the national authorities to make the relevant material available, as had been done in other cases involving the Bosnian and Croatian authorities.[71] In Milošević's case, the situation was all the more farcical because it seemed that Milošević himself had access to some of the archives that the prosecution did not.[72] The majority of the documents from these sources that Milošević chose to produce in court were of limited, if any, probative value, but played well in the court of public opinion in Serbia. The effort to prevent the prosecution from obtaining documents became a political issue for the new Yugoslav president. The Trial Chamber, unfortunately, did not have an ear for the prosecution's protestations to this effect. Instead, it gave the government the benefit of the doubt, which resulted in more obstruction, politicking, and outright lying.[73]

In one case, the Serbian government claimed that it could not obtain a pathologist's report related to a charge in the Kosovo indictment because the pathologist was owed a large sum of money and was unwilling to relinquish the report.[74] In another case, after the prosecution requested certain financial documents, the government replied that it could not find them. Its representative, Vladimir Đerić, summed up the government reponse in a hearing before the Trial Chamber: "The General Secretariat has informed us that there are no such documents in their archives. It took two and a half months for the Prosecution to say. . . . that the requested document might be in the Ministry of Finance," thus accusing the prosecution of not being precise enough when requesting documents.[75]

In some instances, the government claimed that the documentation could not be produced because the governmental bodies and agencies that created them under law did not exist,[76] despite the fact that the prosecution had already produced evidence that confirmed the agencies' existence. When the government did deliver documentation, it frequently was selective, outside the period requested, or exculpatory to the accused.[77] The most important documents requested by the prosecution were the stenographic recordings and transcripts of sessions of the Supreme Defense Council. The council was composed of the presidents of Serbia, Montenegro, and Yugoslavia, and was in charge of all aspects of Yugoslav security policy. It held numerous sessions between 1992 and the end of the Milošević regime, and the recordings and transcripts of those meetings allegedly showed how the regime operated and, most important, demonstrated Milošević's de facto control of Croatian and Bosnian Serbs. The Yugoslav government initially refused to hand over these documents. When it finally did – the "concession" was a direct consequence of another deadline for certification for U.S. financial aid – it requested that the documents be introduced into evidence on a confidential basis.

Although the purported reason for the confidentiality request was national security, an additional factor behind the Serbian request was the pending case against Serbia and Montenegro before the International Court of Justice (ICJ) in which Bosnia and Herzegovina claimed that Serbia was in breach of its obligations under the Genocide Convention. Serbia feared that the Supreme Defence Council documents could be used against it by Bosnia in the ICJ case.[78] Sadly, the Trial Chamber accepted Serbia's "national security" argument. By introducing documents of such importance under protective measures, the Trial Chamber effectively endorsed the Yugoslav government's effort to suppress the full truth of the events alleged in the indictment against Slobodan Milošević. The Supreme Defense Council documents were introduced into evidence during the testimony of Zoran Lilić, a figurehead president of Yugoslavia between 1993 and 1997. During his testimony, a representative of the government was present in the courtroom, and that representative decided whether a given document or part of the document could be introduced openly or confidentially. When the government opted for the latter, the Trial Chamber closed the session to the public for as long as it took to read it into the transcript or discuss it with the witness. This concealed from public view the true extent of Serbia's involvement in crimes in Bosnia and Herzegovina and Croatia. In the process, it betrayed the confidence that hundreds of thousands of victims in the former Yugoslavia had placed in the ICTY. Justice was not seen to be done.

If the tactic of the Yugoslav and Serbian governments was to conceal evidence of their involvement in the policy of ethnic cleansing in Bosnia and Herzegovina, then it seems to have worked. In February 2007, the ICJ found that Serbia was not responsible for genocide in Bosnia and Herzegovina. The court did find that Serbia had violated its obligations under the Genocide Convention by failing to prevent genocide, but only with respect to the massacre in Srebrenica in July 1995 and by its ongoing failure to arrest and transfer General Ratko Mladić to the ICTY.[79] Subsequent allegations of the acceptance on the part of Chief Prosecutor Carla del Ponte to go along with Serbian requests and seal "reasonable portions of the documents" further tarnished the reputation of the tribunal in the rest of the former Yugoslavia.[80] The ensuing revelations by the lead prosecutor in the Milošević case, Geoffrey Nice, that del Ponte's decision went against his and the wishes of other individuals involved in the case, presented perhaps the greatest threat to the credibility of the tribunal. The prosecutor's office publicly rejected any allegation that it had made a deal with Belgrade and emphasized that the decision to keep material confidential lay solely in the hands of the judges.[81] Whatever the reasons behind the prosecutor's decision, the impact of the entire incident had the effect of keeping Belgrade's responsibility out of public scrutiny and, significantly, away from that of the ICJ.[82]

A SELF-INFLICTED DEFEAT

The conduct of the trial has been heavily criticized for two reasons. The first, already mentioned, was the merger of the Croatia and Bosnia indictments with the Kosovo indictment, which massively expanded the scope of the trial. The prosecution case started with the Kosovo charges because those were at a more advanced stage of preparation when the trial started. Yet the events in Kosovo took place chronologically after those in Bosnia and Croatia, thereby diluting the public accounting of the history of Milošević's campaigns. This gave Milošević the opportunity to focus the crucial early moments of public attention on the more politicized circumstances of NATO's bombing, namely the lack of UN backing for the action.[83]

Second, the trial was characterized by extensive delays as Milošević's health progressively deteriorated during the course of the four-year trial, culminating with his death on March 11, 2006. As Milošević was representing himself, his ill health led to constant interruptions, with the Trial Chamber often only sitting for a few hours a day. Over time the chamber adopted a three day a week schedule to accommodate the accused's need to prepare his defense and medical advice about the strain the trial was taking on his health. The fact that after four years of trial Milošević died in his ICTY cell, shortly before his defense case – and the trial itself – was due to conclude, hardly made the trial appear a success.

Despite the lack of a final judgment, these reasons only go part way toward explaining the broader lack of impact of the trial as a whole, which requires deeper consideration of the context in which the ICTY arose and has continued to operate. First, the ICTY is not the Nuremberg Tribunal: it is not part of a broad political project, but rather a sui generis tribunal established by the UN Security Council in lieu of military action. Serbia, unlike postwar Germany, was not occupied following the end of the Milošević regime but was readily readmitted into the international community in good faith.[84] For that reason, the tribunal could only appeal to Western governments – and also, paradoxically, to those same governments in the region that were the most hostile to the ICTY – to apprehend individuals charged by the tribunal with serious violations of international criminal law. Furthermore, despite repeated calls by the ICTY for state cooperation with its orders, the two individuals believed to be chief orchestrators of the policy of ethnic cleansing in Bosnia and Herzegovina, Radovan Karadžić and Ratko Mladić, remained at large at the time of Milošević's death. In some ways, it was an impossible situation for the tribunal: to carry out its mandate – which meant independent and transparent prosecution – it had to rely on the politicians who saw the tribunal's mandate as contrary not only to their nationalist interests but also to other international community priorities in the former Yugoslavia. ICTY Prosecutor Carla del Ponte, in a 2007 interview with leading German weekly *Der Speigel*, stated that the international community refused to apprehend Karadžić for fear of increasing tensions in the region because the order of the day was peace building.[85] At the same time, if the ICTY had not adhered to more rigorous legal standards than those applied by the 1945 International Military Tribunal at Nuremberg – in which the Nazi defendants had no meaningful right of appeal and the prosecution introduced documentary evidence that defendants could not challenge – it would have been heavily criticized for the same swift but flawed justice meted out in Nuremberg.[86]

Second, the ICTY is a UN body: it suffers from many of the weaknesses that have earned the UN system public criticism, ranging from its over-bureaucratization to the lack of will to use the little power it has. Despite the fact that the ICTY's mandate derives from a Security Council resolution under Chapter VII of the UN Charter, which imposes a legally enforceable obligation on all UN member states to comply with its orders, this has made

little difference to the ICTY's ability to force Serbian cooperation in investigations or the arrest of fugitives. As the next chapter of this volume illustrates, it
was political will rather than Chapter VII authority that resulted in increased
governmental cooperation with the Special Court for Sierra Leone.

Third, there is considerable skepticism among tribunal staff about the legal
mandate of the ICTY. In the two years I spent reporting from the tribunal,
numerous officials told me that there was no consensus within the tribunal as
to what constitute "serious violations of international humanitarian law," no
sense of direction, and no agreement as to what the outcome of its work should
be other than to "give victims a voice." Furthermore, the reality of multiple
trial chambers and judicial opinions meant that there was no consistent legal
interpretation of the crimes committed in the former Yugoslavia. The only
widely shared belief was that genocide took place only in Srebrenica, whereas
crimes committed elsewhere before 1995 amounted to "ethnic cleansing,"
which was prosecuted under the rubric of crimes against humanity. To international lawyers "crimes against humanity" may be equally heinous, but to
the public, the paramount power of the term "genocide" remains.

Even if Milošević had lived long enough to be convicted – a verdict that
seemed likely – it would have brought neither satisfaction to the victims of his
campaigns nor an end to the widespread denial within parts of the region that
continue to block any effective "reconciliation process." From the moment
it was formed, the tribunal shied away from establishing a historical record
of the events in the former Yugoslavia in the 1990s. Whatever the Milošević
judgment would have been, there still would not have been a single, universally
accepted historical narrative of his role in the breakup of Yugoslavia and the
criminal campaigns he orchestrated. A judgment of acquittal – although highly
unlikely – would have spelled the end of the tribunal and boosted nationalist
appetites in the region – to the further disappointment and disillusionment of
Milošević's victims in Croatia, Bosnia and Herzegovina, and Kosovo.

EXPORTING INTERNATIONAL JUSTICE AND THE TRIBUNAL'S COMPLETION STRATEGY

The ICTY project was, to some extent, intended to serve as an example
that could spur greater domestic commitment to prosecuting war crimes.
In this regard, a crucial development that coincided with the Milošević trial
and shaped the implications of the trial in the region was the adoption of
the tribunal's completion strategy. The international community, growing
increasingly weary of footing the ICTY's more than $100 million annual price
tag, began to set deadlines for the end of the tribunal's work after fifteen

years of operation. The idea, which gradually took hold toward the end of the prosecution's case, has had mixed consequences for the progress of domestic war crimes prosecutions in the region of former Yugoslavia.

The completion strategy was formalized in a series of UN Security Council resolutions which had a detrimental effect on the impact and perception of the tribunal in the region, primarily in Bosnia and Herzegovina and the former Republic of Yugoslavia. Resolution 1503 called on the ICTY to end all investigations by 2004, all trials by the end of 2008, and all work (including appeals) by 2010. It was understood by many in the former Yugoslavia as giving blanket immunity to those in the important managerial levels of Milošević's criminal enterprise.

The prosecutor's focus now shifted from prosecuting "individuals responsible for serious violations of international humanitarian law" to trying only the most senior individuals. The most important reform, in organizational terms, was the establishment of the bureau, a body of judges tasked with assessing whether an individual whom the prosecutor seeks to indict is senior enough in the hierarchy to try internationally.[87] The tribunal's Rules of Procedure and Evidence were amended to allow for the transfer of individual cases to national jurisdictions. To achieve this integral element of the completion strategy, the legal and juridical landscape of the region had to be reformed to accommodate it.

Unfortunately, the international community ignored the evident lack of political will to prosecute war crimes in the countries of the region. Trials remain a political issue par excellence, and no political elite is willing to relinquish decision-making authority over who to try to a truly independent judiciary. Unwilling to finance sweeping reform of all judiciaries in the region – which was partially achieved only in Bosnia and Herzegovina – the international community opted for establishing separate prosecuting mechanisms and superimposing them on the existing legal system.[88]

Interestingly, the Security Council resolution and the completion strategy drew little criticism, save for the occasional newspaper article. The primary concern of the majority of victims and other interested parties was whether the tribunal would close its doors before Radovan Karadžić and Ratko Mladić were arrested, rather than a fuller analysis of whether there was indeed national capacity and willingness to try war crimes efficiently.

BOSNIA AND HERZEGOVINA: AGAINST ALL ODDS

In Bosnia and Herzegovina, a specialized War Crimes Chamber was established in 2002 by the Office of the High Representative (the international community's caretaker of the post-transition government) as part of the State Court of Bosnia and Herzegovina.[89] The court, which began taking cases in 2004, was modeled on the ICTY and is composed of an office of the prosecutor, chambers, and a registrar, the latter a legal novelty in Bosnia and Herzegovina. The court personnel include a mixture of national and international judges, prosecutors, and others with the international staff scheduled to transition out gradually until the court becomes a fully national institution. The procedural and criminal codes applied by the chamber contain a variety of adversarial features that are foreign to the the the codes previously in force and still used in district and cantonal courts throughout Bosnia and Herzegovina. In addition, the sentencing regime for war crimes is much harsher than under the previous codes. The War Crimes Chamber has jurisdiction not only over cases transferred to it from the ICTY but also over other domestic war crimes cases. As of March 2008, five cases have been transferred to the chamber from the ICTY.

Local prosecutions of war crimes before the War Crimes Chamber have primarily focused on foot soldiers, rather than individuals higher up the chain of command. Unlike trials before the ICTY, few cases have involved senior officials. A notable exception was the case against Momčilo Mandić, who was minister of justice in Radovan Karadžić's Republica Srpska government and alleged to have been responsible for notorious detention camps during the genocidal campaign against Bosnian Muslims and Bosnian Croats. Although named in ICTY investigations and indicted by the War Crimes Chamber for crimes against humanity and war crimes (for which he was subsequently acquitted for lack of evidence in 2008), he was initially arrested in 2003 in Serbia on suspicion of organized crime involvement relating to business activity used in association with the protection of Karadžić.[90]

Milošević's trial did not produce a meaningful debate within Bosnia and Herzegovina regarding his legacy there. On the contrary, it seems to have reinforced the divide between that young country's ethnic communities and their views on recent history. Neither the War Crimes Chamber nor any other court in the country has been able to seriously tackle the war crimes heritage.

Prosecutors cannot rely on the police to investigate war crimes, and state-level organizations are neither equipped nor staffed for the task.[91] Some war crimes suspects have found refuge in the police apparatus. When the State Prosecutor charged eleven Bosnian Serb police officers with genocide for executing 1,500 Bosnian Muslims during the Srebrenica operation, four of them turned out to be active police officers.[92] Hundreds of individuals – including some high up in the hierarchy – who allegedly were involved in crimes in Srebrenica were still employed by the Republika Srpska police for many years after the war, which explains at least in part why the war crimes prosecution record in that part of Bosnia and Herzegovina is so poor.[93]

This is especially important because the War Crimes Chamber will deal with only a few hundred "highly sensitive" cases, whereas others will be transferred to lower courts at the entity, district, and cantonal levels. Lower-level courts are, at best, reluctant and, at worst, unwilling to prosecute war crimes. When they do, trials often take place in hostile surroundings, with witnesses being intimidated and harassed, and prospects for fairness drastically diminished. It thus is possible for two individuals indicted for the same crimes in the same locality and during the same time period to be tried in different courts with completely different outcomes.[94]

The effectiveness of Bosnian prosecutions is further undermined by the fact that individuals indicted for war crimes in Bosnia and Herzegovina often find refuge in Croatia or Serbia on the basis of dual citizenship, which protects them from subsequent extradition and trial.[95]

SERBIA: JUDICIARY ON THE LEASH

Although war crimes prosecutions in Serbia have made some progress, as with the Milošević trial they have failed to make the Serbian public aware of crimes committed in its name or to hold senior officials accountable for wrongdoing, especially if their crimes were committed outside Serbia's borders. Under the Law on Organization and Jurisdiction of Government Authorities in Prosecuting Persons Guilty of War Crimes, which was passed in June 2003, a special War Crimes Chamber and an Office of the Special Prosecutor were established within the Belgrade District Court.[96] In addition, a special police investigative unit was set up, but that unit has been severely underfunded and understaffed, and gets no reliable cooperation from the rest of Serbia's police. In addition, war crimes prosecutions have been marred by the special prosecutor's avoidance of taking action against individuals believed to have been acting in their official capacity.[97]

War-crimes cases before the Belgrade District Court related to crimes committed in Bosnia and Herzegovina are particularly revealing. For example, indictments in two such cases allege that the crimes took place during a "non-international armed conflict" "in the then-Republic of Bosnia and Herzegovina," where "a civil war began between the members of the Serb, Croat, and Muslim ethnicities."[98] This is despite the fact that the international nature of the conflict in Bosnia and Herzegovina was judicially established in proceedings before the ICTY.[99]

One of these cases relates to crimes committed by the Scorpions, a notorious armed unit. Throughout the trial, the prosecution treated Scorpion unit members as part of a "private" group who obtained state-of-the-art weapons and equipment and crossed a heavily guarded border into a war zone on their own initiative, contrary to the existing evidence that the organization was officially part of Serbia's Ministry of the Interior.[100] In addition, the trial chamber capitulated when it came to asserting its authority in the courtroom and in examining witnesses. One such witness was Tomislav Kovač, the deputy minister of the Bosnian Serb Interior Ministry at the time of the massacre in Srebrenica, who signed the order for the Scorpion unit to go to Srebrenica, and who refused to answer questions pertaining to his contacts within Serbia's Ministry of the Interior who arranged for the unit to cross into Bosnia and Herzegovina. In fact, Kovač openly dared the presiding judge to find him in contempt of court for failing to answer the question; the judge dropped that line of questioning.[101]

The reluctance of the Serbian prosecution may be related to the belief among many Serb lawyers that the principles of command responsibility were not part of Serbian criminal law at the time the crimes were committed, notwithstanding the fact that Serbia and, before it, the Federal Republic of Yugoslavia were then bound by the Geneva Conventions which include command responsibility.[102] A more likely explanation, however, is Serbia's ongoing political reluctance to confront its responsibility for Serb war crimes in Bosnia.[103]

BETRAYING VICTIMS, FAILING JUSTICE

In short, the Milošević trial seems to have failed to produce any of the declared goals of the tribunal or the desired effect in the region. While the ICTY was not in a position to ensure an end to impunity for the members of Milošević's criminal enterprise back home, it failed to capitalize on its considerable legal and investigative expertise to contribute to the development of efficient and independent national judicial processes to prosecute Milošević's underlings in the former Yugoslav republics. In addition, the restrictions imposed on the tribunal by the international community's completion strategy have meant that the tribunal squandered its enormous potential to mete out desperately needed justice.

In a way, the ICTY seems to have been the victim of its own legalist policies. In refusing to acknowledge the role that politics played in its work and in war crimes prosecutions in the countries of the former Yugoslavia, its ability to fulfill its broader mandate was undermined by politicians who came to perceive the ICTY as a hindrance to the process of democratization in the region and, in particular, Serbia. That democratization was, in fact, being reduced to appeasement is a different matter altogether and is a subject beyond the scope of this chapter. The greatest achievement of the tribunal may turn out to be the fact that today it holds the largest archive on the dissolution of and ethnic cleansing in the former Yugoslavia, which sooner or later will be used to establish a convincing if not universally accepted historical narrative.

If Milošević were ever to have been held responsible for serious violations of international humanitarian law rather than abuse of power, the tribunal was still the sole logical venue. Trying him anywhere in the region may have had a stronger impact on public opinion, but it also would have been practically and technically impossible. Trying him for any other crimes would have been tantamount to denying his *true* victims in Croatia, Bosnia and Herzegovina, and Kosovo not only their day in court but also their right to truth and justice. That they did not get it makes the failure so much the greater.

NOTES

1. Opening Statement by Geoffrey Nice: "This trial is about the climb of this accused to power, power that the prosecution will invite the chamber to say, in due course, was exercised without accountability, responsibility, or morality. Such climbs cannot be accomplished alone. The help of fellow travelers is required, however quickly they may leave or be made to leave the moving vehicle, and from time to time we should just consider some of these men, co-indictees, some of them in the Kosovo indictment; others named as co-perpetrators in the Croatia and Bosnia indictments." *Prosecutor v. Slobodan Milošević*, IT-02-54, Opening Statement of Geoffrey Nice, Transcript p. 22, February 12, 2002. At the same time, the chief prosecutor, Carla del Ponte, did emphasize to the court that the trial was of an individual, and that the Serbian state was not on trial. See *Prosecutor v. Slobodan Milošević*, IT-02-54, Opening Statement of Carla del Ponte, Transcript p. 4, February 12, 2002, clarifying the individual nature of the prosecution.
2. Gary Bass, "Victor's Justice, Selfish Justice," *Social Research* 69, no. 4 (2002): 1040–1041.
3. Opening Statement by Chief Prosecutor Carla del Ponte: "This is a criminal trial. It is unfortunate that the accused has attempted to use his appearances before this chamber to make interventions of a political nature. I can assure the chamber that in the case before us the prosecution will not allow itself to be drawn into any such exchanges. This is a Trial Chamber, not a Debating Chamber." *Prosecutor v. Slobodan Milošević*, IT-02-54, Opening Statement of Carla del Ponte, Transcript p. 6, February 12, 2002.
4. On its Web site, the ICTY lists "spearheading the shift from impunity to accountability" as its chief achievement in the fifteen years since its establishment. It goes on to claim that "By holding individuals accountable regardless of their position,

the ICTY's work has dismantled the tradition of impunity for war crimes and other serious violations of international law, particularly by individuals who held the most senior positions, but also by others who committed especially grave crimes." "Tribunal at a Glance." Available at http://www.un.org/icty/glance-e/index.htm.

5. For further analysis of the trial of Slobodan Milošević, see Human Rights Watch, *Weighing the Evidence: Lessons from the Slobodan Milosevic Trial*, December 2006; Michael P. Scharf and William A. Schabas, *Slobodan Milosevic on Trial: A Companion*, New York: The Continuum International Publishing Group, 2002; Gideon Boas, *The Milošević Trial: Lessons for the Conduct of Complex International Criminal Proceedings*, Cambridge: Cambridge University Press, 2007; Chris Stephen, *Judgment Day: The Trial of Slobodan Milosevic*, New York: Atlantic Monthly Press, 2005.

6. Laura Silber and Allan Little, *Yugoslavia: Death of a Nation*, London: Penguin Books, 1997.

7. Nebojša Vladisavljević, "Serbia in Turmoil: Collapse of Communism, Mobilization and Nationalism," Ph.D. dissertation, London School of Economics, 2004.

8. Florence Hartmann, *Milosevic: la diagonale du fou*, Paris: Editions Deonel, 1999; Adam LeBor, *Milosevic: A Biography*, London: Palimpsest Books, 2002.

9. Daniele Conversi, "Central Secession: Towards a New Analytical Concept? The Case of Former Yugoslavia," *Journal of Ethnic and Migration Studies* 26, no. 2 (2000): 333.

10. This took place at the urging of Milošević and Serbian member of the presidency of Yugoslavia Borisav Jović, as the latter revealed in his shockingly candid and detailed diary published in 1996. Borisav Jović, *Posljednji dani SFRJ*, Kragujevac: Prizma, 1996.

11. Among many others, the testimony of Mustafa Čandić, a major in Yugoslav Air Force Counter-Intelligence Group, details the importance of the involvement of both JNA Security Administration and Resor Državne Bezbednosti in the armament of the Serb populations in Croatia and Bosnia and Herzegovina. *Prosecutor v. Slobodan Milošević*, IT-02–54, Testimony of Mustafa Čandić, Transcript pp. 12688–12833, October 10, 2002 and November 11, 2002.

12. Ewa Tabeau and Jakub Bijak, "War-related Deaths in the 1992–1995 Armed Conflicts in Bosnia and Herzegovina: A Critique of Previous Estimates and Recent Results," *European Journal of Population* 21, no. 4 (2005): 187.

13. S.C. Res. 827, May 25, 1993, U.N. Doc. S/RES/827 (1993).

14. Gary Bass, *Stay the Hand of Vengeance*, Princeton: Princeton University Press, 2002.

15. Samantha Power, "*A Problem from Hell": America and the Age of Genocide*, New York: Basic Books, 2002, 444.

16. Patrick Ball, *Policy or Panic? The Flight of Ethnic Albanians from Kosovo, March–May 1999*, Washington, D.C.: American Association for the Advancement of Science, 2000, 31.

17. Robert Thomas, *Serbia under Milosevic: Politics in the 1990s*, London: Hurst & Co., 1999.

18. Miloš Nikolić, *The Tragedy of Yugoslavia: The Rise, the Reign and the Fall of Slobodan Milosevic*, Baden-Baden: Nomos Verlagsgesellschaft, 2002.

19. ICTY press release, "President Milosevic and four other senior FRY officials indicted for murder, persecution and deportation in Kosovo," May 27, 1999.

20. Ibid.

21. David Hearst, Martin Walker and Richard Norton-Taylor " Slobodan Milosevic Indicted for War Crimes; Arrest warrant charges leader with responsibility for killings," *The Guardian*, May 27, 1999, p. 1.

22. Supra note 14.

23. French interior minister Jean-Pierre Chevenement, for instance, stated: "I do not approve of this initiative. It does not serve peace." David Hearst, Martin Walker and Richard Norton-Taylor " Slobodan Milosevic Indicted for War Crimes; Arrest warrant charges leader with responsibility for killings," *The Guardian*, May 27, 1999, p.1. It may be worth pointing out that a figure of such influence as Vojin Dimitrijević, the director of the Belgrade Centre for Human Rights, saw the indictment as no more than an obstacle to dealing with Milošević. He is quoted as saying: "Now Milosevic is put into a corner, and there's no incentive for him to make a compromise." David Hearst, Martin Walker and Richard Norton-Taylor, "Slobodan Milosevic Indicted for War Crimes."

24. Amnesty International Press Release, "Yugoslavia: Milosevic Must Be Transferred to the Hague," March 2, 2001.

25. Michael Ignatieff, "The Right Trial for Milosevic," *New York Times*, October 10, 2000, p. 27.

26. "Criminal Report Filed by the Belgrade Police with Belgrade County Prosecutor," *Nezavisne Novine*, April 3, 2001. The results of the investigation did not lead to an indictment, however, until after Milošević's death, so he was never formally charged with embezzlement.

27. Čeda Jovanović, "Pregovori i hapšenje Miloševića," *Nezavisne Novine*, May 8, 2005.

28. Adam LeBor, *Milosevic: A Biography*, London: Bloomsbury, 2002.

29. Convention on the Prevention and Punishment of the Crime of Genocide, January 12, 1951, U.N.T.S. No. 1021, vol. 28 (1951). See also *Bosnia and Herzegovina v. Serbia and Montenegro*, Judgment of 11 July 1996; *Croatia v. Serbia*, Application Instituting Proceedings, July 2, 1999.

30. As part of a resolution reaffirming the Dayton Agreement, the Security Council pointedly reminded the former Yugoslav states of their obligation to surrender indicted persons for trial. S.C. Res. 1357, June 21, 2001, U.N. Doc. S/RES/1357 (2001).

31. "DOS Leaders Agree to Pass a Federal Decree on Extraditing the Accused to the Hague Tribunal," *Serbia-Info Portal*, June 22, 2001.

32. "Savezni ustavni sud u četvrtak doneo (ne)očekivanu odluku: Primena Uredbe o Hagu odložena," *Glas Javnosti*, June 29, 2001.

33. Ibid.

34. "Na osnovu člana 90, tačka druga i člana 135. stav drugi Ustava Republike Srbije, Vlada odlučila: Milošević izručen Hagu," *Glas Javnosti*, June 29, 2001.

35. "Predsednik SRJ Vojislav Koštunica o izručenju Slobodana Miloševića Haškom tribunalu: Ishitreno i ponižavajuće," *Glas Javnosti*, June 29, 2001.

36. Prime Minister Đinđić stated that the primary motive for the decision on transfer of Milošević was "the possibility that before the beginning of the conference a huge number of countries cancel their participation." "Na osnovu člana 90," *Glas Javnosti*, June 29, 2001.

37. Dimitrije Boarov, "Serbs Await Western Aid," *IWPR*, Balkan Crisis Report No. 260, June 29, 2001.

38. "Milosevic Handover Prompts Controversy," *BBC News*, June 29, 2001. Available at http://news.bbc.co.uk/2/hi/europe/1412871.stm.

39. "Court Tries to Deliver Milosevic Warrant," *BBC News*, April 5, 2001. Available at http://news.bbc.co.uk/2/hi/europe/1259369.stm.

40. "EU'S Solana: No Pressure on Serbia to Extradite Milošević," *RFE/RL Newsline* 5, no. 66 (April 4, 2004).

41. Although named in the indictment, Milošević was unable to participate in his aide's trial in Belgrade for the assassination of Ivan Stambolić. Seven individuals were found guilty for the death of Stambolić and an attempt on the life of Serbian politician Vuk Drašković. Nicholas Wood, "Milosevic Aides Found Guilty of Yugoslav Political Assassination," *New York Times*, July 19, 2005, p. 2.

42. *Prosecutor v. Slobodan Milošević*, IT-02-54, Indictment for Case No. IT-01-51-I, 22 November 2001 (Bosnia); *Prosecutor v. Slobodan Milošević*, IT-02-54, Indictment for Case No. IT-01-50-I, 8 October 2001 (Croatia).

43. *Prosecutor v. Slobodan Milošević*, IT-02-54, Decision on Prosecution Interlocutory Appeal from Refusal to Order Joinder, Appeals Chamber, 1 February 2002; Mirko Klarin, "Analysis: Milosevic Wants It Both Ways," *IWPR*, Tribunal Update 253, February 4–9, 2002.

44. Michael P. Scharf, "The Perils of Permitting Self-Representation in International War Crimes Trials," *Journal of Human Rights* 4, no. 4, (2005): 513–520.

45. David Rieff, "Milošević in Retrospect," *Virginia Quarterly Review* 82, no. 3 (Summer 2006): 8–17.

46. Gideon Boas, *The Milošević Trial: Lessons for the Conduct of Complex International Criminal Proceedings*, Cambridge, MA: Cambridge University Press, 2007, 135–136, 146–147, 150; Mirko Klarin, "Analysis: Milosevic Prosecution 'Emasculated'," *IWPR*, Tribunal Update 261, April 8–13, 2002.

47. Mirko Klarin, "Analysis: Milosevic's Revenge," *IWPR*, Tribunal Update 260, April 1–6, 2002.

48. "Attitudes towards the ICTY in 2003," in *The Activity of ICTY and National War Crimes Judiciary*, Igor Bandović, ed., Belgrade: Center for Human Rights, 2005.

49. International Institute for Democracy and Electoral Assistance, "South Eastern Europe: New Means for Regional Analysis," April 4, 2002.

50. Igor Jovanovic, "Pavane for a Dead Dictator," *Transitions Online*, March 17, 2006.

51. Mirko Klarin, "Courtside: Milosevic Trial," *IWPR*, Tribunal Update 257, March 4–9, 2002.

52. *Prosecutor v. Slobodan Milošević*, IT-02-54, Testimony of Nike Peraj, Transcript pp. 4665–4666, May 9, 2002. See also Mirko Klarin, "Analysis: First Milosevic 'Insider' Testifies," *IWPR*, Tribunal Update 265, May 6–11, 2002.

53. Mirko Klarin, "Analysis: Milosevic Needs to Rethink Defense," *IWPR*, Tribunal Update 258, March 11–16, 2002.

54. *Prosecutor v. Slobodan Milošević*, IT-02-54, Testimony of Gen. Klaus Naumann, Transcript p. 6991, June 13, 2002. See also Mirko Klarin, ibid.

55. *Prosecutor v. Slobodan Milošević*, IT-02-54, Testimony of Dragan Karleusa, Transcript pp. 8345–8373, July 22, 2002.

56. Mirko Klarin, "Comment: Milosevic's Greater Serbia Project," *IWPR*, Tribunal Update 290, November 18–22, 2002.

57. *Prosecutor v. Slobodan Milošević*, IT-02-54, Testimony of Milan Babić, Transcript p. 13129, November 20, 2002. Territorial Defense was established by the Yugoslav Communist leadership in response to the Soviet invasion of Czechoslovakia in 1968 as part of the doctrine of an "all people's defense" developed as part of preparations for a similar attack against Yugoslavia. It was inspired by the partisan warfare during the Second World War but was removed from the JNA command structure and placed under the command of local civilian authorities across the former Yugoslavia. See also Marko Hoare Attila, *How Bosnia Armed*, London: Saqi Books, 2004.

58. *Prosecutor v. Slobodan Milošević*, IT-02-54, Testimony of Milan Babić, Transcript p. 13129, November 20, 2002.

59. Mirko Klarin, "Comment: Serbia's 'Secret War'," *IWPR*, Tribunal Update 286, October 21–26, 2002.

60. Mirko Klarin, "Comment: Milosevic's Greater Serbia Project," *IWPR*, Tribunal Update 290, November 18–22, 2002.

61. Mirko Klarin, "Milosevic Trial: Puppet States 'Financed from Belgrade'," *IWPR*, Tribunal Update 308, April 7–11, 2003.

62. Mirko Klarin, Ibid.; *Prosecutor v. Slobodan Milošević*, IT-02-54, Testimony of B-127, Transcript p. 24615, July 16, 2003; Stacy Sullivan, "Federal and Bosnian Serb Armies 'Were as One'," *IWPR*, Tribunal Update 321, July 24, 2003; Stacy Sullivan, "Milosevic Trial: Yugoslav Army Role Examined," *IWPR*, Tribunal Update 341, January 30, 2003.

63. Emir Suljagić, "Milosevic Linked to Srebrenica Massacre," *IWPR*, Tribunal Update 317, June 9–13, 2003. For a detailed examination of the links to Milošević, see *Prosecutor v. Slobodan Milošević*, IT-02-54, Prosecution Submission of Expert Statement of Dr. Budimir Babović Pursuant to rule 94 *bis*, April 25, 2003, para. 3.

64. *Prosecutor v. Slobodan Milošević*, IT-02-54, Testimony of Gen. Rupert Smith, Transcript p. 27329, October 9, 2003; Emir Suljagić, "UK General Links Milosevic to Srebrenica," *IWPR*, Tribunal Update 328, October 10, 2003.

65. *Prosecutor v. Slobodan Milošević*, IT-02-54, Testimony of Wesley Clark, Transcript p. 30373, December 15, 2003; Stacy Sullivan, "Milosevic 'Knew of Srebrenica Plans'," *IWPR*, Tribunal Update 338, December 19, 2003.

66. *Prosecutor v. Slobodan Milošević*, IT-02-54, Decision on Motion for Judgment of Acquittal, paras. 246, 288, 292, 298, 309, June 16, 2004.

67. The decision of the Trial Chamber, however, was not unanimous, with the Korean Judge O-Gon Kwon dissenting as to Milosevic's possession of "*dolus specialis* required for genocide, i.e., the intent to destroy the Bosnian Muslims as a group in whole or in part." Judge Kwon did agree, however, with the other two members of the Trial Chamber that there was sufficient evidence "upon which a Trial Chamber could convict the accused of (i) genocide under the third category of joint criminal enterprise, (ii) aiding and abetting or complicity in genocide, or

(iii) genocide as a superior under Article 7(3)." *Prosecutor v. Slobodan Milošević*, IT-02-54, Decision on Motion for Judgment of Acquittal, Dissenting opinion of Judge O-Gon Kwan paras. 1–2, June 16, 2004.

68. Chief of General Staff of Army of Yugoslavia (Vojska Jugoslavije/VJ) General Nebojša Pavković, currently a defendant at the ICTY in relation to crimes in Kosovo, and Yugoslav defense minister Slobodan Kralović issued a joint decree on March 26, 2001, establishing the Commission of Ministry of Defense and General Staff, with the mandate to "observe the cooperation between Federal Republic of Yugoslavia and Hague Tribunal and suggest ways, forms and extent of cooperation between organs of MoD and VJ with the tribunal." Furthermore, Article 11 of the Rules of Procedure of the Commission states that the Commission shall suggest to the Government "which information, document, report or other document shall be submitted, in other words what kind of cooperation could be realized." Reports of the commission from February and March 2002, weeks after the Milošević trial began, reveal that the commission had put in place a series of plans aimed at "preparing the accused, suspects and potential witnesses" at the ICTY and establishing contact with "legal advisors and attorneys of the accused persons at the Hague Tribunal in order to prepare an adequate defence for the members of the VJ-MoD." Savezno ministarstvo odbrane, no. 486-1, Beograd, Odluka. See also Poslovnik o radu Komisije Generalštaba Vojske Jugoslavije i Saveznog ministarstva odbrane za saradnju sa Haškim tribunalom, April 30, 2001; Analiza dosadašnjeg suđenja pred haškim tribunalom – problemi i predlozi mera, Komisija za saradnju sa haškim tribunalom, February 20, 2002; Rad Komisije GŠ VJ i SMO – informacija, Komisija za saradnju sa haškim tribunalom, March 26, 2002.

69. Čeda Jovanović, "Pregovori i hapšenje Miloševića," *Nezavisne Novine*, May 8, 2005.

70. *Prosecutor v. Slobodan Milošević*, IT-02-54, 54*bis* Motion Hearing, Transcript pp. 21661–21662, June 3, 2003.

71. See, for example, *Prosecutor v. Dario Kordic and Mario Cerkez*, IT-95-14/2, Order to the Republic of Croatia for the Production of Documents, February 4, 1999.

72. Press briefing by Yugoslavia tribunal prosecutor, March 21, 2002.

73. Stacy Sullivan, "Belgrade Accused of Obstructing Hague," *IWPR*, Tribunal Update 315, May 26–30, 2003. Under the Rule 54 bis of the ICTY Rules of Procedure and Evidence a party to the proceedings may apply to the Trial Chamber and ask it to order states to produce documents in writing provided they: "(i) identify as far as possible the documents or information to which the application relates; (ii) indicate how they are relevant to any matter in issue before the Judge or Trial Chamber and necessary for a fair determination of that matter; and (iii) explain the steps that have been taken by the applicant to secure the State's assistance."

74. "There is one where there's been a development, as we understand it, to this extent: That the pathologist who has done the work at Izbica is owed a very large sum of money by the government of Serbia and Montenegro, and until she's paid that money, she's not going to hand over many of the documents that relate to that crime scene. And so if that be right, the documents should be in the possession of the government, but by not paying her bill, they find themselves in the position

of not being able to answer our proper request." *Prosecutor v. Slobodan Milošević*, IT-02-54, 54*bis* Motion Hearing, Transcript pp. 17527–17528, March 10, 2003.

75. *Prosecutor v. Slobodan Milošević*, IT-02-54, 54*bis* Motion Hearing, Transcript p. 21669, June 3, 2003; Stacy Sullivan, "Belgrade Accused of Obstructing Hague," *IWPR*, Tribunal Update 315, May 26–30, 2003.

76. *Prosecutor v. Slobodan Milošević*, IT-02-54, 54*bis* Motion Hearing, Transcript pp. 21661–21662, June 3, 2003.

77. "They would appear to be exculpatory and selectively so and that they are outside the period we've asked for." *Prosecutor v. Slobodan Milošević*, IT-02-54, 54*bis* Motion Hearing, Transcript p. 21660, June 3, 2003.

78. Stacy Sullivan, "Belgrade Accused of Obstructing Hague," *IWPR*, Tribunal Update 315, May 26–30, 2003.

79. *Bosnia and Herzegovina v. Serbia and Montenegro*, International Court of Justice Judgment of 26 February 2007, para. 471.

80. Marlise Simons, "Serbia's darkest pages hidden from genocide court," *International Herald Tribune*, April 8, 2007, p.1; these allegations were rejected by the OTP. Lisa Clifford, "Del Ponte Denies Belgrade Deal Claims," *IWPR*, Tribunal Update 498, April 20, 2007.

81. Lisa Clifford, "Del Ponte Denies Belgrade Deal Claims," *IWPR*, Tribunal Update 498, April 20, 2007.

82. "There was no legal basis for the withholding of the records from the public. It served only one purpose: to keep Belgrade's responsibility from public scrutiny and, significantly, from the International Court of Justice." Letter from Geoffrey Nice, "Hidden from Public View; Campaign Finance Reform; The Tragedy of Iraq," *International Herald Tribune*, April 16, 2007. Available at http://news.bbc.co.uk/2/hi/europe/1259369.stm. See also Nice's letter to a leading Croatian daily, "Carla del Ponte nagodila se s Beogradom," *Jutarnji list*, April 14, 2007. Available at http://www.studiacroatica.org/bol2007/20070414_nagodila.htm.

83. See further discussion of this at Human Rights Watch, *Weighing the Evidence: Lessons from the Slobodan Milošević Trial*, December 2006, p. 58.

84. Once Milošević was out of office, the international community was quick to act on its promises: Yugoslavia was readmitted into United Nations on November 1 and into the Organization for Security and Cooperation in Europe on November 10, 2001. In November 2001, Serbia applied for membership in the Council of Europe and was granted a special guest status as early as January 2002. The EU initially provided Serbia with 200 million euros. In February 2001, the EU lifted long-standing sanctions imposed on the Federal Republic of Yugoslavia and in April allocated the first part of a 240 million euro aid program for Yugoslavia. Furthermore, in mid-July, the EU Council of Ministers invested 300 million euros in macro financial aid for the Federal Republic of Yugoslavia. The United States, for its part, pledged $182 million immediately after the rendition of Slobodan Milošević. Human Rights Watch, *World Report 2002: Federal Republic of Yugoslavia*, 2002.

85. "'Politics Have Interfered with Our Work'," *Der Spiegel*, October 18, 2007.

86. Helena Cobban, "International Courts," *Foreign Policy*, March–April 2005.

87. Rachel S. Taylor, "Judges Change the Rules," *IWPR*, Tribunal Update 353, April 16, 2004.

88. For assessments of these national courts, see Bogdan Ivanišević, *Against the Current: War Crimes Prosecutions in Serbia*, International Center for Transitional Justice, 2007; and Human Rights Watch, *Narrowing the Impunity Gap: Trials before Bosnia's War Crimes Chamber*, February 2007.

89. Law on the Court of Bosnia and Herzegovina, Odluka Visokog predstavnika, Zakon o Sudu BiH, Službeni glasnik BiH (*Official Gazette of Bosnia and Herzegovina*), nos. 29/00, 15/02, 16/02, 24/02, 3/03, 37/03, 61/04, and 32/07, article 13(1).

90. In relation to the organized crime charges see Emir Suljagić, "Tribunal Probes Bosnian Serb Tycoon," *IWPR*, Tribunal Update 310, April 21–25, 2003.

91. Human Rights Watch, *Justice at Risk: War Crimes Trials in Croatia, Bosnia and Herzegovina and Serbia*, October 2004.

92. "Genocide indictees on RS Interior Ministry Payroll," *Balkan Investigative Reporting Network*, Justice Report, March 24, 2006.

93. Nerma Jelačić and Emir Suljagić, "Justice Reports Investigates: Srebrenica Suspect is an RS Official," *Balkan Investigative Reporting Network*, Justice Report, May 5, 2006.`

94. Human Rights Watch, *Still Waiting: Bringing Justice for War Crimes, Crimes against Humanity, and Genocide in Bosnia and Herzegovina's Cantonal and District Courts*, July 2008, sections IV, V, and IX.

95. "Naš su problem dvojna državljanstva," Interview with President of the Court of BiH Meddžida Kreso, *Dani*, March 11, 2005.

96. Helsinški odbor za ljudska prava u Srbiji, Sigurnost građana u nedovršenoj državi, Belgrade, 2005.

97. Bogdan Ivanišević, *Against the Current: War Crimes Prosecutions in Serbia*, International Center for Transitional Justice, 2007.

98. See the discussion of the *Zvornik* case in Bogdan Ivanišević, *Against the Current: War Crimes Prosecutions in Serbia*, International Center for Transitional Justice, 2007, p. 10.

99. For example, the ICTY Appeals Chamber first developed this argument in the Tadić judgment (*Prosecutor v. Duško Tadic*, Case No. IT-94-A, Judgment, July 15, 1999) and then in the judgment in the Čelebići case (*Prosecutor v. Zejnil Delalić et al.*, Case No. IT-96-21-A, Judgment, February 20, 2001). See Bogdan Ivanišević, *Against the Current: War Crimes Prosecutions in Serbia*, International Center for Transitional Justice, 2007, p. 10.

100. "Dokazano da su "Škorpioni" pripadali SAJ-u," *Nezavisne Novine*, June 8, 2005.

101. Veće za ratne zločine, Republika Srbija, Okružni sud u Beogradu, Posl. Br. K.V. br. 06/2005, Transkript audio zapisa sa glavnog pretresa, July 3, 2006.

102. Humanitarian Law Center, "Analysis: Command Responsibility: The Contemporary Law," War Crimes Trials Before National Courts, Belgrade, February 23, 2004.

103. The sentencing judgment against members of the Scorpions seemed to have borne out this possibility to the full extent. Four of the members of the Scorpions – Slobodan Medić, Branislav Medić, Aleksandar Medić, and Petar Petrašević – were convicted and sentenced to fifty-eight years altogether; the fifth member Aleksandar Vukov was acquitted. In its sentencing judgment, however, the judges of the Belgrade District Court went along with the official line that the conflict in Bosnia and Herzegovina was a "civil war" and that members of the Scorpions

were there as a "paramilitary group," rather than investigate their evident links with the top leadership of Resor Državne Bezbednosti and the state of Serbia. Merdijana Sadovic, "Scorpions Judgment Sparks Debate in Serbia and Bosnia," *IWPR*, Tribunal Update No. 497, April 13, 2007. See also "In the Sign of Scorpio," *Oslobođenje, Sarajevo*, April 12, 2007.

10

A Big Man in a Small Cell: Charles Taylor and the Special Court for Sierra Leone

Abdul Tejan-Cole

On March 29, 2006, a United Nations (UN) helicopter carrying former Liberian president Charles Taylor flew over Sierra Leone's capital, Freetown, and landed in the fortified compound of the Special Court for Sierra Leone (Special Court). Cheering crowds flowed into the streets around the Special Court at the sight of the arriving helicopter, and once it landed, Charles Taylor entered cell number three at the court's detention center to await his trial on charges for war crimes and crimes against humanity. Only a few weeks earlier, Taylor had seemed untouchable, comfortably exiled in a Nigerian villa for almost three years in a deal that had been backed by international and regional leaders. During more than a decade of twisting and turning fortunes, Charles Taylor had been emblematic of impunity in West Africa. This chapter chronicles how the existence of an independent prosecutor backed by a joint national-international court, interrupted the all-too-common African tradition of giving former leaders accused of serious crimes a comfortable exit once they relinquish power. Over the years, Taylor rose from a wily official who fled his country to evade corruption charges and reportedly escaped from a U.S. prison, to a successful warlord enmeshed in the power struggles of West African politics, to the elected president of Liberia with a penchant for dramatic displays of power.[1] Bringing Taylor to face justice for his role in the conflict in neighboring Sierra Leone has been a litmus test for the Special Court and has left lingering questions for his victims in Liberia where he may have committed worse crimes. It also set a precedent that has sent ripples across the African continent.

FROM WARLORD TO PRESIDENT: THE RISE OF CHARLES TAYLOR

On December 24, 1989, a group of insurgents describing themselves as the National Patriotic Front of Liberia (NPFL), led by Charles Ghankay Taylor, attacked the border town of Butuo in northeastern Liberia, from neighboring Côte d'Ivoire.[2] This attack marked the beginning of a brutal seven-year civil war in Liberia that grew into a regional conflict engulfing Sierra Leone, Guinea, and subsequently Côte d'Ivoire.[3] Taylor's launch pad was provided by Côte d'Ivoire's president Houphouet-Boigny, who sought a Liberian leader under Ivorian influence to counter Nigerian designs on regional hegemony. Further support for Taylor's NPFL came from powerful regional actors, with troops and transport provided by Burkina Faso and training and weapons by Libya. After the public torture and murder of Liberian president Samuel Doe by a breakaway faction of Taylor's NPFL, the conflict escalated. Other armed groups emerged including the United Liberation Forces of Liberia (ULIMO), led by former members of Doe's cabinet such as Alhaji Kromah, and Roosevelt Johnson.[4] Much of the conflict was formed along tribal lines. ULIMO was founded with the declared objective of rescuing Krahns and Mandingoes from ethnic cleansing instituted by the NPFL's predominantly Gio-Mano fighters, declared enemies of Krahns and Mandingoes who had been similarly persecuted by Doe's military regime.[5]

Despite the intervention of a regional military force known as the Economic Community of West African States Cease-Fire Monitoring Group (ECO-MOG) that at its peak numbered 17,000 troops, the conflict continued to rage. ECOMOG was established by the Economic Community of West African States (ECOWAS), and was composed of troops from the national armies of Sierra Leone, Guinea, and Nigeria. In reality, Nigeria contributed most of the troops, material, and financial backing for the force. Alliances between the various breakaway rebel factions shifted regularly, and cease-fires were agreed and then almost immediately broken, during which the fighting continued. Throughout the war, all factions regularly terrorized the local population. Extrajudicial killings, torture, rape, forced labor, and other atrocities against civilians were widespread. In addition, the country's natural and economic resources became a private enterprise for Taylor and many of the other warlords.

After numerous failed peace agreements, ECOMOG eventually managed to put an end to the mayhem and the UN-sanctioned Abuja Accord was signed on August 19, 1995. It called for a cease-fire, amnesty for warring factions, and a transitional government with executive powers vested in a six-member Council of State that included Charles Taylor as the NPFL representative. Taylor and Kromah became civilian leaders of the newly formed interim Liberian government.

General elections were held in July 1997, and despite reports of NPLF intimidation of voters, Charles Taylor and his National Patriotic Party garnered

75 percent of the vote. This overwhelming victory may be attributed, at least in part, to fear among Liberians that if Taylor lost, he would simply resume fighting. Liberians had watched the international community condone the atrocities committed by Taylor and his men. For seven years, they had brutally murdered and maimed, looted and burnt properties, raped and abducted women, and drugged innocent boys under the eyes of ECOMOG and the United Nations. Yet despite this, in the lead up to the elections Taylor was rewarded with the chairmanship of the transitional presidency; was given control of the national police force headed by his cousin, Joseph Tate; and his troops were largely left armed and were in control of most of the country during the elections. In August 1997, Taylor became the elected president of Liberia.

It is estimated that during the seven years of fighting that preceded his victory, at least one-third of Liberia's prewar population fled the country, more than half was internally displaced, and more than two hundred thousand lives were lost.[6] Women were raped and subjected to other forms of extreme sexual violence, and killings and abductions were prevalent. Liberia's economy was devastated, leaving 80 percent of the population unemployed.[7]

THE TAYLOR PRESIDENCY – THE TYRANNY CONTINUES

Taylor's 1997 triumph did not transform him from a warlord into a states-man. Taylor ruled by centralizing power, rewarding allies, and intimidating antagonists. After years of war, state institutions remained weak, and corruption was rife; high-ranking government officials misused state power to further their political objectives. Taylor and his loyalists monopolized businesses for their own financial interests. Although constitutional rule had been reinstated and Taylor promised a new era for Liberia, human rights abuses persisted as well.[8] Political murders and extrajudicial executions were prevalent, as were abductions or beatings of political opponents, students, journalists, and human rights activists. Press censorship was overt, as Taylor closed media companies and took the owners and operators captive, often tormenting or mistreating them. The Special Operations Division, a special unit of the police forces, and the Special Security Unit, headed by Taylor's son Charles "Chuckie" Taylor, became the instruments of terror.[9] These units murdered, tortured, abducted, raped, and illegally arrested alleged adversaries of the regime.

Signs of a second civil war began to show as early as 1999, when rebels fighting under the name of the Liberians United for Reconciliation and Democracy (LURD) crossed into Liberia from Guinea and for the next year waged war to unseat Taylor. Taylor responded with repression. He arrested and tortured journalists and civil society activists, and charged some of them with espionage.

THE SIERRA LEONE CONFLICT – A TAYLOR-MADE CATASTROPHE

When Taylor launched his 1989 rebellion in Liberia, he had many Sierra Leonean fighters in his NPFL. Since then Sierra Leone's fortunes have been intimately tied to those of Liberia. In March 1991, about 100 fighters trained by Taylor's NPFL, including some of his commanders, invaded the town of Bomaru, a small village in the southeastern corner of Kailahun District in eastern Sierra Leone and announced the presence of the Revolutionary United Front (RUF). A former Sierra Leone army corporal, Foday Saybana Sankoh, was its official commander. From the outset, Charles Taylor acted as mentor, patron, banker, and weapons supplier for this motley collection of Sierra Leonean dissidents, bandits, and mercenaries.

The RUF, in its manifesto "Footpaths to Democracy," claimed to seek political and economic resources for the country's rural population, arguing that the urban elite exploited peasants. "We are fighting for a new Sierra Leone," the RUF asserted, "[a] new Sierra Leone of freedom, justice, and equal opportunity for all. We are fighting for democracy, and by democracy we mean equal opportunity and access to power to create wealth through free trade, commerce, agriculture, industry, science, and technology."[10] Although the RUF claimed to be fighting to oust the corrupt political order and expand access to Sierra Leone's economic resources, its philosophy of salvation quickly degenerated into a movement of brutality and cruelty. With the support of Taylor and the NPFL, the rebels made rapid progress. Years of misrule in Sierra Leone by past presidents Siaka Stevens and Joseph Saidu Momoh provided a suitable platform, of which the RUF took full advantage.

As Sierra Leone's war progressed, Taylor allowed rebels full access to Liberian territory for supply routes and facilitated the flow of weapons to the RUF. The callousness of the combatants on all sides imposed a terrible rule of terror across the country. Thousands of children were abducted and turned into sex slaves or combatants, over a thousand civilians were maimed, and five hundred thousand were forced to become refugees from the war zones.[11] The RUF and its NPFL collaborators brutalized civilians throughout the war. They massacred, raped, burned villages, and looted. The factions reveled in imaginative torture techniques: the NPFL decapitated civilians, sometimes in front of their families, and RUF fighters sliced open the bellies of pregnant women after placing bets on the sex of the fetus. There are no reliable estimates of civilian deaths, but at least seventy-five thousand people perished during the war that engulfed Sierra Leone through most of the 1990s, and well over one million Sierra Leoneans fled their homes.[12] Many spent years in refugee camps, fleeing from country to country as the fighting moved.

The RUF was functionally a faction of the NPFL. Throughout the war, Taylor's forces and the RUF coordinated attacks, exchanged weaponry, and shared fighters and commanders. Taylor was the most efficient and effective entrepreneur among the Liberian warlords, exploiting RUF-controlled territory for personal gain. Taylor and the RUF exchanged arms for diamonds throughout the war, a trade the UN estimated at between $25 million and $125 million annually.[13] With the profits from the diamond trade (the diamonds were worth far more than the weapons and ammunition he supplied the RUF), Taylor created a patronage network, bestowing cars, generous salaries, and luxurious houses on senior aides.[14] His elevation to Liberia's presidency in 1997 gave him international legitimacy, and by the late 1990s, Liberia became a major center for massive diamond-related criminal activity. It had connections to guns, drugs, and money laundering throughout Africa and considerably further afield.[15]

There are various theories as to why Taylor championed the RUF's cause. One was that he acted purely for economic reasons. However, Taylor was also angry with Sierra Leone and some other West African countries that, in addition to backing other factions such as ULIMO, then under the auspices of the Nigerian-dominated ECOWAS, had deployed ECOMOG troops in Monrovia and prolonged Taylor's march to the Executive Mansion to seize power. Furious at being thwarted, Taylor threatened that Sierra Leone, the ECOMOG force's military base, soon would "taste the bitterness of war."[16] It was not long after this threat that the RUF launched its invasion.

Another theory is that Taylor had agreed to support the RUF's leader, Foday Sankoh, long before starting the war.[17] In the late 1980s, Charles Taylor and Foday Sankoh became friends when they each received military training in Libya from the government of Mu'ammar al-Quadhafi.[18] It is speculated that the men signed a pact in Libya to support each other's wars. It was also said to be part of al-Quadhafi's grand scheme to gain political influence in the subregion.[19]

In November 1996, a peace accord was signed between the RUF and the democratically elected Sierra Leone government of President Ahmad Tejan Kabbah. However, the accord failed and the fighting continued. After a breakaway group of young Sierra Leone Armed Forces launched a brief coup in 1997 and joined forces with the RUF, ECOMOG was deployed once again, this time to provide backup to Sierra Leonean forces supporting Kabbah's government.

It was not until July 1999, by which time Taylor was firmly at the helm in Liberia, that the Lomé Peace Accord was signed between the RUF and the government of Sierra Leone.[20] The accord provided for a power-sharing arrangement that granted Foday Sankoh the vice presidency and continued control over Sierra Leone's diamond resources as chairman of a commission on natural resources. It also provided for the creation of a Truth and Reconciliation Commission (TRC) to aid in reconciling the various factions and to provide a forum for victims and combatants to tell their stories and begin a healing process for all Sierra Leoneans. In addition, the accord provided a complete and unconditional amnesty to all combatants for activities occurring after 1991. The UN representative who witnessed the agreement added a provision stating that the amnesty and pardon would not apply to crimes of genocide, crimes against humanity, war crimes, and other serious violations of international humanitarian law committed during the conflict.

THE SPECIAL COURT FOR SIERRA LEONE

In May 2000, the rebels violated the peace agreement when they took UN peacekeepers hostage and despite the amnesty contained in the Lomé Accord, Foday Sankoh was finally arrested. The government was not prepared to face the prospect of actually putting Sankoh on trial, however. In June 2000, President Kabbah wrote to the UN secretary-general requesting the establishment of an independent court to address the violations committed by the RUF during the war.[21] In 2002, the UN and the government of Sierra Leone entered into a bilateral agreement to establish the Special Court for Sierra Leone with the mandate to prosecute "those persons who bear the greatest responsibility for serious violations of international humanitarian law and Sierra Leonean law committed in the territory of Sierra Leone since November 30, 1996."[22] The Special Court began functioning in late 2002. Located in Sierra Leone's capital, Freetown, it was initially expected to complete its work within three years, although more recent estimates see the court's work continuing until at least the end of 2009. The Special Court is often described as a hybrid tribunal, mixing international and national elements about matters such as staff composition and applicable law. Two-thirds of the judges are appointed by the UN, as are the prosecutor and registrar. One-third of the judges are appointed by the government of Sierra Leone, as is the deputy prosecutor.

The decision to create a mixed tribunal of national and international judges was due among other factors to practical considerations and fears about the neutrality and potential destabilizing effects of national trials. The Sierra Leonean judicial system was largely decimated as a result of the war and years of neglect after successive coups. It is only functional in Freetown and lacks the enormous human and financial resources required to undertake postconflict trials. In deciding to establish the court, the UN Security Council noted "the negative impact of the security situation on the administration of justice in Sierra Leone and the pressing need for international cooperation to assist in strengthening the judicial system of Sierra Leone."[23] Although the Security Council also noted that the situation in Sierra Leone constituted a threat to international peace and security in the region, the council did not create the Special Court as an organ of the United Natons, as it had done in creating the International Criminal Tribunals for Rwanda and the former Yugoslavia. As a result, the Special Court is not funded from the regular UN budget, which is dependent on voluntary contributions from states, and its orders are only binding and enforceable within Sierra Leone, with no power to compel cooperation from authorities outside the country.

In addition to the focus on "those who bear the greatest responsibility," the Special Court's jurisdiction imposes individual criminal responsibility on all those who committed crimes, regardless of their position in the chain of command. The statute explicitly provides that "The official position of any accused persons, whether as head of state or government or as a responsible government official, shall not relieve such person of criminal responsibility nor mitigate punishment."[24]

As the Special Court commenced its investigative operations, the name Charles Taylor constantly came up. The investigations coincided with increased fighting in Liberia between Taylor's army and the Liberian rebel groups. Not unsurprisingly, the first case file and, indeed, the first indictment issued by the court was against Charles Taylor – on March 7, 2003.[25] Upon the request of the prosecutor, the court ordered that both the indictment and the accompanying arrest warrant remain sealed from public view.[26] In the months that followed, the Special Court proceeded to issue public indictments for the main leaders of the RUF (including Foday Sankoh, who died in custody of a stroke shortly after his initial appearance before a Special Court judge) and leaders of the Armed Forces Revolutionary Council (AFRC). All of these indictments included factual allegations naming Charles Taylor as the key RUF supporter, yet all the while Taylor continued to serve as president of neighboring Liberia, where the conflict was once again worsening. Most of the others accused by the Special Court were promptly arrested and transferred to the court's custody, including a particularly controversial indictee, Sam Hinga Norman, who at the time of his arrest was minister of interior and was charged with crimes committed by the pro-government forces known as the Civil Defence Forces. Two of the indictees whom the Special Court was not able to arrest were AFRC/RUF figures Johnny Paul Koroma and Sam Bockarie, and allegations persisted that Taylor was harboring them in Liberia or Côte d'Ivoire.[27] Bockarie was later found dead, allegedly killed by Taylor's men to prevent him from testifying.

Speculation about the potential indictment of Taylor hung over the early months of the Special Court's operations and was discussed off-the-record in meetings in the subregion. Human rights groups openly called for Taylor's indictment and public statements by the Special Court prosecutor made it clear that it was only a matter of time.[28]

THE LIBERIAN PEACE PROCESS AND THE UNSEALING OF TAYLOR'S INDICTMENT

In the meantime, the situation continued to deteriorate in Liberia. The governments of neighboring countries explored other means of ending the civil war. Replicating what had become a regional practice, Taylor's opponents backed the new round of Liberian rebel groups in their campaigns to oust Taylor. The largest rebel group, LURD, received support from Guinea, and some evidence suggests that support was provided by Sierra Leone as well. The smaller Liberian rebel group, Movement for Democracy in Liberia (MODEL), found backing in Côte d'Ivoire.[29] The rebels made significant progress in gaining territory and advanced quickly toward the capital, Monrovia. These campaigns greatly reduced Taylor's control over the country, effectively restricting his grasp to little more than Monrovia. By the middle of 2003, LURD forces were regularly threatening the capital.

Diplomatic efforts to avert another catastrophe in Liberia also increased. Headed by representatives of the African Union (AU) and ECOWAS, regional and international discussions were underway regarding how to negotiate Taylor's removal from office. Taylor, however, continued to demonstrate a keen ability to survive through a tight grip on political power, sanctions busting, and a series of convenient alliances. It remained unclear whether the rebel movements would depose him. Moreover, many members of the international community were worried that a military victory by either rebel party would not bring Liberia real peace and a better government. Seizing on Taylor's weakened position, regional and Western diplomats, including those from the United States, intensified efforts to bolster the Liberian peace process. Diplomats found glimmers of hope in reported plans by Taylor to commit to peace and to address serious governance problems in the country. Taking advantage of the added pressure from the rebel military success, they negotiated a new round of peace talks involving all the major parties to the conflict. By June 2003, the stage was finally set for top-level negotiations in Accra, Ghana. African leaders and U.S. diplomats undertook a concerted campaign to convince Taylor to participate personally in the Accra talks. Taylor yielded, and all parties to the conflict were guaranteed their security while attending the conference. Some diplomats considered the Accra talks the best chance in years to create a peaceful, durable solution for Liberia that would also remove Taylor by allowing him a graceful exit from the presidency as part of a negotiated settlement.[30]

Although the legal and diplomatic processes were unconnected, things soon came to a head. On June 4, 2003, while Taylor was in Ghana attending the opening day of the peace talks intended to end the civil war in Liberia, the Special Court prosecutor unsealed the indictment and appealed to Ghanaian authorities (via Ghana's High Commission in Freetown) to arrest their guest for war crimes and transfer him to Sierra Leone.[31]

The timing and means by which the prosecutor publicly announced the unsealing of the indictment were roundly condemned by countries involved in the peace talks. That same day, a Ghanaian Foreign Ministry official denied receiving any documents relating to the arrest warrant, and despite the Special Court's claims to the contrary, it was not certain that the documents had in fact been transmitted to Ghana by its High Commission before the Special Court made it public. The court said it did not notify Ghana earlier because it could not be certain officials would not warn Taylor.[32] Taylor himself was reportedly shocked by the announcement, stating, "What do you mean indictment? It's not possible to indict a head of state."[33]

The Ghanaians promptly refused to enforce the warrant and gave Taylor a presidential plane to return quickly to Liberia. The Ghanaian government complained that it was blindsided and embarrassed by the "surprise" request to send Taylor to the Court. In an interview in the magazine *New African*, Ghanaian president and host of the talks John Kufuor expressed his sense of embarrassment and betrayal:

> Five African presidents were meeting in Accra to find ways of kick-starting the Liberian peace process, and Mr. Taylor had been invited as president of Liberia. We were not even aware that a warrant had been issued for his arrest. Incidentally, the African leadership had taken the initiative to convince Mr. Taylor to resign and allow all the factions in Liberia to negotiate. It was when the presidents were leaving my office for the Conference Center where Mr. Taylor was expected to make a statement that word came in that a warrant had been issued for his arrest. I really felt betrayed by the international

community [and] I informed the United States of the embarrassment that the announcement caused.[34]

Some accused the prosecutor, David Crane, an American, of thinking more about U.S. interests than those of Sierra Leone and the subregion. Both African and American officials who sponsored the talks in Accra were angry that their efforts were thwarted, complaining that the "overzealous" prosecutor was jeopardizing their peace initiative.[35] Some argued that the court might have secured Taylor had it consulted with the Ghanaians prior to the announcement; however, there were real concerns that arresting Taylor in Accra could have led to an increase in hostilities by Taylor's militias.[36] The prosecutor continued to assert that his decision was aimed at supporting the peace process; given Taylor's record of breaking previous agreements, the parties at the peace talks needed to know that they were now negotiating with an indicted war criminal, who, in Crane's opinion, could never be trusted.

THE INDICTMENT

Charles Taylor was originally indicted on seventeen counts of war crimes, crimes against humanity, and other serious violations of international humanitarian law.[37] Although the indictment was later reduced to eleven charges, the crimes alleged include unlawful killings, terrorizing the civilian population, rape and sexual violence, forced labor, and the recruitment and use of child soldiers. He was charged with direct responsibility for the crimes, participating in a joint criminal enterprise, and exercising command and control over subordinate members of the RUF, AFRC, or Liberian fighters. Of particular significance for the dynamics around perceptions of the indictment, Taylor was not charged for offenses committed in Liberia, but only for acts committed in Sierra Leone during that civil war. Because of the limitations on the Special Court's temporal jurisdiction, the prosecution's charges were also limited to offenses between November 30, 1996, and January 18, 2002.[38] Yet the Special Court's indictment of Taylor raised difficult questions for key stakeholders about accountability for crimes committed in Liberia and the impact for the whole region.

THE OFFER OF A GRACEFUL EXIT

In response to learning of the Special Court indictment, Taylor offered to vacate the presidency if he was seen as the impediment to peace. Few believed it was a genuine offer.[39] After Taylor returned home to Monrovia, the rebel forces increased their attacks on the Liberian capital. At the same time, and despite Taylor's departure, the Accra talks continued, ultimately concluding seventy-six days later with a comprehensive peace agreement that finally ended the conflict. As the rebels had insisted that justice for both human rights and economic crimes not be amnestied as part of the negotiations, the peace agreement included a range of measures such as the establishment of a truth and reconciliation commission, judicial reforms, and vetting of the security services. In addition, the agreement called for a transitional government that would not include Charles Taylor.[40]

In the end, the government of Nigeria – backed, reportedly, by the United States, the United Kingdom, the AU, the UN, and ECOWAS – offered Taylor a way out. The specifics of the arrangement have never been made public, but they are understood to have included a safe haven provision and guarantees that he would not be prosecuted provided he withdrew altogether from political activity. Despite Nigeria's offer, until the last moment, there were rumors that Taylor was hoping to broker a deal in which he would only step down on condition that the Special Court charges were dropped.[41] On August 11, 2003, Taylor resigned, handed over power to his vice president and prepared to vacate Liberia's executive mansion. Nigerian president Olusegun Obasanjo had made arrangements for Taylor, his family, and his aides to take up residence at three comfortable villas in Calabar, a quiet town in southeastern Nigeria.[42] Taylor was personally accompanied from Monrovia to Nigeria's capital, Abuja, by the presidents of Ghana, South Africa, Nigeria, and Mozambique (then chair of the AU). In his parting speech he stated, "God willing, I will be back."[43] The president of Sierra Leone, Ahmad Tejan Kabbah, despite his support for the Special Court, reconciled the deal on the basis that it was necessary for peace, stating that "[o]ne day Charles Taylor will be here and would face justice."[44]

GETTING TAYLOR TO THE COURT

Over the months that followed, the Special Court continued to seek ways to build support and to pressure Nigeria to rescind the asylum deal. The Special Court itself was coming under increasing pressure to show results because the voluntary contributions that funded it were running out, and getting hold of Taylor was exactly the credibility boost that the court needed to ensure enough political and financial support to stay afloat. International human rights groups such as Human Rights Watch, No Peace Without Justice, and Amnesty International all campaigned for Taylor to face trial.

In late 2003, the U.S. Congress authorized a $2 million reward for Taylor's capture, yet there was little support politically for acting further out of respect for Nigeria's role in brokering a long-needed peace in Liberia and U.S. concerns over its own bilateral interests in Nigeria.[45] Pressure built slowly to gather sufficient political momentum, with the occasional breakthrough. In March 2004, the UN Security Council – having already placed travel bans on Taylor leaving Nigeria – agreed to freeze the assets of Taylor and his immediate family, barring them from "using 'misappropriated funds and property' to obstruct the restoration of peace and stability in Liberia and the West African sub-region."[46]

Within Nigeria, Taylor's presence was not uncontroversial. A civil claim was filed in the Nigerian courts, challenging the basis on which Taylor had been granted asylum in the first place. The claim was filed against Taylor, Nigerian president Obasanjo, and certain Nigerian federal agencies by two Nigerian journalists who had both suffered amputations by RUF forces while reporting on the Sierra Leonean conflict.[47] Amnesty International sought to intervene in the case, which made it as far as the Nigerian Federal High Court, arguing that Nigeria's own international legal obligations meant that it either had to hand Taylor over to the Special Court or prosecute him itself.

In February 2005, the European Parliament passed a resolution calling on Nigeria's government to send Taylor to the Special Court.[48] Two months later, the U.S. Congress passed a similar resolution.[49] An opening came in May 2005 when President Obasanjo announced that he would turn Charles Taylor over to a newly elected Liberian government if the new administration asked him to do so. However, it was generally agreed that it would be politically difficult for Nigeria to revoke the hospitality it had extended to Taylor, and the Liberian elections were still some months away.

By mid-2005, persistent claims were emerging that Taylor was violating the terms of his Nigerian asylum deal to refrain from political interference in West Africa, including that he had been involved in an attempt to assassinate Guinean president Lansana Conteh in January 2005, that he continued to back armed groups, and that he was attempted to influence the forthcoming posttransition Liberian elections. Special Court investigators accused him of backing a coup plot in Côte d'Ivoire.[50] In August 2005, the leaders of Sierra Leone, Liberia, and Guinea issued a joint statement calling for a review of his asylum arrangements in light of the accusations and a threat to refer the matter to ECOWAS.[51] During a visit to West Africa in July 2005, Louise Arbour, the UN High Commissioner for Human Rights (who had been chief prosecutor at the International Criminal Tribunal for the former Yugoslavia when it indicted Slobodan Milošević), also called for Nigeria to hand him over.

Liberia successfully conducted its first posttransition presidential elections in October 2005 with the support of UN and ECOMOG peacekeepers. Following a runoff, Ellen Johnson-Sirleaf, a former World Bank employee and finance minister under president William Tolbert, became the first elected female president on the continent. Immediately after taking office in January 2006, Johnson-Sirleaf dashed the hopes of many when she stated that the Taylor issue was not a priority.[52] Johnson-Sirleaf came under intense pressure from the human rights community, and international lobbying surrounding Taylor's impunity heated up again.

In a significant departure from previous UN practice, on November 11, 2005, the UN Security Council adopted Resolution 1638, expanding the mandate of the UN peacekeeping mission in Liberia to include the apprehension and detention of former president Charles Taylor in the event of his return to Liberia.[53] The resolution also provided for Taylor's transfer to Sierra Leone for prosecution before the Special Court for Sierra Leone.

Then, after more than two years of declining to pressure Nigeria to send Taylor to the Court, the Bush administration changed its stance. In January 2006, Secretary of State Condoleezza Rice apparently told President Johnson-Sirleaf that the United States felt the right time had come for Taylor to be sent to Freetown to face justice.

President Johnson-Sirleaf, however, had other priorities. Her government was gripped by security concerns. She did not have a standing army, and with Taylor loyalists still armed and roaming the countryside, she felt genuinely threatened. In a bid to win the second round of the presidential elections, she had sought and received the support of many of Taylor's allies, including that of his recently divorced ex-wife, Jewell Taylor. Newspapers alleged that Johnson-Sirleaf had promised not to request Taylor's surrender in return for their support. With some of Taylor's close associates, like Speaker of the House Edwin Snowe, controlling key positions in the legislature in which Johnson-Sirleaf's party had little support, she had a difficult choice to make. When it became clear that the grant of much-needed development assistance from the European Union and the United States was (at least implicitly) linked to bringing Taylor to justice, the new president decided the matter needed to be closed. Johnson-Sirleaf acknowledged that "We also are facing . . . pressure – I must use that word – from the UN, from the U.S., from the European Union, who are all our major partners in development, on the need to do something about the Charles Taylor issue."[54] In the end, despite concerns that Taylor's return would foster unrest, Johnson-Sirleaf stated that the fate of one Liberian should not hold a nation of three million people hostage, and, in March 2006, formally called on Nigeria to transfer Taylor.[55]

THE FINAL TWIST

Following Johnson-Sirleaf's request, Nigeria's Obasanjo told reporters that Liberia was free to come and get him.[56] A final bit of political intrigue concluded the saga: Two days later, Nigerian authorities announced that Charles Taylor had gone missing from his residence in Calabar, Nigeria. Obasanjo claimed to be embarrassed and appalled. According to Nigerian officials, Taylor escaped from his heavily guarded residence in Calabar in a car with diplomatic license plates. The United States warned Nigeria of the "consequences" if Taylor was not handed over.[57]

For twenty-four dramatic hours, Taylor was supposedly on the run, although he is widely believed to have been with Nigerian security forces during this entire time. Newspapers alleged that Nigeria facilitated the "escape agreement" under which Taylor was given 25 million Naira (about $220,000) and asked to find an alternative sanctuary because international pressure was mounting on Nigeria.[58] At the news of Taylor's escape, international pressure mounted on Nigeria. A meeting had been planned in Washington, D.C., between Presidents Bush and Obasanjo for the next day. Obasanjo was told that the meeting with Bush would be cancelled if Taylor remained at large. Because of the mounting pressure, the Nigerian government made a dramatic U-turn, and declared Taylor a fugitive from justice.

Only hours later, Taylor was "captured" by Nigerian authorities at a remote border outpost in Gambura, Maiduguiri, in the northeastern Nigerian state of Borno, close to the Cameroon border, more than 776 miles away from his Calabar mansion. Ironically, Taylor had traveled for many hours only to not quite make it into Cameroon when his villa in Calabar was only thirty minutes away from another point on the Nigeria-Cameroon border.[59] It seemed his alleged escape was merely a ploy to save the Nigerian government from allegations that handing over Taylor violated the Ghana agreement and that Nigeria was caving in to the West. The ploy backfired and Nigeria suddenly had to reverse course. With Taylor's arrest, Obasanjo announced at the White House that Taylor was on his way to Liberia.[60] On March 29, Charles Taylor was flown to Monrovia, and UN peacekeepers then accompanied him by helicopter directly to Sierra Leone.

THE QUESTION OF VENUE

Following Taylor's transfer to the government of Liberia and subsequently to the Special Court in Freetown, the issue of security for the venue of the trial was raised as a major concern. The agreement between the UN and the government of Sierra Leone establishing the Special Court makes provision for the court to sit outside Sierra Leone "if necessary for the exercise of its functions."[61] Officials at the Special Court expressed unease about allowing Taylor to stand trial in Freetown because they feared his appearance in court could prompt a rescue attempt or even lead to renewed fighting in Sierra Leone. Almost immediately upon Taylor's arrival in Sierra Leone, the president of the Special Court at that time, Justice A. Raja N. Fernando of Sri Lanka, made a request to the government of the Netherlands and the president of the International Criminal Court (ICC) to facilitate conducting Taylor's trial in the Hague on the basis of "stability concerns."[62] However, some speculated a political deal involving Liberia, the United States, the AU, and ECOWAS was the primary reason for transferring the trial to the Hague.[63] Allegations that President Johnson-Sirleaf had handed Taylor over to the court with the precondition that his trial be held out of the region were subsequently confirmed by senior staff within the Special Court.[64] The United Kingdom agreed to incarcerate Taylor if he was sentenced to a prison term.

Taylor's defense counsel challenged the ability of the president of the Special Court to decide on a change of venue without first giving the accused the right to be heard on the issue, and the matter was referred to the Appeals Chamber for determination. The Appeals Chamber dismissed the defense motion on the basis that it was a question for the president's administrative functions.[65] The Special Court moved ahead with arrangements for conducting the trial in the Hague. Although the proceedings remain before the Special Court for Sierra Leone, they are being conducted in a courtroom loaned to the Special Court by the ICC. After spending less than three months on Sierra Leonean soil, Taylor was transferred to the Hague, far away from the victims of his wars.

The decision to move Taylor's trial highlights the complex politics and geography of justice in the wake of mass atrocity. According to one Sierra Leonean lawyer:

> as important as these concerns might be, transferring Taylor to the Hague not only poses great challenges for the Special Court, but also undermines the entire rationale for having the Court in Sierra Leone in the first place.... Taylor's transfer to the Hague negatively impacts all these objectives. It would deprive war victims of the justice that they deserve.[66]

The continued reference to so-called security threats blurred together the political and legal considerations. The Special Court had indicted others who arguably posed a security threat equal to, if not more serious than, Taylor in terms of the likelihood of causing potential attacks on the court's Freetown premises. Until his death, Foday Sankoh, the former leader of the RUF, was held in the court without any issue of security ever arising. Similarly, concerns were raised in the case of the leader of the Civil Defense Forces and interior minister Sam Hinga Norman, who despite his indictment continued to enjoy considerable sympathy from the local population for fighting the rebels. The location of the detainees, including Norman, was initially kept secret and the initial hearings were held under tight security measures.[67] The Special Court not only operates from a heavily fortified walled compound, but it has twenty-four-hour security provided by a battalion of UN peacekeeping troops, initially from Nigeria, but since 2006 from Nepal. Although the larger UN peacekeeping presence that had been in Sierra Leone since before the end of the conflict was about to leave the country in 2006, it was not apparent that the court had considered whether there were other options to address these "security" concerns before moving to the Hague option. Internal security assessments were not made public, lending greater weight to the perception that "security" in fact referred to broader considerations of geopolitical stability in the region, rather than direct security threats to the court itself. Observers commented that taking the trial away from Freetown had the effect of making the trial less accessible to the people of Sierra Leone and Liberia, the very people who were most affected by the crimes alleged to have been committed by Taylor.[68]

REACTIONS TO TAYLOR'S ARREST AND DETENTION

The popular reaction to Taylor's arrest was mixed. In Sierra Leone it was overwhelmingly favorable. The *papay* or "big man" who caused them so much grief and agony and who masterminded the conflict in their country was finally going to face justice. Yet many doubted that this would ever happen. No leader in West Africa had ever been tried for atrocities committed against his people, and there are many instances of leaders committing atrocities and getting away with it. The military leaders of the National Provisional Ruling Council government that ruled Sierra Leone between 1992 and 1996 were rewarded with scholarships and cash despite having committed serious violations of human rights. As pictures of Taylor in handcuffs were printed in the newspapers, the myth of the West African "big man" was finally shattered. Justice was no longer like a spider's web that caught only the flies; occasionally hawks could be entangled, too. Sierra Leoneans were jubilant.

On the other hand, some Sierra Leoneans were concerned about security. They were worried that Taylor's detention in Freetown might lead to an attempt from his fighters to release him or, even worse, to the restart of the war, but during the months that Taylor awaited transfer to the Hague, these fears did not materialize.

In Liberia, popular reaction to Taylor's arrest was more mixed. Many in the human rights and civil society community welcomed the news, and his arrest strengthened the small but vocal campaign for a war crimes tribunal for Liberia. However, many other Liberians appeared either indifferent or, worse, indignant at the arrest of their former president, even going so far as to view it as a national humiliation. Others who wanted to see Taylor face trial were unhappy that he was arrested by the Special Court for Sierra Leone, which they perceived as a national court in a neighboring state.[69]

Others were worried that his arrest might lead to further trouble in an already troubled country. Many of his supporters argued that he should not be tried at all.[70] As described earlier, the Comprehensive Peace Agreement laid out a range of reform measures, but no amnesty was included in terms of accountability for past crimes, and the compromise reached was a truth and reconciliation commission without prosecutorial powers. They thought that Liberia's priority at this stage of its transition was reconciliation and not prosecution, which would further divide the nation. What should be paramount in this current Liberian government, they argued, is how to give hope to the people through good and well-implemented policies, improved standards of living, well-equipped hospitals and schools, and effective measures to reduce hunger and starvation and stabilize the economy. They bitterly complained about the breach of the deal that led to his vacating office, despite the fact that Taylor himself had breached more agreements than any other Liberian political leader in the past.

Some also felt that his arrest was not about justice but about the settlement of a vendetta. Despite the long and ambiguous historical connection between the United States and Liberia, one influential press columnist, Baffour Ankomah, suggested that perhaps the United States was trying to settle a personal score with Taylor that "has been dressed up as a 'war crimes' issue for global PR purposes."[71] Some alleged that Taylor did not escape from his Boston prison cell but was released by the United States to wage war on former Liberian President Samuel Doe – whom the United States wanted ousted. Taylor himself had suggested that he had American support for his war. In an interview in *New African*, he stated, "During the war, there was full cooperation between me and Washington, and every move we took, we consulted Washington first."[72] Although Taylor initially listened to his so-called backers, as his forces gained momentum, he ignored U.S. advice, and there came a parting of ways between Washington and Taylor.[73] It is alleged that the relationship further soured when Taylor chose the Chinese over the Americans to exploit Liberia's offshore oil. Given that the United States backed and heavily supported the Special Court, some saw this as a means of getting back at Taylor, particularly given the limited competence of the court to try those who bear the "greatest responsibility" for the war crimes and crimes against humanity.

THE LEGAL PROCEEDINGS AGAINST TAYLOR

The Preliminary Objection – Was Taylor Immune from Prosecution?

Even before Taylor was arrested and brought to the Special Court, he engaged the services of a Sierra Leonean lawyer, Terence Michael Terry, to represent him before the Special Court and to challenge the issuance of the indictment. On July 23, 2003, before his departure from Liberia, he filed a motion "under protest and without waiving the immunity accorded to a head of state," requesting the Trial Chamber of the Special Court to quash the indictment and declare it null and void.[74]

In the motion, counsel for Taylor argued that because the indictment was issued while Taylor was president of Liberia, he enjoyed absolute immunity from criminal prosecution. Terry relied on the International Court of Justice (ICJ) case of *DRC v. Belgium* as the authority for his submission. As is discussed in the introduction to this volume, although the ICJ accepted that heads of state were shielded from prosecution before national courts of another state because of the principle of sovereign equality, it recognized an exception for international courts. The Taylor defense argument submitted that because the Special Court lacked the powers bestowed on, for example, the ad hoc international criminal tribunals established by the UN Security Council, its orders were akin to orders of national courts. The preliminary challenge to the Special Court's jurisdiction then turned on two questions: whether Taylor was entitled to personal immunity and whether the Special Court for Sierra Leone was a national or an international court.

In its response, the prosecution insisted that Taylor could not have it both ways. Under the Special Court's Rules of Procedure and Evidence, challenges to the issue of jurisdiction and abuse of process could only be dealt with after an initial appearance. As such, Taylor could not both evade the processes of the court and submit motions for court rulings.[75]

In relation to the second question, the prosecution took the position that the Special Court was an international court because it was not part of the Sierra Leone judiciary. As such, the immunity recognized by the ICJ case did not apply. The lack of Chapter VII powers under the UN Charter was immaterial to the question of jurisdiction over heads of states; indeed, the ICC lacked such powers and yet had jurisdiction over heads of state for crimes contained in its statute. Customary international law permits international criminal tribunals like the Special Court established under international law to indict heads of state, it argued.

The motion was filed before the Trial Chamber on July 23, 2003, which was then referred to the Appeals Chamber on September 19, 2003. From the outset, the unusual nature of the accused's status as a head of state dominated the course of the proceedings, although by the time the case reached the Appeals Chamber, Taylor had already resigned as president and gone into exile in Nigeria. Amicus curiae briefs were received by the court from the African Bar Association and also international law experts Philippe Sands and Diane Orentlicher. The court conceded the following:

> Technically, an accused who has not made an initial appearance before this Court cannot bring a preliminary motion in terms of Rule 72 (A), nor a motion under Rule 73 of the Rules, and in a normal case such application may be held premature and accordingly struck out. However, this case is not in the normal course. To insist that an incumbent Head of State must first submit himself to incarceration before he can raise the question of immunity not only runs counter, in a substantial manner, to the whole purpose of the concept of sovereign immunity, but would also assume, without considering the merits, issues of exceptions to the concept that properly fall to be determined after delving into the merits of the claim to immunity. Although the Applicant is no longer an incumbent Head of State, a statement of general principle must embrace situations in which an Applicant remains an incumbent Head of State.[76]

The court proceeded to permit a determination of the merits of the application on the basis of its inherent power and discretion, thus creating an exception that was arguably in breach of its own rules of procedure and evidence.

On the merits of the case, the court held that the Special Court for Sierra Leone is an international criminal court, concluding that, "The principle seems now established that sovereign equality of states does not prevent a head of state from being prosecuted before an international criminal tribunal or Court."[77] Relying on the UK House of Lords judgment in the Pinochet case that some crimes should not be covered by head of state immunity when charges are brought before international tribunals, the court dismissed Taylor's application and held that:

> The official position of the applicant as an incumbent head of state at the time when these criminal proceedings were initiated against him is not a bar

to his prosecution by this Court. The applicant was and is subject to criminal proceedings before the Special Court for Sierra Leone.[78]

Although the Appellate Chamber had ruled on the issue, Taylor tried to raise the matter again on his very first appearance in court on April 3, 2006. Not surprisingly, the Trial Chamber considered the matter already settled by the Appeals Chamber decision and proceeded with the preparations for trial.

Taylor on Trial at Last

Taylor's trial formally began on June 4, 2007, in an ICC courtroom in the Hague. When the judges took their seats, however, Taylor was not present in court. His counsel told the court that he had a letter from his client that he wished to read. In the letter, Taylor stated his belief that he was being denied adequate facilities for his defense, as his court-funded legal team was smaller than that of the prosecution. Dramatically declaring that "I choose not to be a fig leaf of legitimacy for this Court," he announced his decision to discontinue his involvement in the process until the matter was resolved.[79] After the prosecutor made his opening statement, the trial was adjourned. In July 2007, the court appointed a new defense team and granted it substantially more time and financial means to prepare for trial. On January 7, 2008, the trial restarted in earnest with the calling of the first witness, and since then there have been no further attempts by the accused to delay the process. In fact, as of mid-2008, the trial was proceeding with none of the theatrics or tactical approaches that many feared would characterize such a trial. After his initial outburst, Taylor has seemingly submitted to the judicial process, attending court sessions and taking notes during testimony. Rather than adopting an approach of trying to challenge every piece of evidence, Taylor's defense strategy has focused on disputing the credibility of the prosecution witnesses – many of whom are insiders from Taylor's own forces – and the strength of the evidence linking him to the crimes committed. The trial is estimated to be completed by May 2009. Around one hundred prosecution witnesses are expected to be called to give evidence.

Nonetheless, early concerns about holding the Taylor trial away from Sierra Leone, the locus of the crimes and the victims, remain on account of the public's poor access to information about the trial.[80] Although live broadcasts of the trial are supposed to be shown to the public in Freetown and Monrovia, in practice this has not always happened.[81] Other problems include limited accessibility for journalists to the Hague courtroom on account of the ICC's failure to facilitate their access to its premises. As a result, few people are now attending the sessions in person. There also is concern over how the court is protecting the witnesses.[82] Threats to several witnesses have been reported, with at least one witness having gone into hiding until his safety is guaranteed.[83]

Yet it now seems that the trial of one of Africa's most notorious warlords is finally able to take its judicial course. Whether Taylor is convicted of some or all of the counts with which he is charged, the Special Court for Sierra Leone, for the moment at least, has been able to do its work. The extent to which this is perceived as justice for the victims of Taylor's crimes in both Liberia and Sierra Leone remains another matter.

CONCLUSION

The prosecution of Charles Taylor by the Special Court for crimes allegedly committed in Sierra Leone continues to be a sensitive topic within Liberia. His prosecution for human rights crimes before the Special Court has coincided with public hearings before the Liberian TRC regarding Taylor's acts in Liberia, and the convergence of the allegations has further discredited his actions. However, there is still a longer-lasting legacy of Taylor's rule that current justice efforts have not been able to address – namely, Taylor's acquisition through corruption and other means of vast wealth as a direct result of the wars in which he engaged. One estimate puts the figure in excess of $100 million per year, although the total figure is unknown.[84] The Special Court has dedicated a certain amount of its prosecution capacity to locating Taylor's assets, but to date this has yielded few results. In 2003, the goal of prosecuting Taylor was seen by many political leaders to be in direct conflict with the desire to secure an end to the civil war and hasten democracy and stability in Liberia. At that time, negotiators from the Bush administration, the UN, the AU, Nigeria, and Liberia were all content to make justice wait, having concluded that the most effective way to end the horrors and bloodshed in Liberia was to remove Charles Taylor peacefully from power. In an interview on CNN, Nigeria's President Obasanjo stated,

> People's memories are always short when they want it to be short. People have forgotten that if Charles Taylor had not moved out, there will never have been peace in Liberia. And the election that had taken place, which had brought Ellen Johnson-Sirleaf, would never have taken place.... So we have played the role that we believed we should play, and whether it's appreciated or not, believe that we have played our role in the interests of peace in that area, in the interests of peace in our subregion of West Africa, and in the interests of peace in the international community.[85]

Yet ultimately Nigeria handed Taylor over to the Special Court. Taylor's transfer to the Special Court was privately condemned by many African leaders. Libyan leader Mu'ammar al-Quadhafi expressed the views of many when, in denouncing Taylor's arrest, he stated, "It means that every head of state could meet a similar fate. This sets a serious precedent."[86] A former senior official with the Special Court for Sierra Leone was quoted in the *International Justice Tribune* as saying, "An African head of state being tried in Europe is highly offensive on a symbolic level."[87] Many criticized Nigeria for failing to refer the matter to the African Union, which had brokered the initial deal. They condemned Nigeria's unilateral decision to hand over one of its own to "a white man's Court" to be tried in the Hague.[88]

By all accounts, Taylor will receive what he denied many of his countrymen: due process and a fair trial.[89] Indeed, the Special Court may only be the beginning of his troubles. The law that established the TRC in Liberia provides that "the Commission shall identify, where possible, persons, authorities, institutions, and organizations involved in the gross violations and abuses of human rights"[90] and ensure accountability for such violations.[91] The commission has powers to recommend amnesty, but these powers shall not apply to "violations of international humanitarian law and crimes against humanity."[92] In light of the atrocities committed in Liberia, it is almost certain that Charles Taylor and his cronies will not be eligible for any reprieve. The commission also has the power to recommend prosecutions. At the inauguration of the TRC on February 20, 2006, Liberian president Johnson-Sirleaf stated that:

> Our country cannot continue to evade justice and the protection of human rights throughout our land, especially of the kind that restores our historical place among civilized nations. Our government will ensure that those culpable of the commission of crimes against humanity will face up to their crimes no matter when, where, or how.[93]

The possibility remains that Taylor could be tried for crimes committed in Liberia. Whether such a trial could take place in Liberia's domestic courts or in a hybrid tribunal similar to the Special Court for Sierra Leone remains to be seen. It will depend to some extent on what the Liberian TRC recommends in terms of prosecutions. A small but vocal civil society group has been at the forefront of a call for the establishment of a war crimes tribunal in Liberia. The campaign has not made much impact, although it has undertaken sporadic demonstrations on the streets of Monrovia.

Regardless of the forum, the Taylor case sets a significant precedent. He is one of the first African head of government ever to face a full-blown trial for war crimes. It signals to African leaders that they can no longer commit atrocities with impunity. West Africa – or for that matter Africa as a whole – is not some distant place where impunity will go unnoticed. This is a welcome development. There should always be a day of reckoning. The thought of that alone should deter current and future leaders.

It is too soon to herald the end of impunity in Africa. Elsewhere on the continent, massive atrocities have been committed against the civilian populations of Côte d'Ivoire, Darfur, and Chad. The implications of the Taylor saga for conflict resolution in the continent are yet to be fully realized. Some assume that Uganda's Lord's Resistance Army leader Joseph Kony's failure to commit to peace, or the ongoing intransigence of Zimbabwe's Robert Mugabe to relinquish power, result from these leaders' inability to trust any impunity deal they might make with the international community.[94] Only time will tell whether such fear is well-founded, but at present many human rights activists and victims of West African's wars rejoice in the fact that justice in Taylor's case is now being done. The big man is finally locked up in a very small cell.

NOTES

1. Mark Doyle, "Charles Taylor – preacher, warlord and president," *BBC News*, June 4, 2003. Available at http://news.bbc.co.uk/2/hi/africa/2963086.stm.
2. See Derek Brown, "The Elected Dictator: Liberian President Charles Taylor," *Guardian*, March 17, 2000. Available at http://www.guardian.co.uk/world/2000/may/17/sierraleone3; see also International Crisis Group, *Liberia: The Key to Ending Regional Instability*, Africa Report no. 43, April 24, 2002.
3. For more information, see International Crisis Group, *Tackling Liberia: The Eye of the Regional Storm*, Africa Report no. 62, April 20, 2003.
4. See Siahyonkron Nyanseor and J. Kpanneh Doe, "Alhaji Kromah: Disappointments and Denials (An Interview)," *The Perspective*, October 25, 2000. Available at http://www.theperspective.org/kromah.html.
5. For further background on the roots of the conflict, see Max Ahmadu Sesay, "Bringing peace to Liberia," *The Liberian peace process 1990–1996*, Accord Issue 1 (1996), available at http://www.c-r.org/our-work/accord/liberia/bringing-peace.php.
6. Ibid.
7. Matthew Clark, "Liberia's Ex-fighters Seek Work," *Christian Science Monitor*, November 1, 2006, p. 6.
8. Human Rights Watch, *Liberia: A Human Rights Disaster – Violations of the Laws of War by All Parties to the Conflict*, HRW report, October 26, 1990 ["Liberia: A Human Rights Disaster"]; Human Rights Watch, *Liberia: Flight from Terror – Testimony of Abuses in Nimba County*, HRW report, May 1990 ["Liberia: Flight from Terror"]. For more recent accounts, see Human Rights Watch, *Liberia: Greater Protection Required for Civilians Still at Risk*, HRW Briefing Paper, September 9, 2003; and Human Rights Watch, *Back to the Brink: War Crimes By Liberian Government and Rebels – A Call for Greater International Attention to Liberia and the Sub Region*, HRW report, May 2002, Vol. 14, No. 4 (A).

9. The U.S. Justice Department indicted Charles "Chuckie" Taylor, Jr., son of the former Liberian president and a U.S. citizen, in December 2006 for torture committed in Liberia. See Curt Anderson, "Torture Trial of Charles Taylor's Son Faces Roadblocks," *International Herald Tribune*, December 17, 2007. Available at http://www.iht.com/articles/2007/12/17/africa/liberia.php?page=1.

10. The Revolutionary United Front's manifesto, *Footpaths to Democracy – Toward a New Sierra Leone*, 1995. Available at http://www.fas.org/irp/world/para/docs/footpaths.htm.

11. Ian Smillie, Lansana Gberie, and Ralph Hazleton, *The Heart of the Matter – Sierra Leone, Diamonds and Human Security*, Partnership Africa Canada, 2000. See also United Nations High Commission on Refugees, 2005 *UNHCR Statistical Yearbook*; for estimates on amputees, see David Pratt, *Sierra Leone: The Forgotten Crisis*, Report to the Minister of Foreign Affairs, the Honourable Lloyd Axworthy, P.C., M.P. from David Pratt, M.P., Nepean-Carleton, Special Envoy to Sierra Leone, April 23, 1999.

12. A Human Rights Watch report estimated the total number of displaced persons at 1 million and deaths at fifty thousand. Human Rights Watch, *Sierra Leone – Getting Away with Murder, Mutilation, Rape: New Testimony from Sierra Leone*, HRW report, July 1999. See also Sierra Leone Truth and Reconciliation Commission, *The Final Report of the Truth & Reconciliation Commission of Sierra Leone*, 2007; UNHCR, 2005 *UNHCR Statistical Yearbook*.

13. A UN Expert Panel on Sierra Leone reported in December 2002 that Liberia had provided military training, weapons, and logistical and communication support to the RUF in return for diamonds from Sierra Leone that were secured and trafficked back to Liberia by rebel forces. See *Report of the Panel of Experts Appointed Pursuant to Security Council Resolution 1306*, Paragraph 19, in Relation to Sierra Leone, December 20, 2000, UN Doc. S/2000/1195 (2000).

14. Lansana Gberie, *War and Peace in Sierra Leone: Diamonds, Corruption and the Lebanese Connection*, Partnership Africa Canada, November 2002.

15. See David R. Francis, "Fueling War," *Christian Science Monitor*, December 5, 2002, p. 11; Greg Campbell, *Blood Diamonds: Tracing the Deadly Path of the World's Most Precious Stones*, Boulder, CO: Westview Press, 2002.

16. CNN Insight, *Deadly Diamonds in Sierra Leone*, aired May 17, 2000.

17. Stephen Ellis, *The Mask of Anarchy: The Destruction of Liberia and the Religious Dimension of an African Civil War*, New York: New York University Press, 2001, 71.

18. Ibid.

19. Ibid, 70.

20. The Lomé Peace Accord, officially titled the *Peace Agreement between the Government of Sierra Leone and the Revolutionary United Front of Sierra Leone*, signed July 7, 1999.

21. Letter dated August 9, 2000 from the Permanent Representative of Sierra Leone to the United Nations addressed to the president of the Security Council, August 10, 2000, UN Doc. S/2000/786 (2000), annex.

22. *Agreement between the United Nations and the Government of Sierra Leone on the Establishment of a Special Court for Sierra Leone*, January 16, 2002 (Special Court Agreement). See also the *Statute of the Special Court for Sierra Leone*, January 16,

2002 (Statute of the Special Court). Article 1 details the competence of the Court. Crimes under Sierra Leonean law subject to the jurisdiction of the Special Court include offenses relating to the abuse of girls under the Prevention of Cruelty to Children Act of 1926, and offenses relating to the wanton destruction of property under the Malicious Damage Act of 1861.

23. UN Security Council Resolution 1315, August 14, 2000, UN Doc S/RES/1315 (2000).

24. Statute of the Special Court, Art. 6(2).

25. *The Prosecutor against Charles Ghankay Taylor*, SCSL-2003-01-I, Indictment, March 7, 2003.

26. *The Prosecutor against Charles Ghankay Taylor*, SCSL-2003-01-I, Decision Approving the Indictment and Order for Non-Disclosure, March 7, 2003.

27. Douglas Farah, "Liberian Alleged to Shield War-Crimes Fugitives," *Washington Post*, May 1, 2003, p. A22.

28. No Peace Without Justice (NPWJ) Press Release, "NPWJ calls for Charles Taylor indictment over Sierra Leone atrocities," April 11, 2003; see also Farah, "Liberian Alleged."

29. LURD primarily consisted of Krahn and Mandingo tribesman, and MODEL was dominated by the Krahn. See International Crisis Group, *Tackling Liberia: The Eye of the Regional Storm*, Africa Report no. 62, April 30, 2003, 4.

30. For further discussion on the process, see Priscilla Hayner, *Negotiating Peace in Liberia: Preserving the Possibility for Justice*, Centre for Humanitarian Dialogue and International Center for Transitional Justice, November 2007; Kathy Ward, "Might vs. Right: Charles Taylor and the Sierra Leone Special Court," *Human Rights Brief* 11, no. 1 (2003): 8.

31. See Statement by Chief Prosecutor for the Special Court, David M. Crane, June 5, 2003.

32. Priscilla Hayner, *Negotiating Peace in Liberia*, 8.

33. As recounted by a close advisor to Taylor, in Priscilla Hayner, *Negotiating Peace in Liberia*, 8.

34. Lansana Gberie, Jarlawah Tonpoh, Efam Dovi, and Osei Boateng, "Charles Taylor Why Me?" *New African*, May 2006, 3.

35. Ibid.

36. Priscilla Hayner, *Negotiating Peace in Liberia*, 8.

37. *The Prosecutor against Charles Ghankay Taylor*, Case No. SCSL-2003-01-I, Indictment, March 7, 2003. The indictment was subsequently amended on March 16, 2006, before Taylor's trial commenced, to bring it in line with prior Special Court decisions regarding greater precision in charging.

38. The conflict officially ended on this date when Ahmed Tejan Kabbah, president of Sierra Leone, announced an end to the hostilities.

39. Gberie et al., "Why Me?"

40. Priscilla Hayner, *Negotiating Peace in Liberia*, 8.

41. Editorial, "Charles Taylor: No Deal," *Washington Post*, August 7, 2003, p. A20.

42. Elizabeth Blunt, "Taylor's New Nigerian Home," *BBC News*, August 11, 2003.

43. Gberie et al., "Why Me?"

44. Clarence Roy-Macaulay, "Sierra Leone President Backs Nigeria's Granting of Asylum to Charles Taylor," *Associated Press*, October 31, 2004.

45. Reed Kramer, "Nigeria: U.S.-Africa Ties, Boosted by Money for Liberia, Face New Complications over Nigeria Sanctions," *Allafrica.com*, November 18, 2003. Available at http://allafrica.com/stories/200311180059.html.

46. UN Security Council Resolution 1532, March 12, 2004, UN Doc. S/RES/1532 (2004).

47. "Nigerians Challenge Taylor Asylum," *BBC News*, July 14, 2004.

48. European Parliament, *European Parliament Resolution on the Special Court for Sierra Leone: The Case of Charles Taylor*, P6_TA(2005)0059 February 24, 2005.

49. *Charles Ghankay Taylor – Transfer to the Special Court for Sierra Leone*, 109th Cong., 1st sess., H.Con.Res. 127, May 10, 2005.

50. See Craig Timberg, "A Warlord's Exile Divides His Hosts: Liberian Ex-President Charles Taylor Doing Business as Usual in Nigeria," *Washington Post*, October 9, 2005, p. A22; Douglas Farah, "A Protected Friend of Terrorism," *Washington Post*, April 25, 2005, p. A19.

51. See "Liberia: West African Leaders Call for Review of Taylor's Asylum Deal," *IRIN*, August 1, 2005.

52. "Taylor 'Not' a Priority for Liberia," *BBC News*, January 27, 2006.

53. UN Security Council Resolution 1638, November 11, 2005, UN Doc. S/RES/1638 (2005).

54. Transcript of interview "Liberia's New President," *Newshour with Jim Lehrer*, March 23, 2006. Available at http://www.pbs.org/newshour/bb/africa/jan-june06/liberia_3-23.html.

55. Ibid. See also Human Rights Watch, "Liberia: President Requests Surrender of Taylor," HRW Press Release March 17, 2006.

56. "Liberia-Nigeria: What Next for Taylor?," *IRIN*, March 27, 2006.

57. Felix Onuah, "Wanted Liberian Warlord Disappears in Nigeria," *Reuters*, March 28, 2006.

58. Gberie et al., "Why Me?"

59. Lydia Polgreen, "Liberian Seized to Stand Trial on War Crimes," *New York Times*, March 30, 2006, p. 1.

60. White House Press Release, "President Bush Welcomes President Obasanjo of Nigeria to the White House," March 29, 2006.

61. Article 10 of the Special Court Agreement.

62. Special Court for Sierra Leone Press Release, "Special Court President Requests Charles Taylor be Tried in the Hague," March 30, 2006.

63. Thierry Cruvellier, "Why Try Taylor in the Hague?," *International Justice Tribune*, n. 44, April 10, 2006. Senior members of the Office of the Prosecutor claimed that a political deal was struck back in October 2005.

64. Craig Timberg, "Liberian President Backs Bid to Move Taylor Trial to Hague," *Washington Post*, March 31, 2006, p. A15.

65. *The Prosecutor v. Charles Ghankay Taylor*, SCSL-2003-01-R72, Urgent Defence Motion against Change of Venue, Appeals Chamber, May 29, 2006 paras. 4, 8.

66. Alpha Sesay, "Trying Charles Taylor: Justice Cannot Be Fully Achieved at the Hague," *Sierra Leone Court Monitoring Programme Newsletter*, vol. 12 (April 12, 2006): 4.

67. See *The Special Court for Sierra Leone: Promises and Pitfalls of a "New Model,"* International Crisis Group Africa Briefing, August 4, 2003. See also International

Center for Transitional Justice, *The Special Court for Sierra Leone under Scrutiny*, March 2006, 23.

68. See, for example, International Center for Transitional Justice Press Release, "Taylor Trial Should Be Moved from Sierra Leone Only as Last Resort," April 3, 2006.

69. Based on reports from the International Center for Transitional Justice representative in Monrovia.

70. Priscilla Hayner, *Negotiating Peace in Liberia*.

71. Baffour Ankomah, "A Pound of Flesh, but in Whose Interest?" *New African*, May 2006. Available at http://findarticles.com/p/articles/mi_qa5391/is_200605/ai_n21391040.

72. Ibid.

73. Ibid.

74. *Prosecution v. Charles Ghankay Taylor*, SCSL-2003-01-I, Applicant's Motion made under Protest and without waiving of Immunity accorded to Head of State President Charles Ghankay Taylor requesting that the Trial Chamber do quash the said approved indictment of 7th March 2003 of Judge Bankole Thompson of the Special Court for Sierra Leone, and all other consequential and related ORDER(s) granted thereafter by either the said Judge Bankole Thomson OR Judge Pierre Boutet on 12th June 2003 against the person of the said President Charles Ghankay Taylor be declared null and void, invalid at their inception and that they be accordingly cancelled and/OR set aside as a matter of Law, July 23, 2003.

75. *Prosecutor v. Charles Ghankay Taylor*, SCSL-2003-01-I, Prosecution Response to Defence Motion to quash the indictment against Charles Ghankay Taylor, July 28, 2003.

76. *Prosecutor v. Charles Ghankay Taylor*, SCSL-2003-01-I, Decision on Immunity from Jurisdiction, Appeals Chamber, May 31, 2004, para. 30.

77. Ibid., para. 52. For further analysis of the immunity decision, see Charles Jalloh, "Immunity from Prosecution for International Crimes: The Case of Charles Taylor at the Special Court for Sierra Leone," *ASIL Insights*, October 2004. Available at http://www.asil.org/insigh145.cfm.

78. *Prosecutor v. Charles Ghankay Taylor*, Decision on Immunity, para. 53. For further discussion of the Pinochet case, see Chapter 4 in this volume.

79. Marlise Simons, "Liberian Boycotts Trial at the Hague," *New York Times*, June 4, 2007, p. 15.

80. Sierra Leone Court Monitoring Programme Press Release, *The Special Court Denies the People of Sierra Leone Access to the Taylor Trial*, July 3, 2007.

81. Ibid.

82. Alexandra Hudson, "Death Threats to Witnesses against Liberia's Taylor," *Reuters*, March 20, 2008.

83. Mike Corder, "Taylor Witnesses Being Threatened," *USA Today*, February 28, 2008. Available at http://www.usatoday.com/news/world/2008-02-28-1743440715_x.htm.

84. Lydia Polgreen, "A Master Plan Drawn in Blood," *New York Times*, April 2, 2006, p. 1.

85. CNN interview with President Olusegun Obasanjo of Nigeria, aired April 1, 2006. Transcript available at http://transcripts.cnn.com/TRANSCRIPTS/0604/01/i_if.01.html.

86. Sarah Grainger and John James, "Head Hunted," *Focus on Africa*, October–December 2006, p. 16.

87. See Thierry Cruvellier, "Why Try Taylor in the Hague?" *International Justice Tribune*, n. 44, April 10, 2006.

88. Olenka Frenkiel, "Africa's Test for International Justice," *BBC News*, February 26, 2008.

89. Peter Mwaura, "Liberia: Can Africa's Most Notorious Warlord Get a Fair Trial?," *The Nairobi*, September 15, 2007.

90. *An Act to Establish the Truth and Reconciliation Commission (TRC) of Liberia*, June 10, 2005. See Section 26(b). Available at http://unmil.org/documents/hr/liberiatrcact.pdf. See also https://www.trcofliberia.org/about/trc-mandate.

91. Ibid., Section 26(d).

92. Ibid., Section 26(g).

93. Speech for the inauguration of the Truth and Reconciliation Commission, February 20, 2006.

94. See discussion at http://www.tompaine.com/articles/2006/04/27/dictating_justice.php.

11

Political Pedagogy, Baghdad Style: The Dujail Trial of Saddam Hussein

Miranda Sissons and Marieke Wierda

On October 19, 2005, Iraqis sat spellbound as the curtains of the Iraqi High Tribunal (IHT) opened and the trial of Saddam Hussein and his seven code-fendants began. The former president radiated condescension, the trial judge looked nervous, and the prosecutor attempted to deliver an oratorical indict-ment of the former Ba'ath regime. Less than two years had passed since the dictator's fall. The momentum to bring him and others to trial had been relent-less. Some fifteen months later, Hussein was hanged in the predawn hours of a cold winter's morning, taunted by his black-masked executioners. The sectarian inflection of the execution was inescapable. Preserved by an illicit video recording, it undid in minutes what others had labored years to achieve.

The distance between the tribunal courtroom and the execution cell was never far. Hussein's trial was a lost opportunity, haunted by the question of what might have been. With millions of victims, ample funding, custody of the main defendants, and prolific documentation and potential evidence, Hussein's prosecution could have been a shining example of how to use law to come to terms with a violent past – and could have contributed significantly to a new Iraqi legal and political order.

The Dujail trial did not fulfill these lofty goals, however, at least in the short term. The IHT's legal process was first compromised and then overwhelmed by the political quest for revenge. Although in mid-2003 there was a real local appetite for accountability,[1] the tribunal's establishment was tainted by the political dynamics of the U.S. invasion and its aftermath. It was further damaged by its context: a wrenching transition that was already difficult by the time the trial opened and almost impossible by the time of the final judgment. Individual trial judges struggled hard to create a new standard

The authors thank Abdul Razzaq al-Saeidi, Mohammed el-Sawi, Clark Gard, Joshua Franco, Valeria Silvestri, Ari Bassin, Lilia Bellahsene, Luke Bolton, and Hani Sabra.

of Iraqi justice and to adapt to new procedures and law. Their efforts were compromised by repeated interference from Iraq's political leaders, their own lack of experience, and disastrous public relations. Events were not helped by the fact that the Dujail case revolved around a little-known episode in the far distant past, rather than more recent and representative regime crimes. The trial's long-term impact will only be known decades after its conclusion; in the short term, it was condemned internationally, excoriated regionally, and celebrated with much joy on the Iraqi street.

This chapter begins by chronicling Saddam Hussein's rise to power and the brutal authoritarianism that followed. It gives an overview of patterns of the regime's human rights violations as well as initial attempts by the international community to seek justice. The discussion then turns to the planning and creation of the Iraq tribunal in the context of the 2003 U.S.-led invasion of Iraq. The chapter then examines the dynamics and challenges of the Dujail trial and reactions at the Iraqi, regional, and international levels.

SADDAM HUSSEIN'S RISE TO POWER

Iraq has a population of 27 million people. Although the majority self-define as Arab, it contains numerous other ethnic groups, including Kurds, Turcomans, Assyrians, and others. Iraqis are religiously heterogeneous; these differences are generally not ethnically defined. With a geographic area of some 169,000 square miles, Iraq is almost twice the size of the entire United Kingdom. Originally called Mesopotamia, Iraq marks the boundary between the Arab world and Persian-speaking Iran to the east. Iraq was formerly a major agricultural producer until oil was discovered near the northern city of Mosul in the early twentieth century. As of 2007, the Iraqi economy was almost completely oil-dependent.[2]

Iraq has a violent and unstable political history. Since it became independent from British rule in 1932, it has experienced eleven coups, five constitutions, seven international armed conflicts, and repeated internal uprisings.[3] Rulers generally depended on two factors: first, the resources that would allow them to maintain the clients and contacts of their patronage networks and, second, control over the coercive apparatus of the state.[4] Changes of power were usually accompanied by political violence, televised sham trials, and speedy executions.

When a small group of Ba'athist military officers seized power in July 1968, their acts fit these well-established patterns. However, the regime they established endured longer and was more repressive than any of its predecessors. Over thirty-five years, Saddam Hussein and his close associates built a complex, patronage-driven, and exceptionally violent state. Hussein's vehicle of rule was the Iraqi regional chapter of the Arab Socialist Ba'ath party. Originally based on the writings of Syrian intellectuals Michel Aflaq and Salah al-Din al-Bitar, the party espoused a vague but heavily nationalist ideology and emphasized a goal of Arab nationalism under the motto of "Unity, Freedom, Socialism."[5]

Hussein rose early to national prominence. He was born circa 1939[6] to a poor rural family in the village of al-Awja, near Tikrit, in Iraq's Sunni heartland. Hussein's father disappeared early, a significant social handicap in most Arab societies. As a young boy, Hussein initially grew up with his stepfather and half-brothers. However, Hussein's most significant relation was his mother's brother, Khair Allah Tulfah. Tulfah was a schoolteacher and former army officer who had been imprisoned for his role in the Rashid Ali rebellion of 1941.[7] An admirer of fascism, Tulfah was also an early proponent of Ba'athism. Hussein went to live with his uncle's family in 1947 and entered school for the first time.[8] A few years later, the Tulfah family moved to Baghdad; Hussein moved with them.

In Baghdad Tulfah gained entry into a network of deeply nationalist, anti-British, Tikriti army officers strongly opposed to Iraq's ruling classes.[9] One particularly significant member of this network was Tulfah's first cousin, Ahmad Hassan al-Bakr. Al-Bakr was active in many of the events of the turbulent 1950s and 1960s, and rose to become prime minister and president of Iraq.[10] His patronage was critical to Hussein's ascent to power.

Hussein's own history during this period is unclear. He reportedly left school and became drawn into political activities, cultivating a reputation for toughness. By 1956, Hussein began mixing with student members of the Ba'ath party. His entrée into national politics most likely occurred in 1958, when a group of army officers overthrew the Iraqi monarchy. Tensions between supporters of coup leader Abd al-Karim Qassem and those of the Ba'ath erupted quickly. Hussein and others orchestrated street violence and other tactics against the government-sponsored militia. Arrested several times, Hussein was imprisoned for murder in November 1958 but released six months later for lack of evidence.[11] Shortly afterward, he reportedly played a minor role in an attempt to kill Qassem.[12] Injured, Hussein escaped to Tikrit and thence to Syria. There he met Ba'ath founder Michel Aflaq, formed an enduring relationship with him, and was accepted as a full party member.[13]

Hussein spent four years in exile in Egypt (where he finished high school), but returned to Baghdad in 1963 when his Ba'athist colleagues, assisted by the United States, overthrew the Qassem regime. His relative, Ahmad Hassan al-Bakr, had played a leading role and was now prime minister. With al-Bakr's sponsorship, Hussein reportedly was given a position in the president's bureau where he aligned himself with the right wing of the party.[14] For a year, he exercised growing influence before the political pendulum tilted, the Ba'ath lost power, and Hussein was once again forced to leave for Damascus. After his return, he was arrested and imprisoned for an attempt to bomb the Presidential Palace; he escaped in 1966 and from hiding opened contact with the Arab Revolutionary Movement, a group of young army officers who, with the Ba'athists, overthrew the corrupt and unpopular government of Abd al-Rahman Arif.

The July 1968 coup was relatively bloodless. A new government of both non-Ba'athists and Ba'athists was established. Within weeks, however, the Ba'athists managed to depose all others and established a purely Ba'athist regime.[15] Hussein used his relationship to al-Bakr, newly installed as president, to consolidate his control over the Ba'ath Party and key intelligence services through the deft use of "Stalinist methods backed by Arab tribal loyalties."[16] Within a year, Hussein was deputy president and the preeminent power apart from al-Bakr, an astonishing position in Arab society for a man only thirty years old. Five years later, Hussein controlled the security services and the Ba'ath party, had created a party militia to counterbalance the regular armed forces, and had crafted a public persona unlike any other Iraqi leader. Al-Bakr was a secondary figure, even though he still held the presidency.

In its early years, the Ba'athist state did not depend on coercive measures alone. With a nod to populism, the state instituted land reform, subsidized basic commodities, and introduced limited social and welfare services.[17] The nationalization of the Iraqi Petroleum Company in June 1972 was immensely popular, removing one of the most important lingering symbols of foreign influence from Iraqi politics just in time to benefit from the fourfold increase in oil prices that followed the Arab-Israeli war of 1973.[18] Hussein was identified as leader of the nationalization process and gained great prestige from it. State coercion was tempered with patrimonialism, and Iraqi living standards and educational levels rose sharply in the years that followed.[19] By 1977, Iraq was ruled not so much by the Ba'ath Party as by the small, highly networked clique of Hussein loyalists that functioned as the Revolutionary Command Council.[20] On July 16, 1979, Hussein pushed al-Bakr aside and assumed the presidency.

The image that Saddam Hussein then created of himself was typical of a cult-of-personality regime. Constant campaigns marketed Hussein as the terror and savior of Iraq. He was variously depicted as both a modern military hero and an early Islamic defender of the peninsula's first Muslims.[21] Ba'athist propaganda served not only to aggrandize Saddam but also to breed a deep mistrust within the Iraqi people of Saddam's perceived enemies and, in some cases, of each other. As noted by contemporaneous critic Kanan Makiya, "Saddam Husain invents and reinvents his enemies . . . he thrives on the distrust, suspicion, and conspiratorialism which his regime actively inculcates in everyone."[22]

Hussein's propaganda machine functioned in multiple registers at every level of society. He controlled and was featured on the front page of every newspaper and in every radio broadcast.[23] Hussein almost always referred to himself in the third person. Mythic imagery was propagated not just through the media but also through art and architecture. "An entire coterie of architects, engineers, construction workers, designers, and artists was deployed to transform Iraqi public space into a tableau memorializing Saddam Hussein."[24] Hussein's iconography was Westernized, Arabized, Islamized, or tribalized as he strategically saw fit. His image was ever-present – in memorials, sculptures, photographs, and other objects, ubiquitous in public and compulsory in homes. The message was clear; he was the regime, and the regime was whatever he chose for it to be. There was no aspect of power Hussein failed to command.

HUSSEIN'S IRAQ: PATTERNS OF HUMAN RIGHTS VIOLATIONS

Hussein and other members of the Ba'ath leadership ruled by a system of "terror and reward," making widespread use of torture, extrajudicial executions, arbitrary detention, and forced disappearances to compel obedience and silence dissent across the country.[25] What distinguished Iraq from many other regimes that indulged in similar practices, however, was its relatively greater capacity. Unlike many other countries, by the late 1970s, Iraq's ruling clique had financial and human capacity to match its deep-seated violence and paranoia. The result was an unusually efficient, spectacularly violent state that, even under the strains of war and a decade of United Nations (UN) sanctions, could ruin its citizens with neither obstacles nor qualms. Max van der Stoel, the UN Special Rapporteur of the Commission on Human Rights, described the repression under the Saddam Hussein regime in his 1994 report to the General Assembly, stating that "the violations of human rights which have occurred are so grave and are of such a massive nature that since the Second World War few parallels can be found."[26]

Wrapped in the rhetorical blanket of Arab and Iraqi nationalism, Hussein and his followers created an elaborate parallel network of Ba'ath party institutions that overruled or subverted state institutions. They also created a full complement of nominally state-based institutions that served only to dignify the will of the regime. The criminal court system was trumped by a system of "special courts"; the death penalty was used routinely and extensively, and Ba'ath security networks and the terror they invoked permeated every aspect of daily life.[27]

Hussein did not limit himself to mere repression, however. His rule also was characterized by savage campaigns of violence against Iraq's ethnic and religious communities. No group was immune. In the north, this included Arabization and other policies that involved destroying nearly five thousand Kurdish villages and forcibly removing their inhabitants; mass disappearances; and the forcible transfer of ethnic minorities from the oil-rich region of Kirkuk. This resulted in the eviction of more than 120,000 Kurds, Assyrians, and Turkomans, and their replacement by Arab families brought in from southern Iraq.[28] In February 1988, Hussein and his cohort launched the eight-phase Anfal campaign, in which between 50,000 to 180,000 Kurds were gassed or executed.[29] Survivors were arbitrarily detained in appalling conditions and then forcibly relocated. Thousands of villages were destroyed.

In the south, the Iraqi majority Shi'a population began stirring against its exclusion from institutions of political power. This coincided with the emergence of the Islamic Republic in Iran and the start of the Iran-Iraq War.[30] Repression against the Shi'a included the expulsion of an estimated half-million people to Iran out of fear that they might support Iran during the war; the imprisonment or disappearance of between fifty thousand and seventy thousand civilians, usually men and boys, who were separated from their families before being executed; and the harsh suppression of the 1991 rebellion in the south, during which unknown thousands were detained, disappeared, or summarily executed.[31] When civilians, rebels, clerics, and army deserters fled into the southern marshlands, the Iraqi Army bombarded the area, carried out forced displacements, and deliberately embarked on a massive drainage project to facilitate military access to the marshes. Thousands of Marsh Arabs fled to Iran, and experts believe that the overall population of the area was reduced from an estimated 250,000 in the early 1990s to no more than 40,000 by 2003.[32]

Iraqi forces also committed multiple violations of international humanitarian law during the Iran-Iraq War and the 1990–1991 Iraqi occupation of Kuwait, including the alleged use of chemical weapons in indiscriminate attacks, summary executions, torture, rape, forced disappearances, collective punishment, and large-scale appropriation of property.[33] This period was followed by an era of UN sanctions that marked an increase in the breadth of human rights abuses and intensification of the Iraqi people's suffering.[34] As standards of living rapidly decreased, public institutions became less effective, corruption ran rampant, and Hussein instituted increasingly cruel methods to maintain control over the Iraqi people.[35]

In all, Saddam Hussein's regime was easily one of the world's worst regimes in recent history and a prime candidate for prosecutions for genocide, war crimes, and crimes against humanity. This makes it all the more tragic that the quest to bring Hussein and his associates to justice was tainted by opportunism, incompetence, and short-sighted political motives.

THE PRELUDE TO PROSECUTIONS

The history of the Dujail trial is inescapably bound up with the 2003 United States–led invasion of Iraq. However, the idea of prosecuting the perpetrators of Iraqi crimes against humanity, genocide, and war crimes predated the invasion by at least a decade. Indeed, the government of Kuwait, the United Nations, and the U.S. Department of Defense had suggested the possibility of prosecutions for Iraqi war crimes committed during the 1990–1991 Iraqi occupation of Kuwait.[36] By April 1992, Middle East Watch was gathering testimonial evidence related to crimes committed in northern Iraq; the U.S. Senate Foreign Relations Committee had agreed to enter official government documents seized in Iraq by the Kurdish resistance into the congressional record; and in summer 1992, international forensics teams were exhuming mass graves at several sites in northern Iraq.[37] Afterward, Human Rights Watch attempted to persuade governments to bring a genocide case against the Iraqi government at the International Court of Justice.[38] The Clinton administration was supportive of such efforts, at least in theory, writing in its 1996 Department of State Country Report on Iraq that "U.S. government policy is to support these efforts to hold Saddam Hussein's regime accountable for its war crimes and crimes against humanity."[39] Government support was hardly aggressive, however, and neither the efforts of Human Rights Watch to bring Iraq to the ICJ, nor the strategy of "quiet diplomacy"[40] by the United States to have a special tribunal created by the Security Council resulted in any action.

In the late 1990s, some initial steps were taken against notorious members of the regime leadership. Prosecutorial mechanisms developed significantly during the decade, and in 1996, a group of U.S. senators and British parliamentarians formed Indict, a U.K./U.S.-based organization founded specifically to bring Iraqi perpetrators to justice.[41] Several former high-ranking regime officials were investigated or charged in jurisdictions such as Switzerland, the Netherlands, Denmark, and Austria, but no cases were brought to trial.[42]

Dynamics changed rapidly in the lead-up to the 2003 invasion. In the months following the September 11, 2001, terrorist attacks in the United States, President George W. Bush and his key leaders formed a strategy of a "war on terror" augmented by a doctrine of U.S. preemptive action against regimes or groups that constituted a sufficient threat to U.S. national security.[43] As summarized by President Bush in his 2002 State of the Union Address:

First, we will shut down terrorist camps, disrupt terrorist plans, and bring terrorists to justice. And, second, we must prevent the terrorists and regimes who seek chemical, biological or nuclear weapons from threatening the United States and the world. . . Iraq continues to flaunt its hostility toward America and to support terror. The Iraqi regime has plotted to develop anthrax and nerve gas and nuclear weapons for over a decade. This is a regime that has already used poison gas to murder thousands of its own citizens, leaving the bodies of mothers huddled over their dead children. This is a regime that agreed to international inspections, then kicked out the inspectors. This is a regime that has something to hide from the civilized world. States like these, and their terrorist allies, constitute an axis of evil, arming to threaten the peace of the world.[44]

Under these doctrines, the United States and its allies continued operations in Afghanistan that had begun in 2001 as the search for the leadership of al-Qa'ida, and prepared to forcibly overthrow the leadership of Iraq. From early 2002, U.S. leadership argued strongly that Iraq's Ba'athist regime was allied with al-Qa'ida and had concealed continued efforts to produce and stockpile weapons of mass destruction.[45] In addition to these security-related arguments, many of which were later criticized as unfounded, the United States used the Ba'ath regime's bloody human rights record as a subsidiary reason to justify armed intervention and regime change.[46]

The United States had signaled its preparedness to change Iraq's regime without resorting to multilateral diplomacy. However, strong U.S. and U.K. lobbying secured partial cover from the United Nations in the form of Security Council Resolution 1441 of November 2002. The resolution declared Iraq in breach of its obligations under previous Security Council resolutions and offered a "final opportunity to comply with its disarmament obligations" or face unspecified "serious consequences."[47] The United States gathered partners for an armed invasion as it simultaneously sought to secure a second Security Council resolution to legitimize the use of force. But world opinion was largely against the proposed invasion, UN monitoring reports were ambivalent, and no resolution was forthcoming.[48] On March 18, President Bush gave Saddam Hussein a forty-eight-hour deadline to leave Iraq; the U.S.-led coalition began combat operations began at 0230 GMT on March 20, 2003.

Early planning for the prosecution of senior regime officials had begun a year earlier, in July 2002. The State Department held a two-day working-group meeting to discuss potential transitional justice initiatives, including prosecutorial mechanisms.[49] Participants included international experts and "free Iraqis" – that is, Iraqi-Americans, exiled Iraqis, and individuals from Iraqi Kurdistan.[50] Although the group and other Washington officials suggested a variety of prosecutorial options, high-level U.S. officials appeared to have preferred a domestic prosecutorial mechanism from the outset. Indeed, the then-U.S. ambassador-at-large for war crimes announced even before the fall of Baghdad that the United States would "work with the Iraqi people to create an Iraqi-led process that will bring justice for the years of abuses that have occurred."[51]

It would be a mistake, however, to depict opinion in Washington, D.C., as unequivocally in favor of accountability: even at the last minute, Saddam Hussein was reportedly offered the possibility of amnesty if he stepped down from power.[52] This was also the practical implication of the forty-eight-hour deadline given to Saddam immediately before the invasion. In a televised address to the nation of Iraq on March 17, 2003, President Bush delivered Hussein a clear ultimatum and amnesty offer: "Saddam Hussein must leave Iraq within forty-eight hours. Their refusal to do so will result in military conflict commenced at a time of our choosing."[53] On the eve of the Bush deadline, Arab governments were still engaged in frantic negotiations over potential exile offers.[54] Opinions appeared to be split – as was the case on many other issues – between certain branches of the State Department (which favored a limited model of regime change) and the more ideologically flavored Pentagon. Although administration rhetoric stressed the need for accountability for Hussein's crimes, it appears that accountability would be abandoned if impunity was of greater political value.

The clear U.S. preference for a domestic Iraqi tribunal – prior to meaningful consultation with Iraqis – caused unease in many constituencies that would ordinarily support prosecutorial initiatives. Many criticized the legality of the U.S.-led invasion, feared the United States had used the regime's human rights abuses as a subsidiary justification to go to war, and believed that accountability issues also would be instrumentalized.[55] Others suspected that U.S. support for an "Iraqi-led" process was motivated by the desire to control it, and so minimize the likelihood that embarrassing details of earlier U.S. support of Saddam Hussein be exposed or that the United States might be held to account for crimes committed in 2003 or in earlier conflicts.[56] Many scholars, governments, and nongovernmental organizations also feared that after thirty-five years of severe repression and executive influence, Iraqi criminal law fell far short of international human rights standards, and the Iraqi judicial system simply lacked the technical capacity to hold trials of such magnitude.[57]

Although the U.S. government consulted Iraqis only minimally during the development of its prosecutions policy, there was keen Iraqi interest in prosecutions. Research conducted shortly after the fall of the regime[58] indicated a broad cross-section of Iraqi society strongly desired that Saddam Hussein and other regime leaders face some form of judicial accountability – and that such trials take place inside Iraq and under Iraqi control. They also asked for trials to be impartial, fair, and able to withstand public scrutiny, both within Iraq and internationally. Many indicated a favorable attitude toward international advice and assistance if they would help ensure the trials' fairness, integrity, and transparency. Nor was the interest confined to Iraq. The Iranian government and the Kuwaiti government both repeatedly expressed their desire for judicial accountability for alleged Iraqi war crimes, both in the media and through diplomatic channels.[59]

REGIME CHANGE AND THE CREATION OF THE TRIBUNAL

The stated goal of the 2003 invasion was regime change. Many media outlets and presidential statements framed the invasion and its aftermath as a clash of values and a clash of presidents: George W. Bush and Saddam Hussein.[60] The United States and its allies focused heavily on the symbolism and media imagery of the fall of the Iraqi regime. One such example was the carefully choreographed photographs of the destruction of Saddam-related monuments in Baghdad, as well as similarly choreographed imagery of the raising of the American flag. Regime crimes and the search for individual wrongdoers was an important part of this imagery. In April 2003, the U.S. Defense Intelligence Agency released a highly publicized deck of playing cards, through which the photographs and short biographies of fifty-two Iraqi officials accused of criminal acts were distributed to U.S. forces and publicized heavily on the Internet.[61]

Coalition planning after the fall of Baghdad was chaotic and insufficient, but it included planning the establishment of an Iraqi-led prosecutorial mechanism. Many high-level regime officials had fled or were in hiding; several dozen others, however, were already in coalition custody. U.S. and U.K. officials worked to develop tribunal plans from April to July 2003[62] and began preliminary contacts with the Iraqi legal community and embryonic civil society groups. When the Coalition Provisional Authority (CPA) announced the creation of the Iraqi Governing Council (IGC) on July 13, 2003, the council set up a four-person legal commission to plan for trials.[63] The commission was composed of four distinguished Iraqi jurists with little international experience, assisted by an exile with little Iraqi experience: Salem Chalabi, the nephew of prominent politician Ahmed Chalabi.[64] From July to late September, Salem Chalabi and others began to rework the draft statute and rules of procedure and evidence.

In comparison with the establishment of other prosecutorial mechanisms, the setup of the Iraqi tribunal was hurried and opaque. International support for the invasion or for domestic-led prosecutions was conspicuously absent: anger at the invasion and concern over the use of the death penalty ran deep.[65] Indeed, UN Security Council Resolution 1443 contained language on the need to bring perpetrators to justice, but conspicuously failed to endorse a particular mechanism or approach. As was the case with many facets of CPA activities, the majority of experienced international actors remained aloof or were excluded. A number of those who sought information or involvement were rebuffed by American officials.[66] These dynamics diminished the tribunal's legitimacy greatly, even before trial proceedings began.

Early planning bore fruit on December 10, 2003, when the CPA delegated authority to the Iraqi Governing Council to create an Iraqi Special Tribunal (IST).[67] The tribunal statute was appended to the CPA order, and the judges were empowered to develop the rules of procedure. The tribunal's title was unfortunate; its wording was reminiscent of the unfair "special" courts of the Ba'athist era. The mechanism of creation was also unfortunate. The establishment of the IST by an occupying power raised serious questions about whether with the tribunal was legal under international humanitarian law. Under international humanitarian law (IHL), including the Geneva Conventions, occupying powers have limited power to alter the legislation of the country they occupy.[68] Many members of the international legal community considered the tribunal illegal.

The tribunal was empowered to try Iraqis and residents of Iraq for crimes against humanity, war crimes, and genocide committed from July 17, 1968, up to May 1, 2003.[69] Under article 14 of the IHT Statute, it also was empowered to hear cases involving lesser crimes, such as corruption of the judiciary or aggression against a fraternal Arab state.[70] The latter linked the tribunal directly to the infamous Mahdawi court, which held a series of trials from 1958 to 1960 in which former Iraqi leaders and others were tried for political crimes.[71] The statute was modeled on those of other international tribunals but with a number of differences, one of the most significant being that the statute did not grant the tribunal personal jurisdiction over crimes committed by Americans on Iraqi soil.[72] Also significant was the statute's retention of the death penalty, which gave many legal experts further grounds for unease and compromised several potential avenues of assistance, including from the United Kingdom.[73]

Yet although the tribunal was unlucky in many aspects, it was fortunate in at least one. Saddam Hussein was captured by U.S. soldiers within days of the tribunal's creation. The former president was discovered in humiliating circumstances on December 13, 2003, hiding underground at a farmhouse near Tikrit. Images of Hussein as a long-haired, disheveled, and confused old man gave the United States a much-needed international media boost. These photographs were designed to contribute to the erosion of his public image and were deemed by many as an attempt to humiliate him in breach of Geneva Conventions.

Hussein's capture contributed a sense of urgency to the tribunal's investigations and operations. However, it also meant that many considered the trial a foregone conclusion. Iraqi politicians were graphic in articulating Hussein's desired fate. Western politicians were only marginally more circumspect. "Let's just see what penalty he gets, but I think he ought to receive the ultimate penalty for what he has done to his people," Mr. Bush told ABC News. "I mean, he is a torturer, a murderer, they had rape rooms. This is a disgusting tyrant who deserves justice, the ultimate justice."[74]

ANATOMY OF THE TRIBUNAL AND ITS WORKINGS

From 2004 to mid-2005, investigations and trial preparations proceeded in stops and starts. Judges were recruited from various sources, many of whom had been lawyers under the previous regime. Hussein and approximately one hundred other high-value detainees were held from the time of their capture in U.S. military custody, most of them reportedly at Camp Cropper near Baghdad's airport. CPA amendments to the Iraqi Criminal Code had legalized indefinite detention without bail for individuals suspected of crimes against humanity, war crimes, and genocide.[75]

The first glimpse the public had of the tribunal's workings was on July 1, 2004. To preempt the argument that Hussein and other detainees were prisoners of war, a legal fiction was created in which detainees were considered as held in Iraqi criminal custody, even though they were physically held in U.S. facilities and guarded by U.S. troops.[76]

Iraqi law requires questioning of the accused within twenty-four hours of arrest. Saddam Hussein and eleven other members of the former leadership were brought before an anonymous chief investigative judge on July 1.[77] The proceedings were held Camp Victory, a former lakeside palace complex, and attended by a mixed group of American and Iraqi officials and journalists. Hussein's questioning was televised, albeit without any sound. Proceedings appeared to have been carefully arranged for the camera. Hussein appeared unkempt and cheaply dressed, and initially seemed to believe that the questioning was in fact his trial.[78] However, he quickly became more assertive and repeatedly challenged the judge's authority. No full transcript of proceedings exists. Saddam and other defendants were reportedly informed of the accusations against them and asked to indicate their choice of legal counsel.[79] There was no indication that defendants had had access to counsel while under U.S. detention.

The tribunal's work was carried out by two groups: tribunal staff and members or subcontractors for the Regime Crimes Liaison Office (RCLO). Composed largely of U.S. personnel, the RCLO was the instrument through which the United States funded, supported, cajoled, and assisted the tribunal. It included Department of Justice lawyers, FBI investigators, U.S. marshals, and arrangements for forensic investigation of several mass graves. The RCLO had a budget of $128 million[80] and was established under National Security Presidential Directive Number 37 (NSPD-37) of May 13, 2004. A high-ranking U.S. legal adviser described the RCLO's work as follows:

> The RCLO has provided logistical assistance where the tribunal has been hampered by poor infrastructure and also legal and law enforcement expertise to the judges as they pursue their investigations. The RCLO funds and coordinates all mass-grave exhumation projects, document management systems, a courthouse construction project and the training and coordination of the tribunal's security. On the legal and investigative side, the RCLO provides training to the judges, international legal research, and strategic investigative guidance.[81]

In reality, the tribunal could not have functioned without RCLO support, particularly with regard to forensic investigations and, during the trial phase, securing the attendance of witnesses. The vast majority of RCLO staff was seconded from the U.S. Department of Justice and lacked any experience in the prosecution of systemic or international crimes, civil law legal systems, or judicial systems of the Middle East and North Africa region. The language barrier proved a further obstacle to input on legal matters.[82]

Yet although the tribunal had RCLO support, it lacked most other kinds of international assistance. The uneasy U.S.-Iraqi-international relationship cost the tribunal dearly in terms of capacity and expertise. Disquiet over the war, the statute, and the retention of the death penalty meant that few individuals with experience in prosecuting international crimes were willing to be associated with the tribunal. The United Nations reportedly prohibited any consultant or staff member from giving technical assistance, removing by far the largest pool of potential experts from the tribunal's reach.[83] Many human rights groups supported this position.[84] Some nongovernmental organizations, such as the International Bar Association, participated in short-term training programs for tribunal judges, and a handful of governments (including the United Kingdom and Australia) contributed toward facilities and training.

Tribunal staff reciprocated the international community's coolness. All tribunal staff members were required to be Iraqi nationals, with Arabic the sole official language of the court. Under the new law, non-Iraqi counsel did not have the right to address the court. The tribunal statute provided for the participation of international expert advisors and, in some limited situations, international judges. Such participation was not mandatory, however, and the tribunal itself was highly resistant to the concept. After much persuasion, the tribunal reluctantly agreed to accept an independent judicial adviser to the Trial Chamber shortly before the Dujail trial opened. Later, it also agreed to an independent international adviser to the defense. Both advisers made vital contributions to the quality and integrity of proceedings.[85]

The international-domestic dialectic profoundly affected the tribunal in other ways. In an attempt to remedy the technical and political questions surrounding the tribunal's establishment, an amended version of the tribunal statute was passed by the Iraqi National Assembly in August 2005. The legislation changed the court's name from the Iraqi Special Tribunal to the Iraqi High Tribunal,[86] as well as making more substantive changes. Many changes were at the behest of political forces and outside the control of the tribunal itself. The new legislation was promulgated on October 18, 2005, the day before the opening of the Dujail trial. The opening of the first session was delayed while the presiding judge telephoned the ministry of justice to confirm which law to apply.

Although the question of the legality of the tribunal's establishment may have been addressed by making it a wholly Iraqi court, political and practical problems remained. The obvious problem was that of legitimacy: a widespread perception remained that the tribunal was controlled by the United States. There also were many substantive legal difficulties. For one, the tribunal's new status left it vulnerable to the inherent weaknesses of the Iraqi legal system. These included the Iraqi Code of Criminal Procedure's lack of flexibility in dealing with crimes as enormous as crimes against humanity, war crimes, or genocide. Even more seriously, they included a long tradition of executive interference with the judiciary.

Although international law provided the substantive legal framework for matters such as the definitions of crimes, the IHT Statute and associated Rules of Procedure and Evidence anchored the tribunal in the Iraqi Criminal Procedure Law of 1971.[87] In practice Iraqi law governed all procedural and many other legal issues, such as the accreditation and disciplining of lawyers. The Iraqi Criminal Procedural Code of 1971 had been amended by the CPA to prohibit the admission of testimony gained through coercive means,[88] but apart from that, it was an antiquated procedural code based on the civil law legal tradition, with little or no thought given to how it might be adapted to cope with the tribunal's mandate. For instance, its investigative judges lacked capacity to carry out full and independent investigations, including the gathering of exculpatory evidence.[89] Likewise, the reliance on civil law procedures diminished the role of the defense, whereas the prosecution enjoyed a role more prominent than that in ordinary civil law proceedings – to the point that the Iraqi judges referred to the tribunal as "the prosecutor's court." The prominent role given to self-representation in the Iraqi system gave ample ground to Saddam Hussein and others to make public speeches and to exert control and influence in the courtroom.

Although the statute was clearly based on the statutes of international tribunals, it also contained some highly problematic provisions. Three proved particularly important. First was the requirement in Article 33 of the statute that no employee could have been a member of the Ba'ath party. This was worded in an ambiguous manner that implied that any Ba'ath affiliation was impermissible – a standard much higher than those used in de-Ba'athification proceedings in other institutions. This left tribunal judges vulnerable to pressure from political actors who wished to rush the process or influence the final outcome. Some twenty tribunal staff members were rendered eligible for de-Ba'athification under this language, many of them judges.[90] As will be discussed later, the language of Article 33 became the single biggest threat to the independence of the Dujail judges.

Second was the power of the executive under Article 4(4) of the statute to transfer judges from the tribunal for any reason. This was a blunt weapon that dissuaded judges from strategies or actions that would draw executive wrath. Used against the presiding judge in the Anfal trial in September 2006, this language conveyed precisely what could happen if judges failed to maintain the confidence of the government. It was also used as a tool to dispose of judges instead of or following their de-Ba'athification.

The third important provision was Article 27 (second), which dealt with the enforcement of sentences. In one short paragraph it prohibited the possibility of a presidential pardon or any other reduction of sentence. It also specified a new requirement that all penalties had to be implemented within thirty days of the final judgment. This language was not part of the tribunal statute of 2003 and was added after other prosecutorial strategies had been decided. It later proved to have fateful consequences.

THE FACTS OF THE DUJAIL TRIAL

The crimes of Saddam Hussein and his followers were legion. Yet like any prosecutorial mechanism, the tribunal would only have the opportunity to focus on a select few. Some fourteen cases were chosen for investigation, including the 1988 Anfal campaign against the Kurds, the 1991 uprising in southern Iraq, the destruction of the marshes after the Gulf War of 1990–1991, the corruption of the judiciary, and others.[91]

In 2003–2004, tribunal staff argued that Iraqi criminal procedure required them to adopt a strategy in which Hussein and other alleged violators were tried in multiple cases relating to multiple incidents. Rather than face trial once for a number of crimes, leading regime figures who were involved in more than one crime would have to undergo multiple trials. The regime's crimes would be exposed, and individual accountability would emerge over the course of several cases.

The tribunal's first trial was that of al-Dujail. Saddam Hussein and seven other defendants were accused of crimes against humanity for actions they took against the Shi'ite residents of the town of al-Dujail following an assassination attempt against the president in July 1982. In comparison with the other cases under investigation, tribunal insiders described it as a quick and simple case that would enable the tribunal to develop its skills outside the limelight. In addition, al-Dujail reportedly was the first investigation to be finished.[92]

This gradualist strategy failed for several reasons. First, the case was not as simple as initially predicted. The facts concerned a retributive attack against the population of Dujail, a mainly Shi'ite town some twenty-five miles north of Baghdad. Local residents allegedly mounted an assassination attempt against Hussein on July 8, 1982, as his motorcade drove through the town. Hussein's bodyguards, the security forces, and the party militia swept into action, and several Dujailis were killed the same day. In the days that followed, hundreds of men, women, and children were rounded up, detained, and sent to the *mukhabarat* (secret police) headquarters in Baghdad. Entire families were held at the intelligence services headquarters in appalling conditions and tortured; at least forty-six died as a result. The Revolutionary Court sentenced some 148 male detainees to death, one-third of whom had already died. Those sentenced to death were executed in a single day at Abu Ghraib prison. Hundreds of their relatives, including women, children, and elderly men, were banished to a desert camp near the Saudi border. While in internal exile, their houses were confiscated, their orchards razed, and their property destroyed. All in all, the crimes of Dujail spanned at least four locations over a period of some five years – hardly a simple case.

The case also touched unanticipated political nerves. The event was little known compared with the other tribunal investigations, and the victims were almost exclusively Shi'a. This later gave rise to the accusation that Dujail was a sectarian-inspired prosecution, a sense that was unfortunately reinforced by the case's connection with the al-Dawa Party, an Islamist party banned under Hussein's rule. It was members of al-Dawa who allegedly planned and perpetrated the 1982 assassination attempt against the president. By the time the trial opened, however, al-Dawa was a leading Shi'a political party and included the Iraqi prime minister among its members. This fact was not lost on Iraqi onlookers, although it is not clear whether U.S. advisors were also aware of this direct connection to contemporary domestic politics.[93]

Another major reason the strategy failed was political pressure. It appears that the tribunal did not originally intend to include Saddam Hussein in the Dujail trial. His name was conspicuously absent from the tribunal's initial press release of February 2005, which named five accused.[94] The exact sequence of events is unclear, but government and public interest were indifferent to strategic or legal reasoning and very interested in trying the former dictator as soon as possible. Hussein was subsequently added to the case somewhere between March and September 2005. Shortly afterward, Article 27 (second) of the statute was added, requiring implementation of all sentences within thirty days. For defendants convicted of death-penalty offenses, the gradualist, incident-based prosecutorial strategy was eviscerated. Most tribunal insiders hoped until the last minute that there would be some way of delaying final judgment until other trials (particularly the Anfal trial) had at least gone through its trial phase. They were to be disappointed. Although Hussein and others were accused of other crimes, they would not live to be tried for them.

TRIAL DYNAMICS: POLITICAL PEDAGOGY, BUT OF WHAT KIND?

The Dujail trial ran for sixty sessions from October 19, 2005, to November 5, 2006. During this period, the wider Iraqi political transition, already faltering, collapsed into widespread violence and increasing sectarianism.

There were eight accused, ranging in seniority from the highest-ranking to low-level Ba'ath officials. The high-ranking defendants included Saddam Hussein; his half-brother and former chief of the intelligence service (the *mukhabarat*), Barzan Ibrahim al-Hassan al-Tikriti; the former deputy prime minister and later vice president and head of the Ba'ath Party militia, the popular army (*jaish al-shaabi*) Taha Yasin Ramadan; and the president of the Revolutionary Court, Awad Hamad al-Bandar. At the other end of the spectrum were local Ba'ath party members. These included Abd Allah Kathim al-Ruwaid and Mazhar Abd Allah Kathim al-Ruwaid, senior Ba'ath party officials in Dujail, and Ali Dayih Ali and Mohammed Azawi Ali, both party officials in Dujail. The defendants were accused of crimes against humanity including willful killing, deportation, imprisonment, torture, forced disappearances, and other inhumane acts.[95] Under Article 406 of Iraq's penal code, the crime of murder is punishable by death.

The trial opened in the unfinished courthouse at a pivotal moment, four days after a constitutional referendum, and seven weeks before national elections. Iraqis across the country crowded in front of their television sets. Leading Iraqi politicians crowded into the twenty-five-seat visitors' chamber, and demonstrations across the country called for the death penalty. All knuckles whitened as Hussein and six other accused entered the courtroom, including the despised former head of the Revolutionary Court, Awad Hamad al-Bandar, and Barzan al-Tikriti, who had served as Iraq's representative to the United Nations in Geneva. The court heard the prosecution's opening statement, read defendants their rights, took initial pleas – and then adjourned for six weeks, during which all parties worked frantically to improve their readiness.

The first phase of the trial consisted of hearing complainants and witnesses. Some of their testimony was both compelling and historic. For example, several complainants testified to the torture they underwent while they were detained in the months and years following the assassination attempt. Female complainants showed tremendous courage in testifying about their detention and torture.[96] One recalled how she was stripped naked, hung by her arms, and shocked by electrical wires attached to her fingers and toes.[97] Many victims withstood strong and often abusive questioning by defense counsel – and verbal outbreaks by the defendants themselves – as they told of the arrest, disappearance, or deaths of friends, brothers, fathers, uncles, sons, and nephews. Even though the majority of witnesses gave testimony from behind a curtain, the power of their experiences was spellbinding.[98] The importance to the victims of participating in the proceedings and recounting their experiences in a courtroom in front of the former Iraqi leadership cannot be overstated. In one of the first examples of their participation in prosecutions for international crimes, complainants were represented by lawyers who were permitted to examine witnesses and defendants.[99]

Yet the presentation of evidence was largely subsumed by the focus on Saddam Hussein. As expected, Hussein was defiant during the early hearings. Well dressed and confident, he regularly faced down the presiding judge. His behavior and appearance contrasted strongly with the images of his arrest and arraignment. Defendants and defense counsel treated him with deference, using forms of address and other behavior that made it clear they continued to acknowledge Hussein as Iraq's rightful president.

Media reporting portrayed Hussein's behavior as continuously disruptive. If viewed over the totality of the sessions, however, this was not the case. Ever-conscious that the proceedings were televised, Hussein generally cultivated an aura of dignity and sorrowful condescension. This was an excellent political strategy, but sometimes it backfired. For example, on March 1, 2006, Hussein interrupted the judge's examination of his subordinates to state that anything that had been done was his responsibility, an admission that was held against him in the judgment.[100] Over time Hussein became increasingly drawn into the legal process, responding to accusations and evidence rather than maintaining a purely political defense. Indeed, it was the testimony of torture and sexual abuse by female complainants that first jolted his composure: after the graphic testimony of the first female witness on December 6, 2005, Hussein and others were visibly taken aback and swiftly sought to distract the court by complaining of their own conditions of detention.[101]

Skillful oratory is highly valued in the Middle East. Hussein exploited the latitude given to him by the court to narrate the political history of the proceedings, mock or patronize the judges,[102] and stir the audience to mourn for the lost glories of the Saddamist past. He referred to the tribunal's lack of legitimacy in every session, ridiculing the occupiers and encouraging loyalists to resist them. Courtroom acoustics also worked in Hussein's favor. The RCLO and the tribunal had designed a system whereby the presiding judge could cut the microphone in cases of inflammatory speech by defendants. But Hussein was a talented orator, and his voice was easily audible without amplification.[103] He also skillfully manipulated publicity in other ways. He went on a hunger strike for part of the trial and alleged that he was tortured and ill treated in custody.[104]

With a charismatic dictator standing only a few feet in front of them, the judges struggled to keep the proceedings on a legal track and diminish their political dimensions. At the trial's outset, it was clear that many within the tribunal intended al-Dujail to set an ambitious new standard for Iraqi justice that was substantively and procedurally fairer than that which had gone before and that would be well regarded internationally. Several continued to fight for that standard even as Iraqi sectarian violence increased. However, there was little public appetite for such a standard. Instead, the demand was for speed. After the first month, the Dujail trial was probably the longest Iraqi trial ever held. Many Iraqis questioned why Saddam deserved fairer justice than his victims. Ordinary Iraqis were never formally consulted about what they thought of the trial, however, and the tribunal conducted virtually no outreach.

The first presiding judge, Rizgar Amin, was criticized bitterly for his inability to control the defendants and for showing them unnecessary courtesy. Many in the Arab world view secular judges as embodying the power of the state. To show any flexibility toward defendants is to show unnecessary weakness; for example, Amin's choice to call Saddam Hussein "Mr. Hussein," rather than "Defendant Hussein," outraged many Iraqi viewers. After weeks of mounting criticism (including from the minister of justice), executive pressure to improve television dynamics, and public petitions for his removal in nine provinces, Amin resigned in January 2006 and returned to Kurdistan.

Amin's departure was a pivotal moment: it led to the first of a series of direct executive interventions that undermined judicial independence and the tribunal's credibility. Amin's nominated replacement was Trial Chamber judge Sa'id al-Hammashi, a former lawyer who showed signs of independence and a strong interest in international norms. Al-Hammashi's name and identity were publicly announced, after which the Higher National De-Ba'athification Commission intervened to remove him. There was little resistance from the tribunal. Al-Hammashi may have been one of the roughly twenty staff members who were reportedly eligible for removal under the statute's very high de-Ba'athification threshold. However, the commission's intervention was most likely prompted by fears that al-Hammashi would fail to deliver the desired death sentence. Although he was swiftly removed from the Trial Chamber, he remained on the tribunal.[105] Judge Rauf Abd al-Rahman, a Kurd, was appointed from outside the Trial Chamber in his place. Judicial independence was shaken. The De-Ba'athification Commission had struck its first blow in the Dujail trial, but not the last.

Saddam Hussein was the cynosure of all eyes, but his lawyers were responsible for his legal defense. Hussein's defense team notionally comprised scores of lawyers across several continents, but the team leader was Khalil al-Dulaimi, reportedly a former intelligence officer with little trial experience. Joined at times by prominent foreign lawyers, including former U.S. Attorney General Ramsey Clarke and former Qatari Minister of Justice Najib al-Nuami, he pursued a political defense strategy that for the most part ignored the alleged facts of the case and at times resorted to obstructive tactics such as repeated walkouts. There were also indications of less savory defense tactics: after two spectacular sessions on May 30 and 31, 2006, four defense witnesses confessed to having committed perjury, allegedly as the result of pressure and threats from al-Dulaimi.[106]

Regardless of the wisdom of their tactics, it was difficult for the defense counsel to do their job. No Iraqi lawyer had any training in international law, and the expertise of foreign counsel varied widely. Three defense lawyers were killed during proceedings. Sadun al-Janabi, counsel for Awad Hamad al-Bandar, was abducted and shot the day after trial's opening. U.S.-brokered security negotiations took place between the defense, the tribunal, the RCLO, and the Iraqi Interior Ministry after al-Janabi's killing. However, Baghdad's security environment, already bad, was deteriorating rapidly and becoming more and more sectarian. There was little trust between the parties, and it appears too little was done too late.[107] Adil Muhammad al-Zubaidi, who represented former vice president Taha Yasin Ramadan, was shot in his car and killed three weeks later on November 8, 2005; a colleague riding with him was injured and subsequently fled to Syria. Khamis al-Ubaidi, co-counsel for Saddam Hussein and Barzan al-Hassan, was killed in June 2006 during the trial's final sessions.[108]

The security situation also made it impossible for the defense to conduct its own investigations, particularly in al-Dujail itself. Nor could they easily gain access to their clients or tribunal offices. Members of the tribunal's own defense office, who were supposed to act as a fallback to ensure the rights of the accused, also had difficulty making adequate security arrangements. As a result, defendants faced difficulties in retaining not only private counsel but even court-appointed attorneys. This seriously affected the quality of their representation.

Security problems were not just the preserve of the defense. At least five tribunal staff members were killed prior to Dujail's opening, and several judges reportedly had relatives killed or injured in retaliation for their tribunal work. Likewise, Dujaili victims, witnesses, and their families reportedly suffered deadly retributive attacks.[109] Iraq's deteriorating security situation affected all aspects of the tribunal's work, massively driving up costs, complicating logistics, and increasing the personal pressures experienced by the judges. Many (including the defense) argued for a change in the trial's venue. These arguments fell on deaf ears. There was a very strong Iraqi desire to hold the trials in the country and a reluctance to transfer the proceedings to the Kurdish regions, which might have deepened accusations of sectarian bias.

The cost of maintaining the status quo was increasing dependence on American logistical and security support. Without the RCLO and U.S. military forces, witnesses and defense counsel could not be brought to trial, the courtroom could not be protected, and judges would not have been able to live in relative safety. Iraqis and Americans became locked in an unhappy dyadic embrace. The relationship had few conditions and little transparency. No matter what they actually did, both sides constantly were criticized. The Iraqis were either too independent of the Americans or not independent enough; the Americans were either exerting too much influence or were not influential enough. The language divide and differences in legal background meant that only a handful of people could navigate these divisions. That they did so is a tribute to their tenacity and dedication during an excruciatingly difficult process.

In addition to security problems, the defense also was disadvantaged by other factors. The tribunal was proud of its commitment to facilitating an adequate defense, which it defined almost entirely as permitting the defendants to be represented by counsel and by providing court-appointed counsel to defendants who could not afford them. Yet laboring under the legacy of decades of dictatorship, tribunal staff found it difficult to shed the assumption that defense lawyers were the enemies of the court. Instead, Hussein's political defense strategy inflamed the judges and other tribunal staff; relationships between the tribunal and defense counsel were glacial.

Practical problems included unclear charges, late disclosure of witness identities, limited responsiveness to defense motions, and restrictions on introducing defense witnesses.[110] Tribunal judges argued that they had provided a far fairer trial and far greater opportunity to the defense than in any previous Iraqi court. Unfortunately, they failed to live up to the protections contained in the tribunal's own statute and guaranteed by Article 14 of the International Covenant on Civil and Political Rights, to which Iraq is a signatory. Having embraced international standards along with the definitions of international crimes, it proved difficult to live by them.

In addition to security and fair trial standards, the tribunal was also faced with other major challenges. Prosecutions for international crimes are a means of determining individual criminal responsibility for horrific crimes. At their best, they also are eloquent tools for revealing the truth of those crimes: the facts, relationships, and logistics that make such crimes possible. The Dujail trial did provide unparalleled moments for victims and complainants to testify about their suffering. However, the Trial Chamber was unable to distill a coherent narrative of events. It was overwhelmed rather than empowered by the evidence, and its members appeared to lack the analytical skills to show how the different organs of the regime functioned; how perpetrators were linked to the evidence as a matter of fact (rather than simply de jure); or wider patterns of state abuse, such as the unfairness of the Revolutionary Court system, that were highly relevant to Dujail.[111] Many of these difficulties can be ascribed to the retention by tribunal judges of investigative and other techniques they used for crimes in the normal Iraqi judicial system: there was little attempt to embrace new techniques that were more appropriate to investigate complex systemic crimes such as crimes against humanity. For example, there was no expert evidence on the manner of the regime's functioning, or on the structure of Iraqi government institutions. Judges said privately that they feared such evidence might be misinterpreted as political. There also were gaps in other important evidence required by the elements of the crimes, including most particularly evidence of intent.[112]

The final major challenge the tribunal faced was outreach. The idea that the tribunal should embrace a strategy to explain itself and its workings to the Iraqi public was difficult for its leadership to embrace. Not surprisingly, staff members lacked any media experience and were accustomed to operating without the need to deliver written reasoned decisions, to explain court proceedings, or even to keep a public record of proceedings. Many feared that transparency would exacerbate political problems, rather than help to resolve them. Thus, the Trial Chamber judges opposed even the release of a written transcript of proceedings, saying it would lead to "misunderstanding."[113] The tribunal included a handful of professional media-related positions, but they appeared to have little impact on or understanding of their work.

That is not to say there was no media strategy. The chief investigative judge was appointed spokesperson, the RCLO and tribunal officials held various media briefings, and the tribunal televised its proceedings. This was a major step toward transparency but proved a double-edged sword. Proceedings were broadcast on local and regional satellite television stations and watched by millions. However, they aired without providing important contextual information, such as public education about the Iraqi justice system, the gradualist prosecution strategy, the tribunal's mandate, or an explanation of what constitutes crimes against humanity. Thus, the audience reacted to day-to-day developments without a broader context in which to understand them. Although security rendered some forms of media and outreach more difficult, it did not preclude basic steps such as regular written, radio, or TV summary updates; a focused outreach program for politicians, legal professionals, or schoolchildren; or a tribunal Web site. By ignoring these and other strategies for educating the public, the tribunal failed to mitigate the proceedings' inaccessibility to the majority of the Iraqi people who, in turn, failed to understand and support its work.

JUDGMENT AND EXECUTION

When the verdicts were announced on November 5, 2006, there were few surprises. Saddam Hussein and his former chief of intelligence, Barzan al-Tikriti, were found guilty of crimes against humanity, including willful killing, forcible deportation, and torture. The two were sentenced to death and two terms of ten-years' imprisonment each. Former president of the Revolutionary Court Awad Hamad al-Bandar was found guilty of the crime against humanity of willful killing and sentenced to death. Former vice president and head of the army Taha Yasin Ramadan was found guilty of willful killing, deportation, torture, and other inhuman acts constituting crimes against humanity. He was sentenced to life imprisonment.[114]

Handed down just two days before the U.S. 2006 midterm elections, the judgment's timing renewed worldwide skepticism about the independence of the proceedings. Nonetheless, Iraqis were happy with the decision, and the rest of the world reacted with relief. Iraqi prime minister Nuri al-Maliki swiftly gave a BBC interview in which he said he expected Saddam to be executed by the end of the year.[115] Few were aware that the De-Ba'athification Commission had intervened again, this time over rumors that not all of the higher-ranking defendants would receive the death penalty. Its threats led to the removal of one judge from the Trial Chamber during the final deliberations and another from the Cassation Chamber to ensure a majority in favor of the death penalty. To be de-Ba'athified meant an automatic loss of job and protection, and loss of residence in the Green Zone. For Trial Chamber judges, this was a virtual death sentence. The commission's October 2006 intervention passed without comment: at the time, no outsiders knew the substitution had taken place.[116]

Despite this interference and many other faults, members of the Trial Chamber delivered what they deemed a fair and fully reasoned judgment of almost three hundred pages. The judgment was released seventeen days after verdicts were announced. It attempted to give detailed reasoning and struggled with international legal norms and jurisprudence, not always successfully.[117] It found that by virtue of Saddam Hussein's position of absolute authority and documentary evidence showing his participation, there was sufficient evidence to convict him of all the offenses charged except enforced disappearances. The RCLO, not surprisingly, hailed it as a milestone for Iraq and the region. Few others troubled to comment, at least in the short term.

Viewed through the lens of international legal experts, the evidence against Hussein was weak. The court relied mainly on inferences to convict him. For instance, there was no evidence of direct orders issued by Saddam Hussein. Although there was plenty of evidence that crimes such as torture had occurred, there was insufficient evidence to show that Saddam had the requisite criminal intent or actual (or constructive) knowledge about the crimes at the time they were committed.[118] On the contrary, there was evidence in the dossier to indicate that Hussein may not have known of these criminal acts when they were committed, although he subsequently received a report outlining what had taken place.[119] Nor was there any evidence to show how the various institutions implicated functioned as part of Saddam Hussein's regime, which would have allowed for clearer and more appropriate inferences.

The case also lacked evidence linking the high-level accused to the crimes charged. On multiple occasions, the court failed to translate "what all Iraqis knew" into legally justifiable facts based on evidence. At one point, the judgment simply declared that "No Iraqi had any doubt about the reality."[120] The Trial Chamber appeared to use inferences inappropriately to bridge important gaps and so achieve the desired outcome: the conviction of Saddam Hussein and the other high-level accused. These kinds of concerns, however, were confined to the ranks of international lawyers.

The case then went to cassation, a form of appeal, which was based entirely on the written record. Unlike the Trial Chamber judges, the cassation judges lacked their own independent legal adviser, although most had significantly greater judicial experience. Also unlike the Trial Chamber, the cassation judges gave up the struggle to apply international norms and instead focused on expediting the proceedings.

The Cassation Chamber was headed by the tribunal president, who was known to be close to the prime minister and appeared susceptible to political influence. The prime minister had several times promised that Hussein would be executed before the end of the year.[121] The Cassation Chamber obliged by issuing its final judgment on December 26, when the RCLO and much of the rest of the world were on holiday.

The haste of the Cassation Chamber's actions appears to have impinged the right of the accused to a full appeal. For instance, the Trial Chamber had announced the verdicts and sentences in the Dujail case on November 5, 2006, but released its written opinion only on November 22 – more than halfway through the thirty-day appeal period. This gave the defense lawyers only eleven days to study the judgment before submitting their appeals on December 3. Subsequent and extensive defense submissions were filed on December 17. The Cassation Chamber announced its judgment just nine days later.

The chamber's written ruling was remarkable for its absence of reasoning and its brevity, being a mere seventeen pages long.[122] It was particularly notable for the fact that, without discussion of reasoning or evidence, the Cassation Chamber ordered Taha Yasin Ramadan's sentence be increased from life imprisonment to the death penalty. To many observers (unaware of last-minute changes to the composition of the trial chamber) the Cassation Chamber judgment marked an important but unwelcome boundary between a tribunal struggling in good faith but limited capacity to deliver a judicial verdict and a purely political process.

Within half an hour of the cassation judgment, the government took steps to implement the execution. The period between the final judgment and the execution was brief but marred by irregularities, as well as tensions between U.S. and Iraqi officials.[123] The Iraqi government had envisaged an immediate execution: the U.S. balked and used various logistical requirements to set January 10, 2007, as the execution date. The Iraqi prime minister's staff member responsible for executions took his scheduled vacation, as did many others.

The prime minister was not to be put off by U.S. planning requirements, however. As much of the rest of the world enjoyed the Christmas holidays and Eid al-Adha – the Muslim feast of sacrifice, Maliki surmounted legal and political obstacles to bring the execution date closer. The normal Iraqi legal requirements for the ratification of death sentences appear not to have been followed. Ordinarily, the Presidency Council is required to ratify the death penalty, but President Jalal Talabani was on record as being opposed to the death penalty and throughout the trial had been clear that he would not endorse it. The following events are hard to piece together, but whether or not the technical ratification requirements were fulfilled, the papers obtained eventually satisfied American political authorities: Maliki bypassed local U.S. commanders, and the final timing and approval of the executions was reportedly resolved directly between the prime minister's office and Washington.[124]

Iraqi interlocutors were less troubled over ratification technicalities than they were over the proposed timing of Hussein's execution: December 30, the morning of Eid al-Adha. The Iraqi Code of Criminal Law clearly prohibits executions on religious holidays. However, there was a loophole: the feast was celebrated on different days by different sects. That year, December 30 was the date celebrated by Sunnis, Hussein's own confessional group. It was, however, the last day of the year before the Eid, and public pressure for Hussein's execution was mounting. Over fierce opposition, the matter was reportedly referred away from secular jurists to major Shi'a religious scholars, who ruled the execution permissible if it took place before sunrise at 7:06 A.M. The timing of the execution alienated many Iraqi jurists, however, and was seen as a deliberate provocation by Sunnis both in Iraq and throughout the region.

Hussein was taken to the gallows at 5:05 A.M. on December 30. U.S. military officials transferred him to Iraqi custody shortly afterwards. He was hanged some forty minutes later.[125] Held in a dank execution cell at the former *istikhbarat* (military intelligence) headquarters, the execution failed to fulfill Iraqi legal requirements and inflamed opinion worldwide. Some of those required to be present under Iraqi law were absent; many others attended who should not have been there, including a number of Dawa Party officials. An official video recording was intended to show the dignity of the event, but a clandestine recording taken on a mobile telephone showed the ugly truth. Hussein in his final minutes was insulted and taunted by officials and by his executioners. His tormentors were unmistakably and proudly Shi'a, and some called on fiery political cleric Muqtada al-Sadr in praise. Hussein remained calm throughout proceedings, and the myth of the brave and fearless leader instantly revived.[126]

REACTIONS TO TRIAL AND EXECUTION

The Dujail trial disappointed almost everyone. For most Iraqis, it was inconveniently long and legalistic; for most international legal experts, it took place before a crippled show court that did little to uphold the rule of law. Many Arab commentators agreed, albeit for different reasons. They saw a tribunal designed to reinforce the triumph of the victors and serve domestic American political purposes; to humiliate Arab dignity; and, by implication, to threaten other regional regimes. In the months following Hussein's execution the trial's initial presiding judge, Rizgar Amin, publicly criticized it as against Islamic custom and illegal under Iraqi law.[127] His successor Ra'uf Abd al-Rahman termed it "uncivilized."[128]

International opinion had always been badly split. Much of this reflected international splits over the legality and desirability of the March 2003 invasion, but not all. The international media commentary on the proceedings was driven by three distinct sources: the technical commentary provided by primarily U.S.-based legal academics and practitioners; human rights groups, some of which were closely monitoring proceedings in Baghdad; and individuals and counsel aligned with various defense teams – particularly that of Saddam Hussein.

The quality of much of the American commentary left much to be desired: unfamiliar with Arab and Continental legal systems, many pundits superimposed the narrative of other international prosecutorial mechanisms onto the tribunal, depending on the English-language information they obtained from the Regime Crimes Liaison Office in Baghdad. Most had never been to Iraq. Theirs was a tribunal of plucky judges and lofty motives: the glass, no matter how empty, was always viewed as half full. This continued until the execution, after which the glass half-full theory became harder to maintain. Officials in those governments that had participated in the coalition or were supporting the tribunal maintained upbeat assessments of the tribunal's proceedings until stunned into shocked silence by Saddam Hussein's execution.

Human rights groups took varying positions. Having opposed the creation of a domestic Iraqi tribunal, they at first took the practical position that the tribunal must be monitored. For them the glass was usually half empty, and thus the process held few surprises in the end. The defense lawyers, by contrast, were part of a far-flung network with multiple centers of power. They deftly played to the circumstances of the invasion and tribunal's establishment, the humiliation to Arab dignity and Arab nationalism, and the fair-trial violations and other issues that dogged tribunal proceedings. Their statements and strategy were aimed toward Arabic regional media, which heavily colored their coverage of proceedings.[129]

Regional Arab dynamics were mixed and varied over time. Many regional and Iraqi outlets relied heavily on Western wire reports for their coverage, mixed with commentary from local politicians, lawyers, tribunal officials, and people in the street. Reactions varied predictably according to the overall editorial position of the outlet. In 2003–2004, a number of voices welcomed the possibility of accountability as an important message to abusive regional leaders, as well as the potential importance that bringing Hussein to justice might have for Iraqi victims. More desired accountability but were troubled by the unlikelihood of it being achieved on the heels of a foreign invasion or via a U.S.-instituted court. For others, shame and anger at Saddam's swift overthrow and ignominious capture lapsed into a lack of interest in tribunal matters until the opening of the Dujail trial, when interest was focused on the dynamics of the interplay between Hussein and the Dujail presiding judges. Victims' voices were quickly obscured in the wake of Hussein's skillful rhetoric. Most media outlets made little or no effort to understand the legal principles behind the tribunal's functioning, the notable exception being the London regional daily *Asharq alaawsat*.

In the few short days after his execution Hussein became a a fallen hero whose dignity in his final moments redeemed what went before. Hussein was lauded as a martyr from Turkey to Jakarta and beyond, even among communities that had little reason to do so. Reaction in neighboring Arab countries such as Jordan was particularly strong, where resentment of both the United States and of Iraqis appeared to grow sharply. Other short-term regional reactions included the passage of amnesty legislation in Afghanistan to assuage warlords who feared suffering Hussein's fate.[130]

Iraqi reactions differed strongly from those of the regional media. Iraqis were deeply interested in the trial and maintained a focus on proceedings even when other major events occurred, such as a constitutional referendum and the election of the first post-Saddam sovereign parliament.[131] Indeed, the rumor in Baghdad at the trial's opening was that the timing had been arranged to benefit the incumbent government in the polls. Public sentiment strongly supported the tribunal, although many feared that the tribunal's deliberations would be manipulated by Ba'athists inside the tribunal to engineer Saddam's survival or rehabilitation.

Most workplaces had televisions broadcasting the (edited) trial sessions, and each day's proceedings were covered on the nightly television news. Feelings ran high and were inflamed by escalating daily violence as well as Hussein's regular panegyrics. Public interest was concentrated on two issues: whether

Hussein would be executed, and when. Demonstrations urging the death penalty were held immediately before the trial's opening, particularly in Shi'ite areas near Dujail and in southern Iraq; counterdemonstrations also were held. Demonstrations were later repeated to protest the length of proceedings and in December 2005 to urge the resignation of Judge Rizgar Amin.

As might be expected, Hussein came off well in most televised courtroom interactions; he was a more capable orator and far more used to calculating media impact than any of the judges or other tribunal staff. Judges Amin and Abd al-Rahman pursued a policy of letting Hussein have his say, perhaps feeling that the short-term problem of nationalist rhetoric was less important than the long-term importance of allowing Hussein freedom to speak.

For many Iraqis, the trial was not so much about the remote crimes of Dujail but the unambiguous extinction of dictatorial dignity. The nationalist rhetoric, the controversy of the invasion, the role of the Americans, the selection of the Dujail crimes as the only case in which Saddam would be tried, and the weak understanding of the trial's legal aspects all contributed to the sense that Saddam, ultimately, was being prosecuted for his loss of power. After all, if his crimes had been important, why focus on the killings of a relatively small number of Shi'ite villagers twenty-five years ago?

In the short term, many Iraqis reacted to Hussein's execution with jubilation. Women painted their hands with henna; men danced in the streets. The major state television station al-Iraqiyya broadcast hours of footage of the execution juxtaposed with crowds celebrating in the streets of Najaf, accompanied by a celebratory children's song.[132] Many shared this simple and immediate joy, however, many were also disturbed by the revanchist overtones of the execution, and in particular the seeming illegality of executing Hussein on an important religious holiday. Many Kurdish Iraqis celebrated Hussein's death but lamented that it had come too soon, depriving them of the opportunity to see him brought to justice for the crimes of the Anfal campaign – for which he was already halfway through trial. It was no surprise that the quick execution of Saddam Hussein left many Iraqis feeling like their chance to be heard had been lost.[133]

It is likely that other groups shared similar mixed feelings, in particular those affected by the 1991 southern uprising. The irony was underscored by the first Anfal trial session to be held after Hussein's execution, in which electrifying audio recordings were played that eloquently spoke to Hussein's leadership role. Playing in front of an empty chair, the voice of the former Iraqi president described to his subordinates how chemical weapons are "very effective if people don't wear masks," assured his vice president that "they will kill thousands," and added that "in areas where you have concentrated populations," dropping containers holding fifty napalm bombs each "would be useful."[134] After that session, however, the accusations against Saddam Hussein were dropped, and the evidence against him was removed from the case. Media interest immediately dropped dramatically, and few, if any, observers sought entrance to the courtroom.

In the months to follow, initial jubilation was tempered by strong regional and international backlash. Strong public criticism from Arab rulers drove an even deeper wedge in relations between Iraqis and the wider Arab world. Even the Iranians indicated their disapproval of the execution.[135] Iraqi politicians were discomfited by the animus against them whenever they traveled abroad, and the Maliki government admitted privately that the manner and timing of Hussein's execution had involved a number of "mistakes." Tribunal judges, too, distanced themselves from both the Dujail trial and the subsequent executions, describing Dujail as an "experiment."[136] In the months to follow, the sentence of Taha Yasin Ramadan was increased to the death penalty, and the remaining executions were carried out. It became clear even to the most optimistic onlookers that the essential meaning of the Dujail trial and the tribunal experiment was not individual accountability, but death to the ancien regime.

CONCLUSIONS

Before and during its proceedings, the Dujail trial was referred to by some commentators as the "trial of the century," depicted as a second Nuremberg that would usher in a new, democratic Iraq that respected the rule of law. These hopes were disappointed. The ultimate legacy of the Dujail trial will be determined in decades to come. Whether it is seen as a landmark step forward or a cynical exercise in political manipulation is an open question. If all trials are exercises in political pedagogy, then what were the lessons to be learned?

To be sure, the narrative was not one of easy victory or of the triumph of international judicial norms over a bankrupt and cruel dictatorship. That was the story the United States and its allies drafted but could not produce. The manifest weakness of the tribunal and the trial's many problems were too serious to credit it as a success.

Yet the Dujail story cannot be reduced to an ill-intentioned exercise in legal rhetoric designed to dignify judicial murder. The high hopes and intentions of many judges, and the efforts with which they struggled to establish a new standard of justice, were genuine and should not be discounted.

Instead, Dujail is a tragedy of missed opportunity. It is rare that a court has funding, jurisdiction, custody of alleged perpetrators, and a dependable source of foreign support. It is a great pity that, despite these advantages, the political sensitivities of the invasion weakened the tribunal both before and after its establishment. Cut off from external expertise, tribunal staff members were forced to rely on U.S. support that compromised them politically and, although vital for their operations, did not have sufficient experience in international criminal prosecutions or regional judicial systems to help them avoid many predictable pitfalls. By 2003, the challenges of prosecuting international crimes were well known and well documented, but political and logistical problems prevented the Iraq Tribunal from benefiting from this knowledge. Furthermore, the tribunal was also undermined deeply by local Iraqi political figures, many of whom neither knew nor cared for an independent judiciary nor for what the tribunal was trying to achieve. The court was right to fear its enemies; perhaps things would have been better had it feared its friends.

NOTES

1. The International Center for Transitional Justice (ICTJ) and the Human Rights Center, University of California, Berkeley: *Iraqi Voices: Attitudes Towards Transitional Justice and Social Reconstruction*, Occasional Paper Series, May 2004, 48–50.
2. See Energy Information Administration, *Iraq: Economic Overview*, August 2007. http://www.eia.doe.gov/cabs/Iraq/Profile.html.
3. Baghdad was the center of the Abbasid caliphate from 750 C.E. until it fell to the Mongols in 1258. It was ruled by successive Mongol and Turkic dynasties and briefly fell under Persian control. It became part of the Ottoman (Turkish) Empire in 1555; the Ottoman provinces of Mosul, Baghdad, and Basra correspond closely to the territory of contemporary Iraq. The British invaded and occupied the provinces during World War I, ending Turkish rule. They then ruled Iraq under a League of Nations mandate from 1920 to 1932, although Britain influenced (and intervened in) Iraqi politics until 1958. See Charles Tripp, *A History of Iraq*, Cambridge: Cambridge University Press, 2002.
4. Ibid., 192.
5. The role played by the party's ideology was of minimal importance once Hussein rose to power. Distinguished historian Hanna Batatu describes Aflaq's ideas as "a mixture of essentially humanitarian nationalism and aspects of the individualism of the Enlightenment, the democratism of the Jacobins, the youth idealization of Mazzini, the class standpoint of Marx, the elitism of Lenin, and over and above that, a strong dose of Christian spirituality and a nationalistically interpreted Islam. The mixture is often mechanical. In other words, 'Aflaq makes no serious attempt to synthesize the ideas that he imbibed.'" See Hanna Batatu, *The Old Social Classes and the Revolutionary Movements of Iraq, a Study of Iraq's Old Landed and Commercial Classes and of Its Communists, Ba'athists and Free Officers*, Princeton: Princeton University Press, 1978.
6. The actual year is disputed but is thought to be either 1937 or 1939.
7. Iraq was then ruled by a monarchy installed by the British in August 1921. The monarchy had entered into crisis in 1939 after the suspicious death of King Ghazi

in a car crash. Ghazi's pro-British and unpopular cousin Abd Allah became regent for Ghazi's infant son. The rebellion was launched by a group of army officers in 1941. The four leaders ("the Golden Square") adopted a pro-Nazi stance and supported a government led by Rashid Ali al-Keilani. The regent fled, and the British initiated a military campaign against the new government on May 19; they regained control of Iraq within eleven days. The coup leaders were executed, Rashid Ali and the Mufti of Jerusalem fled to Germany, and the regent returned. More than three hundred Iraqi army officers were cashiered, including Tulfah. Batatu, *The Old Social Classes and Revolutionary Movements*, 30; see also Said K. Aburish, *Saddam Hussein: The Politics of Revenge*, London: Blumsbury, 2000, 32.

8. Shiva Balaghi, *Saddam Hussein: A Biography*, Westport, CT: Greenwood Press, 2006, 5.

9. Military service has been an important means of social advancement in most countries of the Middle East. According to Aburish, the disproportionate presence of Tikritis in the Iraqi army was partly the result of the patronage of Mawlud Mukhlis, a townsman prominent in Iraqi politics in the 1920s and 1930s. Aburish, *Politics of Revenge*, 23.

10. Al-Bakr was prime minister after the Ba'athist coup of 1963, and president after the coup of 1968.

11. Few facts are clear. Tulfah and Hussein were reportedly arrested for the murder of "Hajji Sa'adun," a Tikriti and political opponent of Tulfah's. Some accounts make this out to be a political killing, others personal. The general conclusion appears that Hussein's arrest was interpreted as a sign of his political commitment and significantly enhanced his reputation.

12. Aburish, *Politics of Revenge*, 46–49. Saddam Hussein commissioned a fictional account of his participation in the assassination attempt, called *The Long Days*.

13. Aburish, *Politics of Revenge*, 35.

14. Tripp, *A History of Iraq*, 170–171.

15. Courtney Hunt, *The History of Iraq*, Westport: Greenwood Press, 2005, 83; see also Aburish, *Politics of Revenge*, 66–77.

16. Aburish, *Politics of Revenge*, 80, 96–129, and 160–174; see also Anne Applebaum, "Hussein in His Place; The Dictator's Regime, and the West's Misreading of It, Followed a Familiar Pattern," *Washington Post*, January 1, 2007, p. A13 (comparisons between Saddam Hussein and Stalin).

17. Tripp, *A History of Iraq*, 205.

18. Iraq oil revenues increased dramatically during this period, from $1 billion in 1972 to $8.2 billion in 1975. See Nicolas Sarkis, "The Depletion of Arab Oil Reserves," *MERIP Reports* 89 (1980): 27–28.

19. Ivan Eland, "Middle East: What Should the United States Do about Saddam Hussein?" *Emory Law Journal* 50, (2001): 833, 836.

20. Amatzia Baram, "The Ruling Political Elite in Bathi Iraq: The Changing Features of a Collective Profile," *International Journal of Middle East Studies* 21, no. 4 (1989): 447–493.

21. William E. Smith, "A Quest for Vengeance," *Time*, July 26, 1982. Available at http://www.time.com/time/magazine/article/0,9171,922944-10,00.html.

22. Kanan Makiya, *Cruelty and Silence: War, Tyranny, Uprising and the Arab World*, New York: W. W. Norton, 1993, 219.

23. Balaghi, *Saddam Hussein: A Biography*, 116.

24. Ibid., 117.

25. ICTJ and UC Berkeley: *Iraqi Voices*, viii–x; see also ICTJ: *Creation and First Trials of the Supreme Iraqi Criminal Tribunal*, October 2005, 4.

26. United Nations Commission on Human Rights, *Report on the Situation of Human Rights in Iraq*, 48th session, E/CN.4/1992/31 (February 18, 1992), para. 154.

27. David Korn, Middle East Watch, *Human Rights in Iraq*, London: Yale University Press, 1990; Human Rights Watch, *Justice for Iraq: A Human Rights Watch Policy Paper*, December 2002.

28. Human Rights Watch, *Claims in Conflict: Reversing Ethnic Cleansing in Northern Iraq*, August 2004.

29. Middle East Watch, *Genocide in Iraq: The Anfal Campaign against the Kurds*, July 1993; and also Joost Hiltermann, *A Poisonous Affair: America, Iraq, and the Gassing of Halabja*, Cambridge: Cambridge University Press, 2007. The estimate of 50,000 is the lowest number cited by Middle East Watch. In proceedings during the 2006–2007 Anfal trial before the Iraqi High Tribunal, the prosecution put the figure of dead at 180,000, although the methodology used to reach this figure is unclear.

30. The war lasted from 1980 to 1988.

31. Middle East Watch, *Endless Torment: The 1991 Uprising in Iraq and Its Aftermath*, June 1992.

32. See Emma Nicholson and Peter Clark, eds., *The Iraqi Marshlands: A Human and Environmental Study*, London: Politico's Publishing, 2002; see also Human Rights Watch, *The Iraqi Government Assault on the Marsh Arabs*, January 2003.

33. See, for example, UN Commission on Human Rights, "Situation of Human Rights in Kuwait under Iraqi Occupation," E/CN.4/RES/1991/67, March 6, 1991; see also Human Rights Watch, *World Report: Iraq and Occupied Kuwait*, 1990.

34. Sanctions were originally introduced by UN Security Council Resolution 661 of August 6, 1990, and were directed at restoring the "sovereignty, independence, and territorial integrity of Kuwait," S.C. Res. 660, August 6, 1990, UN Doc. S/Res/660. The territorial integrity of Kuwait was quickly restored at the conclusion of the Gulf War, but an unintended consequence of the sanctions on Iraq was the humanitarian crisis that ensued. For example, in a 1999 press release, UNICEF credits the sanctions of the 1990s for the reversal of positive trends in infant mortality rates witnessed during the 1980s: "If the substantial reduction in child mortality throughout Iraq during the 1980s had continued through the 1990s, there would have been half-a-million fewer deaths of children under five in the country as a whole during the eight-year period 1991 to 1998." Office of the Press Secretary press release, *President Delivers State of the Union Address*, January 29, 2002.

35. See, for example, reporting on the draining of the Arab marshes and the introduction of cruel and unusual punishments in UN GAOR, 49th Sess., UN Doc. A/49/651 (1994), paras. 43, 51, 63.

36. See, for example, "Iran and Kuwait Should Play Role in Saddam Trial," *Iran Daily*, June 19, 2004; see also "Kuwait Wants to Submit Evidence at Saddam's Trial," *KUNA News Agency*, December 13, 2003.

37. See Human Rights Watch, *Genocide in Iraq*, 1993.

38. See, for example, "Prepared Statement of Kenneth Roth, Executive Director of Human Rights Watch, Before the Senate Foreign Relations Subcommittee on the Near East and South Asia," *Federal News Service*, August 13, 1995.

39. U.S. Department of State, *Iraq Report on Human Rights Practices for 1996 Department of State Human Rights Country Reports*, January 1997.

40. "Press Conference with David Scheffer, Ambassador-at-Large for War Crimes Issues, U.S. Department of State," *Federal News Service*, October 27, 1999.

41. Indict was also associated with Chelabi's Iraqi National Congress. It benefited heavily from U.S. funding under the Iraq Liberation Act of 1998, Pub. L. No. 105-338, 112 Stat. 3178 (1998). This affirmed President Clinton's May 1998 allocation of $5 million to facilitate the indictment of Iraqi war criminals.

42. In November 2002, charges were brought in Denmark against former general Nizar al-Khazraji for alleged violations against Kurdish Iraqi civilians in the context of the Iran-Iraq War. See Diane F. Orentlicher, "Whose Justice: Reconciling Universal Jurisdiction with Democratic Principles," *Georgetown Law Journal* 92, no. 1 (2004): 1057. In 2004, after the U.S.-led invasion, Dutch businessman Frans van Anraat was arrested in the Netherlands and put on trial. He was found guilty of complicity in genocide and war crimes and sentenced to fifteen years' imprisonment on December 23, 2005. See, for example, Anne Penketh, "Dutch Court Says Gassing of Iraqi Kurds Was 'Genocide'," *The Independent*, December 25, 2005, p. 20. In its judgment, the court stated:

> "The accused [van Anraat] consciously and solely acting in pursuit of gain, has made an essential contribution to the chemical warfare program of Iraq during the nineteen eighties. His contribution has enabled, or at least facilitated, a great number of attacks with mustard gas on defenseless civilians. These attacks represent very serious war crimes.... It is the opinion of the court that the proven facts and the consequences thereof are serious to the extent that even imposing the maximum penalty will not do sufficient justice to the victims." District Court of the Hague, Public Prosecutor's Office number 09/751003-04, the Hague, December 23, 2005 at §17. Available at www.rechtspraak.nl/ljn.asp?ljn=AX6406.

43. "The United States has long maintained the option of preemptive actions to counter a sufficient threat to our national security. The greater the threat, the greater is the risk of inaction – and the more compelling the case for taking anticipatory action to defend ourselves, even if uncertainty remains as to the time and place of the enemy's attack. To forestall or prevent such hostile acts by our adversaries, the United States will, if necessary, act preemptively." Chapter V, The National Security Strategy of the United States of America, September 2002. Available at http://www.whitehouse.gov/nsc/nss/2002/index.html.

44. The speech continues: "We will work closely with our coalition to deny terrorists and their state sponsors the materials, technology, and expertise to make and deliver weapons of mass destruction. We will develop and deploy effective missile defenses to protect America and our allies from sudden attack. [Applause.] And all nations should know: America will do what is necessary to ensure our nation's security." Press Secretary, *State of the Union Address*, 2002.

45. See, for example, the full text of Colin Powell's presentation to the United Nations Security Council, *U.S. Secretary of State Addresses the U.N. Security Council*, February 5, 2003.

46. For a sample of U.S. criticisms of Iraq, see Press Secretary Press Release, *Iraq: A Decade of Deception and Defiance. Saddam Hussein's Defiance of the United Nations*, September 12, 2002. Available at http://www.whitehouse.gov/ news/releases/2002/09/iraqdecade.pdf.

47. UN SCR, 4644th Sess., UN Doc S/RES/1441 (2002). The U.S. position was that military action taken under 1441 was in fact authorized by UN S.C. Resolution 678 of 1990. The latter authorized "all necessary means to uphold and implement" resolution 678 and "all subsequent relevant resolutions." See Press Secretary press release, *Press Briefing by Ari Fleischer*, March 7, 2003. Available at http://www.whitehouse.gov/news/releases/2003/03/20030307-6.html#13.

48. Jon Henley, Gary Younge, and Nick Paton Walsh, "France, Russia, and Germany Harden Stance," *The Guardian*, March 6, 2003. Available at http://www. guardian.co.uk/world/2003/mar/06/russia.iraq.

49. The report was shelved almost immediately because of Washington-based bureaucratic struggles. See Report of the Working Group on Transitional Justice in Iraq and the Iraqi Jurists' Association, *Transitional Justice in Post-Saddam Iraq: The Road to Re-Establishing Rule of Law and Restoring Civil Society, A Blueprint*, March 2003. Copy on file at the ICTJ. The working group reportedly first met in mid-2002 and released its plan at the U.S. Institute of Peace on May 21, 2003.

50. Office of International Information Programs, U.S. Department of State, *Working Group on "Transitional Justice in Iraq" Meets in Washington*, July 12, 2002. Available at http://usinfo.state.gov/xarchives/display.html?p=washfile-english& y=2002&m=July&=20020712172351sdomowit@pd.state.gov6.261843E-02.

51. Prosper repeated the concept of the process being "Iraq-led" several times in follow-up questioning. See U.S. Department of Defense Briefing, "Geneva Convention, EPW's and War Crimes," April 7, 2003. Available at http://www. defenselink.mil/transcripts/transcript.aspx?transcriptid=2281.

52. See Michael P. Scharf, "From the Exile Files: An Essay on Trading Justice for Peace," *Washington & Lee Law Review* 63 (2006): 339.

53. Julian Borger, "Bush Gives Saddam and His Sons 48 Hours to Leave Iraq," *The Guardian*, March 18, 2003, Available at http://www.guardian.co.uk/world/ 2003/mar/18/iraq.usa1.

54. Bahrain reportedly made an offer to host the Iraq president, whereas Saudi Arabia had said publicly that it would not host Saddam and his family in exile. Emily Wax, "Arab Leaders Fail in Last Minute Efforts: Mubarak Blames Iraq, Cautions Coalition: Bahrain Signals that It Would Give Hussein Sanctuary," *Washington Post*, March 20, 2003, p. A21.

55. See, for example, the statement by Irene Khan, secretary-general, Amnesty International, *Human Rights in the Balance*, MDE 14/011/2002, September 25, 2002: "This selective attention to human rights is nothing but a cold and calculated manipulation of the work of human rights activists."

56. For a discussion of such complicity, see Barry M. Lando, *Web of Deceit: The History of Western Complicity in Iraq, from Churchill to Kennedy to George W. Bush*, Scarborough, Canada: Doubleday, 2007.

57. See Human Rights Watch: *Justice for Iraq*, December 2002. See also Amnesty International, *Iraqi Special Tribunal – Fair Trials Not Guaranteed*, May 2005. See also Cherif M. Bassiouni, "Post-Conflict Justice in Iraq: An Appraisal of the Iraq Special Tribunal," *Cornell International Law Journal* 38 (2005): 327.
58. ICTJ and Human Rights Center, Berkeley, *Iraqi Voices*, May 2004.
59. See "Play Role in Saddam Trial," *Iran Daily*, June 19, 2004. See also "Submit Evidence at Saddam's Trial," *KUNA News Agency*, December 13, 2003.
60. See Press Secretary Press Release, *President Bush: Monday "Moment of Truth" for World on Iraq*, March 16, 2003, available at, http://www.whitehouse. gov/news/releases/2003/03/20030316-3.html. See also Press Secretary Press Release, *President Says Saddam Hussein Must Leave Iraq Within 48 Hours*, March 17, 2003, available at, http://www.whitehouse.gov/news/releases/2003/03/20030317-7.html; Michael Ignatieff, "The American Empire: The Burden," *New York Times*, January 5, 2003, p. 22; Dana Milbank, "For Bush, A Sense of History – And Fate: Response to Iraq Reflects Self-Beliefs," *Washington Post*, March 9, 2003, p. A1.
61. Hussein was the ace of spades. See Linda Kozaryn, "Deck of Cards Helps Troops Identify Regime's Most Wanted," *American Forces Press Service*, April 12, 2003. Available at http://www.defenselink.mil/news/newsarticle.aspx?id=29113.
62. The planning was first undertaken by officials at the Pentagon's Office of Reconstruction and Humanitarian Assistance (ORHA). After ORHA's dissolution, the responsible officials worked from the Crimes Against Humanity Investigations Unit (CAHIU) of the Office of Human Rights and Transitional Justice of the Coalition Provisional Authority The CAHIU was charged with supporting the tribunal's investigation and operational endeavors while local capacity to undertake the work could be developed. See Tom Parker, "Prosecuting Saddam: The Coalition Provisional Authority and the Evolution of the Iraq Special Tribunal," *Cornell International Law Journal* 38, no. 3 (2005): 899–909.
63. The CPA was the administrative and executive entity established by the occupying powers in Iraq following the fall of the Ba'ath regime. It functioned from May 2003 to June 28, 2004.
64. Members were Judge Wa'el Abd al-Latif, Judge Dara Nur al-Din, Ahmad Shya'a al-Barak, and Naseir al-Chadirchi. The senior commission staff member was Salem Chalabi, a U.S.-trained lawyer who formerly worked at an international commercial law firm. See U.S. Department of State, *Interim Report on Plans for the Prosecution of Saddam Hussein and His Top Associates for Genocide, Crimes against Humanity and War Crimes*, August 14, 2003, copy on file at the ICTJ. The IGC was created by Coalition Provisional Authority Regulation Number Six of July 13, 2003. Available at www.iraqcoalition.org/regulations/20030713_CPAREG_6_Governing_Council_of_Iraq_.pdf.
65. The United States failed to secure a second UN Security Council resolution to authorize military action, even though it sought to do so. In sharp contrast to the support the United States gained for the Gulf War of 1990–1991, few nations other than the United Kingdom and Australia were prepared to directly participate in the "Coalition of the Willing." Although some forty-nine countries were technically coalition members, only five contributed troops to the invasion force: the United States, the United Kingdom, Australia, Poland, and Denmark. On concerns related

to domestic prosecutions mechanisms, see, for example, Human Rights Watch Press Release, "U.S. Plans for Iraq Tribunals 'A Mistake'," April 7, 2003.

66. The CPA and IGC failed to respond to several requests from international human rights groups, including the ICTJ, to see and comment on the draft statute. Once established, the tribunal did share early drafts of its Rules of Evidence and Procedures with the ICTJ and other nongovernmental organizations. The ICTJ understands from tribunal staff that comments from human rights organizations were reviewed and some points incorporated.

67. *Coalition Provisional Authority Order Number 48: Delegation of Authority Regarding an Iraqi Tribunal*, CPA/ORD/9 Dec 2003/48 (2003) ("IST Statute").

68. Iraqi criminal law did not include the offenses of genocide, war crimes, and crimes against humanity: by including them, the Tribunal Statute effectively amended existing Iraqi criminal law. According to international humanitarian law (IHL), an occupying power is limited in the changes it can make to the penal laws of the country it occupies. Convention (IV) respecting the Laws and Customs of War on Land and Its Annex: Regulations concerning the Laws and Customs of War on Land (the Hague, October 18, 1907), Article 43; Convention (IV) relative to the Protection of Civilian Persons in Time of War (Geneva, August 12, 1949), Article 64. The occupying power's competence to introduce new penal provisions is limited to circumstances in which it is necessary for their own security and in the interests of the population. The ability of occupying powers to prosecute protected persons for acts committed before the occupation is also highly limited, although they may prosecute conduct prior to the occupation if it entails a breach of the laws and customs of war (Geneva IV), Article 70. These legal doubts as to the tribunal's validity were somewhat ameliorated in October 2005, when the (revised) statute of the Supreme Iraqi Criminal Tribunal was promulgated by the Iraqi Transitional Government.

69. Supreme Iraqi Criminal Tribunal Law, No. 10 of 2005, *al-Waqa'ia al-Iraqiyya* (the official gazette of the Republic of Iraq), No. 4006, October 18, 2005. Effective on publication ("IHT Statute") at Article 1(2). English text available at http://www.ictj.org/static/MENA/Iraq/iraq.statute.engtrans.pdf; Arabic text available at http://www.ictj.org/static/MENA/Iraq/IraqStatute.ara.pdf.

70. Ibid., Article 14(2–4). The lesser crimes were drawn from Law Number 7 of 1958, the Punishment of Conspirators Against Public Safety and Corrupters of the System of Governance Law.

71. The Special Supreme Military Court was created immediately after the Iraqi revolution of 1958 to try officials of the former regime. It was chaired by Colonel Fadil al-Mahdawi, a relative of the president. The commander-in-chief of the armed forces referred cases for investigation and trial. The court legitimated and was the mouthpiece for the new regime. See Benjamin Shawdran, *The Power Struggle in Iraq*, New York: Council for Middle Eastern Affairs Press, 1960, 60–74.

72. Supreme Iraqi Criminal Tribunal Law, No. 10 Article 1, *al-Waqa'ia al-Iraqiyya*, no. 4006, October 2005.

73. Supreme Iraqi Criminal Tribunal Law, No. 10, Article 24, *al-Waqa'ia al-Iraqiyya*, no. 4006, October 2005. Article 24 states, "The penalties imposed by the Tribunal shall be those prescribed by the Penal Code no. 111 of 1969." Paragraph 25, section 2 of the Iraqi Penal Code allows for felonies to be punishable by death.

Penal Code no. 111 of 1969, available at, http://www.ictj.org/static/MENA/Iraq/iraq.penalcode.1969.eng.pdf.

74. "Bush Calls for Saddam Execution," *BBC News*, December 17, 2003.

75. "Coalition Provisional Authority Order Number 31: Modifications of Penal Code and Criminal Proceedings Law," CPA/ORD/10 Sep 2003 (2003) at sec. 6 ("Modifications to Bail Arrangements").

76. This was intended to preempt later arguments that Hussein and others were entitled to prisoner of war status and so could not be tried. An uneasy gap between this fiction and reality persisted up to the moment of Hussein's execution, in which many in Washington, D.C., and elsewhere questioned the legality of Hussein's transfer for execution. Miranda Sissons and Marieke Wierda, personal communication with an Regime Crimes Liaison Office official, December 27, 2006.

77. See Iraqi Code of Criminal Procedure No. 23 of 1971, Article 123. Technically, proceedings on July 1 were three days after "arrest," because the dissolution of the CPA had taken place on June 28. The handover ceremony had been brought forward two days ahead of schedule to minimize security concerns.

78. Personal communication from John F. Burns, February 2006. Hussein reportedly relaxed visibly as soon as he caught sight of foreign journalists, perhaps believing that their presence meant he was unlikely to be immediately executed.

79. See John F. Burns, "Defiant Hussein Rebukes Iraqi Court for Trying Him," *New York Times*, July 2, 2004, sec. A. See also "Transcript of First Half of Saddam Hussein's Appearance before Tribunal," *Agence France Presse*, July 2, 2004. For a list of incidents related to the charges against the accused, see "Preliminary Charges against 11 of Saddam's Lieutenants and Aides," *Agence France Presse*, July 1, 2004.

80. U.S. Department of State, *Quarterly Update to Congress: Section 2207 Report on Iraq Relief and Reconstruction*, April 2005.

81. John B. Bellinger III, legal advisor, Office of the Legal Advisor, U.S. Department of State, *Supporting Justice and Accountability in Iraq*, presentation at Chatham House, London, February 9, 2006. Available at http://www.state.gov/s/l/rls/61110.htm.

82. Miranda Sissons, personal observation and communications in Baghdad, 2005–2007.

83. This was reinforced by a later decision that prevented direct UN monitoring of tribunal proceedings.

84. Human Rights Watch, *Letter to US Regarding the Creation of a Criminal Tribunal for Iraq*, April 15, 2003.

85. Miranda Sissons, personal communications and trial observation, 2005–2008.

86. The tribunal's name in Arabic is *al-mahkama a-jana'iyya al-'iraqiyya al-'uliyya*. This can be translated as the Higher Iraqi Criminal Tribunal or Supreme Iraqi Criminal Tribunal. The tribunal decided its English title was the Iraqi High Tribunal.

87. Rule 45 of the Supreme Iraqi Criminal Tribunal Rules of Procedure and Evidence (October 2005) states: "The trial proceedings shall be in accordance with the Code of Criminal Procedure No. 23 of 1971, and with the present rules."

88. Coalition Provisional Authority Memorandum Number 3 (Revised): Criminal Procedures, CPA/MEM/27 June 2004, sec. 3(d)(7). Available at http://www.ictj. org/static/MENA/Iraq/iraq.cpamem03.062704.eng.pdf.

89. Tribunal procedure envisioned each defendant facing not only multiple charges, but entirely separate trials for different moments in which they are alleged to have committed grave violations of human rights. This requires multiple investigative judges to separately research and refer for trial crimes that are, in reality, not discrete and easily-separable, but in fact depend upon evidence of systematic high-level rights abuses over time. The result is that Tribunal procedure is at odds with the necessity of evaluating grave violations of human rights in terms of patterns of abuse that go beyond individual instances or events. See ICTJ, *Creation and First Trials*, October 2005, 18.

90. Miranda Sissons, personal communications, IHT officials and Higher National De-Ba'athification Commission officials, 2005.

91. Other cases investigated include the persecution of religious political parties, the persecution of secular political parties, the invasion and occupation of Kuwait, the execution of merchants in 1992, and others.

92. Information in this and the following section is primarily drawn from direct and extensive personal observation of the Dujail trial over five ICTJ monitoring missions, 2005–2008. The authors are also indebted to the ICTJ's Baghdad-based trial monitor, who attended more than 70 percent of the Dujail proceedings.

93. The Prime Ministership was held by Dawa Party members throughout the Dujail trial. Prime Minister Ibrahim al-Ja'afari held office at the trial's opening in October 2005, and Prime Minister Nuri Jawad al-Maliki held office for the rest of proceedings.

94. See, for example, Iraqi Special Tribunal Press Release, *Investigation of al-Dujail Crimes Concludes*, February 26, 2005. Available at http://www.iraq-iht.org/EN/0014a.html. The press release named five accused: the names of Saddam Hussein and Ali Dayeh Ali, a local Dujaili Ba'ath party official, were absent. The release explicitly states "in the future, other detainees, including senior officials of the ex-regime, especially Saddam Hussein, accused of other crimes still being investigated will be referred to the trial chamber."

95. Under Iraqi criminal law, the tribunal used a two-step charging process, meaning the accused were notified of the accusations against them at the beginning of the trial, and a charging instrument issued by the Trial Chamber judges much later in proceedings, after both witness and documentary evidence had been heard.

96. *BBC Monitoring Middle East*, "Iraqi TV Carries Fourth Session of Saddam Trial," *Al-Sharqiyah*, December 6, 2005. (Witness AA recalling how she was tortured with electricity, beaten with hoses, and prodded to confess.)

97. The witness testified that she was detained, tortured, and subjected to mock hanging and the mock execution of her parents. ICTJ Observer notes IHT session nine, February 1, 2006 (unpublished document on file with authors).

98. There was significant international pressure to provide adequate protection for witnesses as well as defense lawyers. See, for example, Human Rights Watch, *Iraq: Saddam Trial Faces Big Challenges – Protection for Witnesses, Defense Lawyers Must Be Ensured*, November 24, 2005.

99. Iraqi Code of Criminal Procedure, para. 168.
100. "Saddam Hussein is telling you that he is responsible – responsible. So do you think I'm going to deny responsibility or rely on others? Saddam is going to take responsibility. It's a critical time. And Saddam is not going to duck his responsibility." "Saddam Hussein Makes Admission before Trial Adjourns," CNN News, March 1, 2006. Transcript available at http://transcripts.cnn.com/TRANSCRIPTS/0603/01/ywt.01.html.
101. Miranda Sissons, trial observer notes, session December 6, 2005 (unpublished document on file with authors).
102. A favorite being to correct the presiding judge's grammar: both Rizgar Amin and Ra'uf Abd al-Rahman were Kurds, and Hussein was emphasizing the fact that Arabic was not their mother tongue. Both judges appeared to have made the strategic decision to allow Hussein ample latitude to speak. Some observers wondered whether they had confused the right of self-representation with the right to adequate defense. Miranda Sissons, trial observation notes various sessions 2005–2006 (unpublished document on file with authors).
103. Canceling of amplification had two results, however: the defendant's words would not be broadcast, and they would not be transcribed.
104. At one point, Hussein stated that he was so badly beaten with the butt of a rifle that the bones in his feet had become exposed. John F. Burns, "Hussein Accuses U.S. Guards of Torture," *New York Times*, December 22, 2005, p. A1. Saddam is reported to have gone on at least five hunger strikes and in July 2006, having been on strike for two weeks, was hospitalized and given a feeding tube so that he could still stand trial. Damien Cave, "As a Tactic, Starving Is Found Wanting," *New York Times*, July 30, 2006, http://www.nytimes.com/2006/07/30/weekinreview/30cave.html?partner=rssnyt&emc=rss]. According to off-record personal communications, Hussein ended his strike immediately after the session in which verdicts were handed down.
105. The chairman of the Higher National De-Ba'athification Commission, Dr. Ahmed Chelabi, wielded considerable political influence and was at that stage aligned with the hard-line Shi'ite Sadrist parliamentary bloc.
106. The witnesses were later relocated outside Iraq by tribunal or RCLO officials.
107. We have heard many recriminations on this issue. The Ministry of Interior at this stage was led by Bayan Jabr from April 2005 to May 2006 and was notorious as a base for Shi'ite militia activity. See, for example, John F. Burns, "Torture Alleged at Ministry Site Outside Baghdad," *New York Times*, November 16, 2005. Defense counsel told the authors that a preliminary deal involving relocation of lawyers and families had been agreed but that the government of Iraq failed to give final agreement. The RCLO told the authors that defense counsel had at times refused to take advantage of protections that were provided.
108. Al-Ubaidi was abducted and killed on June 21, 2006, during the trial's final stages. Al-Ubaidi also represented Barzan Ibrahim al-Hassan.
109. Personal communication, Iraqi official, February 2006. Witness protection arrangements, although initially planned for, were in reality ad hoc. Several witnesses who gained long-term protection did so via personal connections in the prime minister's office.

110. Much of the discussion in this section draws from Miranda Sissons and Ari S. Bassin, "Was the Dujail Trial Fair?" *Journal of International Criminal Justice* 5, no. 2, (2007): 272–286.
111. Evidence of a pattern of unfair trials by the Revolutionary Court, headed by Awad Hamad al-Bandar, would have greatly helped prosecution efforts to prove that the trial and subsequent execution of the Dujail defendants were unfair. Sissons and Bassin, "Was the Dujail Trial Fair?" 272–286.
112. See ICTJ, *Dujail: Trial and Error?* November 2006. See also Human Rights Watch, *Judging Dujail*, November 2006.
113. Miranda Sissons, personal communication, Trial Chamber judge, November 2005.
114. Former Ba'ath party officials Abdallah Ruwaid and Ali Dayih Ali were both found guilty of willful killing as a crime against humanity and sentenced to fifteen years' imprisonment; former senior Ba'ath party leader Mizher Ruwaid was sentenced to fifteen years' imprisonment for willful killing and seven years' imprisonment for torture. Charges against Muhammad Azawi Ali, a former Ba'ath party member from Dujail, were dismissed for lack of evidence. No defendants were found guilty of the crime of enforced disappearances.
115. Thair Shaikh, "Saddam Tells All Iraqis to Settle Their Differences," *The Independent*, November 8, 2006, sec. World.
116. Access to the courtroom required detailed security vetting procedures – not to mention a link to the prime ministerial adviser that controlled the twenty-five available seats. Furthermore, the tribunal had decided that because of security restrictions, the identities of four of five Trial Chamber judges would remain secret: only the presiding judge was included in television broadcasts, along with defendants and the chief prosecutor. Hence, few people realized that there were at least six changes to the five-member panel: only one judge served throughout proceedings.
117. Human Rights Watch, *The Poisoned Chalice: A Human Rights Watch Briefing Paper on the Decision of the Iraqi High Tribunal in the Dujail Case*, June 2007.
118. See, for example, Dujail Trial Judgment, Iraqi High Tribunal, Trial Chamber (Case No. 1/C 1/2005), November 5, 2005, 105, and 111–112.
119. The authors extensively reviewed evidence contained in the Dujail trial dossier as part of their research. Dujail Trial Dossier, unpublished document on file with the authors.
120. Ibid., 248.
121. See Thair Shaikh, "Saddam Tells Iraqis to Settle Differences," *The Independent*, November 8, 2006, p. 24.
122. Iraqi High Tribunal, Cassation Chamber (Case No. 29/c/2006), Dujail Case December 2006.
123. The narrative of events provided here is based on an extensive series of interviews in Baghdad in February–March 2007. See also John F. Burns, "In Days before Hanging, a Push for Revenge and a Push Back from the U.S.," *New York Times*, January 7, 2006. Available at http://www.nytimes.com/2007/01/07/world/middleeast/07ticktock.html?pagewanted=1].
124. Miranda Sissons, personal communication, member of Prime Minister's Office, Baghdad, 2007.

125. In a briefing after Saddam's execution, U.S. military spokesman Major General William B. Caldwell IV described the transfer as taking place at 5:21 A.M., after which point "we had absolutely nothing to do with any of the procedures or any of [the] control mechanisms or anything from that point forward." John F. Burns, "Days before Hanging."

126. John F. Burns, "Days before Hanging."

127. Lauren Frayer, "Sunni Areas Erupt in Rage over Saddam," *Associated Press*, January 2, 2007. Para. 290 of the Iraqi Code of Criminal Procedure of 1971, which provided the procedural rules for the trial (see n. 69 above), reads: "The death penalty cannot be carried out on official holidays and special festivals connected with the religion of the condemned person."

128. See Ghassan Sharbil, "Interview with Judge Ra'uf Abd-al-Rahman Rashid," *Al Hayat*, May 2, 2007.

129. See BBC Monitoring Middle East, "Saddam's Plea of Innocence "out of place" Legal Adviser to Husayn Family," *Al-Arabiya TV*, October 28, 2005. See also BBC Monitoring Middle East, "Al-Jazeera Talk Show Discusses Saddam Husayn's Trial," *Al-Jazeera TV*, June 17, 2005.

130. Marieke Wierda, personal communications from a variety of Afghan and international officials, Kabul, 2007.

131. A constitutional referendum was held October 15, 2005; national parliamentary elections were held December 15, 2005.

132. In translation, the wording is roughly: "We call out to execute him today/That's his punishment, Haddam the tyrant./Al-intifada and what happened in al-Kufa./The dome of Ali was attacked by tanks/All these crimes are obvious/ O blind me, so many people died through oppression./The sects of people call out to you today./To rid us of the tyrant/For the mass graves we shout with you/O judge we hope to accelerate his execution." "Haddam" is a play of words based on Hussein's first name. It means "the demolisher."

133. See, for example, Najmaldin Karim, "Justice, but No Reckoning," *New York Times*, December 30, 2006, sec. A.

134. John F. Burns, "Hussein's Voice Speaks in Court in Praise of Chemical Atrocities," *New York Times*, January 9, 2007, p. A1.

135. BBC Monitoring Middle East, "West Using Saddam's Execution as 'Cover'," *Siyasat-e Ruz*, January 1, 2007.

136. Miranda Sissons, personal communications in confidential interviews with tribunal staff and government figures, Baghdad, March 2007.

12

Conclusion

Ellen L. Lutz and Caitlin Reiger

In December 2006, as the news filtered out about General Augusto Pinochet's death at the age of ninety-one in Chile, both his supporters and detractors took to the streets. Despite granting himself an amnesty when he stepped down from power, Pinochet spent the final years of his life under criminal investigation and indictment for massive human rights violations and corruption. His detractors lamented that he had gone to his grave without standing trial; his supporters cheered, "No le condenaron" – "They never got him."[1]

Pinochet's case, like the others in this book, raises questions about the relationships between justice and power, justice and popular demands for accountability, and justice and societal change. Motivated by changes in international and domestic political willingness for holding former heads of state or government accountable, national judges increasingly have overturned amnesties and other legal impediments to prosecuting leaders for crimes committed on their watch.

The existing transitional justice literature that analyzes trials of those responsible for serious human rights or humanitarian law violations shows that trials have the potential for a strong positive impact on the rule of law in situations when a country is transitioning from an authoritarian regime to a democratic one, or from conflict to peace. For trials to be successful, however, there must be a confluence of circumstances: (1) the new government must be eager to differentiate itself from the conduct of its predecessor; (2) the country, as a whole, must have already embraced democracy and the rule of law as the governance principles to which it should adhere; (3) the new leaders must be relatively untainted by histories of significant involvement in past crimes; (4) civil society, by and large, must support (or at least not passionately oppose) trials; and (5) the judicial system must be reasonably efficient and independent. In some cases, such as Greece, Argentina, and the former East Germany, these conditions were in place almost immediately after the governance transition occurred. In others, such as Chile, the Czech Republic, and Uruguay, years or decades separated the criminal events from the trials of their perpetrators, but when prosecutions did occur, the requisite conditions were in place and the trials further legitimized democratic governance.[2] In many postconflict settings, however, these circumstances are far more difficult to satisfy, particularly when the judicial system (and public trust in it) has been devastated by the conflict or the peace remains fragile. The cases in this book do not alter those findings. Instead they push the inquiry further by also looking at cases that do not fit into the classic transitional pattern.

Even when there has been a complete transition from a rights-violating or corrupt regime to an accountable, democratic government, it is not possible to divorce efforts to prosecute former heads of state from other political considerations. The waxing and waning of political fortunes still dominates the extent to which former leaders are held judicially accountable for their crimes at all. Instead of being neutral adjudications of right and wrong, the courtrooms in which their trials take place become the playing fields for political contest.

For example, in many of the cases in this book, the accused still enjoyed significant popularity and power bases, even after his alleged misdeeds were exposed. In domestic settings such as those in the cases of Augusto Pinochet, Alberto Fujimori, Joseph Estrada, and Saddam Hussein, it may be easy for the former leaders' supporters to claim that justice efforts are politically motivated. This is even more likely when there has been a tradition of courts being used to silence political opponents. In such circumstances, those calling for prosecutions face the added challenge of establishing that their purpose is different from what came before. It takes time for a new government to establish that the country is governed by the rule of law and that the courts are fair, impartial, and independent, all of which is necessary to ensure that prosecutions are in fact, and are seen to be, legitimate. Such trials alone may not build trust in public institutions, but they can be an important component, especially when complemented by other measures such as judicial and police reforms.

The need to demonstrate judicial impartiality and independence was one of the motivating factors in the development of international justice processes, and it continues to be a reference point in the requests of national governments for international assistance.[3] Yet as the cases of Slobodan Milošević and Charles Taylor show, trials before international or hybrid courts are not immune from political manipulation. In a letter read to the court at the opening of his trial before the Special Court for Sierra Leone, Charles Taylor boldly declared that he had chosen not to appear because he did not want to be "a fig leaf of legitimacy for this process."[4] It was a moment reminiscent of the posturing that had characterized the defendants' responses in the Slobodan

Milošević and Saddam Hussein trials, both of whom similarly attempted to impugn the credibility of the entire judicial exercise. Politicization of international trials of ex-leaders is particularly likely where the international community has played an active role in the conflict or transition. In such cases, there are likely to be loud and persistent claims of "victor's justice," or, as was heard with respect to the former Yugoslavia, Rwanda, and Sierra Leone, "victor's hypocrisy" – the notion that the international community was salving its conscience by establishing courts to try former leaders for crimes that it had not stopped in the first place.

Some of the conclusions we present in this chapter are not specific to prosecutions of heads of state or government but are indicative of attitudes toward human rights or corruption trials in general. Others are very much related to the particular significance that attaches to pursuing those at the pinnacle of power. As Martti Koskenniemi and others have pointed out, putting a head of state on trial highlights the inherent tensions between individualizing guilt and reflecting the context of a criminal regime that is manifest when a head of state is put on trial.[5] This book acknowledges that the didactic function of these judicial proceedings invites accusations of being show trials, although they are entirely different processes from power plays dressed up in legal garb. The global trend today seems to be moving toward more genuine trials of former leaders responsible for egregious crimes.

In this chapter, we examine the conclusions that emerged from our data set of sixty-seven indictments of heads of state and government since 1990, the regional surveys of changing attitudes in Europe and Latin America, and our eight case studies. We begin by looking at the role of international engagement – and intervention – in decision making about trials of leaders. From there, we turn to the relationship between states' willingness to try senior officials for human rights crimes and their willingness to try them for corruption. Next we highlight some of the difficulties, as well as some of the benefits, of using ordinary criminal justice processes to deal with the extraordinary challenges of prosecuting a former head of state. Finally, we take up the "peace versus justice" dilemma by considering the timing of ex-leaders' trials.

We conclude this book with reflections on the "justice cascade" concept that Ellen L. Lutz and Kathryn Sikkink wrote about in an article in 2001. They documented a broad norms shift in Latin America between the late 1970s and the mid-1990s that led to increased regional consensus in trying former human rights abusers.[6] The findings from this book suggest that although there are many positive indicators, it is premature to declare that the justice cascade they observed in Latin America is today a consolidated global phenomenon.

Nevertheless, the sheer volume of high level prosecutions in recent years suggests that leaders who want to ensure their own comfortable retirement would be well advised to behave themselves while in power. Even those at the pinnacle of global power have reason to fear the consequences if they do not.

INTERNATIONAL INFLUENCE

On certain occasions, the international community has chosen to take the matter of holding heads of state accountable out of national governmental hands altogether. In the case of Slobodan Milošević, it acted by threatening to take away foreign aid that Serbia desperately needed unless he was sent to the International Criminal Tribunal for the former Yugoslavia (ICTY) in the Hague. In the case of Charles Taylor, it put pressure on Nigeria, a peace-negotiation partner state, to turn him over to the Special Court for Sierra Leone to stand trial, and on Liberia, a posttransition government in desperate need of international assistance. In the cases of all the international tribunals and most hybrid tribunals, the international community has declared not only that a trial must take place but that the trial process will be internationally driven. In Iraq, the United States, exerting its influence over the transitional Iraqi leadership, controlled the decision making that led to the creation of the court that tried Saddam Hussein – although the tribunal then slipped out of U.S. control. In the latest hybrid tribunals for Cambodia and Lebanon, it remains to be seen whether international influence will be enough to ensure that top leaders are held accountable for their crimes.

As international organizations and negotiators become more invested in accountability, they often usurp the role once played by domestic and international human rights advocates. For example, although the role played by human rights advocates may have been significant at certain moments, Liberian and Sierra Leonean voices were not central to the story of Charles Taylor's demise. However, international human rights groups did serve as crucial partners for the Special Court in the campaign to exert pressure on Nigeria. Nor did human rights advocates play much of a role in the decision to set up a court to try Saddam Hussein and his henchmen in Iraq. To the contrary, although international human rights groups had been campaigning for justice for victims of the Ba'athist regime since the Gulf War of 1990–1991, governments around the globe, including the United States, turned a deaf ear to them until the U.S. invasion of Iraq in 2003. Once the process was underway, however, human rights organizations often were the only ones documenting the political interference that ultimately undermined the trial's international legitimacy.

Nonetheless, domestic and international human rights advocates have continued to make significant contributions in less geopolitically charged cases. In the Philippines, the Alien Tort Claims Act litigation in U.S. courts, which was brought by U.S. and Philippine attorneys on behalf of victims of human rights violations and financial crimes by Ferdinand Marcos, set an important external precedent for prosecuting Philippine leaders for crimes they committed while in office. Some even saw the subsequent domestic prosecution of Joseph Estrada as a proxy for the Philippine government's failure to bring Marcos to account, although, as Abby Wood shows in her chapter, the actual relationship was not so much one of proxy as one of progression of the rule of law in the post-Marcos era. The combined efforts of domestic and international human rights advocates led to Augusto Pinochet's arrest in Chile and to the further solidification of justice norms in Latin America, which in turn led to the indictment of previously untouchable heads of state like Uruguay's Juan Bordaberry.

The indefatigable efforts of internal and international activists, boosted by the window of opportunity afforded by Belgium's short-lived universal jurisdiction legislation and a dedicated Belgian judge, have played a major role in Hissène Habré's house arrest and forthcoming trial in Senegal. The role of universal jurisdiction cases, however, should not be overstated. Although external legal remedies remain important options in a diverse global justice toolkit, Gary Bass reminds us that the political will to prosecute is always harder to generate when the victims are not one's fellow citizens.[7]

Any consideration of international influence must address whether the ad hoc international criminal tribunals have helped or hindered domestic progress in seeking justice for those most responsible for human rights atrocities. One of the more classic political trials described in this book, the Kagame regime's pursuit of former Rwandan President Pasteur Bizimungu, took place against the backdrop of the International Criminal Tribunal for Rwanda (ICTR), which the Rwandan government continues to resent as an infringement of its own sovereignty. All of the ICTR prosecutors to date have failed to indict any Rwandan Patriotic Front members for atrocities against Hutus for fear that they will lose the much-needed cooperation of Paul Kagame's government, a circumstance that may in fact have emboldened the Rwandan government to use the judicial process to eliminate political opponents by implicating them in the genocide. Yet at the same time, the continued presence of the ICTR and its threat to transfer some of its cases to third countries has arguably been a significant factor in Rwanda's recent decision to abolish the death penalty in the hope of facilitating transfers of these cases back to its domestic courts.

In the case of the ICTY, the impact of international influence has been similarly mixed. Within Serbia, where there was little progress in domestic war crimes cases for many years after the end of the conflict, the presence of the ICTY was seen by some as a hindrance. It provided nationalist forces with a convenient forum to blame as a tool of Western political interests. At the same time, the remoteness of the proceedings in the Hague meant that many victims also were dissatisfied, leading some to see the ICTY as being more interested in accommodating international diplomats than on establishing justice for the communities in whose name (and on account of whose suffering) the tribunal had been established. Some local human rights advocates have lamented that the ICTY has usurped the political imperative of pursuing accountability, conveniently providing reluctant national political elites with an excuse to do nothing.

In the case of ICTY, it must be recognized that it was created in the midst of a full-blown armed conflict, when national trials were inconceivable. In recent years, there has been a resurgence of domestic war crimes prosecutions, not just in Bosnia-Herzegovina, where the ICTY actively helped establish the War Crimes Chamber of the Court of Bosnia and Herzegovina, but also in Croatia and Serbia, and to some extent in Kosovo. Removing the highest-level and most difficult cases, such as Milošević, from the domestic arena also provided the time and space needed for domestic accountability to emerge at a pace more in tune with the region's ability to face its past.[8]

A somewhat different and perhaps more direct influence on domestic trials has emerged with the advent of the International Criminal Court (ICC), the statute of which requires states parties to ensure that their domestic laws are consistent with the Rome Statute. In many cases, this has led governments to introduce new laws or amend existing legislation to remove legal and procedural barriers to domestic accountability for the most serious international crimes. As of January 2007, 49 of the 104 countries that were then members of the ICC had enacted implementing legislation.[9] Although in many of these instances, this has been limited to the issue of cooperation with the ICC, in others the process has involved substantive changes to their criminal laws, including the definitions of crimes.[10]

HUMAN RIGHTS VS. CORRUPTION TRIALS

One of the issues this book explores is the relationship between states' willingness to prosecute senior officials for human rights crimes and their willingness to prosecute them for corruption. Both categories of offenses pose particular challenges for effective prosecution. They can span wide ranges of crimes, some of which are far more damaging than others. Both can happen either as isolated incidents or as widespread or systematic patterns or practices. Moreover, both involve multiple actors and multiple links in the chain of command. In some legal systems, this gives prosecutors acting within the legitimate scope of their discretion choices about whom to prosecute; in other systems, even when there is little prosecutorial discretion, it may be more a matter of resource allocation and political will. What is fascinating is that popular opinion sometimes finds the dishonesty of a senior governmental official far more disturbing than that official's participation in murder, torture, or even genocide. However, as the Pinochet and Fujimori cases show, once a leader lands in the political doghouse for corruption, any remaining public tolerance for human rights violations is likely to dissipate as well. It seems that once civil society in a country wakes up to the fact that their leader is a common crook, any respect citizens may have had for that leader's decisions in other domains evaporates.

Things can also work the other way around. In places where aggressive prosecutors are investigating human rights or humanitarian law violations, they may stumble onto evidence of ill-gotten wealth that otherwise might never have come to light. Of course, the overlap between the two types of crimes is often necessary: systematic human rights violations, like other governmental activities, cost money. If a government is trying to maintain some pretense of being democratic, as Fujimori tried to do in Peru, it is unlikely to put a line item for death squads in the national budget.

Human rights advocates tend to focus on accountability for the worst bodily integrity violations such as murder and torture rather than other civil and political rights violations, let alone violations of economic and social rights. Although international clamor, particularly by nongovernmental organizations, is stronger for human rights trials than for corruption trials, states often find that it is less costly to try former leaders for financial crimes than for human rights crimes. One reason is that corruption can be committed by an individual (or family) without much outside help, whereas human rights and humanitarian law crimes tend to implicate far larger numbers of people, including politically powerful actors who have a vested interest in blocking human rights prosecutions. In addition, corruption is a crime that affects an entire population more or less equally, whereas human rights crimes tend to target specific subpopulations. Thus, corruption trials are less likely than human rights trials to create or exacerbate social schisms within the society.

The cases in this book show that although human rights crimes are almost always accompanied by corruption or other financial crimes, the reverse is not always true. Grand corruption (the type involving senior government officials) takes place even in countries with outstanding human rights records.

Moreover, as Italy's prosecutions of Silvio Berlusconi and France's trials of Jacques Chirac's inner circle show, political popularity can trump even the most fervent efforts to prosecute. Most countries seem to have some tolerance for corruption as long as it remains modest and discreet. However, once a leader's corruption brings embarrassment to a country, prosecution becomes far more probable. As they say in Peru, "God forgives sin, but not scandal."

Yet even where corruption is exposed, prosecution might not be a government's preferred policy choice. Public figures may be concerned that if they set a precedent for prosecuting corrupt officials, their own peccadilloes will land them in the dock at some future time (a fear that underlies U.S. government resistance to the ICC and to ratifying international human rights treaties or making those it does ratify self-executing). There also are legitimate reasons why states may prefer not to prosecute senior political figures. For one, the state's ability to recover illicitly acquired wealth may depend on the cooperation of the corrupt public official. Under such circumstances, the state is likely to engage in an economic calculus to decide whether to prosecute or indemnify the public official in exchange for his or her cooperation. Another problem involves the difficulties of obtaining sufficient evidence to win a conviction in court. Without it, states risk putting a corrupt politician on trial only to see that person exonerated, thereby demonstrating to others that crime can pay. Moreover, all trials are expensive, and highly charged political trials can cost a fortune that a government may prefer to spend in other ways. Finally, there are alternative sanctions, including loss of power, prestige, and access to illicit (not to mention legitimate) financial gain by being publicly exposed, humiliated, or voted out of office or forced to resign, that may be more devastating to corrupt public officials than being sent to jail. Where corruption crimes did not cause gross human suffering, governments often find it less costly to let publicity and electoral politics deliver the sanctions.

THE PROBLEMS WITH ORDINARY JUDICIAL PROCESSES IN EXTRAORDINARY CASES

Another problem highlighted by the cases in this book is the difficulty of using ordinary criminal justice processes to deal with the extraordinary challenges of prosecuting a former head of state. One of the repeated criticisms of such trials is that their emphasis on procedural fairness makes it easy for politically savvy defendants such as Slobodan Milošević or Saddam Hussein to manipulate them for their own purposes. One of the foundational assumptions underlying all judicial systems is the authority of the court, personified in its judges. Judges are used to exercising their authority over ordinary defendants, but doing so is much more difficult when former presidents or other once-powerful leaders are in the dock. One reason is that such trials tend to be conducted in the glare of the media spotlight. Even if media attention only takes place during key moments, such as the issuing of the indictment, the opening of the trial, and the rendering of the verdict, what it captures is high drama. Whereas most judges are unaccustomed to conducting judicial business in such an environment, the political leaders on trial are in their element in a politicized arena and usually are highly skilled at playing to a public audience. Judges in ordinary courts rarely have training in media relations, whereas political leaders surround themselves with spinmeisters and other media-savvy advisors. As a consequence, political leaders are well positioned to upend the basic balance of power between the assumed authority of the court and an accused standing trial.

Another element of the legal process that is subject to political hijacking by high-profile defendants is the right to self-representation. This tactic has been used by Milošević and other high-profile defendants at the ICTY including most recently by Radovan Karadžić, as well as by Sam Hinga Norman at the Special Court for Sierra Leone. Whereas the right to self-representation is not a standard feature of civil law inquisitorial legal systems, it is a feature of common law adversarial systems whose traditions dominate international tribunals. One of the criticisms of the judges' handling of the Milošević trial was that they bent over backward to ensure that he was accommodated in ways that other defendants or counsel would not have been, including ignoring his deliberate and repeated snubs at the authority of the courtroom by referring to the judges as "Mister" and remaining seated when the judges addressed him.

Once an accused exercises the right to represent himself, he gains the additional right to cross-examine witnesses testifying against him. In cases of high-level commanders, establishing superior criminal responsibility requires proving an unbroken chain of command, and that usually involves the testimony of witnesses from inside the very command structure that the accused once controlled. Former leaders frequently continue to enjoy the support of segments of such national institutions as the armed forces. Hence, cross-examination of a former subordinate by his one-time commander can be not only intimidating but threatening and can lead to silence, perjury, or other ways of undermining evidence that the prosecution needs to prove its case.[11] This is even more problematic in domestic settings, where independence of the judiciary may be fragile or where witness-protection programs are nonexistent.

Although trials of heads of state have moments of high drama, many prosecutions against senior leaders drag on for months and years, as is shown by the Pinochet, Estrada, and Milošević trial processes. Often the reasons are legitimate attempts to ensure that the defendant receives a fair trial or result from delays introduced by the defense as part of a deliberate strategy. The Estrada case, for example, dragged on for six years, in part to reduce the number of issues the defense could raise on appeal. Although a trial that is too brief may be regarded as unfair – or even a show trial – if it is at the expense of the accused's due-process rights to prepare his case or challenge the evidence against him, a trial that drags on also can face legitimate human rights criticism. Judges dealing with these cases therefore have the unenviable task of ensuring that enough care is taken to preserve the perception of fairness to the accused, without allowing this to be manipulated to an extent that it becomes a farce. Delays can be a double-edged sword for the trial's broader legitimacy. The longer they last, the greater the likelihood that the public will lose interest, thereby lessening their potentially restorative value to society.

In the aftermath of Milošević's death, considerable criticism was heaped on the ICTY prosecutor for prosecuting crimes that occurred throughout the decade-long history of the Balkans wars, rather than on a single chapter, such as Kosovo. In contrast, the trial of Saddam Hussein for a single incident in a decades-long campaign against his people has been criticized for not adequately reflecting the magnitude of the suffering he inflicted. Of course, had Milošević not died and Saddam Hussein not been executed immediately after the Dujail case ended, the criticisms might have been different.

Balancing trial manageability with historical completeness and fairness to the accused remains a fundamental challenge in many of these cases, especially given the age of many former heads of state by the time they stand trial. The aging Khmer Rouge leaders currently in the dock before the Extraordinary Chambers in the Courts of Cambodia and their regular need for hospital visits and medical monitoring highlights this dilemma. Too often, by the time senior leaders cede power and political momentum in favor of trials gathers, it is a race against the clock before old men die.

The impetus toward creating an authoritative historical record that encompasses the systematic or large scale nature of the crimes is all the greater when the leaders are the only ones likely to face trial or no alternative forms of official truth-seeking processes are planned. In Chile, Peru, Sierra Leone, and now Liberia, the existence of Truth and Reconciliation Commissions that have documented and exposed the extent of historical crimes and where responsibility lies has taken pressure in this regard off the trials. In contrast, in the former Yugoslavia and Cambodia, the internationally assisted tribunals bear perhaps greater burdens to acknowledge publicly the suffering of victims and the systematic nature of the crimes precisely because they are the primary transitional justice mechanisms in play.

SHATTERED MYTHS

Why is it worth undertaking the challenges of overcoming political intransi-gence, choosing the right moment, and conducting a trial that may continue for months or years? One of the primary benefits is that trials can shatter a prevailing atmosphere of impunity. As Miranda Sissons and Marieke Wierda note in relation to Saddam Hussein, for many ordinary Iraqis, the Dujail trial was about "the unambiguous extinction of dictatorial dignity."[12] In this regard, the line between upholding respect for the rights of the accused and degenerating into a show trial may be a fine one. Yet properly conducted trials demonstrate that no one is above the law, no matter how rich, how powerful, or how seemingly untouchable he is. This was the message conveyed in early April 2006, as images flashed around the Internet of former Liberian president Charles Taylor, handcuffed and surrounded by United Nations peacekeepers, being transferred to the Special Court's custody in Sierra Leone. Moreover, the "big man in a small cell" image seems to be contributing to increasing institutionalization and respect for the rule of law in both countries. It similarly was a powerful moment for international justice in July 2008 when Radovan Karadžić was arrested in downtown Belgrade after a decade on the run from the ICTY.

Trials for mass atrocity also have ritual power. They create a formal moment that separates the present from the past. Through trials, the actors and acts of the past are condemned, creating fresh opportunities for new leaders and new political structures enhanced with built-in safeguards. This, in turn, helps reassure the populace that the past is in the past and that a better future is on the horizon. As Justice Robert Jackson stated at Nuremberg, a trial can demonstrate how the new regime distinguishes itself from the past by offer-ing rights – such as a fair trial – to leaders of the predecessor regime that they denied to their victims. Hannah Arendt observed following Adolph Eich-mann's trial in Jerusalem, that trials of individuals can become stand-ins for trials of the predecessor regime. While this can blur their focus on individual criminal responsibility, the symbolic power of trials to clean the slate thereby creating space on which to design a better political future cannot be over-looked.[13]

Ultimately, the symbolic value of head of state trials depends on the quality of the process and the "demonstration effect" it is seen to have for strengthening the rule of law. If conducted transparently and in a way that inspires the general population's confidence in the process, they can contribute to ending pervasive traditions of impunity, and demonstrate that no one is above the law, no matter how far up the political or military chain of command. The risks of politicization, however, are never far away. The cases in this book show some of the ways these risks – and these potential benefits – are playing out.

THE RIGHT TIME FOR JUSTICE

Accepted wisdom in some circles would have us believe that trials are inherently risky in the aftermath of transitions where peace or democracy is not yet fully consolidated.[14] Yet in the cases discussed in this book, trials of heads of state or government have not contributed to a return to violence or collapse of the transition. Indeed, as the cases of Milošević and Hussein show, prosecutions of heads of state or other senior leaders at the time of or immediately after a transition prevented them from establishing conditions of impunity for themselves. In the case of Charles Taylor, there is evidence to suggest that his indictment by the Special Court eroded his ability to continue as president and made his exile in Nigeria a temporary arrangement rather than a formal amnesty.[15] The only case in which further violence followed a trial was in Iraq. There, however, the particular circumstances of the insurgency and U.S. military occupation relegated Hussein's trial to either a very minor causal factor or an irrelevancy.

It cannot be denied that in cases of ongoing conflict, the parties and peace negotiators are usually reluctant to put justice on the table for fear of prolonging the conflict or hindering dialogue on other elements of a negotiated agreement.[16] It is hard to dispute that leaders of abusive regimes, such as Robert Mugabe in Zimbabwe or Sudan's Omar al-Bashir, or even rebel leaders such as Joseph Kony of the Lord's Resistance Army in northern Uganda, are likely to do everything possible to entrench their positions and hang on to power longer if they fear they will face prosecution. However, these leaders are just as likely to cling to power for other reasons, such as their enjoyment of power and the perks that come with it.

What this suggests is that although it is difficult to make a general rule regarding the right time to prosecute, it is possible to find the right time for justice in any particular circumstance. Sometimes it will take months or even years for the political and popular momentum to gather, for judicial institutions to be sufficiently strong, for the peace to be consolidated, and for the other conditions for a successful trial to be met. In the meantime, a range of interim activities can help ensure that justice can be achieved down the line. These include preserving key documents and other evidence, challenging amnesty laws and other legal hurdles, or advocating for legislative or constitutional reform. Truth commissions or other official inquiries can be undertaken as important first steps, rather than mutually exclusive alternatives, to trials. Vetting initiatives can prevent the recurrence of violations by removing human rights abusers from the security services. Finally, institutional reforms and training can strengthen judiciaries so that they are better prepared when the right time for trials arrives.

THE JUSTICE CASCADE

In 1985, when President Raúl Alfonsin decided to try the nine junta leaders for crimes in connection with Argentina's "dirty war," the decision to do so was made in Argentina. Although the trial of the colonels in Greece may have had some remote resonance for Alfonsin and his advisors, the decision was made without significant external influence. Since that time there has been so much global attention to and experience with holding senior officials accountable, that such influence-free policy decision making is no longer possible.

The fact that several of the most high-profile developments in recent years occurred within close proximity in time from each other meant that explicit reference was often made to the influence of one case on the next, and at the same time a sense of normative momentum building. Milošević's indictment by the ICTY occurred only a few short weeks after the House of Lords decided Pinochet could be extradited for his crimes. The International Court of Justice, in ruling on immunity for senior officials, had the benefit of the recent examples of both Pinochet and Milošević to build on. In June 2003, when the prosecutor of the Special Court for Sierra Leone announced in a press statement that the unveiling of the indictment against Charles Taylor had caused him to flee back to Liberia, it coincided with the heady early days of the Milošević trial when press coverage was still high. Prosecutor David Crane explicitly made reference to the precedent of another head of state on trial before an international court to bolster his appeal for the enforcement of the Special Court's arrest warrant, quoting his counterpart at the ICTY at the time Milošević was indicted on the moral and legal obligation of a prosecutor to proceed in light of the evidence at hand, regardless of political considerations.[17] In turn, ICC supporters can point to the Special Court's pursuit of Charles Taylor as a precedent for the ICC prosecutor's request for an arrest warrant to be issued against Sudanese President Omar al-Bashir.

Yet it is still not always clear what motivates governments to prosecute former leaders. One hypothesis is that new leaders of states making the transition from an authoritarian or totalitarian regime to democracy feel that a trial is in their political best interest.[18] This calculus might be based on domestic considerations, such as demonstrating to the populace that the new government is making a "fresh start" by seeking judicial condemnation of the old regime, as occurred with the trial of the nine military junta leaders in Argentina in 1985. It also might be based on international considerations, such as demonstrating the state's worthiness to join the community of democratic nations or attracting foreign aid from countries that have made the rule of law a central component of their development assistance, as was the case for both Serbia and Liberia in relation to Milošević and Taylor, respectively.[19] Whereas in Serbia the conditionality of aid was explicitly linked to cooperation with the ICTY, in Liberia such pressure was exerted in a less direct but equally effective way.

Another hypothesis is that states conduct trials because they are responding to pressure from a hegemon or are asserting their own hegemony over a weaker state.[20] For example, the news analyses of the trial of former East German president Egon Krenz accused Germany of using his trial to "get even" with East Germany and its leaders.[21] Perhaps this, rather than self-interest alone, better explains Serbia's decision, in the wake of enormous international pressure that included a threatened cutoff of much-needed foreign aid, to send Milošević to the Hague to stand trial at the ICTY.

In previous writing, Ellen L. Lutz and Kathryn Sikkink posited that a broad norms shift in Latin America between the late 1970s and the mid-1990s led to increased regional consensus, reinforced by popular, political, and legal support, for an interconnected bundle of human rights norms, including the norms against torture and disappearance and the norm for democratic governance. In one article, they found that the legitimacy these norms now possess is reinforced by diverse legal and nonlegal practices, including a significant increase in the number of criminal indictments and trials of those responsible for past human rights abuses.[22] In another article, they concluded that although in 1985 Argentina presaged the trend toward trials with its groundbreaking prosecution of its dirty war–era leaders, the buildup of international interest in trying former rights abusers encouraged national courts throughout Latin American to entertain such cases. In that article, they termed this trend a "justice cascade."[23]

As the two regional chapters in this book show, in Europe and Latin America, if a state decides not to try a senior government official for human rights or corruption crimes, it must justify its decision not to do so to civil society and the regional and international community, not the other way around. In these regions, the evidence that governments are trying ex-leaders because they believe it to be their duty to prosecute those most responsible for serious human rights and corruption crimes is stronger now than it was when the Lutz and Sikkink articles were published several years ago. The latest round of trials in Chile and Argentina, as well as the recent indictment of ex-president Bordaberry in Uruguay, all display strong normative underpinnings.

It is less clear that governmental absorption of a cascading justice norm is motivating the conduct of governments in other parts of the world. In some instances the evidence of external coercive pressure is blatant. In others the rationale seems at least partially instrumental. Governments in the early phases of a transition to democracy may want to demonstrate their effort to make a "fresh start" to the populace by seeking judicial condemnation of the old regime. Others may want to "lock in" international justice norms as a hedge against extremists from either end of the political spectrum who threaten democratic consolidation.[24]

Earlier we discussed the now well-established correlation between democracy and the rule of law, and state willingness to try leaders for human rights and corruption crimes. The more consolidated democratic norms are, the more consolidated the justice norm is likely to be. One demonstration of this is the fact that three-quarters of the countries that indicted former heads of state are democratic, as measured by the 2007 Freedom House "Freedom in the World" report, whereas only about half of the countries in the world are democratic when measured by the same criteria. The correlation is not perfect. For example, although Spain is now fully democratic and is one of the global leaders in using its courts to try perpetrators of crimes that took place in other parts of the globe, it has not engaged in accountability for the atrocities committed by the Franco regime.

Similarly, states that have joined the ICC are more likely to indict and prosecute their leaders for their human rights or financial crimes in their domestic courts. In part this may be explained by the specific legal duty to prosecute that ICC states parties accept when they ratify the Rome Statute, yet it may also reflect a broader commitment to the importance of accountability. Currently, just over half (54 percent) of the nations in the world are parties to the ICC. Of the forty-one states that have indicted heads of state, thirty-five (more than 85 percent) have joined the ICC.

In many instances, multiple reasons for trying senior offficals seem to be operating simultaneously with different governmental actors articulating different reasons for their interest in doing so. This is certainly the case with respect to Peru's decision to bring Fujimori to trial. That case, along with Rwanda's indictments of thousands of ex-*génocidaires* and Cambodia's agreement after lengthy negotiations with the United Nations to proceed against former Khmer Rouge leaders, further illustrates that the rationale for trying heads of state is more likely to be normative when none of the current leaders are themselves under threat of being tried.

Similarly, in many instances, the motivation seems to shift over time. Those shifts can be in multiple directions. Thus, whereas the basis of Chile's interest in prosecuting Pinochet probably shifted from instrumental to normative, the rationale for trying Hussein in Iraq probably began as normative and shifted to a mix of less wholesome reasons, including vengeance and the desire to decapitate his political movement at a time when conflict was escalating and political power holders were changing. It therefore is not possible to create a simple continuum of rationales for acceptance with coercion on one end and norm embedment on the other. In contrast, as the case of Zambian ex-president Frederick Chiluba suggests, there is a greater likelihood that the reasons will be normative when the country has undergone a transition that has strengthened democracy.

Despite the positive trends, politics can still trump legal process. For example, the long-standing tradition that former heads of state will find security in exile is still prevalent. Fujimori enjoyed the absolute protection of Japan, which even acknowledged him as a citizen, until he elected to return to Peru via Chile. Even Chile, whose courts are now prosecuting the crimes committed by Pinochet and his cronies, initially displayed scant enthusiasm for extraditing Fujimori to Peru. Carlos Menem of Argentina also enjoyed safety from extradition in Chile until his 2004 arrest warrant was canceled. For its part, Argentina refused to extradite former junta members Jorge Videla and Emilio Massera to Germany and Spain, respectively, for crimes committed during Argentina's dirty war. Mexico is protecting Guatemalan ex-president Alfonso Portillo; France is sheltering Haitian ex-president Jean Claude ("Baby Doc") Duvalier, and the United States is providing safe haven from extradition for former Bolivian president Gonzalo Sánchez de Lozada, who is charged with killing demonstrators in October 2003; it also may be harboring Prosper Avril of Haiti.

Exile also has protected many African leaders from going to jail, although in some cases ex-leaders have been convicted in absentia. On December 12, 2006, Ethiopia's former dictator Mengistu Haile Mariam was convicted of genocide in absentia after a decade of legal proceedings. He enjoys the protection of Zimbabwe. Madagascar's former leader Didier Ratsiraka was convicted of embezzling $8.7 million as well as violating state security and was sentenced to fifteen years in prison, but instead lives in exile in France. One of the continent's most notorious "bad guys," Uganda's Idi Amin, escaped prosecution altogether by fleeing to Saudi Arabia, and Chad's former leader Hissène Habré enjoyed a comfortable exile in Senegal until Chadian and international human rights advocates persuaded prosecutors in Belgium to seek his extradition. Only now does it appear likely that Senegal, where Habré is now under house arrest, will bring him to trial. Finally, in a peace-for-justice deal reportedly cut between the United Kingdom, the African Union,

Liberia, Nigeria, and the United States, former Liberian president Charles Taylor enjoyed protection in Nigeria for nearly three years until international pressure mounted to the point that Nigeria sent him back to Liberia in the knowledge that this would lead to his immediate transfer to the Special Court for Sierra Leone.

CONCLUSION

Since the fall of the Berlin Wall, global trends generally have been in the direction of democracy, the rule of law, the reduction of corruption, and the promotion of human rights. Even where these trends have been honored in the breach, states now give lip service to these values, and, increasingly, civil society – nationally and internationally – is raising the bar on states' ability to evade honoring them in practice. Side by side with these trends, there has been a dramatic rise in the prosecutions of heads of state or government for crimes that undermine these values. This transformation is not just cosmetic, nor can it be explained by hegemonic pressures or instrumental political calculus alone. Something bigger has occurred – something that is at least in part normatively grounded. It is most embedded in Europe and Latin America, where it is by no means perfectly executed. However, the trend reaches beyond these regions to parts of the world where the rule of law, democracy, anticorruption, and human rights norms are weaker but are moving in a positive direction. More empirical attention to measure and assess these trends is needed. Nonetheless, the findings presented in this book show that the justice norm is becoming embedded around the globe and that politicians should assume high office only if they are prepared to govern honestly and justly. For if they sanction human rights violations or dip their hands into public coffers, they can no longer assume they will get away with it. If current trends continue, their retirement years are likely to be filled with legal wrangling, extreme limits on their freedom of movement, the humiliation of criminal prosecution, and, quite possibly, an old age behind bars.

NOTES

1. Footage contained in *The General and the Judge*, directed by Elisabeth Farnsworth, ITV films (2007).
2. Naomi Roht-Arriaza and Javier Mariezcurrena, *Transitional Justice in the Twenty-First Century*, Cambridge: Cambridge University Press, 2006; Naomi Roht-Arriaza, *The Pinochet Effect: Transitional Justice in the Age of Human Rights*; Philadelphia: University of Pennsylvania Press, 2004; Kathryn Sikkink and Carrie Booth Walling, "The Impact of Human Rights Trials in Latin America," *Journal of Peace Research* 44, no. 4 (July 2007): 427–445.

3. See, for example, the letter requesting the establishment of the Special Tribunal for Lebanon, "Letter dated 13 December 2005 from the Charge d'affaires of the Permanent Mission of Lebanon to the United Nations Addressed to the Secretary-General," December 13, 2005, UN Doc S/2005/783, annex.

4. *The Prosecutor v. Charles Ghankay Taylor*, SCSL-2003–01-T, transcript of trial proceedings, June 4, 2007, p. 10.

5. Martti Koskenniemi, "Between Impunity and Show Trials," *Max Planck United Nations Yearbook* 6 (2002): 1–32.

6. Ellen L. Lutz and Kathryn Sikkink, "The Justice Cascade: The Evolution and Impact of Foreign Human Rights Trials in Latin America," *Chicago Journal of International Law* 2, no. 1 (2001): 1–34.

7. Gary Bass, "Victor's Justice, Selfish Justice," *Social Research* 69 (2002): 1035–1044.

8. For a full discussion of the impact of the ICTY in Serbia, see Diane Orentlicher, "Shrinking the Space for Denial: The Impact of the ICTY in Serbia," *Open Society Justice Initiative*, May 2008.

9. Amnesty International USA, "The International Criminal Court, Summary of Draft and Enacted Implementing Legislation. Available at http://www.amnestyusa.org/document.php?lang=e&id=ENGIOR400412006.

10. See Matthias H. Goldmann, Rain Liivoja, Cornelia Schneider, Ann Swampillai, and Isabelle Walther, "Symposium on Project on ICC National Implementation Legislation," *Finnish Yearbook of International Law*, 16 (2005).

11. Gideon Boas examines this question at length in his book, *The Milošević Trial: Lessons for the Conduct of Complex International Criminal Proceedings*, Cambridge: Cambridge University Press, 2007.

12. See Chapter 11.

13. Hannah Arendt, *Eichmann in Jerusalem: A Report on the Banality of Evil*, rev. and enl. ed., New York: Penguin, 1994.

14. Jack Snyder and Leslie Vinjamuri, "Trials and Errors: Principle and Pragmatism in Strategies of International Justice," *International Security* 28, no. 3 (Winter 2003/2004): 5–44.

15. Priscilla Hayner, *Negotiating Peace in Liberia: Preserving the Possibility for Justice*, Centre for Humanitarian Dialogue and the International Center for Transitional Justice, November 2007.

16. Christine Bell, *Peace Agreements and Human Rights*, Oxford: Oxford University Press, 2000.

17. Statement of David M. Crane, chief prosecutor, Special Court for Sierra Leone, June 5, 2003.

18. See generally Mark Oseil, *Mass Atrocity, Collective Memory and the Law*, New Brunswick, NJ: Transaction, 1997.

19. See, for example, Andrew Moravcsik, "The Origins of Human Rights Regimes: Democratic Delegation in Postwar Europe," *International Organization* 54 (2000): 217.

20. See, for example, Stephen D. Krasner, "Sovereignty, Regimes and Human Rights," in *Regime Theory and International Relations*, V. Rittberger and P. Mayer, eds., Oxford: Oxford University Press, 1993, 139–167; John G. Ikenberry and Charles Kupchan, "Socialization and Hegemonic Power," *International Organization* 44 (1990): 283.

21. Rick Atkinson, "Holding Ex-Rulers Accountable; Germany Struggles with 'Victims Justice'; Courts Stymie Prosecution of Eastern Abuses," *Washington Post*, September 24, 1995, p. A26.

22. Ellen L. Lutz and Kathryn Sikkink, "International Human Rights Law and Practice in Latin America," *International Organization* 54 (2000): 633, 654–657.

23. Ellen L. Lutz and Kathryn Sikkink, "The Justice Cascade."

24. Andrew Moravcik, "The Paradox of US Human Rights Policy," in *American Exceptionalism and Human Rights*, Michael Ignatieff, ed., Princeton: Princeton University Press, 2005, 147–197.

List of Prosecutions of Heads of State or Government January 1990 to June 2008

Country	Name	Title	Term of office	Year indicted	Crimes charged	Year trial began	Disposition
LATIN AMERICA							
Argentina	Reynaldo Bignone	Military head of state	1982–83	1996, 1999, 2007	Human rights	–	Indicted in Spain and Italy. In Argentina he was charged in connection with clandestine detention centers and a month later for his involvement in the kidnapping of children. Currently under house arrest awaiting trial.
	Armando Lambruschini	Military head of state	1980–81	1985, (2003)	Human rights	1985	Sentenced in 1985 to 8 years, pardoned in 1990 by Menem. Rearrested in 2003 pursuant to a 1998 Spanish warrant but died in 2004. He was also tried in absentia in Italy.
	Emilio Massera	Military head of state	1976–1981	1996, 1998, 2003, 2004	Human rights	1999	Sentenced in 1985 to life in prison for assassination, illegal confinement, and torture, then pardoned by Menem in 1990. He was also convicted in 1999 and 2004 for the disappearance of children, fined 210,000 pesos, and faced arrest warrants in Spain and Germany. His pardon was held unconstitutional but he was declared incapable of standing trial due to poor health.

(*continued*)

Country	Name	Title	Term of office	Year indicted	Crimes charged	Year trial began	Disposition
	Carlos Menem	President	1989–1999	2001, 2002, 2003, 2007	Illegal arms transfers Financial crimes	2008	Held in pretrial house arrest and then cleared for lack of evidence. A subsequent investigation into alleged embezzlement failed because Chile would not extradite him. After the arrest warrants were canceled, he returned to Argentina in 2004, still facing charges of embezzlement. Trial underway.
	María Isabel Martínez de Perón	President	1974–76	2007	Human rights	–	Indicted in Argentina but Spain refused to extradite her in 2008.
	Fernando de la Rúa	President	1999–2001	2008	Human rights	–	Charged with deaths resulting from a riot during an economic crisis. Case went before the Court of Cassation which found that there was insufficient evidence to proceed.
	Jorge Videla	Military head of state	1976–1981	1998, 2001, 2003, 2004	Human rights	–	First tried and convicted in 1985 of multiple cases of homicide, aggravated false arrests, torture, torture resulting in death, and robbery. Sentenced to life imprisonment, then pardoned by Menem in 1990. Pardon ruled unconstitutional. Subsequently indicted in Argentina for further abductions, and in Germany, although extraditions were denied. He was put under house arrest in 2007 and in jail in 2008.
Bolivia	Gonzalo Sánchez de Lozada	President	1993–97; 2002–03	2005	Human rights	–	Trial has not yet begun. Resides in United States, which is blocking extradition.
	Luis García Meza	Military head of state	1980–82	1987	Human rights	1993	Found guilty in 1993 in absentia. Began serving 30-year sentence in 1996.
Brazil	Fernando Collor de Mello	President	1990–92	1992	Financial crimes	1993	Impeachment barred him from holding public office for 8 years. In 1994, exonerated of all charges by the highest court. Elected governor of his province in 2006.

Country	Name	Title	Term of office	Year indicted	Crimes charged	Year trial began	Disposition
Chile	Augusto Pinochet	Military head of state	1974–1990	1998, 2000, 2004, 2005	Human rights, Financial crimes	–	Arrested on Spanish arrest warrant while in United Kingdom. House of Lords approved extradition but not extradited for health reasons. Returned to Chile. Immunity stripped by Chilean Supreme Court. Found unable to stand trial in 2002 because of vascular dementia; case dismissed. Public display of mental competence led to new human rights indictments. Appeals court ruled that he had immunity, and the case was dropped in 2005. Immunity stripped again in 2005 for the killing of dissidents. Acquitted the following day because of ill health. Indicted again that year for the disappearance of six people. In 2006, an appeals court let financial crime charges stand and in September 2006, immunity was lifted for kidnapping and torture. Died in December 2006.
Costa Rica	Rafael Ángel Calderón	President	1990–94	2004	Financial crimes	–	Under pretrial house arrest for a year. Trial has not started; the investigation continues.
	José María Figueres	President	1994–98	–	Financial crimes	–	Charged with taking kickbacks but not indicted because of insufficient evidence. Lives outside the country.
	Miguel Ángel Rodríguez	President	1998–2002	2004	Financial crimes	–	In pretrial house arrest for more than a year. Trial has not started; the investigation continues.
Ecuador	Abdalá Bucaram	President	1996–97	1997	Financial crimes	–	Charges dismissed. Was out of country until 2005. Returned when charges were dropped.
	Lucio Gutiérrez	President	2003–05	2005	Human rights; threatening national security		Brazil granted him asylum. He returned to Ecuador, and in March 2006, the case was dismissed.

(*continued*)

Country	Name	Title	Term of office	Year indicted	Crimes charged	Year trial began	Disposition
Guatemala	Efraín Ríos Montt	Military head of state	1982–83	1999, 2000, 2004	Genocide, Torture, Terrorism, Financial crimes	–	Rigoberta Menchú filed a case against him in Spain. Arrest warrant issued in 2006; gained senatorial immunity in 2007. Guatemalan Constitutional Court denied extradition Dec. 2007. Case continues in Spain. In Guatemala he was held in pretrial house arrest but both financial and human rights charges were dropped.
	Fernando Romeo Lucas García	Military head of state	1978–1982	1999	Human rights	–	Spanish indictment. Arrest warrant issued in 2006. Died in 2006.
	Alfonso Portillo	President	2000–04	2004	Financial crimes	–	Extradition approved by Mexico; extradited Oct. 2008 but no action taken.
	Óscar Humberto Mejía Victores	Military head of state	1983–84	2001	Human rights	–	Arrested 2006 on Spanish warrant as part of Menchu case for genocide and other related crimes. He was held until Dec. 2007 when extradition to Spain was denied. Case against him continues in Spain.
Haiti	Prosper Avril	President	1988–1990	1994, 1996	Human rights	1994	First convicted in 1994 and fined $41 million. Arrested in 2001 on outstanding warrant from 1996. Freed in 2004, when Aristide was ousted. Fled the country.
	Jean-Claude Duvalier	President	1971–1986	1999	Human rights	–	Complaint filed in French court but dismissed. Resides in France.
Mexico	Luis Echeverría	President	1970–76	2004	Human rights	2004	Blocked on statute of limitations grounds in July 2006; ruling reversed in November 2006. Genocide charges dismissed 2007.
Nicaragua	Arnoldo Alemán	President	1997–2002	2002	Financial crimes	2002	Serving 20-year sentence under house arrest. Prison term for money laundering reduced to 5 years meaning he will finish 15 years ahead of schedule. Began serving time in prison, moved to house arrest and later to "Nicaraguan arrest."

Country	Name	Title	Term of office	Year indicted	Crimes charged	Year trial began	Disposition
Paraguay	Alfredo Stroessner	President	1954–1989	2000, 2001	Human rights	–	Indicted for murder by Paraguay. Extradition from Brazil requested and refused. Indicted for participation in Operation Condor by Argentina. Extradition from Brazil requested and refused. Died in 2006.
	González Macchi	President	1999–2003	2002	Financial crimes	2003	Convicted in 2006 of embezzlement. Sentenced to 8 years in prison and to house arrest during the appeals process.
	Raúl Cubas Grau	President	1998–99	1999, 2002	Acts against the state (murder of the vice president), Human Rights	–	Apparently never convicted for the first indictment. Subsequently convicted for the murder of seven protesters and sentenced to house arrest.
Peru	Alberto Fujimori	President	1990–2000	2003, 2005	Human rights; financial crimes, arms smuggling	2008	Japan refused to extradite. Later went on his own to Chile, which extradited him to Peru. Trial underway.
Suriname	Desi Bouterse	President	1980–87	2007	Human rights, smuggling	2007	Trial underway in Suriname. Case before a court martial as most defendants are military personnel. Also convicted in absentia by a Dutch court on cocaine-smuggling charges, and investigated by Dutch court for torture charges but time barred.
Uruguay	Juan Bordaberry	President	1972–76	2005	Human rights	2007	In pretrial house arrest; still awaiting trial.
Venezuela	Carlos Andrés Pérez	President	1974–79, 1989–1993	1993, 1998	Financial crimes	1993	Convicted in 1996 and sentenced to twenty-eight months in prison. At the time of sentencing, only six months remained. New charges filed in 1998 but dropped because of senatorial immunity; he was reelected after charges filed. The case was reopened in 1999; he appears to have asylum in the United States. In 2008, Venezuela's Supreme Court ruled that case could continue.
	Jaime Lusinchi	President	1984–89	1992	Financial crimes	–	Dismissed in 1992, reopened in 2000. Lives in self-imposed exile in Miami. In 2008, Venezuela's Supreme Court ruled that case could continue.

(continued)

Country	Name	Title	Term of office	Year indicted	Crimes charged	Year trial began	Disposition
EUROPE							
Albania	Ramiz Alia	Head of state/ president	1985–1992	1992, 1997	Financial crimes, Human Rights	1994, 1997	Pretrial house arrest 1992. Convicted in 1994 and sentenced to 9 years in prison, reduced to 5 years. Indicted for genocide and crimes against humanity. Escaped to France. Case dismissed on *nullem crimen sine lege* grounds.
Belarus	Mikhail Chyhir	Prime minister	1994–96	1999	Financial crimes, abuse of power	2000	Found guilty in 2000, sentenced to 3 years; 2 suspended and $200,000 fine. Later cleared of abuse of power charge.
Bosnia	Dragan Čović	Co-president	2003–05	2005	Financial crimes, smuggling persons	2006	Croat co-president; found guilty of corruption in 2007 and sentenced to 5 years in prison. Must remain in country pending appeals.
Bulgaria	Todor Zhivkov	Head of state/ president	1954–1989	1991	Financial crimes	1991	Convicted in 1992 and sentenced to seven years' house arrest; acquitted on immunity grounds in 1996. Died in 1998.
Czech Rep.	Jozef Lenárt	Prime minister (and acting president in 1968)	1963–68	1997	Human rights, treason	–	Acquitted 2002 because of lack of evidence.
Germany	Erich Honecker	Head of state	1971–1989	1990	Human rights	1993	Trial halted for health reasons. Died in Chile in 2003.
	Egon Krenz	Head of state	1989	1995	Human rights	1995	Convicted and sentenced to 6.5 years in 1997. Released in 2004 to probation after serving four years.
Italy	Silvio Berlusconi	Prime minister	1994–96, 2001–06, 2008–	1994, 1996, 1997, 2000	Financial crimes, illegal financing of a political party, bribing a judge	1996	Found guilty of illegal financing, corruption, and bribery in 1999. Further convictions sustained in 2000 on similar charges. Sentenced to 28 months and a further 33 months in prison. All sentences overturned on appeal on statute of limitations grounds. Acquitted in 2005 of all corruption-related charges.

Country	Name	Title	Term of office	Year indicted	Crimes charged	Year trial began	Disposition
Poland	Wojciech Jaruzelski	Prime minister/ president	1981–1990	1995, 2007	Human rights	–	Suppression of protest. In 1996 cleared of all responsibility for imposing martial law but in 2007 was charged with creating a criminal organization. Trial yet to start.
Serbia (Federal Republic of Yugoslavia)	Slobodan Milošević	President	FRY 1997–2000	1999, 2003	Human rights, assassination of political opponents (including former Serbian president Ivan Stambolic)	2002	Serbian proceedings began in February 2004, but Milošević was being tried in the Hague, so his indictment was suspended. He was also under active investigation for embezzlement, but charges were brought against coaccused after Milošević's death. Died during ICTY trial in 2006.
AFRICA							
Chad	Hissène Habré	President	1982–1990	2000, 2002	Human rights	–	Indicted in Senegal (then dismissed); immunity lifted in Chad; will be tried in Senegal, where trial is expected to begin in 2010. Belgian arrest warrant and extradition request remain pending.
Ethiopia	Mengistu Haile Mariam	Head of state	1977–1991	1994	Human rights	1994	Living in Zimbabwe, which will not extradite him. Tried in absentia for genocide and crimes against humanity beginning in 1994. Sentenced to life in prison in 2006. Ethiopian high court concurred and sentenced him to death for genocide in 2008.
Liberia	Gyude Bryant	Transitional Head of state	2003–06	2007	Financial crimes	2008	Case ongoing.
	Charles Taylor	President	1997–2003	2003	Human rights	2007	On trial before the Special Court for Sierra Leone.

(*continued*)

Country	Name	Title	Term of office	Year indicted	Crimes charged	Year trial began	Disposition
Madagascar	Didier Ratsiraka	President	1975–1993, 1996–2002	2003	Financial crimes, violating state security	2003	Tried in absentia and found guilty of embezzling $8.7 million. Sentenced to 10 years' hard labor for financial crimes and a further 5 years in prison in 2003. Sentence not begun; remains in exile in France.
Malawi	Hastings Kamuzu Banda	President	1963–1993	1995, 1997	Human rights, financial crimes	1995	Acquitted of human rights charges and found unfit for trial on financial charges. Died in 1997 at approximately 100 years of age.
Mali	Moussa Traore	President	1968–1991	1991	Human rights, financial crimes	1991	Sentenced to death in 1993. Commuted to life with hard labor in 1997. Pardoned in 2002. During 11 years of imprisonment, conditions gradually improved, but no luxuries (phone, radio, TV).
Nigeria	Olusegun Obasanjo	President	1976–79, 1999–2007	1995	Involvement in a coup plot	1995	Initially sentenced to death by secret tribunal. Sentenced to life in prison in 1995. Later reduced to 15 years. Pardoned in 2002.
Republic of Congo – Brazzaville	Bernard Kolelas	Prime minister	1997	1998	Human rights, financial crimes, treason	2000	Convicted in absentia and sentenced to death. Kolelas went into exile in France but in 2005 was allowed to return and was granted an amnesty.
	Pascal Lissouba	President	1992–97	1998, 2001	Human rights, financial crimes, treason	2001	Convicted in absentia and sentenced to death. Living in exile in London.
Rwanda	Pasteur Bizimungu	President	1994–2000	2001	Human rights, financial crimes	2002	Acquitted of endangering state security; guilty of human rights and financial crimes. Sentenced to 15 years in prison in 2004. Pardoned by President Paul Kagame in 2007.
	Jean Kambanda	President of caretaker government during genocide	1994	1997	Human rights	1998	Indicted by International Criminal Tribunal for Rwanda. Pleaded guilty. Sentenced to life in prison in 1998. Serving sentence in Mali.

Country	Name	Title	Term of office	Year indicted	Crimes charged	Year trial began	Disposition
South Africa	P. W. Botha	President	1978–1989	1998	Ignoring a Truth Commission summons	1998	Convicted and sentenced in 1998 to a $1,600 fine plus one year in prison. Suspended three years. Set aside on appeal. Died 2006.
Zambia	Frederick Chiluba	President	1991–2002	2003, 2007	Financial crimes	2003	Sentenced to a $58 million fine in 2004. In 2007 found unfit to stand trial because of poor health. Also lost civil case in United Kingdom.
	Kenneth Kaunda	President	1964–1991	1997	Plotting to topple Chiluba	Unclear	Status of formal legal process uncertain. Imprisoned for six months and released in 1997.
Zimbabwe	Canaan Banana	President	1980–87	1998	Sodomy and indecent assault	1999	Sentenced to one year in prison in 1999. Served 8 months.
MIDDLE EAST							
Iraq	Saddam Hussein	President	1979–2003	2004	Human rights	2005–2006	Sentenced to death; executed in 2006.
Israel	Moshe Katsav	President	2000–07	2008	Sexual harassment	2008	Originally entered into plea bargain but rescinded in 2008. Now on trial.
ASIA							
India	P. V. Narasimha Rao	Prime minister	1991–96	1996	Financial crimes, bribery	1997	Case dismissed in 2002 because of lack of evidence.
Indonesia	Suharto	President	1967–1998	2000	Financial crimes	–	Trial never began because case dismissed. Acquitted on appeal. Died 2008.
Pakistan	Nawaz Sharif	Prime minister	1990–93, 1997–99	1998, 1999	Financial crimes, forgery, attempted murder, terrorism, kidnapping	1999, 2000	Indicted repeatedly for corruption during the Bhutto government. Convicted of corruption in 2000 and sentenced to 14 years in prison. Convicted of hijacking and terrorism but acquitted of attempted murder and kidnapping. Sentenced to 2 life sentences, reduced to a single life sentence, and then pardoned 5 months later. Exiled to Saudi Arabia but returned to Pakistan in 2007.

(continued)

Country	Name	Title	Term of office	Year indicted	Crimes charged	Year trial began	Disposition
	Benazir Bhutto	Prime minister	1988–1990, 1993–96	1998	Financial crimes	–	Indicted during Sharif government. Convicted in 1999 of money laundering and sentenced to 5 years in prison and a fine of $8.6 million. Supreme Court ordered a new trial in 2001. Husband served jail time for financial crimes. Was also indicted by a Swiss court for illegal financing of a political party. Assassinated in 2008.
Philippines	Joseph Estrada	President	1998–2001	2001	Financial crimes	2001	Found not guilty of perjury but guilty of plunder and sentenced to life imprisonment in Sept. 2007. Given executive clemency the following month. Faces renewed investigation in perjury case.
South Korea	Chun Doo Hwan	President	1980–88	1995	Human rights, financial crimes, treason	1996	Convicted in 1996 of suppressing rebellion, human rights violations, and bribery. Sentenced to death, commuted to life, and then pardoned. Fined $270 million.
	Roh Tae Woo	President	1988–1993	1995	Human rights, financial crimes, treason	1996	Convicted in 1996 of suppressing rebellion, human rights violations, and bribery. Sentenced to 22 years, commuted to 17 years, and then pardoned. Fined $250 million.

Selected Bibliography

BOOKS AND REPORTS

Aburish, Said K. *Saddam Hussein: The Politics of Revenge*. London: Blumsbury, 2000.

Amnesty International. *Universal Jurisdiction: The Scope of Civil Universal Jurisdiction*. July 1, 2007. http://www.amnesty.org/en/library/info/IOR53/008/2007/en.

Arendt, Hannah. *Eichmann in Jerusalem: A Report on the Banality of Evil*. Rev. and enlarged ed. New York: Penguin, 1994.

The Aspen Institute, Justice and Society Program. "State Crimes: Punishment or Pardon." Papers and report of the Conference, November 4–6. Wye, MD: The Aspen Institute, 1989.

Balaghi, Shiva. *Saddam Hussein: A Biography*. Westport, CT: Greenwood Press, 2006.

Bass, Gary. *Stay the Hand of Vengeance: The Politics of War Crimes Trials*. Princeton: Princeton University Press, 2002.

Batatu, Hanna. *The Old Social Classes and the Revolutionary Movements of Iraq, a Study of Iraq's Old Landed and Commercial Classes and of Its Communists, Ba'thists and Free Officers*. Princeton: Princeton University Press, 1978.

Boas, Gideon. *The Milošević Trial: Lessons for the Conduct of Complex International Criminal Proceedings*. Cambridge: Cambridge University Press, 2007.

Brody, Reed. "The Prosecution of Hissène Habré: International Accountability, National Impunity." In *Transitional Justice in the Twenty-First Century: Beyond Truth versus Justice*, edited by Naomi Roht-Arriaza and Javier Mariezcurrena. Cambridge: Cambridge University Press, 2006.

Clancy, Craig, and Steven Chan. *Zambia and the Decline of Kaunda 1984–1998*, edited by Craig Clancy. New York: The Edwin Mellen Press, 2000.

Conaghan, Catherine M. *Fujimori's Peru: Deception in the Public Sphere*. Pittsburgh: University of Pittsburgh Press, 2006.

DesForges, Allison. *Leave None to Tell the Story: Genocide in Rwanda*. New York: Human Rights Watch, 1999.

Doronila, Amando, ed. *Between Fires: Fifteen Perspectives on the Estrada Crisis*. Manila: Anvil, 2001.

Due Process of Law Foundation. *Victims Unsilenced: The Inter-American Human Rights System and Transitional Justice in Latin America*. July 2007. Available at http://www.dplf.org/uploads/1190403828.pdf.

Ensalaco, Mark. *Chile Under Pinochet: Recovering the Truth.* Philadelphia: University of Pennsylvania Press, 2000.

Ewell, Judith. *The Indictment of a Dictator: The Extradition and Trial of Marcos Perez Jimenez.* College Station: Texas A&M University Press, 1981.

Front Line, *Front Line Rwanda: Disappearances, Arrests, Threats, Intimidation and Co-option of Human Rights Defenders, 2001–2004.* Dublin: Front Line, 2005.

Gloppen, Siri, Roberto Gargarella, and Elin Skaar, eds. *Democratization and the Judiciary: The Accountability Function of Courts in New Democracies.* London: Frank Cass, 2004.

Gourevitch, Philip. *We Wish to Inform You That Tomorrow We Will Be Killed with Our Families.* New York: Farrar, Strauss & Giroux, 1998.

Human Rights Watch. *The Trial of Hissène Habré: Time Is Running Out for the Victims.* January 2007. http://www.hrw.org/backgrounder/africa/habre0107/index.htm.

The International Center for Transitional Justice and the Human Rights Center, University of California, Berkeley. *Iraqi Voices: Attitudes Towards Transitional Justice and Social Reconstruction.* Occasional Paper Series, May 2004.

Ivanišević, Bogdan. *Against the Current: War Crimes Prosecutions in Serbia.* International Center for Transitional Justice, 2007.

Johnston, Michael. *Syndromes of Corruption: Wealth, Power, and Democracy.* Cambridge: Cambridge University Press, 2005.

Kajeguhakwa, Valens. *Rwanda: De la terre de paix à la terre de sang et apres?* Paris: Fayard, 2001.

Keefer, Philip. "Democratization and Clientelism: Why are young democracies badly governed?" *World Bank Policy Research Working Paper* 3594, May 2005.

Kritz, Neil J., ed. *Transitional Justice: How Emerging Democracies Reckon with Former Regimes.* Vols. 1–3. Washington, DC: United States Institute of Peace, 1995.

Lutz, Ellen L., and Kathryn Sikkink. "International Law and Domestic Human Rights in Latin America." In *Legalization and World Politics*, edited by Judith Goldstein, Miles Kahler, Robert Keohane, and Anne-Marie Slaughter. Cambridge, MA: IO Foundation and the Massachusetts Institute of Technology, 2001.

Moghalu, Kingsley C. *Global Justice: The Politics of War Crimes Trials.* Westport, CT: Praeger Security International, 2006.

Nino, Carlos Santiago. *Radical Evil on Trial.* New Haven: Yale University Press, 1996.

Oseil, Mark. *Mass Atrocity, Collective Memory and the Law.* New Brunswick, NJ: Transaction, 1997.

O'Shea, Andreas. *Amnesty for Crime in International Law and Practice.* The Hague: Kulwer Law International, 2002.

Pottier, Johan. *Re-imagining Rwanda: Conflict, Survival and Disinformation in the Late Twentieth Century.* Cambridge: Cambridge University Press, 2002.

Power, Samantha. *"A Problem from Hell": America and the Age of Genocide.* New York: Basic Books, 2002.

Prunier, Gerard. *The Rwanda Crisis: History of a Genocide.* New York: Columbia University Press, 1999.

Roht-Arriaza, Naomi. *The Pinochet Effect: Transnational Justice in the Age of Human Rights.* Philadelphia: University of Pennsylvania Press, 2005.

Roht-Arriaza, Naomi ed. *Impunity and Human Rights in International Law and Practice.* New York: Oxford University Press, 1995.

Roht-Arriaza, Naomi, and Javier Mariezcurrena. *Transitional Justice in the Twenty-First Century*. New York: Cambridge University Press, 2006.

Rose-Ackerman, Susan. *Corruption and Government: Causes, Consequences and Reform*. New York: Cambridge University Press, 1999.

Sands, Phillippe. *Torture Team: Rumsfeld's Memo and the Betrayal of American Values*. New York: Palgrave Macmillan, 2008.

Schabas, William A. *An Introduction to the International Criminal Court*. Cambridge: Cambridge University Press, 2001.

Scharf, Michael P., and Gregory S. McNeal. *Saddam on Trial: Understanding and Debating the Iraqi High Tribunal*. Durham: Carolina Academic Press, 2006.

Schiavo-Campo, Salvatore, and Mary Judd. *The Mindanao Conflict in the Philippines: Roots, Costs, and Potential Peace Dividend*. World Bank Social Development Papers: Conflict Prevention & Reconstruction, Paper no. 24. February 2005.

Shklar, Judith N. *Legalism: Law, Morals and Political Trials*. Cambridge, MA: Harvard University Press, 1964, 1986.

Silber, Laura, and Allan Little. *Yugoslavia: Death of a Nation*. London: Penguin Books, 1997.

Stover, Eric, and Harvey Weinstein, eds. *My Neighbor, My Enemy: Justice and Community in the Aftermath of Mass Atrocity*. New York: Cambridge University Press, 2004.

Taylor, Telford. *The Anatomy of the Nuremberg Trials: A Personal Memoir*. Boston: Little Brown & Co., 1993.

Tripp, Charles. *A History of Iraq*. Cambridge: Cambridge University Press, 2002.

Truth and Reconciliation Commission. *Final Report*. Lima, Peru, 2003.

Villa-Vicencio, Charles, and Erik Doxtader, eds. *The Provocations of Amnesty: Memory, Justice and Impunity*. Trenton: Africa World Press, 2003.

Waugh, Colin M. *Paul Kagame and Rwanda: Power, Genocide, and the Rwandan Patriotic Front*. London: McFarland, 2004.

Williams, Charles. *Petain, How the Hero of France Became a Convicted Traitor and Changed the Course of History*. New York: Palgrave Macmillan, 2005.

Wilson, Richard A. *The Politics of Truth and Reconciliation in South Africa: Legitimizing the Post-Apartheid State*. Cambridge: Cambridge University Press, 2001.

JOURNAL ARTICLES

Bass, Gary. "Victor's Justice, Selfish Justice." *Social Research* 69, no. 4 (2002): 1037–1046.

Bassiouni, M. C. "Universal Jurisdiction Unrevisited: The International Court of Justice decision in case concerning the arrest warrant of 11 April 2000 (Democratic Republic of the Congo v. Belgium)." *The Palestine Yearbook of International Law* 12 (2002–2003): 27–48.

Cassese, Antonio. "When May Senior State Officials Be Tried for International Crimes? Some Comments on the *Congo v. Belgium* Case." *European Journal of International Law* 13, no. 4 (2002): 853–875.

Koskenniemi, Martti. "Between Impunity and Show Trials." *Max Plank Yearbook of United Nations Law* 6, no. 1 (2002): 1–32.

Lutz, Ellen L., and Kathryn Sikkink. "The Justice Cascade: The Evolution and Impact of Foreign Human Rights Trials in Latin America." *Chicago Journal of International Law* 21 (2001): 1–34.

Marks, Johnathan H. "Mending the Web: Universal Jurisdiction, Humanitarian Intervention and the Abrogation of Immunity by the Security Council." *Columbia Journal of Transnational Law* 42 (2004): 445–490.

Parker, Tom. "Prosecuting Saddam: The Coalition Provisional Authority and the Evolution of the Iraq Special Tribunal." *Cornell International Law Journal* 38, no. 3 (2005): 899–909.

Scharf, Michael P. "From the Exile Files: An Essay on Trading Justice for Peace." *Washington & Lee Law Review* 63 (2006): 339–376.

Scharf, Michael P. "The Perils of Permitting Self-Representation in International War Crimes Trials." *Journal of Human Rights* 4, no. 4 (2005): 513–520.

Sissons, Miranda, and Ari S. Bassin. "Was the Dujail Trial Fair?" *Journal of International Criminal Justice* 5, no. 2 (2007): 272–286.

Szeftel, Morris. "'Eat with Us: Managing Corruption and Patronage under Zambia's Three Republics, 1964–99." *Journal of Contemporary African Studies* 18, No. 2 (2000): 207–224.

CASES

Barrios Altos Case, Judgment of March 14, 2001, Inter-Am Ct. H.R. Ser. C, No. 75 (2001).

Democratic Republic of the Congo v. Belgium, Case Concerning the Arrest Warrant of 11 April 2000, ICJ, 14 February 2002, General List No. 121.

Dujail Case, 1/C 1/2005, Judgment of the Trial Chamber, Iraq Special Tribunal, November 22, 2006. Available at http://www.ictj.org/static/MENA/Iraq/DujailJudgment.eng.pdf.

Prosecutor v. Charles Ghankay Taylor, SCSL-2003-01-I, SCSL, Decision on Immunity from Jurisdiction, May 31, 2004.

Prosecutor v. Slobodan Milošević, IT-02-54, ICTY, Decision on Motion for Judgment of Acquittal, June 16, 2004.

R v. Bow Street Metropolitan Stipendiary Magistrate, ex parte Pinochet Ugarte (Pinochet I), [1998] 37 I.L.M. 1302.

R v. Bow Street Metropolitan Stipendiary Magistrate, ex parte Pinochet Ugarte (Pinochet II), [2000] A.C. 119.

R v. Bow Street Metropolitan Stipendiary Magistrate, ex parte Pinochet Ugarte (Pinochet III), [2000] A.C. 147.

Index